Children's Literature

CHILDREN'S LITERATURE
THEORY, RESEARCH, AND TEACHING

KAY E. VANDERGRIFT

1990
LIBRARIES UNLIMITED, INC.
Englewood, Colorado

LIBRARIES UNLIMITED, INC.
P.O. Box 3988
Englewood, CO 80155-3988

Library of Congress Cataloging-in-Publication Data

Vandergrift, Kay E.
    Children's literature : theory, research, and teaching / Kay E. Vandergrift.
    xiv, 277 p. 22x28 cm.
    Includes bibliographical references.
    ISBN 0-87287-749-3
    1. Children--Books and reading. 2. Children's literature--History and criticism--Theory, etc. 3. Children's literature--Study and teaching. 4. Children's literature--Research. I. Title.
Z1037.A1V36 1990
809'.89282--dc20

                     89-29959
                       CIP

FOR JANE

Table of Contents

Preface

This book began with my own love of children's literature and my belief in the power of both that literature and the children for whom it is created. It reflects many of my concerns as a teacher of children's literature and grew in response to two divergent but complementary calls heard fairly consistently from colleagues in the field. The first was for more and better theoretical and critical knowledge of children's literature and the second for practical assistance in the teaching of that literature. A variety of responses to both of these have come forth, but the cries continue and our needs are still not met. As the body of literary theory grows and those of us who teach children's literature become increasingly involved with that theory and corresponding research activities, an even greater need exists for some means to bring theory and practice together.

There has been an increase in more lengthy and more theoretically based critical analyses of works for children and young people, but too often this work is assumed to be esoteric, isolated from and unrelated to either children or the teaching of children's literature. Many who teach children's literature dismiss this work as being that of those who have little sense of the child for whom the literature was created and even less for the practical problems of bringing that child and the literature together. On the other hand, there has been a proliferation of books about children's literature that describe both literary works and activities associated with these books but have little relation to theory, research, or even the practical problems of one's own teaching. We are interested in *what* our colleagues do, but we are more interested in *why* they do it. Even the most exciting practices cannot just be transported from one situation, setting, and group of people to another. What teachers need is a continuing dialogue grounded in the theory and research of both literature and teaching that is focused on the particular problems of the field of children's literature.

The purpose of this book is to set forth a triad of literary theory, research, and teaching as the basis for such a dialogue. The first three chapters approach this triad from a theoretical base, although there are attempts throughout to relate theoretical ideas to the practice of teaching children's literature. Later chapters contain specific demonstrations of how literary theories, theories of teaching, and scholarly research in children's literature actually inform the practice of teaching. Although this book is primarily directed to those who engage in the teaching of children's literature in colleges and universities, it is also useful to those who want to share literature with children. During many of the almost twenty-five years I have been teaching adults, I was also teaching children; and many of the activities and assignments here have worked equally well with both groups. In fact, many of the ideas and worksheets in this book were first developed with elementary or junior high school students and only later used with adults.

Since teachers, especially beginning teachers, often teach their students the way they were taught, it is especially important for those who teach adults to develop materials and teaching strategies with enough depth to allow real intellectual growth for students of different ages and different levels of experience and knowledge. One intent of this work is to share ideas about the teaching of children's literature that demonstrate respect both for that literature and for all those who enter into engagements with it. Much of what is contained here I learned from my students, both children and adults, and I invite readers to share what they take from this book with those whom they teach. Through such sharing, we can enrich each other, the field, and both child and adult students.

Chapter 1, "Literary Theory and Children's Literature," provides a map outlining the whole world of literary theory. The intent is not to present detailed information about and analysis of any particular aspect of that world, but rather to remind readers of some of the primary landmarks. Those who wish to obtain more information about literary theory in general, or about any one theoretical approach mentioned here, should refer to the bibliography on literary theory for appropriate sources. Using a different metaphor, one might think of this discussion of literary theory as Henry James described criticism, as a house with many windows. This chapter builds the structure or the framework for a house of literary theory and sketches the floor plan so that one might see a layout of rooms within that house. The author hopes to encourage readers to use the bibliography to become more familiar with the various rooms, recognizing that this is, and will remain, a house-in-the-making so that rooms are continually being added or changed. Readers will undoubtedly find one or two rooms in which they feel more comfortable than in others and will use their own knowledge and experiences to add those personal touches that make a particular room their own. I find myself settling most comfortably into a room called transactional or reader-response theory; but, as I settle there, I also carry with me some accoutrements from other rooms in which I have spent time. Thus, in my own theoretical model, with which this chapter ends, one will recognize traces of both archetypal and formalist ideas in what is basically a transactional approach to literary theory.

Chapter 2, "Research and Children's Literature," also presents generic categories and a display of a variety of approaches to research in children's literature. It does not review specific research that has been done in the field but provides a topical analysis and identifies some potential paths for future researchers. I have found this kind of overview especially helpful in working with advanced students planning their own research in children's literature. Since the overall intent of this book is to show the connections from theory to research to teaching, the only specific research activity described in the chapter is that which relates to my own theoretical model described in Chapter 1.

Chapter 3, "Teaching and Children's Literature," presents the third of that triad of disciplines which form the foundation of knowledge necessary to inform the teaching of children's literature. Of the three disciplines, teaching is the one least studied by faculty members in colleges and universities. There seems to be an unfortunate assumption among those in higher education that anyone who is knowledgeable about subject matter will, therefore, be able to teach. Most teachers, however, know that this is not so. New teachers, especially, are often desperate for help and deserve whatever assistance is available, or they may settle into that all-too-familiar pattern of expecting adult students to accommodate their learning to the inadequacies of their teachers. This chapter sets forth a literary model of teaching consisting of composition, craft, and criticism and draws from research and knowledge in general education to help teachers think about their work. As in previous chapters, the content is very selective, identifying only that which this author has found especially useful in her composition of teaching.

Chapter 4, "Development of Course Syllabi in Children's Literature," is a very practical one, demonstrating my own decision-making process as I attempt to translate theoretical knowledge from literary theory, research, and teaching into a preactive plan for the conduct of literature classes. This particular process may not work for everyone, but it is one I have developed over many years and find useful for my own teaching. Of course, the description of this process makes it appear far more orderly that it actually is. In reality, it is much more flexible and variable. The design and development of the "History of Children's Literature" syllabus is used for most of the examples in this chapter because it represents a kind of "middle distance," that is, content that is known to most teachers but is not usually the primary course taught. Thus, it is hoped that readers will be more likely to focus on the process rather than debating the merits of particular items of content.

The actual syllabi developed for my classes are presented in Chapter 5, "Examples of Syllabi for Various Courses." These syllabi are not here for others to copy, although readers are free to do so, but rather as examples of ways of articulating the intent of teaching to students. Some readers may find only segments of an individual syllabus useful in their own teaching but should be able to select from these examples that which will work for them. Since all these syllabi were developed by one person and represent that teacher's knowledge, style, and personal philosophy, there may be more similarities than differences among them. One characteristic evident in all of them is the emphasis on the development of critical and evaluative skills rather than on the study of established literary works. This is directly the result of my own first course in children's literature in which I studied the "best books." Since this course was more than a quarter of a century ago, I would be unable to "sell" most of those books to today's young people, even if they were still available. If I had not continued my own study of literature for children and young adults, I might still be waiting for the reviewers and the book selection aids to tell me which titles are worth sharing. Particularly in a publishing world in which many books go out of print almost before they can be included in such reference tools as the *Children's Catalog*, it is vital that teachers read and evaluate new works as they appear.

Another characteristic of these syllabi is the inclusion of rather lengthy reading lists. Although some students may find these intimidating, the value of the lists is substantial. Students are presented with a more comprehensive map of the field and are given increased options from which to select their own readings. Three of the five syllabi reflect the usual course offerings in the field; the fourth and fifth represent advanced level courses focused in the history of the field or in literary theory itself. The first three normally draw large numbers of students while the others are clearly designed as seminars.

Chapter 6, "Worksheets for the Teaching of Children's Literature," presents a series of worksheets that are intended to help focus student attention on particular aspects of course content. These are merely tools used in teaching, and they are developed, modified, or discarded as emphases in teaching or student needs change. Many of these worksheets are used with other teaching tools such as films, videotapes, or slides as well as with children's books themselves. The numbers assigned to these worksheets are merely accession numbers and not indicative of any priority or emphasis. A list of worksheet titles is included in this chapter.

Continuing education is the focus of Chapter 7, "Continuing Education in Children's Literature." After a brief discussion of some of the more common means for both teachers of children's literature and their students to remain current with new work in the field, an analysis of one institute, focused on heroism, is provided as an example. Also included in this chapter is an expression of concern for the future if we do not plan for differing levels of continuing education programs that meet the needs of teachers, scholars, and researchers, as well as those of beginning students and practitioners. Although not explicit in this chapter, international children's literature is one area in which there is a great need for continuing education. Scholarly work in other, especially non-English-speaking, countries is relatively inaccessible to both teachers and students of children's literature in the United States. In fact, only a limited number of children's books produced in other countries ever become available in the United States.

The bibliographies at the end of this book are, from one perspective, representative of a microcosm of literary theory, research, and teaching as seen from a primary focus on children's literature. This emphasis is evident in the length of the children's literature bibliography compared with the others. The subcategories within that bibliography are somewhat arbitrary, more related to my teaching than to outside criteria. Thus, one seeking information on Beatrix Potter, for example, might find some relevant works listed under Picture Books and Illustration and others under Studies of Authors and Illustrators. Only books are contained here, although a great deal of critical content is available in journal articles. The teaching bibliography is especially eclectic, containing many books not specifically about teaching but important to me as a person in the way I think and feel about my work as a teacher. No annotations are given because contents are often obvious from titles and because further elaborations would reveal more about me than about the authors of these works. Consistent with my philosophy of teaching and my understanding of the reading process is the belief that each reader makes his/her own meaning in relation to a text.

In some ways, these three bibliographies represent the various ways I think about bibliographies in general. They may be used as containers of content and for recognition of key writers and thinkers in a field (children's literature), as a brief sampling of the content and key figures of a field (literary criticism), or as a collection of personally significant or influential ideas that come together in me as a person (teaching). Thus, these lists are highly selective and idiosyncratic—a cluster of works that have informed or inspired my own teaching.

The items listed in the three bibliographies are in one numerical sequence. For the convenience of the reader, an author or work mentioned only briefly in the text is identified by its item number in parenthesis after the reference. Children's books are identified in the footnotes at the ends of chapters.

Throughout the book figures are used to visually present ideas expressed in the text. These figures also are perceived as teaching tools and may not communicate adequately out of context. The model of "The Child's Meaning-Making Process in Response to a Literary Text" (Figure 7) represents the basic triad of concerns underlying this book.

No book is totally and uniquely the product of a single author. My philosophy of teaching and learning is rooted in the belief that ideas and insights are to be shared. To all of those colleagues who have shared their work and their ideas with me, I express my gratitude. Students, many of whom are now colleagues in the teaching of literature, have, over many years, helped me to see young people and their literature in new ways and have given both joy and substance to my work.

Betty Jean Parks translated my rough sketches for the figures into finished products. Her tolerance for my missed deadlines and for frequent overnight mail with pleas for instant assistance was just one of many examples of her continued friendship and support.

David Loertscher of Libraries Unlimited acted with care and concern in the final production of the manuscript.

Leland B. Jacobs, my own teacher of children's literature, although not involved in the preparation of this manuscript, is, nonetheless, present in its pages. It was he who first introduced me to teaching in this field, shared his vision of children and their literature with me, and has served both as inspiration and as sounding board throughout my career. Much of my work as a teacher can be traced directly to my association with Jake as my teacher, my colleague, and my friend.

Very special appreciation is due to Jane Anne Hannigan, without whom this project would never have been completed. Her encouragement, support, and many hours of criticism and discussion added immeasurably to the content of this book. She kept me going when I would otherwise have given up and truly embodies the kind of selfless giving of ideas and effort which is the essence of teaching.

Finally, I wish to thank my mother, Lillian Vandergrift, for her understanding and patience as I worked to complete this manuscript. Her willingness to read and discuss children's books and her insightful responses to them reminded me of my earliest experiences with literature, and her spirited approach to life is a continued source of inspiration.

Kay E. Vandergrift

 **Literary Theory and Children's Literature**

INTRODUCTION

In an age of science and technology when even literary theory bears such names as structuralism and semiotica, we may begin to think of this theory as being very precise and scientific. We must remember, however, that the purpose of such theory is to bring readers closer to literary works. In the past several decades both literary criticism and the theory that supports that criticism have shifted from a base in the literary community of readers and writers to the scholarly community of professors and university students. In the process, literary theory has become more fragmented and, many would say, more isolated, both from the literary works themselves and from the readers and writers connected to those works in the non-academic world. There appears to be no particular theory that dominates virtually all aspects of literary writing and discussion as was evident throughout much of our history. Not only are there many different approaches to literary thought centered in universities in this country, but it also seems that most of these "schools" of criticism are scarcely cohesive enough to be called schools, and are often not necessarily concerned with cohesiveness, let alone dominance in the marketplace of literary ideas. In fact, one sometimes wonders if there is any relationship between the various literary theories practiced in universities and the world of practicing readers, writers, and critics. Those of us who care about children's literature and young readers need to be knowledgeable about the theoretical work of the general literary community, but we are also probably more mindful than some of our colleagues that literature requries readers. Only that theory which, in some way, brings readers closer to the work will ultimately serve the field.

Theory as Metaphor

Those who become lost in what Geoffrey Hartman (710) and others have called the "wilderness" of contemporary literary theory, will find it useful to keep in mind that all theories are themselves products of the imagination. All theories are fictions, if you will, and they are much more tentative and more imprecise than the fictions of story. A theory is a metaphor imposed on discrete phenomena in order to explain those phenomena, identify commonalities, and show relationships among individual and unique objects. Literary theory, therefore, is a metaphor about metaphors. Theories are fictions without the full strength of "make believe" engendered by a fictional work of art, but, nonetheless, they are fictions which may lead to insight and discovery. We try to confirm our belief in theories by experience and experiment, but are, at the same time, fully aware that they are refutable and ever susceptible to modification or disproof.

Theories are judged by their applicability and their usefulness. As new phenomena are created or discovered or existing ones perceived in new ways, theory is revised to assimilate this new information. Thus, all theories are in a process of continuous revision, and when a particular theory can no longer encompass new ideas or new works of art, new theories are developed. Each theory opens our eyes to new perceptions and new perspectives, but it conceals as well as reveals certain aspects of the literary work and the literary experience. Each offers a system of useful, but incomplete, organizing constructs which continually lead to new solutions, new problems, and new theories.

Like all fiction, literary theory requires a willing suspension of disbelief, that condition of mind philosophers refer to as the world of "as if." We enter into Mr. McGregor's garden or the land of Oz *as if* those places really exist while, at the same time, acknowledge that they are not to be found in the actual world of our everyday existence. So too we must learn to accept the statements of a literary theory *as if* the premises were valid, use that theory as a lens to examine the particular aspects of the literary work or the literary experience on which it sheds light, and make what meaning we can of what we see with that light. The lenses I use to find my way through the wilderness of literary criticism are closest to those of the reader-response critics, particularly to the transactional theory of Louise Rosenblatt (804). My personal literary history has also been influenced by early studies based on the formalist approaches of the now-old "New Critics" and the archetypal theories of Northrop Frye (690). It is from this combination of perspectives that I view the theory, research, and teaching of children's literature.

Literature is, first of all, to be experienced, to be enjoyed, to be appreciated, to be loved. Each reader, in the process of experiencing a literary work, both brings meaning to and takes meaning from that work. Thus, the meaning made from having experienced that work is personal and idiosyncratic and is based on all that the reader has known and experienced outside that work. Meaning is also communal in the understanding of the human condition as expressed in and communicated by the work. Without that initial appreciation of and engagement with the work, the experience remains meaningless. The fact that teachers have assigned a particular text or even read that text aloud to students (either children or adult students of children's literature) does not necessarily mean that those students have read meaning into or out of that text. Without that process of meaning-making which is reading, there can be no progression to critical or theoretical judgment. Once this reading occurs, however, any further consideration of literary works has some general notions about the nature of literature, that is, some semblance of literary theory, at its core. Even the discussion of personal events from one's own life in response to a literary text is, in one sense, an implicit acceptance of the assumption that literature illuminates or instructs actual life experiences.

Relation of Theory, Research and Criticism

Theory, then, needs to be seen in a total context of literary criticism and literary research, two other means of approaching or responding to the literary experience. As we attempt to distinguish between literary theory and literary criticism, we find that criticism comes both before and after theory. We must be aware of, experience, and respond to unique works of art before we can conceive of a literary theory; and then, in order to refer to a work of art, we must distance ourselves from our experiencing of it with the abstractions of language. Any discussion of literary works requires some degree of distancing, abstraction, labelling, and generalization, or, in other words, theorizing, even if that theoretical activity is implicit and subconscious. As literary theory is more consciously and precisely developed and general principles established, individual texts may be viewed as manifestations of an abstract structure which should in turn aid in the analysis or interpretation—the criticism—of unique works of art. The normal progression in this development is:

1. The reader experiences a unique work of art.

2. There is some pre-critical response. ("I like it.")

3. The reader takes the first steps in critical response with some theory at least implicit. ("I like it because....")

4. There is a comparision and contrast among works and among various responses to a particular work.

5. The reader develops some general notions applicable to all literary works. (a general theory)

6. There is a testing of that general theory in relation to specific works.

7. The reader revises theory in response to that testing.

These seven stages are illustrated in Figure 1.

FIGURE 1

STAGES IN THE DEVELOPMENT OF LITERARY THEORY

(What new knowledge or understandings of literature will I bring to subsequent readings?)

REVISE THEORY (7)

READER EXPERIENCES WORK (1)

(An internal act ordinarily not "visible" either to the reader or to an outside observer.)

(Is each additional work examined illuminated in some way by the developing theory?)

TEST THEORY (6)

PRE-CRITICAL RESPONSE (2)

(How do I feel about this work or in response to it?)

(How does this work relate to other works? Are there some things which seem to be true of all literature, or at least of all works similar to this one? Rephrase specific questions to become general questions. Relate them to each other in organized system.)

DEVELOP GENERAL THEORY (5)

BEGINNING CRITICISM (3)

(What in the work evoked these personal reactions? What questions are suggested by the work?)

COMPARISON & CONTRAST (4)

(How is this work like and un-like other works? How is my experience of this work like and unlike my experiences of other works?)

You will note that this process of meaning-making and theorizing begins again with each work experienced, although obviously the meanings we bring to a text and the context in which we consider it are enhanced by previous encounters with literature. Thus, theory and criticism are two sides of the same coin. They are inter-penetrating and inseparable literary activities.

Research, on the other hand, occurs (or should occur) after theory and depends upon some sort of organized or theoretical means of imposing order on discrete phenomena. A theory leads to a taxonomy because we must have names and categories to bring order to and make sense of our theorizing. To see the uniqueness of an individual work presupposes that there are some principles of differentiation. Theory, therefore, implies a methodology which might be used in the validation of that theory, that is, in the process of research.

Why Theory?

Why is knowledge of literary theory important to those of us whose primary area of interest is children and their literature? There are two basic reasons. First, many of us have declared that children's literature is an important and equal part of all literature and have been somewhat resentful that the rest of the literary community has not fully accepted our literature and our work. But one does not become a part of a scholarly community, or any other community, by declaration. Participation in a community requires constant care, sensitivity to the whole, and just plain hard work. If we do not work diligently to remain informed about adult literature, criticism, research, and literary theory, we cannot expect other members of the literary community to take our work seriously. It is also our study of adult literary theory that helps us to interpret and appreciate children's literature more fully.

Second, children, with their unbridled curiosity, their constant "why?" questions, and their attempts to group like things and like works together, are at the early exciting stages of theoretical activity. Questions such as "Is it believe or make-believe?", posed prior to hearing a story, or requests for "another book like this one" are examples of a child's beginning sense of literary relationships, which is the very beginning of theory. Our adult understanding of literary theory helps us to recognize big ideas in child-sized language and to find ways to keep that beginning theory-making activity and that excitement about literature alive and growing. Some teachers of children's literature might say of literary criticism as Marianne Moore has said of poetry:

> I, too, dislike it: there are things that are important
> > beyond all this fiddle.
> Reading it, however, with a perfect contempt for it,
> > one discovers in
> it after all, a place for the genuine.[1]

It is that "place for the genuine" we must seek in all our teaching of children's literature, a place where literary scholarship, literature itself, and all those who make meaning in transaction with that literature are respected and valued.

In the preceding comments, I have revealed something of my own prejudice and my own stance within that "wilderness" of contemporary literary theory and criticism. Most of us find it difficult to divorce ourselves and our individual perceptions of literature from the idea of meaning. Until recently, the various schools of literary theory shared a concern for meaning. There was disagreement about where that meaning resides, but not a great deal of doubt about its existence. Theorists of deconstructive criticism suggest, however, that the bond between signifier and signified is arbitrary, which is a denial of both perception and reference. From this perspective, the words of the text never mean what they say or even what anyone thinks they mean. The text is perceived as an instable object composed of words deprived of referential meaning because language itself is unreliable. Deconstructionists appear to believe that language does not convey meaning but complicates and ultimately cancels it. Words lead only to other words, not to a known or knowable world, or to ideas, or even back to a speaking self. If we were to give this theory a name from a children's story, we might call it "the theory of *Outside Over There*." This concern with the inability of language to convey meaning is, of course, not a new one. It might be said that the deconstructionists have carried to the extreme Percy Bysshe Shelley's romantic notion of the "imperfect medium of language." In fact, in spite of their apparent radical departures from previous literary ideas, deconstructive and other contemporary theories may be perceived as being natural developments of an ever-spiraling concern with the various elements of the literary experience, each returning to, and enlarging upon, previous work.

APPROACHES TO CRITICAL THEORY

The various primary approaches to critical theory are illustrated in Figures 2 and 3. Figure 2 illustrates those aspects of the life of a literary work that have traditionally been taken into account in an examination of literature or the literary experience. The diagram is intended to represent the four primary approaches to meaning. The literary work itself is central because to have any kind of literary theory or

FIGURE 2

ASPECTS OF A LITERARY WORK

(APPROACHES TO CRITICISM)

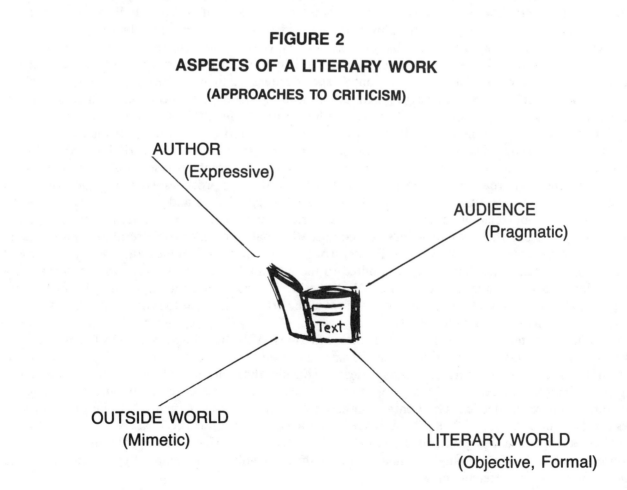

AUTHOR
(Expressive)

AUDIENCE
(Pragmatic)

OUTSIDE WORLD
(Mimetic)

LITERARY WORLD
(Objective, Formal)

literary criticism, one must first have something that has been identified as literature to serve as the starting point of discussion or study, and the basic referent to which the study must return. The circle of meaning in which the work exists contains many possible meanings generated by each of the four coordinates.

Mimetic theories are those that emphasize relationships to the world outside the work; pragmatic theories emphasize the audience; expressive theories emphasize the author; and objective or formal theories emphasize literary knowledge or the structure of the work itself.

Two of the best sources of information about these approaches to literary theory are Meyer Abrams (615) and William Wimsatt (843). Both recognized that, in order to deal meaningfully with all the diverse and highly individualistic forms of literary study, one must impose some theoretical framework upon the field that will artificially "hold still" what is a dynamic, relative, and ever-changing human concern. Abrams did this as clearly as any when he suggested that all critical theories could be discussed in terms of the various emphases and alignments that can occur among the four coordinates. Wimsatt is more concerned with relationships between subject and object in a work of art and treats the four coordinates or main types of literary theory in terms of tensions between opposing pairs. Wimsatt calls these the genetic (Author), the affective (Audience), the contential (World), and the formal (Literary Knowledge). He places a fifth type of theory, the tensional, in the center of the four coordinates and focuses his attention on the axis between contential and formal types of literary analysis, that is, between art as technique, style, and structure and art as a statement of a true message. Another means of categorizing contemporary literary theories divides them into three basic groups based on the process of explication or interpretation: phenomenological theories explore the mode of existence of the literary work; hermeneutic theories are concerned with the reader's understanding of self when confronted with the work; and gestalt theories concentrate on the perceptive powers of the reader as brought into play by the literary work.

Figure 3 presents an alternative but complementary view of the sources of meaning among the various elements of the literary experience. The author, in composing a literary work, has intent, whether that intent be simply "to tell a story" or to contain specific ideas, feelings, or meanings within the form of the work. The work always contains the potential for meaning whether that meaning was intended or not, or whether it falls short of or differs from the author's intent. Thus, the content actually conveyed to readers by the vehicle of the formed literary work may differ significantly from what the author had in mind. Readers, then, not only receive some content conveyed by the form of the work, but also have their own intent in engaging in a transaction with that work. (Louise Rosenblatt distinguishes between efferent and aesthetic approaches to literature, that is, between those approaches which are concerned with what may be taken from the work to be used in other life experiences and those which seek only the enjoyment and appreciation to be found in the experiencing of that work.) Thus, readers extend the content, by bringing their own meanings into contact with that work, ultimately resulting in a recreated meaning for each reader. In this way, the literary work is a vehicle of communication, over both time and space, that contains meaning but is not limited to the meaning intended by its author or to that of a particular reader or community of readers. Both the literary world and the larger outside world from Figure 2, although not visible here, are omnipresent in the other elements as the context in which this process of recreating meaning takes place.

Although differences among literary theories have most often been identified according to which of the four basic variables assumes primary significance, most theories, at least until recently, have acknowledged the influence of all four, and, to some degree, consider the relationships among them. All criticism begins with an encounter with a literary object and then that object is related, either implicitly or explicitly, to some framework that focuses attention on certain aspects of its being and determines the kinds of results that can be achieved. The critic as reader or audience is one critical context that cannot be totally eliminated and is used, to greater or lesser extent, by all critics. As Henry James (737) described it, the house of fiction is one of many dissimilar windows through which many pairs of eyes watch the same show but see many different things.

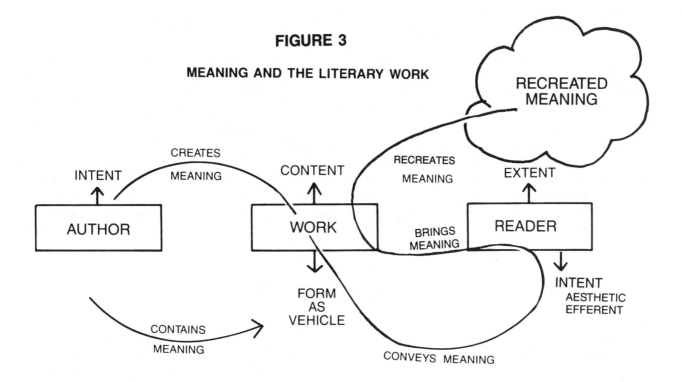

FIGURE 3

MEANING AND THE LITERARY WORK

Perhaps the most obvious evidence in children's literature of these many pairs of eyes is seen by examining multiple picture book versions of a single traditional tale. The dramatic differences between Trina Schart Hyman's vision of Snow White and Nancy E. Burkert's have resulted in fascinating comparisons between the two.[2] When one adds historical renderings of Snow White as well as other contemporary visions, the varieties of interpretation of a single text are powerfully demonstrated. This would be equally true for virtually any traditional tale as evidenced in the continuing flow of new editions of folk and fairy tales each year. The various interpretations of folk and fairy tales are not dependent upon illustration alone for their impact. What has kept these stories alive over time and through many cultures is the ability of different peoples to recognize themselves and what is important in their lives within these very simple texts. Literary critics, as well as other readers, bring their differing perspectives to bear on these works and interpret them in light of a number of critical and theoretical perspectives as seen in "Three Little Pigs: From Six Directions."[3]

What critics and literary theorists have been able to see either in a work or in the literary experience has also been determined, in part at least, by the times in which they live. Each era has preconceptions of the world and of literature that both reveal and conceal certain aspects of understanding and experience. There are no neat beginnings and endings to these eras, and there were always individuals writing and talking about literature whose ideas deviated greatly from the mainstream.

Mimetic Theories

The beginnings of mimetic theories of literary criticism are usually traced back to the work of Socrates, Plato, and Aristotle. Although their basic concerns were not necessarily literary or aesthetic theory and their perceptions of mimesis differed, all three shared the belief that works of art are imitations.

They did not agree upon whether art imitates things or the forms of things, the world of the senses or the world of shadows; but this view of art as imitation dominated aesthetic theory until the end of the seventeenth and the beginning of the eighteenth century. Mimesis has been evident since then in the work of individuals such as Shelley, who in his *Defense of Poetry* proclaimed that all poems imitate the same essential forms which are the residences of value and models for all human activities and products, and in that of Stendhal, who referred to the novel as "a mirror on wheels." More recently, contemporary critics such as Gerald Graff in his *Literature Against Itself* (705) and Eugene Goodheart in *The Failure of Criticism* (703) called for a return to a more rational, referential, mimetic understanding of literature.

Using a mimetic approach to children's literature, one might ask, "How does the modern sociological novel reflect late twentieth-century American life?" or "Are the works of Judy Blume and Robert Cormier accurate representations of the lives of young people today?" The content analysis studies of family patterns, sex roles, racial and ethnic diversity, and the like are, for the most part, mimetic studies of literature as they attempt to determine if the characteristics of the fictional world correspond with those of the actual world.

Pragmatic Theories

Throughout most of the eighteenth century, literary theory was dominated by pragmatic ideas or a means-end concept of evaluating works in terms of their usefulness for practical academic or moral instruction. These ideas were stated earlier by Sir Philip Sidney in his *The Apologie for Poetry* when he said the end of poetry was "to teach and to delight." Horace emphasized the pleasurable end but believed that "graver" readers would not be pleased without moral matter, and many will recall Dr. Samuel Johnson's phrase "to instruct by pleasing." Pragmatic theories shifted attention from the nature of the world to the nature of human beings, but they were also concerned with rules of imitation and the craft of the creator, thus looking back to mimesis and forward to the expressive theories most evident in nineteenth-century Romanticism.

There should be little difficulty thinking of pragmatic theories in relation to children's literature. Unfortunately, those who work with children's literature have traditionally been too pragmatic, often at the expense of the literature itself. We have overemphasized what children's literature is "good for" rather than "good" literature. This is understandable, of course, when we acknowledge that children's literature has always been didactic in that it represents, at least in part, one generation's impulse to pass on information, ideas, and values to the next. Although most works from the early history of children's literature appear depressingly, or sometimes humorously, didactic to today's audiences; one must wonder if the works of Mrs. Trimmer in the eighteenth century or of Mrs. Molesworth and Charlotte Yonge in the nineteenth century will appear any more "preachy" to future audiences than some of the problem novels of the 1960s to the 1980s. It is true, however, that even those works considered the best, and the most pleasing, of children's literature are also useful for their ability to instruct. The works of C. S. Lewis, J. R. R. Tolkien, W. H. Hudson, and others which James Higgins (231) has called mystical fancy lend themselves readily to this approach for their presentation of basic human or "spiritual" values. One might also consider a popular modern novel such as Laurence Yep's *Child of the Owl*[4] from the perspective of pragmatic criticism. This work certainly has the capacity to delight readers; but in their enjoyment of the story, readers probably also learn some specifics of Chinese-American life in San Francisco. More significantly, a reader may take from this story a more general appreciation for another way of life, for an older generation, and for a sense of tradition and continuity amidst change.

Rosenblatt would identify any intent to make these kinds of meanings from a literary work as efferent rather than aesthetic. Although most literature, upon reflection, yields more than just the aesthetic satisfaction of the reading itself, evidence of an overly moralistic or practical approach to children's literature is revealed in the emphasis on thematic, problematic, or curricular concerns in bibliographies of children's books and in adult-led discussions of those books. One may wonder when reading bibliographies or discussion guides how an author who has spent many months on a book and placed a great deal of self and a wide-ranging world view into that book reacts when that work is simply labelled "Getting Along With Siblings" in a list of others "with the same theme." As many authors have said, they compose a story world; others then label the theme and act as if that theme were more important than the imagined world created by the author. This is not to say that such bibliographic tools are not helpful in that all-important task of finding appropriate books for young readers, but we must guard against allowing the external "problem" of the protagonist or of potential readers to overpower the telling of story.

Expressive Theories

The Greek philosopher Longinus was the chief historical source of the notion of the work as a reflection of its author, but we probably know this theory best through William Wordsworth's "spontaneous overflow of powerful feelings" in the preface to the *Lyrical Ballads* or John Stuart Mill's "feeling expressing itself in moments of solitude" ("What Is Poetry" and "The Two Kinds of Poetry—Essays," 1833). The mirror that was held to the world or to the hidden nature of the world by mimetic theorists was, in the hands of expressive theorists, held up to the author, and the sincerity and intensity of that author's emotion as revealed in language became cardinal values. Leo Tolstoy (830) referred to an "infection theory" in which literature is viewed as emotional communication, and Susanne Langer wrote of art as the dynamic form of feeling (746). Even I. A. Richards, better known as a formalist, discussed an emotive theory in which literature has no meaning (proposition), only expression, in his work with C. K. Ogden (777). A somewhat different author-centered approach is found in the work of modern critic and theorist E. D. Hirsch (719, 720). Hirsch insists upon accepting the author's meanings of the texts, defines interpretations as the construction of *another's* meaning, and believes that any perspective other than the author's will, at best, reveal a significance extrinsic to the meaning of the work.

There are many works of children's literature that, because of the beauty of the language and the emotions conveyed, lend themselves to an expressive approach to criticism. Barbara Wersba's *The Crystal Child*, especially when read aloud, encourages one to bask in the mystical beauty of its language and feeling.

The statue was dead. She stared into the sunset with cold eyes, and its colors were her colors. When the moon came she would turn into moonlight. When it was dawn she would become dawn for a while and sparkle with rainbows. She had no life beyond these moments. She was made of rainbows and the moon.[5]

Or consider the more realistic, but equally powerful and mysterious, feeling of events under Jane Yolen's *Owl Moon*:

> The owl's call came closer,
> from high up in the trees
> on the edge of the meadow.
> Nothing in the meadow moved.
> All of a sudden
> an owl shadow,
> part of the big tree shadow,
> lifted off
> and flew right over us.
> We watched silently
> with heat in our mouths,
> the heat of all those words
> we had not spoken.[6]

For a very different sense of the power of language, recall the pure joy expressed in the "silly talk" of *Rain Makes Applesauce*[7] or the perpetual pleasure of Lewis Carroll's "Jabberwocky."

Expressive theories, however, focus on the expression of the author. In response to questions about the composition of *Sweet Whispers, Brother Rush*,[8] Virginia Hamilton described her own creative process:

> An image occurs in my mind. A book follows. One day, I had an image of a teen age girl coming home through urban streets. She sees a young man whom she falls in love with. I know immediately that the young man is not as she sees him. And I know that she is unaware of his true nature.
>
> This is how *Sweet Whispers, Brother Rush* occurred to me. It simply began with a swift, yet somewhat vague image that had a street as its setting. And it was compelling enough for me to take the time to write it down. I find that setting down such an image tends to make it grow. The street expands into a larger setting. I follow the young woman home, observe how she is dressed and know what she thinks about the young man. Upon entering her home, I see how she lives. I discover she is alone with her brother. I know her name, Sweet Tree. I know her brother is frail, physically, and limited, mentally. His name is Dabney and he is called Dab. I know that their mother, Vy, is rarely home. The apartment in which Tree and Dab live is at once their security and their isolation. Enter the young man in the street who is not as he seems at first to Tree. The three of them are enclosed in a shadow world where the past and the present exist side by side. It is a place full of kindness, full of sorrow. It is a place where love and caring wither, and grow again stronger than ever.
>
> All of us carry our pasts around with us in the present as physical traits, mannerisms, sweet nostalgia. We also carry the past as family history and historical fact. I have written *Sweet Whispers, Brother Rush* as sincere entertainment, in memory of past ghosts who stay with me. And it is through the creative process of the known, the remembered and the imagined that I am able to tell the tale.[9]

Hamilton's statement seems to point more toward earlier expressive theories than to Hirsch's search for authorial meaning. One might, through biographical and historical criticism and through analysis of the work itself, attempt to discover and interpret Hamilton's original meaning; but, if such meaning exists, it appears to be not so much "intended" as inherent or subconscious. Hamilton's explanation does, however, satisfy, if somewhat mystically, some of that curiosity many readers feel toward the authors of the books they read and enjoy.

Objective Theories

Although roots might be traced to Aristotle's *Poetics*, objective theories were rare in the early history of literary studies and really began to emerge in the late eighteenth and early nineteenth centuries. The belief in "art for art's sake," that art does not imitate the world but creates its own autonomous world, has been preeminent during much of this century and is probably the theory used to instruct many who now teach children's literature. Those of us who find our own personal realities often chaotic and disordered have taken heart in the ability of the imagination to impose order and create a coherent, unified world, to, as Robert Frost said of poetry, "make shapes out of chaos." Kant wrote of the purposefulness of art without purpose and the need for a "disinterested" contemplation of its beauty, that is, an appreciation of the reality of the object without regard to its utility. This may sound very close to Rosenblatt's aesthetic approach; but, in practice, it resulted in the close analysis of themes, images, or words within a literary text remembered by many of us from our own high school or college classrooms. Such literary study depends upon close reading of the work itself to reveal the independent, balanced structure subject to its own internal requirements of unity, probability, and progression which is called "story". Because of our familiarity with this approach to literary theory and the influence of texts such as Rene Wellek and Austin Warren's *Theory of Literature* (837) or Cleanth Brooks and Robert Penn Warren's *Understanding Poetry* (643), many of us still tend to think of the particular brand of objective criticism labelled the "New Criticism" as the one "true" literary criticism distinct from external or extrinsic studies of author, audience, or the outside world.

Of course, close analysis of the formal elements of story has been simplified for the comprehension of children and young people. Various forms of language and linguistic analysis become vocabulary study, often with too little attention paid to literary or metaphoric meanings in the pursuit of the literal. Occasionally, some of the obvious symbols from the title pages of children's books (*The Hundred Dresses, The Jazz Man,* etc.)[10] are pointed to and discussed and more subtle symbols are searched for in the text. Some children's literature textbooks, however, still present elementary introductions to theme, plot, characterization, and style as if these four were the only literary elements, ignoring the fact that mood or setting may be key elements in a particular story and that point of view is probably the element most characteristic of the novel as a genre. Tracing themes has been almost as common in children's literature as in work for adults, but style remains elusive and ill-defined and so is virtually ignored in this typical four-pronged approach.

TWENTIETH-CENTURY LITERARY THEORY

Before more closely examining contemporary literary theory, let us think once again of that shift of focus from one component in the chain of literary communication to another and try to link these literary changes to changes in society. Obviously, all four of the basic components exist in a cultural context and cannot be completely separated from the social and intellectual climate in which they have their being. What an author is able to create or an audience is able to perceive is, to some extent at least, limited and shaped by the time and place in which those human beings live. The progression of concern from an emphasis on norms or *codes* of literary forms in Classical poetics, to the *encoder* in Romantic expressionism, to the text and the *message* of formalism, to the *decoder* in reader-response theories might be perceived of as a move from elitism to democratization in the understanding of literary experience. Of course, all of these approaches have coexisted over time, and it is only the emphasis that has changed. Recent works are now challenging the reader-centered approach which has been prominent in recent years. E. D. Hirsch's *Cultural Literacy* (902) and Allan Bloom's *The Closing of the American Mind* (855), both surprising best sellers of 1987, have caused many to rethink the openness and emphasis on the learner (reader) rather than the content of education (literature) and will undoubtedly have an effect on approaches to literary study into the last decade of the twentieth century.

During the twentieth century, literary criticism and theory in America have shifted the focus of attention from *interpretation* to *structure* to *response*. Pre-twentieth-century criticism was concerned primarily with *value*. Historical scholarship dominated the early twentieth century until it gave way to formalistic approaches, especially the New Criticism. The movement toward the New Criticism began in the 1890s, grew in strength through the 1930s, and reigned supreme throughout the 1940s and 1950s. This growth of New Criticism coincided with the growth of mass education and with the creation of more complex literary works requiring greater explication. The introduction of these new works into the curriculum and the move from lecture to discussion as a means of education made methodology more important than the reader's prior knowledge in literary study. The decline of belief in the "social function" of literature and of the cultural snobbery of the "sensitive and knowledgeable elite" led to a democratization of the literary experience and, ultimately, to a move from formalist approaches toward reader-response or reception theories.

The Early Years: New Criticism

New Criticism was undoubtedly the most influential of the formalistic approaches that dominated the first seventy-five years of twentieth century literary criticism, but there were other formalist groups as well. Vanderbilt University fostered a group known as the "Fugitives" who worked there with John Crowe Ransom (794). R. S. Crane (656) and Wayne Booth (639, 640) were the best known of the Chicago Critics or the Neo-Aristotelians who saw fiction as more dynamic than the somewhat static forms of the New Critics. They emphasized plot but also paid attention to action and setting. In addition, this period saw the beginnings of mythic criticism and the work of individuals such as Yvor Winters (846) and R. P. Blackmur (633) who formulated their own systems for literary study. All these approaches emphasized literary technique or methodology to illuminate form and theme in reaction to earlier extrinsic studies of literary history and biography that focused attention away from the literary work itself. For the most part, the work of the formalists was theoretically weak but critically productive. There was great variety among the various formalistic approaches, but they were united in the acceptance of two basic premises—the primacy of the work itself and the need for a close reading of the text.

I. A. Richards's *Principles of Literary Criticism* (801) and *Practical Criticism* (800) were two of the most influential early works of formalistic criticism followed by studies, based on their own writing, by T. S. Eliot (675, 676), Allen Tate (823), Robert Penn Warren (833), and others. Between 1945 and 1955 there were two major influences on literary theory. The post-war emphasis on science placed historical and impressionistic studies of literature in even greater dispute and encouraged the institutionalization of the New Criticism to the extent that what had been general attitudes and tentative approaches became dogma. The most influential text in this institutionalization of the New Criticism was undoubtedly Brooks and Warren's *Understanding Poetry* (833), first published in 1938 but used as a college text well into the 1960s.

The New Criticism was created, in part at least, to explain the work of contemporary authors, and as those authors receded into history, so did this critical methodology. There were, however, other factors which led to its decline. The method was best suited to the short poem and did not prove as useful in the study of the novel. For example, Brooks and Warren's *Understanding Fiction* (644) was not as well-received or as effective for teaching as was *Understanding Poetry* (833). In addition, and more serious, the method kept literature so isolated from history, culture and human response that it lost any relationship to the lives of many readers. Finally, the close ties to education which led to its almost total acceptance as "the one true critical approach" led also, in the hands of poor teachers, to its misuse in an attempt to prescribe readers' reactions to and interpretations of literature. Contrary to this movement, and certainly to a lesser degree in this early period, literary studies followed society in a move from consensus to diversity.

Since many of those who have been teachers of children's literature in the last few decades were themselves students of the New Criticism, it is to be expected that at least some variants of this approach would be evident in the field of children's literature. The inappropriate analysis of poetic forms before children develop a love for poetry itself, which Leland B. Jacobs refers to as "verse vivisection," is a typical misuse. Similar misuses have abounded in work with children and story. Some teachers and librarians have either not trusted children to read, often what we have selected for them to read, or have presumed a sacred trust to see that young readers "really comprehend" their reading. The response to both of these concerns has too frequently been an emphasis on the facts within the text or the literal interpretation of those facts, ignoring that fictional meaning is literary or metaphoric, not literal. This response, of course, is not what the New Critics had in mind, but it has often been considered a "safe" method that is easily administered by teachers, even it it is self-defeating to focus on the factual content of a work of art. One suspects that many teachers using this approach were primarily concerned with assuring themselves that youngsters had decoded the text and were uncertain about how to deal with the more complex encoding or interpretive and comprehensive skills of reading. Even the analysis of structure, syntax, diction, symbol, and metaphor common to the work of the New Critics often became an end in itself rather than a means of increasing understanding and enjoyment of the literary composition. The consequences were years of dreary discussions and those even more dreary and belabored dissections known as book reports.

Beginning in the Fifties: Archetypal Criticism

Two 1957 publications heralded the move from what almost appeared to be literary study as devotional practice to literary study as theology. Wimsatt and Brooks' *Literary Criticism: A Short History* (844) summarized the past, predicted the demise of the New Criticism, and presented a prologue of some of the changes which were to follow. Frye's *Anatomy of Criticism* (690) was a landmark work representing a radical shift in Anglo-American literary theory and criticism. *Anatomy of Criticism* marks the move from critical analysis of individual works to the development of an overall theoretical approach to the whole body of literature and is one of the first major critical works of this period not produced by a practicing artist. Frye shares a concern for the autonomy of individual works of art with the formalists, but harks toward the structuralists who are to follow in his concern for the structural similarities and archetypal patterns of various genres. Unlike advocates of either of these critical approaches, however, his theory focuses on individual works primarily as representatives of groups or genres in a total organization or system of literary knowledge rather than as unique creative compositions. The focus is on how the works are the same rather than how they differ. The archetypes he identified exist in all aspects of popular culture as well as in what might be called "good literature." In response to an earlier article of Frye's, Brooks asked "Is the aim to make criticism a purely descriptive, value-free social science?" To a large extent Frye answers "Yes" to that question and has consistently stated that value judgments have no place in criticism. This posture enables him to treat popular culture and classical literature equally as representative of mythic groups. More important to present readers, however, is the fact that Frye has recognized the equality of children's literature and the need for the education of the child's imagination through literature.[11]

Glenna Davis Sloan's *The Child As Critic* (86) and Kay Vandergrift's *Child and Story: The Literary Connection* (102) contain specific details on the use of Frye's theory with young people, and Frye himself was supervisory editor of a series of literature textbooks entitled *Literature: Uses of the Imagination*.[12] In addition, there have been numerous genre studies in children's literature, some of which have been specifically based on Frye's work.[13] All of these should be useful to those working with children, but teachers of children's literature are also urged to read at least *Anatomy of Criticism* and *The Educated Imagination* to determine the applicability of this critical theory to their own work.

The Sixties: Social and Literary Diversity

As the somewhat more unified social and political attitudes of the 1950s gave way to the conflicts and diversity of the 1960s, literary theory also became a many-headed beast. The student movement with its demand for relevance and the more general unrest resulting from the Vietnam conflict proved fertile ground for the growth of a variety of approaches to literature as it interacts with history, biography, sociology, and psychology. Frederick Crews' collection of parodies, *The Pooh Perplex* (657), is a delightfully ironic look at many of these approaches. The social activism of the 1960s was reflected in a diversity of activity in the literary community, including many studies of racism, sexism and other "isms" in literature. At the same time, however, there was a move toward examination of literature as a linguistic structure and several new theoretical approaches to literary studies.

One needs a very detailed and complex map to find a way through what appears to be the maze of contemporary literary thought. Consequently, one trait required of students of literary theory is "a tolerance for ambiguity." An informed and receptive but somewhat skeptical tolerance may be the attribute most needed by those trying to make some sense of what is happening in the field. It seems that, among the many forms of contemporary literary activity, two major strands are evident—structuralism and reader-response. Deconstructionism, mentioned earlier, began as a reappraisal of structuralism and does not seem to have a powerful influence in this country, and certainly not in the study of children's literature.

Both structuralism and reader-response theories were, in part, reactions to that social unrest of the 1960s when this country was perceived by many as the leader of a dehumanized, technological, warring world. The structuralists, to some, embraced the scientific form of textual analysis as a means toward human—and humane—meaning. Reader-response theorists, on the other hand, turned from the text to focus on readers. Young people who were "doing their own thing" in an effort to avoid becoming "things" in this dehumanized world embraced what Wimsatt and Beardsley (845) had earlier called the "affective fallacy" or the confusion of the work with its results, its affects on readers.

Structuralism

Structuralism came into prominence in the American literary community during the 1960s and 1970s. Although many still perceive it as a relatively new approach to literary theory, it is clear that most of the ideas of structuralism are direct descendants of the Russian Formalist movement of the 1920s, only recently practiced to any great extent in the West. Claude Levi-Strauss's (755) concepts of structural anthropology in the analysis of myth are widely known here and have been influential in the popularization of structuralism in linguistics, philosophy, and psychoanalysis, as well as in anthropology and literary theory. F. de Saussure's work (808) in linguistic theory is an even more direct source of the intellectual origins of literary structuralism. One work of Russian Formalism that is widely known to children's literature specialists is Vladimir Propp's *The Morphology of the Folktale* (785), largely through Andre F. Favat's *Child and Tale* (491) which was based, in part, on Propp's work.

Structuralism, in whatever discipline, is basically a way of thinking about the world that is concerned primarily with the perception and description of basic structures. This approach is the result of a twentieth century shift in the perception of reality that occurred first in the physical sciences and then in the social sciences and the humanities, which posits that the world is not comprised of independently existing objects that can be perceived objectively. Each observer possesses personal biases that determine what objects are perceived, and how they are perceived, and it is this relationship between observer and observed, rather than the object itself, that is the "stuff" of reality. This view refers, of course, to *semiology*, a general science of signs which investigates all human activity as "signifying systems," the elements or components of which derive meaning in relation to each other and to the system itself. Saussure analyzed the sign and identified its two components: the "signifier" (the sound or written sign used to communicate the message) and the "signified" (the mental or conceptual representation of the "signifier"). The signified is not a thing but an idea, notion, or image of a thing which comes to the mind when the signifier is expressed. The nature of the message conveyed by any sign is culturally determined, that is, signs have no natural significance, only cultural or conventional ones. Flowers, for instance, have no meaning in and of themselves, only that which we attribute to them. A single rosebud presented by a young man to his sweetheart has a very different significance than that same flower woven into a funeral wreath.

Literary structuralists believe that literature is non-referential; they neither discover meaning nor assign meaning to a work, but attempt to identify how one uses various semiotic conventions in making sense of texts. Structuralists have, in recent years, suffered from others' associations of their work with that of those deconstructionist or absurdist theorists who deny the ability of language to express reality, deny the validity of all forms of literary criticism and, sometimes, even of knowledge in general. Some structuralists, on the contrary, see themselves as advocates of a "human science" capable of identifying the structures that make up a coherent universe and regard their work as an affirmation of the human mind's ability to make sense of the world. Structuralism is, however, not an ideology but a method, a way of approaching and rationalizing a particular field of inquiry.

In looking at structuralism, or any literary theory, those who are in the community of concern for children's literature must ask themselves two questions: How does this theory relate to the study of children's literature? and How does this theory inform our work with children in the process of sharing the literary experience? More specifically, one might ask such questions as: Will a structuralist approach be as useful in examing modern realistic fiction as for traditional literature, popular culture, and fantasy? What semiotic conventions communicate meaning in the illustrations of a picture story book? What kind of literary experiences could be planned for young children to aid in their growth as "competent readers" with a mastery of a wide variety of semiotic conventions? Recent and significant attempts to answer some of these questions, based primarily on the work of Roland Barthes and Jonathan Culler, are found in the Children's Literature Association Quarterly's "Structuralist Approaches to Children's Literature,"[14] including Roxburgh's interpretation of *Anno's Counting Book*[15] and Stott's structuralist approach to *The Hobbit* in *The Reading Teacher*.[16]

Reader-Response Theories

Two major overviews of reception aesthetics or the reader-response school of literary study, both published in 1980, trace the roots of this approach from "New Criticism" and encompass all literary ideas since, including structuralism. The subtitle of Jane P. Tompkin's *Reader-Response Criticism* (797) is

"From Formalism to Post-Structuralism," and Susan Suleiman and Inge Crosman's *The Reader and the Text* (796) identifies six varieties of audience-oriented criticism: (1) rhetorical, (2) semiotic and structuralist, (3) phenomenological, (4) subjective and psychoanalytic, (5) sociological and historical, and (6) hermeneutic. Each of these groups has many branches or divisions within it, and a single critic may be placed under any one of several of the labels depending on the specific article or book being discussed. Recall the need for that "tolerance for ambiguity."

Rhetorical studies, such as much of the work of Wayne Booth, are primarily concerned with the total situation of communication, its meaning, ideological content, or persuasive force. Semiotic or structuralist approaches are included in the Suleiman and Crosman volume, in spite of the concentration on the text, because of their conception of that text as indeterminate—a product of the reader's mind. In Barthes's words, the "object of structuralism is not man endowed with meanings, but man fabricating meanings." Phenomenological studies, best known through the work of Iser who in turn uses Ingarden's work as a point of departure, focus on aesthetic perception and the role of imagination in the construction of meaning. Here the text is an indeterminate skeleton of four different strata of schemes (Sound, Meaning, Represented Objectivities, and Aspects) and readers give form to a work by adding their own determinations to each of these strata.

Psychoanalytic or subjective studies are concerned with the ways in which a reader's personality shapes reading and interpretation or, in the words of Norman Holland, provides for "the management of psychological fantasy" (723). Sociological and historical approaches examine the reading public at a particular time within a given sociocultural context. Stanley Fish popularized the notion in this country that meaning is a process or an event—something that happens in time and within a particular "interpretive community"—in a theoretical approach he has called "affective stylistics" (684). The work of Marxist critic Georg Lukacs (761) is also a form of historical or sociological approach to literature. The hermeneutic group of critics seem less unified in approach than the others. Their critical approaches range from authority in interpretation, as in E. D. Hirsch's *Validity of Interpretation* (720) and *The Aims of Interpretation* (719), to that of members of the "Yale Mafioso" such as deconstructionist Paul deMan (663). It seems that the authors of these overviews of reader-response theory possess a double dose of that ability to see everything in the light of and in support of the particular lens or construct through which each of us views the world, a characteristic that is inherent in the acceptance and use of any theoretical metaphor.

One literary theorist whose importance to reader-response criticism is acknowledged, if only in footnotes to the introductions in both the Tompkins and the Suleiman and Crosman books, is Louise Rosenblatt who has already been identified as a primary influence on my own work. Tompkin's note indicates that

> Rosenblatt deserves to be recognized as the first among the present generation of critics in this country to describe empirically the way the reader's reactions to a poem are responsible for any subsequent interpretations of it. Her work and later the work of Walter Slatoff raise issues central to the debates that have arisen since.[17]

Suleiman apologizes for the fact that

> Rosenblatt's pioneering work in the field of subjective criticism came to my attention only after this essay was in proof.... Rosenblatt's book, *Literature As Exploration* (New York, 1938), challenged the objectivist assumptions of the New Criticism as they affected the teaching of literature in high schools and colleges.... Although her work was influential among those most concerned with questions of pedagogy, its relevance for literary theory was recognized only recently, when it was rediscovered by Bleich and others.[18]

Rosenblatt presented her "transactional theory", which accounts for both reader and text, in *Literature As Exploration* (803), first published in 1938 and now in its fifth edition. She further develops this theory in *The Reader, The Text, The Poem* (804). Although few critical texts have the longevity of *Literature As Exploration*, Rosenblatt's work has not been given the serious attention it deserves, perhaps for two reasons, neither of which alienates her from many of us. First, she is an educator; and second, she is a woman.

The fact that Rosenblatt is unabashedly an educator whose workplace was a school of education, rather than an English department in the graduate faculties, of a major university is especially interesting in light of the movement of literary theory from the community of author/critics to multiple communities of scholar/critics. Unfortunately, the distinction made between scholar and teacher is too often that which separates those who create highly specialized closed communities and use such specialized language that they speak only to themselves from those who want to communicate their ideas and their enthusiasms to the widest possible audience. Admittedly, this is a biased view, but the scholarly study of literature in recent years seems to have been extremely fragmented with the writings of those of one theoretical persuasion almost incomprehensible to other scholars. Perhaps a few more critics like Rosenblatt who combine scholarship and teaching would help to return literary theory closer to the masses of people who read, write, and care about books.

The second thing that may have worked against Rosenblatt as a literary theorist is her gender. Until recently, there is no mention of a woman theorist in the history of literary theory from Aristotle to deMan. Generally, this entire arena in the history of ideas has been almost totally dominated by men. The mainstream of literary criticism and even what has been called "serious" as opposed to "popular," reading has been primarily a male domain.

Feminist Criticism

The woman's movement of the 1970s led to an awareness of a new feminist criticism. General histories of the social or intellectual life of women, such as *Clio's Consciousness Raised, Perish the Thought* (653) and *The Feminization of American Culture* (669), include references to literary life as one of the few avenues open to women. The avenues open to women, however, were as writers, not ordinarily as critics of works written by men. Nonetheless, seeds planted in these works gave rise to a growing number of articles and full-length books of feminist criticism.

Although there is still some doubt, even from a few feminist critics, that there is anything resembling a fully-formed feminist critical theory, there appears to be as much commonality in approach among feminists as there is within some other theoretical groups. Like reader-response criticism, feminist criticism began during the social unrest of the 1960s and grew prominent in the 1970s. Some major early works were in direct response to questions of female graduate students[19] who resisted the New Criticism's exclusion of women writers and female consciousness in the accepted literary canon. The identification with women writers and the work of those writers, along with a sense of repression, trivialization, and misinterpretation of female texts, led to new studies of the images of women in literary works and, consequently, a feminist revision of the literary canon itself.

These early feminist critics set out to demonstrate that the male experience as reader, writer, and critic is different from, and sometimes alien to, the female experience. They pointed out that the experiences female critics bring to a work are different from those of male critics and that critical language itself, although assumed to be objective, was, in fact, masculine. They also believed that female works were not just lost, but were deliberately supressed by male critics who had previously convinced women that their interest in these texts was a sign of immature tastes. Armed with the work of female psychologists such as Carol Gilligan (893), feminists practiced criticism as political action, that is, they set out to reinterpret the literary world and change that world (Toril Moi, 772) by changing the consciousness of those who read. Much of feminist criticism has focused on either biographical criticism of rediscovered female authors or on the establishment of an alternative historical criticism that ties literary events to feminist social concerns as well as to male ones. In these new versions of literary history, the suffrage movement may be as important to literary consciousness as was industrialization or a world war.

Feminist approaches to literature should be of particular concern to those who work with children's literature because at least half of the authors and readers we work with are female. The Children's Literature Association, in a 1982 *Quarterly*, also looked at children's literature from the perspective of feminist criticism, but there is much work yet to be done.[20] One might, for instance, investigate whether female authors of children's books present different views of sex roles and family life than those of their male counterparts, although all aspects of gender theory have now been rejected by many in the feminist criticism movement. New authors and characters in fantasy and science fiction stimulate an interest in and need for new studies of the female hero in these genre. Since politicalization is an integral part of feminist criticism, perhaps a feminist approach offers a means to examine the socio-political aspects of the writings of Florence Crannell Means. My own research on Means is moving in this direction as I examine "contextual voids" in young people's understanding of her work. That this investigation could be linked to feminist criticism is a possibility.

In attempting to impose some order on contemporary literary criticism, it appears that old diagrams and representations are no longer adequate. Modern critics are looking beyond the four traditional coordinates of the literary experience to explore and discuss new relationships between, among, and within both works and readers. The world of literary experience has expanded to include all the elements in Figure 4. These are not new elements, but new points of emphasis in the theoretical approaches to literature.

FIGURE 4

FOCAL POINTS OF LITERARY THEORY

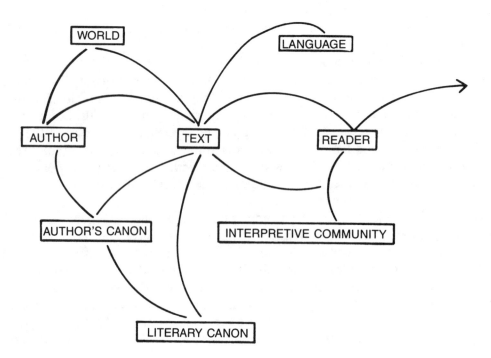

The text remains central in the schema because the work, no matter what the critic relates it to, is, at the very least, still the point of departure for any critical response. This representation demonstrates the possibility of looking beyond the single text to consider that text in relation either to the author's total work or to the entire literary canon. In similar fashion, a critic may look beyond an individual reader to a group of readers who share interpretive strategies. Language is also added as a coordinate to represent structuralist and semiotic approaches to criticism.

In Figure 5, I have placed some of the individual critics or schools of criticism in relation to the various elements. The placements are not intended to be either exact or stable, but rather tentative and

FIGURE 5

MAP OF LITERARY THEORIES

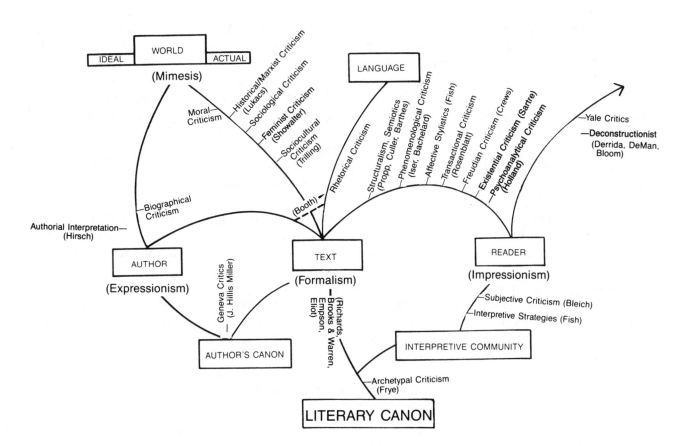

changing indications of the relationships of particular theories to the various elements and to each other. The work of many contemporary critics has moved from one position to another on this diagram, usually from a formalistic analysis of the text toward the reader or beyond. Because of these changes in the focus or stance of particular critics and our varying understandings or interpretations of their work, a diagram such as Figure 5 is most useful as a point of departure for discussion of various critical theories. The diagram has been used with students almost as a game board—"If you put Fish here, then Rosenblatt will have to go there."; "If the Yale Critics are to the right (certainly not a political 'right') of the reader, the psychoanalytic critics will have to be closest on the left."

CHILDREN'S LITERATURE AND LITERARY THEORY

Now is an appropriate time to ask again what all this theory has to do with children, with their literature, with the transaction between the child and literature, and with our role as facilitators of that transaction. Some connections and some questions have been raised along the way, but let us now examine some concerns unique to our particular aspect of literary study. Obviously, the child reader or listener differs in some ways from the reader assumed by those whose critical work we have been considering. With all due respect for the vast capabilities of children, we must admit that they are not yet at the height of their abilities (intellectual, emotional, and experiential) to comprehend and appreciate literary works. In spite of their uniqueness as human beings, we are more likely to be able to make some generalizations about the social, emotional, intellectual, or moral development of first graders than we could about forty year old elementary school librarians or teachers of children's literature. Does this mean that a theory of children's literature concerned with audience or reader must include some consideration of theories of child development and child psychology and education? Even if the theory itself does not contain such content, the successful use of any theoretically-based practice must account for these disciplines.

Children's literature is a part of all literature, probably no better and no worse than that intended for other audiences. But what of literary forms such as the picture-story book, concept books, reasoning books, simple affirmations of everyday experiences, or even the wordless informational books which are found almost exclusively in the field of children's literature? Are there unique ways to study such works? Might we combine theories of the graphic arts and theories of literature, along with child development theories in our analysis of picture-story books? How can we examine the nature of the transaction between child and story when the child is not yet able to articulate that experience, and what right have we to invade that private world when our subjects have not yet reached the age of consent?

The Adult Intermediary

Adults not only have the right, but an obligation to do something about the role they play in the child's literary experience. Obviously our beliefs about the child, literature, and the transaction between the two will determine our perception of this role. Regardless of the theoretical literary stance we take, however, we must still answer, as specifically as possible, the questions: "How does one learn literature?" and "Is there a literary equivalent of linguistic development?" For instance, before psycholinguistic knowledge of language learning was available to teachers, we taught children *about* language and hoped this practice would lead to proficiency in its *use*. James Moffett (933) made it quite clear that learning language is not learning about language, but learning to use it both as a source of experience and as a resource for personal growth.[21] Those who are interested in children as composers as well as consumers of literary works make the obvious connections here. Finally, in whatever work we do with groups of children, how can we preserve and protect the unique and personal literary experience of each child while, at the same time, helping the entire group to grow in an appreciation of and love for literature?

As adults (parents, teachers, librarians), we often intervene in the process through which young people respond to and make meanings from literary works. In fact, for many of us, it is a part of our professional responsibility to do so. In schools and libraries, the adult intermediary's role intersects both the reader's world and the world of the text as in Figure 6. To increase enjoyment, appreciation, and comprehension of a text, we try to illuminate that text and help young readers make connections between and among themselves, the work, and a larger literary and social world.

FIGURE 6

**ADULT INTERVENTION IN
CHILD'S EXPERIENCE OF STORY**

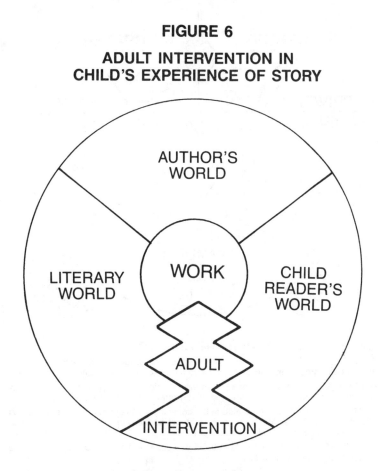

Vandergrift's Model

My own theoretical model of the child's meaning-making in response to a literary text (Figure 7) represents an approach to literary study in which a young person responding to a literary work interacts both with other young readers and with an adult intermediary. This model represents an engagement with literature in both a personal and social context. Young readers must be allowed time for the private experiencing of a text, represented by the upper portion of this model, before they participate in a public discussion of that text and their experiences of it. Time alone, however, is not enough. Readers must learn to respect their own transactions with a text, recognizing that any authentic meaning made in response to a work of art is a valid meaning, but that other, differing meanings are also valid and acceptable. Since meaning is defined as a event in time, all readers' meanings change as they think about and,

FIGURE 7

MODEL OF THE CHILD'S
MEANING–MAKING PROCESS
IN RESPONSE TO A LITERARY TEXT

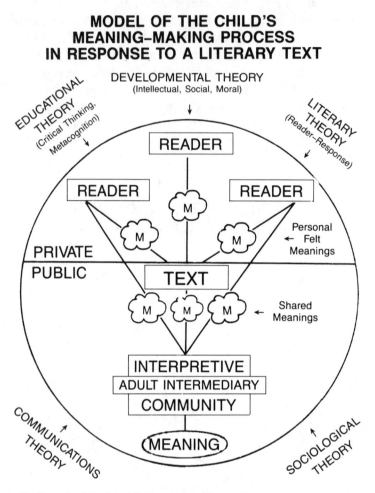

In the Study the following definitions are used:

TEXT: Story or metaphor which stimulates thought about feelings; assumed to be immediately comprehensible, even by the young child, but never fully comprehended.

READER: An active maker-of-meaning in the experience of responding to a text, that is, bringing meaning to and taking meaning from a symbolic form.

MEANING: An event in time, located in the consciousness of a reader so that the text disappears into the reader's experience of it just as the dancer cannot be separated from the dance or the musician from the music.

INTERPRETIVE COMMUNITY: A group of persons who share, exchange and create meanings in response to a text.

ADULT INTERMEDIARY: The adult who shares symbolic experiences with young people and, at best, is both a member of their interpretive community and one who is responsible for encouraging and maintaining the process illustrated in this model.

therefore, gain some aesthetic distance from that work of art. Thus, the meanings made in the immediacy of the transaction between reader and text change during personal reflection after the reading, and are then modified even more in the attempt to express those felt meanings in language to communicate them to others. Of course, one's own meanings are further modified in the process of sharing and in the discussion of alternative meanings in an interpretive community.

An interpretive community can be thought of on several different levels. Frye (692) distinguishes ways of perceiving an event between Eastern and Western cultures. Alan Purves's (790) research demonstrates differences of perceptions based on national boundaries, and many of us can identify distinct differences between various groups of children with whom we work. Perhaps it is most useful to keep these three levels in mind while recognizing that an interpretive community is, like meaning, an event in time. Those who meet regularly with a particular group of readers may remember times when that group remained a congregation of individuals rather than a community, and other times when the dynamics of interaction went beyond community to communion.

The primary role of the adult intermediary in this model is that of establishing an atmosphere of respect and trust. Young people must learn to respect and trust themselves and their own interpretive powers as well as each other and the adult who participates in their interpretive community. Without this, there is a danger that the adult or one or two members of the group will dominate the discussion and impose their predetermined meanings on others. During the discussion, the adult intermediary will preserve this attitude of respect and trust by ensuring that all who wish to may share ideas and meanings; that their ideas and meanings are heard and considered by others; and by encouraging all participants to track their own meaning-making process by referring back both to the text and to themselves. Of course, any meaning which develops from interactions within an interpretive community is itself an event in time and will be modified, interpreted, and changed in each participant's reflection on or discussion of that meaning.

The various theoretical disciplines surrounding the graphic representation of this process in the model are there to remind us that much of what happens in the meaning-making process is not visible, either to the adult intermediary or to an outside observer.[22] Rather, the sensitive adult participant in or observer of the process is bringing meanings to the situation from these, and probably many other, theoretical as well as personal means of making sense of human experience.

One must keep in mind, however, that this model merely attempts to "hold still" or make static enough for observation what is, in reality, a dynamic, on-going process. Making-meaning exists in a moment in time and any meaning, even a community meaning, is itself an event in time that is likely to change from moment to moment, response to response.

SUMMARY

This all-too-brief overview is intended merely to open a window to the fascinating, difficult, often contradictory world of literary theory. A knowledge of and appreciation for this theory is necessary for those who teach children's literature and want to share the excitement of the pursuit of literary ideas with students. We may not teach this theory in introductory classes, but what we do teach must be informed by theory. Even the very definition of children's literature has a grounding in theory. Whether children's literature is a specific group or type of texts or a particular variety of literary experiences is obviously a theoretical question. How one determines those texts or experiences is a theoretical activity. In the chapters that follow readers will trace the threads of such theoretical thought through research activities to both preactive and interactive teaching with adult students who ultimately may apply those ideas in professional practice with young people.

NOTES

[1]Marianne Moore. "Poetry," in *The Blue Guitar: A Selection of Modern Verse*. (1968). Edited by Donald Rutledge and John M. Bassett. (Toronto, Canada: McClelland and Stewart, Ltd.), p. 134. This book, along with several others in my personal collection contains the full thirty-eight-line poem originally published in *Selected Poems* (1935) and in *Collected Poems* (1951). *The Complete Poems of Marianne Moore*, published in 1967 in honor of Moore's eightieth birthday and containing "all the poems she is willing to preserve," contains only four and a half of what were the original first five lines, that is, what is

quoted here with the omission of the words "there are things that are important beyond all this fiddle." This raised a question that Ms. Moore answered very succinctly in four words on an otherwise blank page prior to the contents page in the 1967 volume: "Omissions are not accidents. MM."

[2]Perry Nodelman, for example, has explored this relationship in a number of presentations, see *Image and Maker* (133).

[3]Robert D. Robinson. (1970). "The Three Little Pigs: From Six Directions," in *Aspects of Reading*. Edited by Eldonna L. Evertts. (Champaign, IL: National Council of Teachers of English.)

[4]Laurence Yep. (1977). *Child of the Owl*. (New York: Harper & Row).

[5]Barbara Wersba. (1982). *The Crystal Child*. (New York: Harper & Row), 221.

[6]Jane Yolen. (1987). *Owl Moon*. Illus. by John Schoenherr. (New York: Philomel).

[7]Julian Scheer. (1964). *Rain Makes Applesauce*. (New York: Holiday House).

[8]Virginia Hamilton. (1982). *Sweet Whispers, Brother Rush*. (New York: Philomel Books).

[9]Virginia Hamilton wrote this statement at the request of Anne Beneduce, her editor, who asked her to share more of how this unusual story took form in her mind. (Letter from Ann Beneduce to Kay Vandergrift, not dated, but after ALA Annual Meeting, July, 1982).

[10]Eleanor Estes. (1944). *The Hundred Dresses*. (New York: Harcourt, Brace, Jovanovich); Mary Hays Weik. (1966). *The Jazz Man*. (New York: Atheneum).

[11]An early introduction and Frye's best-known work related to literature as a means of educating the child's imagination is, of course, *The Educated Imagination* (692). A more recent treatment of this topic is contained in Northrop Frye, *Criticism in Education*, the First Leland B. Jacobs Lecture. (Available from the Friends of Leland B. Jacobs, 24 Starview Drive, Neshanic, New Jersey 08853.)

[12]*Literature: Uses of the Imagination*. (1972). Will T. Jewkes, General Editor; Northrop Frye, Supervisory Editor. (New York: Harcourt, Brace, Jovanovich).

[13]Janice Antczak. (191) and Barbara Ripp Safford. (1983). "An Archetypal Analysis of Children's Fantasy." D.L.S. dissertation, Columbia University.

[14]"Structuralist Approaches to Children's Literature," (Fall 1982). Edited by Anita Moss. *Children's Literature Association Quarterly*. 7 (3): 33-58.

[15]Stephen Roxburgh. (Fall 1982). "Anno's Counting Book: A Semiological Analysis," *Children's Literature Association Quarterly*. 7 (3): 48-52.

[16]Jon C. Stott. (November 1982). "A Structuralist Approach to Teaching Novels in the Elementary Grades," *The Reading Teacher*. 136-143.

[17]Tompkins (797), xxvi.

[18]Suleiman (796), 45.

[19]Both Fetterley's *The Resisting Reader* (683) and Spacks' *The Female Imagination* (819) were based on such questions.

[20]Anita Moss, Editor. (Winter 1982). "Feminist Criticism and the Study of Children's Literature," in *Children's Literature Association Quarterly.* 7(4)3-22 + .

[21]James Moffett. (1968). *A Student-Centered Language Arts Curriculum, Grades K-13: A Handbook for Teachers.* (Boston: MA: Houghton Mifflin).

[22]The model developed by the author draws from a number of disciplines and from twenty-five years of practical experience working with young people and literature for its theoretical base. The brief mention of some of these sources is not intended to demonstrate specific relationships between previous work and the current study, but merely to identify and pay tribute to those whose work has influenced my own. The perception of the reader as one who both brings meaning to and takes meaning from a literary text is grounded in the transactional theory of Louise Rosenblatt (803, 804). Other reader-response theorists and critics whose work informs this study are Stanley Fish (684) for his work in interpretive strategies and interpretive communities, and Wolfgang Iser (733, 734), for his discussions of gaps or "areas of indeterminancy" in a text. Alan Purves (689) and Robert Protherough (496) are among those who have documented the recreative powers of school-age children in response to literary texts. From developmental psychology and education have come work on critical thinking and metacognition. John Dewey's classic work on the development of thinking skills (880) has been reexamined and expanded in recent years as educators study the development of higher order thinking skills across all areas of the school curriculum, (Costa, 879; Elizabeth Robinson [1983]. "Metacognitive Development," in *Developing Thinking*. Edited by Sara Meadows. [London: Metheun], 106-141) and in relation to specific subjects such as reading (Linda Baker and Ann L. Brown. [1984]. "Metacognitive Skills and Reading," in *Handbook of Reading Research*. Edited by P. David Pearson. [New York: Longman] 353-94; Eleanor Kulleseid. [1986]. "Extending the Research Base: Schema Theory, Cognitive Styles, and Types of Intelligence," *School Library Media Quarterly*. 15:41-48). The whole-language approach (Kenneth S. Goodman and others. [1987]. *Language and Thinking in School*, 3rd ed. [New York: Richard Owen Publishers]) to language arts instruction, the speech act theory of literary discourse (Pratt, 784), and the importance of informal writing as a way of ordering and shaping thought about literature (J. D. Marshall. [1987]. "The Effects of Writing on Students' Understanding of Literary Texts," *Research in the Teaching of English*. 21:30-63; Richard VanDeWeghe. [1987]. "Making and Remaking Meaning: Developing Literary Responses through Purposeful, Informal Writing," *English Quarterly*. 20:38-51) have provided examples of the connections between and among reading, writing and thinking. Also important to the understanding of the process through which community meanings are created are studies of communication and paralinguistics (Colin Cherry. [1978]. *On Human Communication: A Review, A Survey, and A Criticism*, 3rd ed. [Cambridge, MA: MIT Press.]) and of the sociology of knowledge (Berger and Luckmann, 854).

Research and Children's Literature

INTRODUCTION

Research in children's literature offers the opportunity for a rigorous examination of the literature of the child and connections that link the child, the author, the text, the larger world of literature, and the world outside literature. Not everyone concerned with children's literature will assume the role of researcher, but all should be at least consumers of research. The intent of this chapter then, is, first, to provide a framework for the reaction to and the use of that research in work with children and literature and, second, to serve as an introduction for those who intend to pursue research activities in children's literature. The intent of this chapter is not to analyze and discuss previous research but to identify and discuss the range of research designs that might be employed in children's literature.[1]

Those contemplating literary research must do so with caution. Research, by its very nature, strives toward objectivity. Literary works, on the other hand, are subjective compositions perceived subjectively and may actually be destroyed by some types of objective analysis. More accurately, the literary work survives independently of the research activity even if the researcher loses sight of the totality of that work in an analysis of some aspect or part of it. An "objective" analysis of language in a particular book or group of books, for example, is sometimes undertaken without accounting for the delicate and complex interrelationships of that language with characterization, setting, and other compositional elements. Those who are dismayed by non-standard language or four-letter words in a children's story have an obligation to recognize, at the very least, the relationship of that use of language to the development of believable characters in a specific time, place, and situation. Those who study social roles and racial, ethnic, religious, or sexual groups in literature must also keep this total compositional context at the forefront of consciousness, recognizing that story does, of necessity, have antagonists, villains, flat, static, and even stereotypical characters. Without such characters, story could not exist. The embodiment of a story's antagonist as an old, white, Anglo-Saxon, American, Protestant man does not imply that either the author or the work is taking an antagonistic or prejudicial stance toward the elderly, WASP's, men, or any other group of people. In any aesthetic composition, the whole is indeed greater than the sum of its parts, and those doing research on various parts of literary works must keep this in mind. Research should never become a means for the destruction of literature, rather, it should increase both our understanding of and our appreciation for that which we study.

The Research Design

In planning or analyzing research, one might examine the design for the following basic five-fold pattern:

1. Statement of the problem to be addressed

2. Statement of the hypotheses to be tested

3. Clearly articulated methodology

4. Means or technique of analysis

5. Appropriate means to report the findings.

This basic pattern is virtually the same for all kinds of research. As an investigator determines a problem or a teacher reads research reports, each must examine the significance of the problem, that is, answer the "so what?" question as a means to test the significance of the study. In seeking hypotheses to test, the researcher focuses the direction of the study or at least suggests a set of questions to be investigated. Not every study will have hypotheses, but the lack of them may cause the researcher to lose focus and direction by entering too many yellow brick roads while looking for the emerald city. Sometimes this is a matter of not taking the time to delve sufficiently into the nature of the investigation to design the necessary hypotheses. Well designed hypotheses should lead naturally to a choice of methodologies and then to means of analysis and reportage. In fact, either in designing research or in analyzing the research of others, it may be helpful to use columns, flowcharts, or other means to verify that each hypothesis grows out of the problem statement and that methodology, analysis, and reportage follow logically. Sometimes this kind of graphic analysis will reveal a flaw in the design. The concept of a mini-storyboard is frequently used in management training exercises to facilitate the presentation of a concept or idea to an audience. For some this may also be an alternative means of describing or analyzing a research design. Thus, a flowchart of the design, a diagram of parts, a visual representation of items or events in the study, or a rather free-style flow of circles and squares indicating relationships may help to clarify and define the problem and focus the research.

For those conducting research, it may also be helpful very early in the research process to write a short but personally meaningful statement concerning that research and its importance and keep that statement ready and available as the study takes shape. The conduct of research is sometimes tedious and it is easy to lose either impetus or direction. Such statements help sharpen the focus and direction of research activities. Sometimes the sparks of imagination and creativity may be almost extinguished by the details of research, but, if the problem is truly significant, that spark will ignite again and again each time the darkness of drudgery descends.

It is also necessary to separate the content of the research from its methodology. It is not uncommon to hear that a great many studies in children's literature have focused on either reader interests or content analysis. This may be true, but the comparison is confusing because the first is a topic of research while the second is a methodology. One might study reader interests using survey, case study, or experimental methods; content analysis might yield information about any number of literary, historical, or sociological concerns. This confusion of content and method has been a serious impediment to the development of a solid base of research in children's literature because it is difficult to sort out relationships and determine how one research study builds on others in the field. Without clarification of content, methodology, and the conditions under which research has been conducted, it is impossible to replicate a study or to accumulate data collected from comparable research. Children's literature research in this country has suffered from fragmentation and idiosyncracy. The time is now right to establish a national research agenda that would reexamine and reaccess the many studies related to children's literature that have been conducted, replicate those deemed appropriate, and design new studies which build on both existing knowledge and new perceptions of the field.

Overviews of Research Directions

During the last quarter century there has been a tremendous increase in research in children's literature. A few of the bibliographical essays and lists demonstrating the differing directions that research has taken are presented in the bibliography at the end of this chapter. Sara Fenwick, in her 1979 *Library Trends* article on historical research in children's literature provides a useful analysis of the various directions taken by historians.[2] Her categorization and specificity of titles is a good starting point for one pursuing research using historical methods. Gillian Avery in "The Researcher's Craft: Designs and Implements" offers a more personal account of her encounters with the Darton collection, which she labels "idiosyncratic" in nature.[3] *Dissertation Abstracts International, Phaedrus* and *Children's Literature Association Quarterly* are among the best resources for both research results and information about research-in-progress in children's literature. W. Bernard Lukenbill and Sharon Lee Stewart (494) have provided invaluable assistance to researchers by consolidating entries for fifty-five years of dissertations in one volume. The work of the International Reading Association (IRA) has also been helpful in locating and identifying research although the Dianne Monson and Bette Peltola publication is considerably out-of-date. One should also be aware of the research reports of the National Council of Teachers of English (NCTE) and particularly the work of Alan Purves who has, over a number of years, been studying young people's responses to literature.

Phaedrus is a major source of information on the international aspects of research and, for the most part, this annual gives a solid portrait of activity in the field of children's literature throughout the world. Thus, each item in the research bibliography represents a source that leads to the findings of scholars and researchers in the various sub-divisions of children's literature as well as the allied fields of reading, schooling, and linguistics.

CATEGORIES OF LITERARY RESEARCH

In order to make sense of existing research, it is useful to categorize it in some way. Two of the best known organizations of literature studies are those of Wellek and Warren (837) who distinguish between intrinsic and extrinsic approaches to the study of literature and of the Modern Language Association (MLA) which divides scholarship in modern languages and literature into five groups: (1) linguistics, (2) textual scholarship, (3) historical scholarship, (4) literary criticism, and (5) literary theory. The MLA categorization moves from the word and sentence (linguistics), to the text (textual), to the context (historical) and then to the practice (criticism) and theory of literary interpretation. When one eliminates theory and criticism, which are not necessarily research activities, the first and second MLA categories correspond to Wellek and Warren's intrinsic approach and historical scholarship includes all forms of extrinsic approaches.

Robert Spiller accepted this view of literary history when he defined it as "concern with describing and explaining the expression *in literature* of a people during a period of time, in a place, and usually in a specific language.[4] Although this definition may appear to be almost all-encompassing, others believe that literary history may be either more or less than this. Some would include a concern for literary theory or criticism not evident in Spiller's statement. Marxist scholars would examine the sociology of audiences, of authors, and even of critics; others place emphasis on the reader; still others would examine changes in the meanings of language. The deconstructionists might deny us the use of history since texts, in their eyes, have no meaning or referentiality. In other words, it appears that some of what is called historical scholarship in literature partakes of theory, criticism, and various kinds of extrinsic interpretations. Neither authors and audiences nor literary works themselves can be separated from their historical contexts, but including many different kinds of research activities under any one label may not be very helpful either to researchers or to the consumers of research results.

Research, like theory, can begin at any of the various coordinates represented in Figure 2. It is also useful to think of research activities as being innertextual, intratextual, or extratextual, that is, looking within a particular text, among texts, or beyond texts. Using this schema, studies focusing on the work are innertextual, those concentrating on literary knowledge are intratextual, and all studies of the world, the author, or the audience are extratextual. Whether we call this final group of studies extrinsic, historical, or extratextual, it seems useful to divide them at least into the three foci represented in Figure 2 (audience, author, world).

Extratextual Studies

AUDIENCE STUDIES

Ordinarily, when we think of an audience in relation to children's literature, we imagine an actual child reading or listening to a story. Literary scholars, however, might consider four different story audiences. In addition to the actual child, there is an authorial audience or the author's abstract construct of prospective readers and the knowledge they assumedly possess. Then there is the narrative audience or the reader who has willingly suspended disbelief in the engagement with the text and, finally, the ideal narrative audience which includes all those who share the ethics, beliefs, and interpretations of that text.

Many early studies of children's literature focused on the child as audience, by identifying readers' interests in or preferences for types of literature. The most common methodology used for these studies was the survey which enables a researcher to sample a large population and correlate interests or preferences to such variables as age, sex, schooling, or social, economic, or ethnic groups.[5] Questionnaires, interviews, checklists of titles, and the analysis of school reading records and library circulation records are all means of data collection. Case studies or experimental methods may also be used for interest or preference studies,[6] or to investigate the influence of literature upon readers, as in research into attitudes toward literature, changes in attitude or behavior as a result of reading, or the influence of literature on the child's self-concept or academic performance. Although literature is commonly used as a supplement to informational content in the school curriculum, there have been few substantial studies of the actual benefits of this relationship.

EDUCATIONAL OR DEVELOPMENTAL STUDIES

One might look to educational or developmental theory and study the works of John Dewey, Horace Mann, W. H. Kilpatrick, Maria Montessori, Jerome Bruner, Jean Piaget, or Johann Pestalozzi to establish a context and a set of questions to examine literature for children. Applebee is probably the best known of those who combine developmental psychology and pedogogical studies in their research in children's literature. Michael Benton, John Gardner, and Barbara Leondar are also among the increasing number who study this literature in relation to these contexts.[7]

More recent reader-response studies seem to fall at different points on a continuum between the reader and the text, with those at one end taking a psychoanalytical approach to readers and those on the other examining texts to determine built-in expectations of or requirements for authorial audiences. On the one hand, researchers study what actually happens as one reads, sometimes even by measuring physical responses, or how readers describe the process of reading. On the other, they investigate cultural or contextual variables that affect reading.

Examples of audience-centered studies of literature range from impressionistic responses to phenomenological considerations of methods of cognition, to Marxist dialectical studies, to Freudian analyses of literary texts and readers in relation to universal needs and fears. Investigations of the creative work of children as evidence of response to literature have also fascinated researchers for some time and continue today.

Purves's investigation of literature education in ten countries combined a number of perspectives to look at literary experiences of young people. He studied student responses, but determined that those responses were shaped, at least in part, by the nature of the text. The relation to the world outside the text was also noted in the differences in responses across national boundaries. For our purposes, it is interesting to speculate just how much of this "national character" of response is dependent upon dominant modes of literary instruction in the various countries. Such speculation might lead to the design and execution of a series of international research studies much needed in this field.

Certainly, there are other ideas that might be examined in literature for young people. How do literary texts relate to the culture of the adolescent and to what extent does a study of these works reveal changes in adolescent culture and behavior patterns? The feminist analyses of children's literature which have proliferated over the past decade or two might benefit from a thorough grounding in some of the recent adult feminist criticism mentioned in the previous chapter. Such criticism of children's literature might also be enriched by the use of a schema from the world of psychology or human development. Gilligan's *In A Different Voice* (893) provides a fascinating and very sound basis for such a study.

AUTHOR STUDIES: LITERARY BIOGRAPHY

Author-centered research is primarily literary biography which Barbara Lewalski suggests will require the literary biographer to "find and examine all the available material by or pertaining to the author; published and unpublished works, diaries, letters, manuscripts, working papers, public records, oral testimonies from family or friends, if available, and information about the persons, places, institutions and activities important for his subject's life."[8] Then, of course, the writer of such a literary biography is faced with the task of melding all of the research into a literary and expository document. The danger in such studies is threefold:

1. Over-enamourment of the subject and the work of the subject which fosters biases presented as truth. (Less frequently, in the children's field, this takes a negative approach and attempts to "debunk" an author.)

2. Too much dependence on chronological development which often does not reveal the author and the work in the most interesting or dynamic fashion.

3. Concentration on the life of the author and on the society that shaped that person to the virtual exclusion of the literary work which was the original reason for the selection of the subject.

In studying primary documents related to the life of an author, researchers may place more weight on gossip and small talk located in letters and transcribed from interviews than common sense or justice would permit. An important question that must be resolved in the ethics of research is: To what extent does the production of books for public consumption entitle researchers to enter the private byways of the author's life? This is not to deny the validity of using personal papers or holographic materials collected in libraries in our pursuit of knowledge, but one must ask if there is a point at which biographical research becomes invasion of privacy. It is recognized, of course, how eagerly all readers delight in stories and anecdotes about the authors whose work we enjoy. In a conversation with Larry Yep he confirmed that the grandmother in *Child of the Owl*[9] was indeed based on his own grandmother and that the child protagonist, although a female, was basically himself with the outer trappings of a young female cousin of his. Although this is a delightful bit of information that confirmed what I had suspected, does it entitle a researcher to make substantive comments on the relationship of Yep's life and the characters in *Child of the Owl*? Or would the fact that Yep was a part of Leslie Fiedler's research team, which produced *Freaks*,[10] permit me to infer anything about his relationship to outsiders in society?

In determining subjects for biographical research, one might identify those authors whose work holds special personal significance and ask why they are important. A favorite example is Florence Crannell Means who was an author ahead of her time in respect to sociological issues and concerns. A reader wonders about the person who could write so perceptively about Japanese-Americans during World War II in *The Moved-Outers*,[11] about Blacks in *Shuttered Windows*,[12] and about Native Americans in *Our Cup Is Broken*.[13] Means's sensitivity to the human concerns of different cultural groups and the placement of her books in a period of history that was certainly less accepting of these cultures than she appeared to be causes a research psyche to catch fire! Another example is Ann Nolan Clark, whose *In My Mother's House*[14] is considered a landmark work by many in education. She approached the teaching of reading in a fashion similar to that of Sylvia Ashton Warner, and her writing bears testimony to her concern for Native American children. The questions raised about these two authors point out the difficulty of using any system to categorize research activities. Only a combination of biographical and sociological research would shed light on these questions and on the importance of the work of Means and Clark.

Literary biographies of children's authors and illustrators range from relatively simple factual accounts of their lives to complex analyses which attempt to trace the development of creativity or of specific creations in the events of their lives. These biographies suffer from the same psychological speculation from a distance common in much general biography, but this phenomenon seems to take two distinct paths in studies of children's authors. On the one hand, the circumstances of the life are used to demonstrate that a person such as Beatrix Potter never, or only very late in life, fully matured as an adult and thus maintained a child-like simplicity and view of the world that was reflected in her work. On the other hand, a case is made for a kind of perverse obsession with children or with a particular child that enabled the author to shape those adult fantasies about children into imaginative texts. In many instances, this has resulted in psychological speculations about such writers as Carroll, Barrie, and Alger as "dirty old men."

Two recent developments in the approach to literary biographies of those who create for young people are represented by the Twayne "Young Adult Authors" series and a number of autobiographical volumes from children's authors themselves. Books in the Twayne series focus on a critical analysis of the author's work and are as much a source-book for that criticism as an interpretation of the life. Since these books are about contemporary authors, they usually include personal interviews; but, as in any biography of a living person, they may lack the perspective of time and may be over-influenced by personal attachment or the fear of offending the subject. The "Self-Portrait" books published by Addison-Wesley, are a series of first-person picture books by distinguished picture book artists intended for young readers. This autobiographical approach is also seen in the many individual accounts of their lives and work, sometimes fictionalized, by writers for older children such as M. E. Kerr, Katherine Paterson, Beverly Cleary, and Madeleine L'Engle.

Researchers might learn a great deal about children's literature through biographical or autobiographical studies of key authors. It is important to remember in research on literary biography that it is the work, in this instance the literary work, of the author that makes that life important to us and, thus, a thorough understanding of the literary achievement of the author placed in the context of the author's life is required.

AUTHOR STUDIES: INFLUENCE

Although literary biography is ordinarily most closely aligned with historical and sociological concerns, it can also combine with other types of literary study. For instance, many years ago I watched a film made by Puffin Books about Alan Garner and his work. The lasting impression of this film is that of the mood created by the setting. The scenes of Garner's house and its surroundings cause speculation about the influence of that environment on Garner's novels, particularly on the creation of settings. This very tentative notion is just a clue that could eventually result in a researchable question that would require intense work to answer. Such research, however, would have to examine Garner's use of setting in the various novels as well as the actual settings of his life experiences.

Research into Garner's use of setting might indeed be an aspect of literary biography or the analysis of a particular literary element, but it could also fit into another type of literary research which has been labeled "influence study." This is the study of sources used by an author, or more precisely, "source study asks what an author has used of what he/she has read (or seen or heard) in creating plot, characters, themes, structure, imagery, or style: its guiding principles should be tact and a sure sense of relevance."[15] A problem with this kind of study is often one of basic design. The approach that matches computer analysis of texts to prove reliance upon earlier texts, particularly through word counts and phrase frequency may, however, be somewhat suspect.

The questions of significance are inevitably "How does influence work?", and "How does one recognize with certitude whether one thing influenced a second or if both were influenced by still another?" Certainly the current interest in retold tales and myths of earlier times leads to questions of influence. Influence might be examined in fantasy since many books in this genre depend on the mythic tradition, and some aspects of this dependence might make for fruitful research. Higgins has offered some insights into the nature of influences on writers of mystical fancy in *Beyond Words* (231). It is easier to assess the influence of William Blake on Maurice Sendak or the relationship of the private press movement to Walter Crane because the artists themselves have provided much of the evidence.

One can easily suggest some factors that may have influenced the work of Elaine Konigsburg, Katherine Paterson or, Daniel Pinkwater. To demonstrate this influence, however, the investigator should have not only a detailed knowledge of these authors' lives but of a broad range of both cultural and societal history, not just vague notions of the past two or three decades. For example, did Konigsburg's attendance at many conferences inspire her to express some entrancing notions about conference-going in *Journey to an 800 Number*?[16] Katherine Paterson has often discussed her missionary upbringing in another country, but how does one measure this influence on her works? Was what I perceived to be Pinkwater's key statement in *young adult novel*, the result of Pinkwater's schooling experience?

Mr. Winter declared the day's exercises over, and by executive order abolished all elections in the school until further notice. This is why the Wild Dada Ducks—and apparently Kevin Shapiro—do not take school elections seriously. Mr. Winter has the last word.[17]

Or was the interpretation of this as the key statement influenced by my own educational experiences? From a totally different perspective, is this book really Pinkwater's playful reaction to an art movement? Although such questions are fascinating, research that could lead to documentary evidence in relation to them is clearly very difficult to collect.

CONTENT ANALYSIS STUDIES

Emphases on the relationship of the literary work to the world outside that work are most frequently represented by content analysis studies which focus on contemporary sociological concerns. Although content analysis might appear to be a form of innertextual study or a close examination of content within a text, its focus is most often on the text's representation of an external reality. It is in such studies that we have been especially susceptible to confusing methodology and content, or at least to talking about the research as if the method were more important than what is derived from that method. Key to any content analysis study is the formulation of the rules of interpretation or analysis and the definition of terms. Terms which are precisely defined in another discipline may be difficult to apply to literary works in which the various aspects of that definition are not necessary or even appropriate to the aesthetic composition. For instance, sociologists make clear distinctions between the terms "rural" and "suburban," but the information about the setting of a story may not contain enough elements to make a clear sociological distinction, allowing each reader to imbue that setting with personal comprehension and meaning.

Content analysis is designed to permit the researcher to make inferences about the content of communication. The tools used in such studies are a series of precisely ordered and defined schedules for collecting and coding data. Once the rules of data collection and interpretation are established and the terms to be used are clearly defined and systematized, they must be rigorously applied to the content selected. Normally at least two coders are required to insure some degree of objectivity in interpretation. Consistency is a hallmark of quality, assuming, of course, that all aspects of the research design were carefully developed in the first place. The range of studies in content analysis in our field has been tainted, to some measure, by personal biases of the investigators in the inferences that have been drawn. In many instances, this is the result of investigators relying only on their own coding. It is obviously very difficult to be objective if one has also devised the coding system and determined what will be coded. It is undoubtedly true that all of our perceptions are skewed to some extent, but a researcher must make every effort to rid the work of personal biases and should not attempt to design a research study to use as propaganda to put forth a particular point of view on social or moral issues.

Of course, previous misuses do not constitute a rationale for dismissing a whole methodology, but they should alert us to exercise special care in considering this approach to exploring a problem. The greatest danger is that the methodology becomes dominant and the researcher loses sight of the real purpose of the study, that is, the illumination of literary works.

We must not forget that all people, including authors, are a product of their times and they, like the rest of us, grow and change in their views and in their awareness of social concerns and injustices. A number of content analysis studies, with the benefit of hindsight, have chastised writers and their works for an insensitivity to an issue or to human rights, or have drawn far-reaching conclusions from an examination of earlier works. It is important to be aware of such insensitivity wherever it is found and to help young readers recognize and deal with this content. On the other hand, we should not attempt to judge a 1940s work against the social consciousness of the 1980s. Ignorance, lack of information, or a particular social consciousness, which the researcher might also have shared in the past, may have been a variable that accounts for much of the problem. Casual attributions to something else, such as author prejudice, may be, and often are, erroneous, especially since editors and publishers, then as now, made decisions about what was acceptable and marketable. Marguerite De Angeli's *Bright April*,[18] for instance, may appear prejudicial and stereotypical to contemporary readers, but this book was, in some ways, a breakthrough in the positive treatment of Blacks when it was published in 1946. Of course, April was a "Negro" in this story, but today's readers and researchers must acknowledge that this was the appropriate term at the time of writing.

SOCIOLOGICAL STUDIES

Sociological studies are among the most popular form of extratextual research, and often that popularity is what triggers one who seeks a topic for investigation. Some authors or works are criticized in terms of their treatment of nonresponsiveness to a societal question or concern. Young adult "problem novels" are frequently examined in this way. For example, the drug context might be explored as a phenomenon of the 1960s and 1970s with *Go Ask Alice*[19] or *A Hero Ain't Nothin' But a Sandwich*[20] examined as documentable evidence. Questions come to mind related to cults, life styles, sexual activity, suicide, abortion, and the right to die as represented in books for young people. Each of these areas of concern has a strong theoretical and research base in other disciplines that may be used for developing a schema to examine the literature dealing with these topics.

There is no question that *The Grapes of Wrath*[21] is often cited as testimony to what the depression did to people in this country, and indeed it became fictional evidence for asserting some of what Dorothea Lange and Pare Lorentz documented in photographs. Are there children's books that have that same capability? Do *The Hundred Dresses, Roosevelt Grady, Blue Willow, Home Before Dark,* or *Strawberry Girl* permit the child to grasp a sense of the life of migrant workers in particular times and places?[22] How might we address this question through research? To what extent did the blacklisting and banning resulting from McCarthyism effect children's authors and their works? How might we use this context to examine books published during that time, even those such as *Ben and Me*[23] which was censored in some schools and libraries because it was considered un-American?

HISTORICAL STUDIES

Closely aligned with sociological studies are historical analyses of literary texts that are often combined with the examination of historical fiction as a genre. Alethea Helbig's article in *Children's Literature Association Quarterly* on the forest as setting in the Mantlemass novels offers a fascinating example of the complexity and interrelationships of such research.[24] The author's hypothesis combines innertextual concentration on the compositional element of setting with intratextual relationships within Barbara Willard's work, and within the genre of historical fiction and extratextual historical concerns to provide fresh insight into this literary chronicle.

An interesting problem that emerges in historical studies of children's literature is a concern for those periods of civilization for which no records exist. This can be seen in the examination of two books for young people—*Spirit on the Wall*[25] by Ann O'Neal Garcia and *The Lady of Rhuddesmere*[26] by Victoria Strauss. Both of these are compelling stories that raise some interesting questions for historians. In the first instance, the author has created a story that may be less believable to some readers because of our understanding of the social patterns and the role of woman among Cro-Magnon people. Checking with a number of anthropologists elicits differing views on the acceptability, from an historical point of view, of the contents of the book. The second work raises the question of whether the information on Manichaeism might be over-simplified or even incorrect. Since the period of time and the plot is dependent on a rather obscure portion of theological history, it will require some work to determine the accuracy of the historical information central to this work of fiction.

How close must the relationship between history and fiction be? How does an author create the sense of a living society in historical novels? Details about settings, costumes, and customs are important attributes of historical fiction, but accurate information about these is not always available. The question is one of "poetic license." Must an author maintain absolute accuracy in the creation of an historically grounded fictional world, or are minor deviations acceptable if they serve the plot? On the other hand, when does "wise conjecture" about that for which there are no historical records become misrepresentation of history?

Another significant question is whether an author has interpreted history accurately or used it as means to moralize. This question could be examined in an analysis of several series books, including some well-known biographical series which focus on particular traits or influences in the lives of famous people. Even the works of Foster, Fritz, or Collier might be examined to determine the degree of moralizing and the relation of that moralizing both to historical fact and to the impact of the literary work. Lisl Weil's *I, Christopher Columbus*[27] raises a number of questions about the treatment of this figure. The author/illustrator's respect for the child reader is evident in her approach, and many historical and biographical facts are presented, although some might find her first-person narrative unacceptable. An examination of biography for young people demonstrates that dealing with real heroes and real villains provides many problems to the author as well as to the critic and researcher.

An alternative form of historical study of children's literature is that which examines the history and development of this literature itself. Many historical studies look at the content of literature created at different times to investigate historical periods in children's literature and relate those periods to general historical events. Extratextual research also takes the form of general surveys (Meigs, 424), period studies, regional surveys, surveys of ethnic literature, and investigations of intellectual or social trends— feminism, Darwinism, conservatism. One example of a study that traces a history of an idea is *Poor Monkey* by Peter Coveney.[28] His tracing of the image of childhood in literature is worth examination and study, although many readers might not agree with Coveney's notions.

We have only begun to see the investigation of historical children's literature. One of my concerns is to see historical methods applied to the children's literature of the twentieth century. The richness of our tradition of children's literature lies in this century, and we sometimes seem to avoid research that testifies to this. We are nearing the very end of the century and need to examine the strengths and weaknesses of this literature in the hope of moving into the twenty-first century with a greater understanding of developments in the field. In a national symposium, sponsored by the Library of Congress, several of these issues were discussed and later reported in *School Library Journal* by Vandergrift and Hannigan.[29]

RELIGIOUS AND MYTHOLOGICAL STUDIES

Another context which researchers may use to gain insight into children's literature is the religious. Theological and mythical concepts evident in the work of fantasy writers such as C. S. Lewis, George MacDonald, J. R. R. Tolkien, and Susan Cooper are well known. Religious references are readily discernable to readers of Madeleine L'Engle's *A Wrinkle in Time* trilogy, but her realistic fiction might also be examined for its rich religious underpinnings. In fact, religion may be making a comeback in contemporary fiction for young people with many recent books dealing directly with this topic. Theological or religious analyses of such works as *Ganesh, The Tempered Wind*,[30] or perhaps even the work of Virginia Hamilton, could well shed interesting new light on these works.

A more obvious connection between particular works and mythological concerns is that between Jamake Highwaters' Ghost Horse-Cycle stories and Native American myth.[31] One might use this author's own studies of mythology to examine his fiction for children.[32] One could also use the work of theologians such as Martin Buber, Karl Rahner, Paul Tillich, Abraham Heschel, or Teilhard de Chardin to develop schema for the examination of children's literature, from that literature that stresses such broadly religious motifs as the battle between good and evil to those that relate more specifically to religious groups or doctrines.

Innertextual Studies

Studies of the literary work itself (innertextual), or of that work in the context of the whole body of literary works (intratextual), are probably still the most influential studies in respect to their effects on teaching. Perhaps it is the belief that intrinsic studies are more valued and more appropriate than extrinsic ones, or that many of these studies are more easily controlled in the classrooms, or just the emphasis of New Criticism in many teachers' own education that has resulted in this influence. Regardless of the origins, it appears to be true that studies of children's literature still focus most often on the internal elements and structures of literary works. Research, however, is needed to verify this.

TEXTUAL STUDIES

Textual scholarship, or the verification of accuracy of the printed text in relation to the author's original creation has had little emphasis in studies of literature for children and youth. Perhaps the immediacy of experiencing literature with young people or the concentration on New Criticism, which has sometimes been accepting of any version of a text as an independent entity available for study, has drawn our attention away from this form of research. There has been a great deal of interest in returning to the "original" written versions of traditional folk and fairy tales, particularly in the wake of work by Sendak[33] and Bettleheim (197). Such oral transmissions, however, cannot be subjected to the same kind of scrutiny as original manuscripts. Neither can one author's intention and the personal and historical context in which creation took place, often sought after by the textual scholar, be studied in relation to these works.

Literature published for children does stimulate a number of textual questions related to the publishing history of key works in the field. Many works considered children's classics were originally published for adults and have been available in various edited versions for children. Other classics were originally published as serials in periodical literature and only later released in book form, and one might wonder if there were accommodations made to these differing formats. In addition, children's books tend to stay in print for a much longer period than most adult books. This longevity, along with a perceived pragmatic or acculturating function of children's literature, raises questions about the editing of older works in light of contemporary social consciousness or educational concerns.[34]

Picture books present many fascinating questions for the consideration of textual scholars. If it is the combination of text and illustrations that is the artistic entity of a picturebook, must we not be concerned with the effect of repeated printing on the quality of the visual expression? Many texts are available with a number of different visual interpretations, and some artists have been asked to replicate their original award-winning illustrations in a new medium as the technologies of publishing change.[35] Paperback editions of children's picturebooks also raise interesting textual questions. Not only does the quality of the paper change illustrations, but many picturebook editions even change the size and the shape of the original work. Preference studies have demonstrated that children often are concerned with these aspects of books, so this certainly is a topic worthy of study. Recent interest in the history of children's literature has led to the publication of facsimiles of early books for young people which may, in less carefully researched editions, lead to misinformation about these works. It is hoped that such questions and considerations will result in a renewed interest of textual studies in children's literature.

NEW CRITICISM AND BEYOND

New Critics tend to accept the text as presented and look into the self-contained world of that work to study rhetoric or form. Close analysis of euphony, rhythm or meter, style and stylistics, symbol, image, metaphor, and mythic elements are common in such studies. Some of the critical activities of this group are closely related to those of linguistic scholars who might define their work as examining *what* is said and *how* it is said. Until recently, however, linguistic scholarship was generally considered too "scientific" to shed much light on literary compositions. Now semiological and structural studies embrace the scientific basis of literary study. They begin with linguistics, that is, the orderly arrangement of sounds, words, and sentences into a coherent whole and then move from language and the literary work to principles of structure that enable them to see a work, a genre, or all of literature as related systems. When the selection of texts to be studied is organized according to structural principles, genre studies or archetypal studies of a large body of literature result.

Intratextual Studies

GENRE STUDIES

One of the easiest of intratextual literary studies to grasp and to design is that of tracing the history of a genre. Lewalski suggests that the primary concern for the scholar is "how to identify and describe the continuities and changes in the element in question and how to assess the various causal factors bearing upon this development."[36] Children's literature is only in the beginning stages of genre study, with most work being done in science fiction, fairy tales, and fantasy. One area of research that is potentially exciting is that of historical fiction. One who reads Lukacs's theoretical work on historical fiction (761) may find sufficient structure to formulate a study of this genre. The works of Sutcliffe, Aiken, Willard and Harnett are rich in both historical detail and in literary form and might lend themselves to such investigations. Aiken's own writing about the nature of historical writing could give additional insight into her fiction.[37] Relatively new writers for young people such as David Wiseman and Lensey Namioka have developed their stories around the everyday citizen affected by and reacting to historical events as have many of their predecessors. Of course, any intratextual study of historical fiction is likely to overlap extratextual historical research.

THEORETICAL STUDIES

Another type of intratextual literary analysis is that of theory-building or the testing of existing literary theory. Such research might begin with the following assumptions:

Assumption #1: One might select any literary theory that will permit an examination of some aspect(s) of the literature or the literary experience, to be used as the conceptual framework of the study.

Assumption #2: Any study that includes a conceptual framework drawn from literary theory presupposes a thorough grounding in that theory as well as in literary theory in general.

Assumption #3: There is a distinction to be drawn between a literary theory which encourages one to focus on an individual work and one which encourages one to address a body of works. The former might be termed the micro-theory approach, the latter a macro-theory approach. The former might be drawn, for instance, from the theories of Barthes or Eco and the latter from Frye or Propp.

Assumption #4: It is possible to modify a theory; and in some instances modification is essential to the research design.

Assumption #5: Although literary theories focus primarily on non-discursive literature, some may be applicable to discursive literature. For instance, structuralist theories might contribute to the serious investigation of informational books for young people.

Assumption #6: Although literary theories have been developed primarily to permit us to examine print literature, some may be applicable to other forms of communication. For instance, the semiotic movement has permitted serious investigation into cinema.

Assumption #7: Literary theories should be perceived and acted upon from the basic premise that they are fluid rather than static. They permit one to hold a literary work or a group of such works in a temporary state of stillness.

Assumption #8: Any systematic examination will permit the scholar to make generalizations — the process of which is, in fact, a part of research.

Theory leads to a taxonomy which in turn may lead to testing and validating that theory. Implicit in this statement is the presumption of developing a structure, a model or a schema, either taken directly from a theorist or one extrapolated from the work of one or more theorists. For example, if Northrop Frye's concept of romance intrigues you (as it did Janice Antczak in her book on science fiction), you may want to test the validity of his theory by applying it to a body of children's literature. Thus, you are able to make a judgment about those works relative to Frye's principles of romance.

To apply a theory to a body of literary works, tools, instruments, or some means to control the study must be devised. Often this takes the form of a schema or a matrix. There is no magic or mystery to this, just plain old-fashioned hard work. One might compare the creation of a matrix or schema to the design of a questionnaire, it looks easy but requires intense work and objective scrutiny. Sometimes a scholar gets bogged down in the design of instruments and begins to believe that this part of the research is wasted energy. Sometimes too, the investigator will see the instruments of the study as an infringement on creativity and scholarship and becomes impatient to get to the "books themselves." Achieving the results of the analysis of many individual titles, however, becomes practically impossible without a schema or set of instruments to control the data. Experience demonstrates that those who acquire the discipline and control such work requires are most likely to complete their research, and recognize, at least in retrospect, the value of such schema or instruments. Consumers of research will also learn much from these instruments and may be able to comprehend and evaluate the results only if the instruments are available.

Vandergrift's Model

My own current research draws from a number of disciplines for its theoretical underpinnings as represented in the model (Figure 7) presented in the previous chapter. The way in which those theoretical approaches come together in a research design is dependent upon personal, educational, and professional history. My interest in a transactional theory of literary response, which leads to an examination of both texts and readers, no doubt stems from a combination of early studies of New Criticism and many years of dealing with the responses of young people in classrooms and libraries. The examination of texts is based on a formalistic analysis of compositional elements (character, plot, setting, point of view, mood/ tone, and language/symbol) and more recent interest in what Iser has labelled "gaps" or "areas of inde- terminacy" in a text. As an educator, I relate Iser's literary theory with Rumelhart's work in cognitive psychology. Rumelhart is concerned with schema theory, or the way in which learners store information in organized ways, so that prior knowledge facilitates the acquisition of knowledge or the process of meaning-making in reponse to a text. Essentially what a reader does is to attempt to fill the empty "slots" of a partially completed schema. From a literary perspective then, the act of reading becomes a complex metaphoric dance between the "gaps" in the text and the "slots" in the reader's mental schema.

The model represents a group of readers (only three symbolized here, but usually many more partici- pate) who are together in a reading environment, often a classroom or a library, sometimes for extended periods of time and thus are thought of as an interpretive community. Although this is a community of readers, a particular reader's initial engagement with a text is ordinarily a private event with meanings internally experienced in the consciousness of that reader and not necessarily shared. No one else can par- ticipate in that first act of meaning-making even if all are listening to a reading of the same story. If an adult intermediary is reading aloud, the quality (tone, emphasis, enthusiasm, etc.) of the reading may influence young people's meaning-making. One fruitful area of research is to study responses to different readings of the same text.

Whether or not the text is read aloud, after the reading, the adult intermediary uses all personal knowledge about individual readers and brings all available literary, educational, sociological, and com- munications knowledge to bear in studying the meaning-making situation. The task of the adult intermediary is to help develop and maintain the interpretive community and to ensure that each participant finds both private and public space within that community. The intermediary will observe outward behaviors for clues to literary response, provide ample time for the experiencing of personal felt meanings, and encourage young people to enter into discussion with confidence in and respect for both their own initial meanings and those of others.

Once the process of meaning-making moves from the private to the public domain, the role of the adult intermediary is both to keep the discussion going and make certain there is time for reflection, to encourage young people to share their own meanings and to listen to the meanings of others; and, finally, to refer readers back both to the text and to their own lives in an effort to track their own processes of meaning-making. The entire procedure then is one of metacognition in which participants are assisted in gaining an awareness of their own thought processes as meanings grow and are shaped both personally and socially. It is important to note here that what appears to be a single, solidified group meaning in the visual representation of the model is not nearly as neat as that. There is ordinarily a movement toward some kind of shared meaning, but not all will ascribe to it. Even if it were unanimously shared, that meaning itself would be an event in time and would shift and change to some degree, even within the same interpretive community.

METHODOLOGY

The methodology employed to conduct research to test the model includes an analysis of both written and oral responses using a classification of responses to literature derived from results of studies of critical thinking and literary response (Figure 8). Additionally, a form of ethnographic research is used in which the social discourse within interpretive communities is observed, described, and interpreted to elicit the processes which inform and texture meaning-making behaviors. Both participant observation by the investigator and audio-tapes of group discussions are used to analyze oral communication.

FIGURE 8

**CLASSIFICATION OF RESPONSES
TO LITERATURE**

I. **PERSONAL**—Reader's subjective and affective reactions to engagement with a text; Describing personal thoughts, feelings, memories or beliefs.

II. **DESCRIPTIVE**—Recalling or retelling the story; Answering "who," "what," "where," "when" and "why" (if answer is given in text) questions; Defining words; Identifying the main idea; Identifying medium used in illustration.

III. **CLASSIFICATORY**—Placing the work in a literary and/or historical context; Identifying genre; Comparing and contrasting works.

ANALYTIC—Identifying uses of literary elements in the composition of a text (e.g. language, structure, point of view, etc.).

INTERPRETIVE—Making inferences about a work and its parts; Interpretation of meaning; Relating work to some other way of viewing phenomena (e.g. psychology, sociology, etc.).

EVALUATIVE—Judging the work's merit or quality on personal, literary, social or moral criteria.

In this form of reader–response criticism, one begins with a subjective response (Personal), moves to a more objective position (Descriptive, Classificatory and Analytic) in an attempt to identify the characteristics of the work that triggered personal responses and then to a combination of subjective and objective responses (Interpretive, Evaluative) to use both personal and external criteria in interpreting and judging a text.

PHASES OF STUDY

I.   A PRE-READING INTERVIEW: Although it is difficult or impossible to measure a reader's tacit knowing in relation to literature, the answers to these questions reveal expectations that may affect comprehension, interpretation, and evaluation.

   A.   What kind of stories do you like to read?

   B.   Why do you read stories?

   C.   What do you know about stories?

   D.   What do you expect when you read a story?

   E.   What kinds of things usually happen in stories?

II.   A READING LOG: Readers are asked to keep a log as they read or listen and are encouraged to record any thoughts, ideas, or responses during that process or immediately thereafter. They are encouraged to key their responses to segments of text so that both they and the investigators will be more able to relate their initial reactions more specifically to that text.

III.   POST-READING WRITTEN RESPONSE: Immediately after the reading, students are asked to respond to the following questions which correspond to the categories in Figure 8. These questions are read aloud by the adult intermediary and youngsters are instructed to record their initial responses quickly to capture ideas without worrying about the mechanics of writing. The responses to many of the questions range throughout the classification schema; however, the classes of response most commonly elicited are recorded in parentheses after each question.

A.   What is the story about? [DESCRIPTIVE, INTERPRETIVE]

B.   List key words or phrases that describe this story. [DESCRIPTIVE, INTERPRETIVE]

C.   Did this story evoke any particular *feelings* as you read or heard it? [PERSONAL]

D.   What, if anything, in the story prompted strong *emotions*? Why does this affect you as it does? [PERSONAL, ANALYTIC]

E.   Who is the most interesting character? Why? Does this character change during the story? [ANALYTIC, INTERPRETIVE]

F.   Were there any clues in the text that helped you anticipate the outcome? [ANALYTIC]

G.   Were you aware of any connections between this story and your own *memories*? [PERSONAL]

H.   Does this story remind you of any other stories? If so, what? [CLASSIFICATORY]

I.   Did particular *beliefs* surface as you read? What prompted them to surface? Did they affect your response? [PERSONAL/EVALUATIVE]

J.   What *questions* were left unanswered? [INTERPRETIVE]

K.   If you read this story previously, how does this reading differ from earlier ones? [PERSONAL]

L.   What do you want to share with others from your reading? [PERSONAL, INTERPRETIVE, EVALUATIVE]

These particular questions were devised to convey to young people that investigators are more interested in their responses to story than to the recollections of it. They are intended to be questions that every child can answer by referring to the text rather than to themselves if they choose, but ones that would facilitate the process of meaning-making. Both the questions themselves and the spirit in which they are asked are considered part of an "enabling" or "empowering" process to help students learn to respect their own recreative abilities while, at the same time, being aware of the stimuli for those reponses in the text.

IV.   GROUP DISCUSSION (taped). Discussions begin with the last questions raised in Phase III and, in most instances, range freely over, around, and beyond all those questions and any responses recorded in the logs in Phase II. The adult intermediary encourages participation, reminds participants to go back to their written responses and to the text to support their ideas, and generally tries to facilitate the process of making meaning.

ANALYSIS AND FINDINGS

Analysis of the oral and written responses to the first two phases of the study are ordinarily done by three experienced literature teachers, one of whom is also the adult intermediary in the process. In the Pre-Reading Interview, the teachers look for responses that indicate preferences for particular types or genre ("mysteries," "stories about real people"), moods ("funny" or "scary" stories), or content ("the occult," "describes how something happened or how something works"). The second question is intended to reveal student expectations or preferences for either efferent ("I have to," "Helps me do better in school") or aesthetic ("to relax," "I love to," "I get to be somewhere else for a while") approaches to reading. Students who reply "I get to be somewhere else for a while" and then go on to say "It helps me to understand other people," indicate that they are able to extract an original personal experiencing or knowing of a story (aesthetic) from some more generalized knowledge or understanding to be used outside the story (efferent).

The last three questions of this interview schedule are intended to give some indication of respondents' knowledge of or preconceptions about story forms. Comments such as "Stories have a beginning, a middle, and an end,"; "Characters have to resolve problems,"; "Stories aren't real, but they should be true,"; "I expect stories to have a sense of place and a mood—and leave you with something to think about,"; "The good guys always win in the end"; or "Everything works out" are indications that students have reasonably well-formed perceptions of and expectations from story.

The reading logs are used in two ways. First, students use them to refresh their own memories and get back to their initial responses during the group discussion. This proves to be highly informative, both to students and to the researchers, as we note how quickly many readers "forget" their own thoughts and feelings as the group discussion moves in other directions. Even if these "forgotten" responses are integrated into student interpretations as they move through the story or discuss it with others, they serve as references to the original meaning-making process. Second, logs are analyzed by the researchers in an attempt to follow the process of meaning-making in individual readers. Whenever possible, responses are categorized according to the classification system identified in Figure 8. Since log notes are very personal and idiosyncratic, many are difficult for the researchers to interpret or classify according to the schema in Figure 8. Previous experience with children and texts leads us to look also for four general bimodal patterns of response and try to indicate students' positions on continua between two points (Figure 9). The first two bimodal patterns refer to the form of the response and the third and fourth bimodal patterns refer to referents for responses.

FIGURE 9

BIMODAL PATTERNS OF RESPONSE TO A LITERARY TEXT

FORM OF RESPONSE

QUESTION ←——————————————————————→ STATEMENT

PREDICTION ←——————————————————————→ FLUID
(FIXED)   (OPEN)

REFERENT OF RESPONSE

TEXT ←——————————————————————→ SELF

GENERALIZATION ←——————————————————————→ PERSONALIZATION

Thus, we look for the form of recording, whether responses are more often written as statements or as questions. Some students raise questions as they read and then answer their own questions as they gain information or insight from the story, but there are those who record almost all of their responses as questions. Many students also copy brief quotes from the text into their logs. In some cases, punctuation (a question mark or an explanation point) gives some indication of the copier's intent. Subsequent conversations with these students often support our premise that they copy words or phrases or segments of text that they have questions about; those that are keys to their understanding; those considered to be powerful and affective uses of language; or those that, for whatever reason, they just want to "keep." In as much as possible, these statements and questions are also classified according to the schema in Figure 8.

A second continuum of responses is that between readers who try to get an early "fix" on the story and anticipate its outcome (CLASSIFICATORY) and those who, in the words of one student, "go with the flow" (PERSONAL). In both written and oral responses, some readers seem to need to classify a text very early in their reading and then interpret and evaluate the text according to that classification. One factor which seems to be related to these modes of response is the type of fiction respondents prefer in reading for pleasure. Those who prefer "genre" fiction (mystery, science fiction, romance) appear to be more likely to keep a greater aesthetic distance from a literary work and concentrate more on form than on feeling. Those who select primarily realistic fiction for their personal reading are more likely to identify with the protagonist and "live through" the text. Of course, such responses appear to be the result as much of the nature of the text as of that of the readers; but the mode of response seems to persist with some readers regardless of the particular text, indicating that these patterns of response warrant further study.

A more obvious third pattern of response is that between those who refer primarily to the text and those who refer primarily to themselves. This is the difference between "The plot is confusing," (INTERPRETIVE) and "I'm confused," (PERSONAL); between "This character is...." (ANALYTIC or INTERPRETIVE) and "This character reminds me of...." (PERSONAL)

Closely related to this third pattern is a fourth continuum between generalization and personalization or from "All kids sometimes feel their parents hate them," (INTERPRETIVE) to "I remember when my mother...." (PERSONAL)

In public discussions within the interpretive community, young people are encouraged to examine and evaluate the story from a variety of vantage points and to share their questions or insights with others. The adult intermediary not only keeps the discussion going — or slows it down to give students an opportunity to reflect — but also helps participants to recognize that the origins of their personal responses are as much in their prior knowledge or experiences as in the story. Transcripts of these discussions are coded according to the classification schema in Figure 8. During the discussions, adult intermediaries encourage students to think back to their responses during earlier phases of the study. In each group, respondents had referred to some sort of "neat resolution" of story problems in the Pre-Reading Interview. Students are encouraged to consider their interpretive community as a kind of "think tank" in which each member is an invited guest, who is highly respected for unique contributions. As in a "think tank," however, personal insights and ideas come under the close scrutiny of other thinkers, so that each learns from the others and expands the possibilities of meaning. On the other hand, there is no pressure for anyone to "buy into" or accept what appears to be a group meaning or consensus.

The ability of young people to make meaning from a literary work has been clearly demonstrated in the research using this model.[38] Students are able to engage in the metacognitive process of "tracking" their own meaning-making by identifying referents both from the text and from personal experiences that influence their perceptions, interpretations, and evaluations. Most importantly, they seem to grow in their trust of and respect for their own personal meanings as well as those of others, and in an understanding and appreciation of the social construction of meaning.

Of major concern to those of us who work with young people is the role of the adult intermediary in the literary experience. In some studies, students heard the text read aloud, rather than reading it themselves. This almost certainly influenced responses because less able youngsters could concentrate on meaning without having to decode. On the other hand, a particular adult intermediary's own responses to a text cannot, nor should they necessarily be, eliminated from the reading. It would be possible to "neutralize" the effect of the specific adult intermediary by using a tape, but this could have a detrimental effect on establishing the sense of community so necessary for this type of research. Thus, the influence of the particular intermediary's reading is considered a topic for possible future research.

Of even greater concern is the way in which adult intermediaries can manipulate meaning-making in the process of discussion by ignoring responses they do not know how to deal with—or those they disagree with—and by reinforcing what they believe to be "the truth" of the work. Analysis of a number of taped discussions revealed that this was done in very subtle ways, even by the most well-intentioned adults. All of us who lead discussions risk listening *for* the responses we want or expect rather than listening *to* responses that may stretch our own capabilities for encountering meaning. Thus, the collegial process of the adults involved in these investigations alerted each of us to some of our own personal mannerisms or teaching strategies that either inhibit or enhance learning and the making of meaning.

FUTURE STUDIES

Not only is there much research yet to be done based on the model described above, but many other literary studies remain to be undertaken. One possibility is a study of the use of evocative language in children's books, particularly as it is used to create mood and tone. The fact that many of these books are read aloud to young children sparks an interest in language and what the human voice can evoke from an audience. One might go further to investigate how different oral interpretations of the same text influence a listener's interpretation. One might go even further and suggest that visual language be added to a study, particularly one of looking at picture books for young children in relation to contemporary filmmaking. There are innumerable areas of potential research in children's literature that cannot be developed here. Many are now integrating literary theory and theoretical ideas from other disciplines into children's literature research, but there are other such combinations which might prove elucidating which are as yet untapped. Might we use or adapt theory from science or mathematics to develop a structure for the analysis of concept or informational works? Could we adopt the stance of the revisionists in history and approach analysis of historical books with this theoretical frame?

OBSTACLES TO RESEARCH

Anyone who has either studied research or engaged in research activities knows that there are problems to be resolved in order to produce satisfactory results. The tellers of traditional tales would have us believe that there are basically three obstacles to be overcome. Unfortunately, however, the number of obstacles confronting the researcher is far greater. Some of these obstacles are common to most research; others are most frequently encountered in a particular type of research.

The major obstacles besetting the researcher in children's literature do not radically differ from those of researchers in other fields. Four specific obstacles are of concern; the first two are so interrelated that they might even be perceived of as one. Although I have listed the first two together, they are indeed separate problems and need to be seen clearly as such if we are to overcome them.

Bibliographical and Physical Access

The first difficulty is that of bibliographic access. The second is that of physical availability. We need to know, first of all, what exists, both in the literature itself and in the scholarship about that literature. Then we need to know the locations of various collections and the specific details of holdings within those collections. A general access to collections is improved by the latest edition of *Special Collections in Children's Literature* (540) by Carolyn Field which brings together a vast resource on children's literature in the United States. This book, however, only gives the briefest indication of the actual contents of collections. The detailed inventories of collections required for scholarly purposes are only recently becoming available, but are still virtually nonexistent. Scholars require the kinds of information that permit them to make decisions about their use of time and financial resources. Such information might include the register of a specific manuscript holding with details regarding the content of the various folders in the collection.

The Walter Farley papers from the collections of the Columbia University Libraries are an example of inadequate access. Although Farley's works have been among the most read, translated, and reprinted in children's literature, the available information about this collection in the Columbia University catalog is little more than an acknowledgment of its existence, and even this reference does not exist in the Field work.

To know precisely what is in this collection, a researcher would have to come to the library and get permission to go through the actual boxes of materials. On the other hand, Field does note that the Robert Cormier papers are at Fitchburg State College in Massachusetts and that they include several unpublished manuscripts. Without Field's volume, few would think to look for such a potentially rich resource in that location. The brief entry in Field, however, does not give enough detail to know the nature of Cormer's unpublished manuscripts or the terms of use attached to the collection. The unevenness of coverage revealed in these examples is not intended as a criticism of what is a very useful and powerful tool, but as an indication of the difficulty of the task. A smaller institution with fewer resources is more likely to report specific holdings than a large research institution in which materials related to children's literature may not be considered a major aspect of the collection.

British scholars face similar problems in the effort to identify resources. An issue of *Signal*[39] called for help from the Centre for Children's Books in London to compile information on the holdings of institutions throughout the country. Research experience at the Bodleian and the Victoria and Albert Library, as well as the British Library Reference Room, attests to problems of access to holdings when details on editions and contents of manuscripts are incomplete. It is possible that computer capabilities may allow greater access to rich resources both in our own country and worldwide, but this will happen only if we insist on the scholarly need for such a network. The purpose of such insistence is to facilitate the future work of scholars and to make known the specific riches of the holdings within various institutions. At present, however, bibliographic access to scholarly resources in children's literature is still a very time consuming, often unreliable, process.

Some believe that this lengthy pursuit of data, often a result of inadequate means of access, is in itself, a desirable goal. On the contrary, anything which enables the user of a collection to more speedily access needed materials is to be desired. Although there may be occasions when serendipitous information leads to important discoveries, there is little value in sustaining lengthy engagements with a topic if those engagements are not productive. Precise and accurate attention to appropriate details is the very essence of research. Fenwick pointed out that access to doctoral research is very difficult.[40] Even with all of the computerized data bases available, we still find gaps that often exclude a set of pertinent studies. The intricacies of designing and searching data bases are still not refined enough to permit a sense of certainty that one has found all pertinent data in a given search. Bibliographies are often limited by what is indexed and many journals which publish studies of children's literature are not indexed. This is of grave concern to scholars in this field. Haviland, in her various reference books, has at least attempted to provide additonal access points, as has *Phaedrus*; but significant materials still fall by the wayside and are virtually lost to scholars and researchers.

In addition to these more general aspects of inadequate access, there are unique cases in which the potential of a lost piece of data may be critical to research in progress. In authorial or textual criticism of the work of the Lobels, for instance, it would be unfortunate if the researcher had available only the regular publisher's edition of *On Market Street*. At the time of publication there were 250 signed copies of this book available which included a three-page, bound-in insert by Anita Lobel exploring the intent of the author/illustrator. The probability is that this special edition may be unavailable in most collections and may seldom appear in bibliographies, thus allowing a scholar to speculate or devise theories about the origins of the book independent of the Lobel's own published statement.[41]

There is also the problem of acquiring the physical access to materials that have been determined to exist. Like other rare materials, many older children's books will be in rare book collections with restrictive hours and rules for usage and photocopying. Of course, many materials important to the study of the history of children's literature no longer exist because the popular literature of children has not always been considered worthy of preservation and young people have been known to "love their books to pieces" through repeated uses. Although rich and extensive collections of children's literature do exist in the United States, as well as in many other countries, many institutions are not seeking manuscripts or books to add to those resources. This lack may be reflective of attitudes about scholarship in children's literature and the ranking this discipline receives in various priority systems, either those of the university itself or of the university library. Perhaps scholars from various departments within the university who do research in children's literature need to come together to find more effective ways of sharing the results of their scholarship and to exert influence on the larger institution. Common sense and reasonableness must sometimes dominate our rigor. A researcher must find the balance between giving up a search too easily and succumbing to an irrational passion to be absolutely positive that all has been seen and analyzed which can ultimately result in the research never being completed.

Cost

A third obstacle related to a particular type of research is that of the cost of working with historical children's books, especially with the illustrations of such books. Reproducing old and rare items is costly and often not permissible. In order to conduct research in illustration, some study will need to be devoted to what is permissible and economically feasible for the scholar who approaches this area of investigation. In this country, because of changes in the tax laws, more and more of the original art work of illustrators is being shunted off to the private buyer rather than being contributed to library or museum collections. Consequently, access to scholars is becoming more difficult. Individual works of Trina Schart Hyman, Maurice Sendak, Kit Williams, the Dillons and others are being purchased by private collectors from sources such as the Bush Gallery or Justin Schiller's Gallery which specialize in children's book illustration. The result is fragmentation and unavailability of the work of these artists. In the past, because of the tax benefits to the creator or donor, at least some of this art might have been given to institutions where it would be preserved and made available to scholars.

The trend towards private sale of art work is, however, neither new nor unjustified. Artists deserve the financial rewards of these sales, and many of us are pleased to have their work in our homes. We should be aware, however, that the dimensions of this practice are growing and may be an obstacle to future research. On the other hand, the traveling exhibits of the Lena Y. deGrummond Collection from the University of Southern Mississippi provide the opportunity to display original illustrations from contemporary children's books, thus, affording all of us the pleasure of viewing and studying the work of various artists.[42] Another positive instance is Rutgers University's honoring of illustrator Roger Duvoisin with a retrospective exhibition at the Jane Voorhees Zimmerli Art Museum. The exhibition of approximately one-hundred original illustrations, preliminary sketches, color separations, jacket covers, dummies, galley proofs, and published books draws primarily from the Rutgers Collection of Children's Literature at the Zimmerli Art Museum.[43]

Language Barriers

A fourth obstacle is the inaccessibility of a wide range of international studies and materials. The need for the scholar to read in foreign languages is increasing for certain areas of concern; and the need is not only for knowledge of the traditional languages of French and German, but the less familiar ones such as Danish, Swedish, Russian, and other Slovak languages. A great deal of criticism and research in these countries is still not translated, and the scholar must develop a means to use this information. Perhaps even greater obstacles than language barriers are cultural variances that require an increasingly greater degree of understanding in order to interpret context.

These obstacles, although not unique to children's literature, have been of concern in our field for some time as seen in Henne's calls for bibliographers of children's literature more than a decade ago.[44] Recent attempts to meet the needs of researchers are evident in publications from the Kerlan Collection (534) and the Osborne Collection (538, 539) as well as the records of the Stratemeyer syndicate publication (473) and the accurate and quite beautiful reproductions from the Osborne Collection.[45]

Of course the greatest obstacle to any scholarly research is ignorance, and ignorance of primary sources is all too common in the field of children's literature. It is alarming to note the numbers of pseudoscholars who make use of secondary sources and seem to have no notion of the availability of the original item. No matter how much one trusts the work of Meigs and Field and others, such trust is not a license to avoid the difficult and painstaking work of checking original sources.

Obstacles to Empirical Studies

Although the obstacles just enumerated apply to all literary research, they are most frequently associated with some form of historical or formalistic literary study. There are additional obstacles or problems that need consideration in working with empirical studies of the transactions between children and their literature. The first concern is for the privacy of the child. Many of the studies proposed in the name of psychological or reader-response theory may invade the privacy of child readers. Psychoanalytic critics such as Holland had the consent of the respondents in his research; but many younger children are not yet of an age to give informed consent. Although schools ordinarily protect children, they sometimes permit qualified researchers to enter their domains without providing adequate protection for children nor informing parents of the nature of the research. This concern for children cannot be expressed too strongly; ethical research practices require that a sound judgment regarding their rights as subjects be made before any study is undertaken. One must also warn of the intrusion of the computer into the reading habits and patterns of young people. There is no question that this tool is powerful and can provide invaluable data, but we must also be alert to technological invasions of privacy. *BookWhiz* and *BookBrain* are examples of products that offer a positive approach to the use of this technology.[46]

Another problem in working with empirical studies is the need to understand both the level of measurement we are seeking and the corresponding statistical tests that will help in the analysis of the data. The capability of the computer to manipulate statistical data has led some researchers to assume that any and every set of statistics will enliven their work. Statistics are only useful when they permit us to say what cannot be said as strongly any other way. They permit us to offer some degree of confidence about our findings with the expectation that the reader will accept our recommendations and move to some specified set of actions. There is a danger that parents, teachers, librarians, and other researchers will be led to believe that any research with statistical analysis is both valid and useful. Too many content analyses studies have used statistics to demonstrate hypotheses that have been tested in a biased and often imprecise fashion. For many years we have assumed that children's reading interests could be statistically determined and have made a number of questionable generalizations about such findings.

For instance, studies which measure preferences for different types of literature such as adventure, sports, romance, and science fiction, etc., based on age and sex are probably measuring the wrong things. Neumeyer, among others, points this out and suggests that we adopt some of the methods of the structuralists to study the reading interests of children.[47] He refers to his research that examined the preferences of children for works such as *Peter Rabbit*,[48] by looking at Peter as a scamp, Peter as a naughty boy who gets caught, Peter who is the risk taker, etc. This approach is not the same as indicating that *Peter Rabbit* is an adventure story or an animal story and, therefore, children who say they like Peter obviously like adventure or animal stories. It is the acceptance of such broad categorization that is so dangerous because it is misleading. One might apply similar criticism to many of the studies that have explored the "isms" in literature. Too many of these studies examine isolates in the text rather than the entire work. When a work is not looked at holistically, there is at least some question about the findings.

Another problem discerned in dealing with empirical studies is one inherent in observational or case studies. The control of the environment and the recording of the necessary data are a serious problem for a research team. Applebee (488) and Butler (388) relied on findings of others or on the observation of children in their own families, and many of us operate as participant observers in the research setting. There are many methods that might be used in recording observational data and probably no one of them is wholly adequate.

POTENTIAL RESEARCH QUESTIONS

An examination of the current picture of research in children's literature, has raised some research questions that might prove fruitful for investigation. Some of these are listed below with the hope they may lead to an interesting intellectual dialogue which is among the most exciting of educational experiences.

- Might we look forward to an increase of scholars using a particular literary theory as the conceptual framework for investigations of literary genres, works, or authors?

- Will historical research move into the twentieth century and use more contemporary works as the objects of investigation in children's literature?

- Will we see reader-response studies that explore the literary experience through documented case studies?

- Could new methodological approaches be devised that would permit more substantive examination of the concept of "influence?"

- Will we approach media, other than the book, as a fertile field for serious investigation in terms other than causal studies related to children's behavior?

- May we expect a series of studies that strengthen our perception and heighten our understanding of communication through illustration?

- Will we explore the significance of "popular culture" as children's literature?

- How might we begin to examine the nature of informational books in terms of their approaches to content?

- How might we design a semiotic study of such poetry as that by R. L. Stevenson or A. A. Milne which has remained popular with successive generations of children?

- Is there any match between learning theories and the various informational series for children?

- How might one design a study to test Rosenblatt's transactional theory with beginning readers?

COMMUNICATION: SHARING RESEARCH RESULTS

A final consideration in discussing research is that of communication. Unless we are able to write with competence and with style as well as with accuracy, we are in risk of joining that cluster of literary theorists who have created such a private enclave that they can talk only with one another. There is joy in open and clear writing about research in children's literature that illuminates the thought processes of another and shares the results of intellectual efforts. Much of adult literary theory and research in recent years has been distinguished by its incomprehensibility to most intelligent readers. Researchers in children's literature do not need to share that characteristic to be precise in sharing our work with a larger community of scholars.

An essential ingredient that must be present in our work with children's literature is a thorough and deep knowledge of and a respect for the body of that literature. There is increasing cause for concern that some researchers who posit theories and compile evidence seem to value neither the literature nor the child. True scholarship is grounded in literary theory and methodology while at the same time steeped in children's literature and an understanding and appreciation of childhood.

There is an exhilaration in research—the thrill of the chase; the excitement of an argument; the taste of an awesome idea—that can be shared with adult students. We recognize ourselves in the role of student wishing to learn and to turn new corners either through our own work, or through that of our students or colleagues. We listen to Cullum's call in the following passage and remind ourselves that the role of teacher-researcher is one of child-like openness, risk-taking, and the continual process of learning all over again:

Teacher, come on outside!
I'll race you to the seesaw!
No, you won't fall off!
I'll show you how!
Don't be afraid, teacher.
Grab my hand and follow me.
You can learn all over again!...[49]

NOTES

[1]Special gratitude is due to Jane Anne Hannigan, Professor Emerita, Columbia University who generously shared her paper on Research in Children's Literature presented at the Fifteenth Annual Seminar, "Loughborough International Seminar in Children's Literature," University of Tennessee, Knoxville, August 16-20, 1982 and who has shared her knowledge and insight on all aspects of this chapter.

[2]Sara Innis Fenwick. (Spring 1979). "Scholarly Research About Historical Children's Books," in The Study and Collecting of Historical Children's Books, edited by Selma K. Richardson. *Library Trends*. 27: 529-549.

[3]Gillian Avery. (1980) "The Researcher's Craft: Design and Implements," in *Research About Nineteenth-Century Children and Books*. Edited by Selma K. Richardson. (Urbana, IL: University of Illinois Press.)

[4]Robert Spiller. (1970) "Literary History," in James Thorpe, Editor. *The Aims and Methods of Scholarship*. (New York: Modern Language Association of America), 55.

[5]George W. Norvell. (1950). *The Reading Interests of Young People*. (Boston, MA: D. C. Heath).

[6]G. LaVerne Freeman and Ruth S. Freeman. (1933). *The Child and His Picture Book*. (Chicago, IL: Northwestern University Press).

[7]Michael Benton. (Summer 1979). "Children's Responses To Stories," *Children's Literature in Education*. 10 (2): 68-85; and Barbara Leondar. (1975). "Metaphor and Infant Cognition," *Poetics: International Review for Theory of Literature*. 4: 273-287.

[8]Barbara Kiefer Lewalski. (1981) "Historical Scholarship," in Joseph Gibaldi, Editor. *Introduction to Scholarship in Modern Languages and Literatures*. (New York: The Modern Language Association of America), 56.

[9]Laurence Yep. (1977). *Child of the Owl*. (New York: Harper & Row).

[10]Leslie Fiedler. (1978). *Freaks*. (New York: Simon & Schuster).

[11]Florence Crannell Means. (1945). *The Moved-Outers*. (Boston, MA: Houghton-Mifflin).

[12]Florence Crannell Means. (1938). *Shuttered Windows*. (Boston, MA: Houghton-Mifflin).

[13]Florence Crannell Means. (1969). *Our Cup Is Broken*. (Boston, MA: Houghton-Mifflin).

[14]Ann Nolan Clark. (1941). *In My Mother's House*. (New York: Viking Press).

[15]Barbara Kiefer Lewalski. "Historical Scholarship," p. 60.

[16]Elaine L. Konigsburg. (1982). *Journey to an 800 Number*. (New York: Atheneum). Konigsburg verified this idea as part of the "real" events behind her book during her speech at the Fifteenth Annual Seminar "Loughborough International Seminar on Children's Literature," University of Tennessee, Knoxville, August 16-20, 1982.

[17]Daniel Pinkwater. (1982). *young adult novel*. (New York: Thomas Y. Crowell) 42.

[18]Marguerite de Angeli. (1946). *Bright April*. (New York: Doubleday).

[19]*Go Ask Alice*. (1971). (Englewood Cliffs, NJ: Prentice Hall).

[20]Alice Childress. (1973). *A Hero Ain't Nothin' But a Sandwich*. (New York: Coward-McCann).

[21]John Steinbeck. (1939). *Grapes of Wrath*. (New York: Viking Press).

[22]Eleanor Estes. (1944). *The Hundred Dresses*. (New York: Harcourt, Brace, Jovanovich); Louisa Shotwell. (1963). *Roosevelt Grady*. (Cleveland, OH: Collins World); Doris Gates. (1940). *Blue Willow*. (New York): Viking Press); Lois Lenski. (1945). *Strawberry Girl*. (Philadelphia, PA: Lippincott). A more recent example would be Sue Ellen Bridgers. (1976). *Home Before Dark*. (New York: Alfred A. Knopf).

[23]Robert Lawson. (1939). *Ben and Me*. (Boston, MA: Little Brown).

[24]Alethea K. Helbig. (Spring 1982). "The Forest As Setting and Symbol in Barbara Willard's Mantlemass Novels," *Children's Literature Association Quarterly*. 7, 1: 35-39.

[25]Ann O'Neal Garcia. (1982). *Spirit on the Wall*. (New York: Holiday House).

[26]Victoria Strauss. (1982). *The Lady of Rhuddesmere*. (New York: Frederick Warne).

[27]Lisl Weil. (1983). *I, Christopher Columbus*. (New York: Atheneum).

[28]Peter Coveney. (1957). *Poor Monkey*. (London: Rockliff.) This work was later revised and published under a new title: *The Images of Childhood*. (Baltimore, MD: Penguin Books, 1967).

[29]Kay E. Vandergrift and Jane Anne Hannigan. (April 1985). "A Celebration of Tradition in Children's Literature," *School Library Journal*. Vol. 31, No. 8: 33-37.

[30]Malcolm J. Bosse. (1981). *Ganesh*. (New York: Thomas Y. Crowell); and Jeanne Dixon. (1987). *The Tempered Wind*. (New York: Atheneum).

[31]Jamake Highwater. (1984). *Legend Days*. Part I of the Ghost Horse Cycle. (New York: Harper & Row); (1985). *Ceremony of Innocence*. Part II of the Ghost Horse Cycle. (New York: Harper & Row); (1986). *I Wear the Morning Star*. Part III of the Ghost Horse Cycle. (New York: Harper & Row).

[32]Jamake Highwater. (1982). *The Primal Mind: Vision and Reality in Indian America*. (New York: New American Library); Jamake Highwater. (1983). *Ritual of the Wind: North American Indian Ceremonies, Music, and Dance*. (Van der Marck).

[33]Selma G. Lanes. (1980). *The Art of Maurice Sendak*. (New York: Harry Abrams), 191-207.

[34]Dr. Dolittle books had been criticized for their visual and verbal images offensive to Blacks. Because the stories, for the most part, were good adventures, new editions have been issued which remove the offensive segments without destroying the essence of the story. Selma Lanes in a review of the new editions wrote: "Happily, none of this well-intended editorial tinkering has had the slightest effect on the tales' enduring charms." Selma G. Lanes. (August 28, 1988) "Doctor Dolittle, Innocent Again," *The New York Times Book Review*.; Hugh Lofting. (1988). *The Story of Doctor Dolittle*. Centenary Edition. (New York: Delacorte); Hugh Lofting. (1988). *The Voyages of Doctor Dolittle*. Centenary Edition. (New York: Delacorte).

[35]Kathleen T. Horning. (Winter 1988). "Are You Sure That Book Won the Caldecott Medal? Variant Printings and Editions of Three Caldecott Medal Books," *Journal of Youth Studies in Libraries*. 1 (2): 173-176.

[36]Barbara Kiefer Lewalski. "Historical Scholarship," p. 66.

[37]Joan Aiken. (1982). *The Way to Write for Children*. (London: Elm Tree Books); and Joan Aiken. (1985). "Interpreting the Past," *Children's Literature in Education*. 16: 67-83.

[38]Kay E. Vandergrift. (in press). "Meaning-Making and the Dragons of Pern," *Children's Literature Association Quarterly* and Kay E. Vandergrift. (Winter 1987). "Critical Thinking Misfired: Implications of Student Responses to *The Shooting Gallery*," *School Library Media Quarterly*. 15: 86-91.

[39]"Endpapers," (May 1982). in *Signal*. 38: 129.

[40]Sara Innis Fenwick. "Scholarly Research About Historical Children's Books," 530-534.

[41]Anita and Arnold Lobel. (1981). *On Market Street*. Deluxe edition, No. 154, with an introduction by Anita Lobel. (New York: J. G. Schiller and Greenwillow Books), 44pp. This copy, one of the limited edition of 250 numbered and signed copies, contains the authors' introduction. The other edition is identified only as a first edition, published in 1980 by Greenwillow Books and contains only forty pages. Each of the two first editions was searched in OCLC and RLIN, the two major bibliographic utilities, on April 22, 1983, with the result that only the forty-page first edition was found in RLIN, while both the first and deluxe editions showed up in OCLC, plus a sound recording and filmstrip by the same authors and with the same title. This finding was contrary to expectations, since RLIN, is made up of institutions with research collections which might have been more aware of an interest in acquiring variant or unusual editions of the work. Nevertheless, OCLC contained the variant entry, a copy held by Florida State University, as well as the nonprint versions of *On Market Street*, and the ordinary first edition. Although the variant edition appears in OCLC there is no clue as to the significant content of the introduction, so important to the literary researcher.

[42]The Lena Y. deGrummond Collection of Children's Literature at the University of Southern Mississippi may be contacted through the Curator.

[43]For further information contact Philip Cate, Director, Jane Voorhees Zimmerli Art Museum, Rutgers University, New Brunswick, NJ 08903.

[44]Frances Henne. (October 1975). "Toward A National Plan to Nourish Research in Children's Literature," in James Fraser, Editor, Children's Literature Collections and Research Libraries. *Wilson Library Bulletin.* 50, 2: 131-137.

[45]Selected works from the Osborne Collection have been reproduced in a special collection available from Chatto, Bodley Head & Cape Services, 99 Main Street, Salem, New Hampshire 03079 at $695.00 for the complete set. This set does represent an extraordinary venture of providing future scholars and even the contemporary child with replicas of many of the books that children have found delightful through two centuries.

[46]Educational Testing Service. (1987). *BookWhiz* (Princeton, NJ: Educational Testing Service); and E. A. Hass. (1987). *Bookbrain.* (Phoenix, AZ: Oryx Press).

[47]Peter F. Neumeyer. (December 1967). "A Structural Approach to the Study of Literature for Children," *Elementary English.* 883-895.

[48]"That youngsters like *Peter Rabbit* or *The Swiss Family Robinson* may mean no more than these two books are written in just the way that happens to hit it off with children." from Peter Neumeyer. "A Structural Approach," p. 883.

[49]Albert Cullum. (1971). *The Geranium on the Window Sill Died But Teacher You Went Right On.* (New York: Harlin Quist, Inc.), 60.

RESEARCH TOOLS FOR BIBLIOGRAPHIC ACCESS IN CHILDREN'S LITERATURE

Avery, Gillian. (1980). "The Researcher's Craft: Design and Implements," in *Research About Nineteenth-Century Children and Books.* Edited by Selma K. Richardson. Urbana, Champaign, IL: University of Illinois, pp. 7-22.

Bekkedal, Tekla K. (October 1973). "Content Analysis of Children's Books," *Library Trends.* 22, 2: pp. 109-126.

Benton, Michael, Editor. (1980). *Approaches to Research in Children's Literature.* Southhampton, England: The Department of Education, The University.

Fenwick, Sara Innis. (Spring 1979). "Scholarly Research about Historical Children's Books," in *The Study and Collecting of Historical Children's Books.* Edited by Selma K. Richardson. *Library Trends.* 27, 4: pp. 529-549.

Field, Carolyn E., Editor. (1982). *Special Collections in Children's Literature.* Chicago, IL: American Library Association.

Haviland, Virginia and others, comps. (1966). *Children's Literature: A Guide to Reference Sources.* Washington, DC: The Library of Congress. (plus various supplements.)

Kelly, R. Gordon. (Spring 1973). "American Children's Literature: An Historiographical Review," *American Literary Review.* 6, 2: pp. 89-107.

Lukenbill, W. Bernard, and Sharon Lee Stewart. (1988). *Youth Literature: An Interdisciplinary Annotated Guide to North American Dissertation Research, 1930-1985.* New York: Garland Publishing.

Monson, Dianne L., and Bette J. Peltola, comps. (1976). *Research in Children's Literature: An Annotated Bibliography.* Newark, DE: International Reading Association.

Purves, Alan C. (1981). *Reading and Literature: American Achievement in International Perspective.* (NCTE Research Report No. 20.) Urbana, IL: National Council of Teachers of English.

Robinson, Helen M., and Samuel Weintraub. (October 1973). "Research Related to Children's Interests and to Developmental Values of Reading," *Library Trends.* 22, 2: pp. 81-108.

Vandergrift, Kay, and Jane Anne Hannigan. (April 1985). "A Celebration of Tradition in Children's Literature," *School Library Journal.* Vol. 31:33-37.

RESEARCH TOOLS FOR LITERARY STUDY

Altick, Richard D. (1963). *The Art of Literary Research.* Revised Edition. New York: W. W. Norton & Co., Inc.

Boillot, F. (1924). *The Methodical Study of Literature.* Paris: Les Presses Universitaires De France.

Clifford, James. (1970). *From Puzzles to Portraits: Problems of a Literary Biographer.* Chapel Hill, NC: University of North Carolina Press.

Crane, R. S. (1971). *Critical and Historical Principles of Literary History.* Chicago, IL: The University of Chicago Press.

Gibaldi, Joseph, Editor. (1981). *Introduction to Scholarship in Modern Languages and Literatures.* New York: The Modern Language Association.

Goldsmith, Evelyn. (1984). *Research Into Illustration: An Approach and A Review.* Cambridge, England: Cambridge University Press.

Hoffman, Daniel, Editor. (1979). *Harvard Guide to Contemporary American Writing.* Cambridge, MA: The Belknap Press of Harvard University Press.

Kehler, Dorothea. (1987). *Problems in Literary Research: A Guide to Selected Reference Works.* Metuchen, NJ: Scarecrow Press.

Lovejoy, A. O. (1960). *The Great Chain of Being: A Study of the History of an Idea.* New York: Harper & Row. (reprint of 1936 edition.)

Thorpe, James, Editor. (1970). *The Aims and Methods of Scholarship in Modern Languages and Literatures.* Second Edition. New York: Modern Language Association.

Teaching and Children's Literature

INTRODUCTION

If literature, literary theory, and literary research are continuing sources of fascination and pleasure, one of the greatest joys comes in the interaction with these elements and with other human beings in the act of teaching. It is in teaching that the opportunity exists to share enthusiasm for all aspects of literary study and research and appreciation of children with others who have similar concerns. As students and teachers share ideas and interests, they encounter not only new works and new relationships but open their eyes to new interpretations of established practices and materials. Thus, teaching is a very important means of nurturing our own growth in the discipline and in the profession, and of keeping us fully alive to the literature with which we work.

Faculty in higher education not only specialize in one or two content areas, but also allocation of their professional time is indicative of the role of scholar/teacher. In addition, those who teach children's literature to adults are almost always working with students who have elected to attend the particular class and already have some commitment to the field. Often students are preservice or even inservice teachers or librarians who work directly with literature and with children, or they are students in English departments or American studies or popular culture programs with special interests in children's literature relevant to those disciplines. Thus, one who teaches children's literature to adults must be both scholar and teacher; must be knowledgeable in the subject area; must be able to make that subject matter come alive for those who view it from a variety of perspectives; and must ultimately relate that literature back to its primary audience—children.

This chapter introduces seven models of teaching common in the college/university setting and then proposes a new "literary" model which looks at both the artistry of the teaching composition and the skillful use of the crafts of teaching which make that composition possible. Finally, it will explore the criticism of teaching, positing that the appropriate means of interpreting and evaluating any compositional form is criticism.

The primary research of those who teach children's literature is the literature itself, as discussed in the previous chapter; but there is also a need for research on teaching in higher education itself which does not have to be delegated totally to those in graduate schools of education. Most such research combines the content to be taught with particular teaching methods or technologies; but a body of more general research on motivation, student characteristics, faculty attitudes, learning environments, and evaluation techniques also exists. There are many topics within these areas which are fruitful arenas for research. Additional knowledge about existing methodologies and the development of new approaches to teaching in higher education is also needed. Research and demonstration projects funded by the U.S. Department of Education provide impetus for such work, but much more is required if practice is to be influenced in any substantive way.

SEVEN MODELS OF UNIVERSITY TEACHING

"Sitting at the Feet" Model

There are a number of basic forms of teaching in colleges and universities, many of which reflect a narrow and unhealthy view of teaching and, in fact, of the whole educational process. The first is the "Sitting at the Feet" model in which it is assumed that students come to sit at the feet of the "greats" in the field to catch whatever pearls of wisdom may drop from their lips and soak up the ambience of greatness. Students are expected to piece their own sense of the discipline together from whatever personal and professional tidbits are revealed. Of course, "greatness," in whatever degree, does not come early or with ease; and, in most instances, the teacher in this model is merely resting upon past laurels and reminiscing about previous accomplishments and "the good old days." This approach inspires some students and arouses their own aspirations for greatness and perhaps even points the way. As education, however, it is self-defeating because education, even in its study of history, should look forward rather than back. Education should point toward where students might go rather than to where we, as teachers or scholars, have been.

"Content Synthesis" Model

A second model of teaching in colleges and universities is that of "Content Synthesis." In this model, the teacher analyzes historical material, keeps up with the field by reading all the latest books and articles in that subject area, and tells students what they need to know. Often this model takes the form of a synthesized list of influential scholars, key events and "great truths" over time, and, unfortunately, frees students from the obligation of reading much original material or thinking for themselves. In one sense, a teacher is a "gatekeeper" and a certain amount of content synthesis is necessary, but this form of presentation is probably an inefficient means of instruction in an age in which so many technological media are available to transmit the same content. Even for those students who absorb more through a human transmitter—probably a minority today, given all the other media in common use—it might well be more beneficial to use the uniquely human qualities to help individual students sort, select, and synthesize their own store of information gained from other sources.

"Show and Tell" Model

A related, but in many ways an opposite, form of teaching might be called the "Show and Tell" model. In this model, the teacher also selects and presents material to the class, but often without the benefit of synthesis and historical perspective. What is shared is frequently the most recent activity or idea that caught the professor's interest in the professional literature or at a conference. The benefit, of course, is timeliness; but the disadvantage is fragmentation. There is a danger that students will complete the class having no sense of the totality of the field. Furthermore, the dependence on chance always keeps students in the role of audience with no way of anticipating or preparing for course content and little sense of articulation of the whole.

"Worship with Me at the Shrine" Model

A fourth, somewhat less common, model is one in which the professor invites students to "Worship with Me at the Shrine." In this approach, the teacher basks in the reflected glory of the discipline that is held up as if it were an awe-inspiring, multi-faceted crystal ball. This places the student in a similar position in relation to the content as does the "Sitting at the Feet" model. In both instances the student is assumed to stand at a distance, to look upon the content with a sense of wonder, and to be duly impressed. The primary difference between the two models is that, in the first, the professor is the subject of awe within the crystal ball; while in this one, the professor is more like an informed guide who is sharing enthusiasm and previous experiences with the class. Of course, students are often led to suspect that, in reality, the professor really does belong inside that crystal ball and it is modesty that prohibits that revelation.

"The Classicists" Model

Practitioners of the fifth model might be called "The Classicists." These are the professors who have a seemingly unending supply of quotations and all-purpose excerpts from "great literature" which they can, and do, pull forth for every occasion and in response to every question. Students cannot help but be impressed with this apparent breadth and depth of knowledge, and it is often only in retrospect that they realize that the professor's learned soliloquy had little or nothing to do with the topic under consideration.

A variant, and less impressive, form of this model is that of the teacher who, for a period of time at least, finds in one theory, in one work, or in one thinker the answer to everything and proceeds to conduct classes as if that were so. Often the particular scholar or theory that serves as the base for such attention is in a discipline only tangentially related to the course content. Although any of us might learn a great deal from theology, the work of Kierkegaard, or any of a number of means of imposing order on the world, I doubt that a course in children's literature is the appropriate forum for such work. In fact, I reject basing even a course on literary theory on a single theorist unless that course is part of a larger constellation of courses on the topic, and this emphasis is clearly communicated in the course description. There is always a certain amount of "bandwagoning" in teaching; and it is inevitable that we will emphasize whatever topics or theories are of particular interest or a part of our research at the moment. This is not a cause for concern; in fact, such timely topics often inject life and spirit into our classes and introduce students to the excitement of scholarly activities. The danger lies with those who can see nothing but their own interests and their own immediate research and insist that all student work be related to their pet topics. Graduate schools are infamous for professors who organize their classes so that all student work can be incorporated into the professor's own research before those students have a thorough grounding in the larger field of study.

"Educational Exchange" Model

The sixth model, one which at least acknowledges that students are knowledgeable, thinking human beings, is that of "Educational Exchange." In this model, which is especially prevalant in graduate schools where students often are experienced professionals—sometimes more experienced than their graduate school teachers—ideas, information, and experience are shared among class members. The two basic variants of "Educational Exchange" are student reports and brainstorming. In the first variant, the teacher provides a list of topics from which each student chooses, or is assigned, a subject for a class presentation. Some teachers conduct an entire semester's work in this way and, in so doing, relieve themselves of the responsibility of teaching. Of course, some solid learning may result from a superior student's presentation or from a talented teacher's responses to student ideas and discussions, but too often this is not the case. This model leaves too much to change by allowing individual students to select specific content and determine directions for the entire class. The second variant encourages students to expound, often at great length, upon their own narrow practice or even casual and untried notions about a topic. Disgruntled students, intolerant of teachers who refuse to teach, as indeed they should be, refer to this model as the process of sharing ignorance.

"Community of Scholars" Model

This leads to the seventh model which is closer to what I believe education is all about. Some professors think of a college or university class as a "Community of Scholars." Such a community is, of course, a wonderful model if students are sufficiently grounded in both the discipline and in the methods and techniques of scholarship. An advanced graduate class in which the teacher serves as guide and critic as students share their own research activities is often thought of as the epitome of university teaching. These exchanges may, if the professor is precise and skilled in response, be very beneficial to the student who is presenting work and perhaps even to others who are attuned adequately to the topic. Unfortunately, professors attempt to use this model with students who are not yet sufficiently prepared in the subject matter to benefit from the approach. As a result, these classes become another type of educational exchange in which many students are merely sharing their ignorance. Without a solid overview of the field of study, some sense of commonality of individual research interests, and an understanding of the relationship of research to the field as a whole, the "Community of Scholars" model fails as a strategy for teaching.

A more negative form of this model is the "Present and Attack" approach, all too commonly used in research classes at the doctoral level. Students required to take a research methods course during the first year of a doctoral program have the right to expect instruction in the methodologies, tools, and techniques of research as a discipline. Instead, they may be required to produce a draft of a dissertation proposal, often long before they are prepared to select a topic. Then the majority of class sessions are allocated to individual students to present these premature proposals for extensive criticism by those who have no more knowledge of methodology and less knowledge of the topic. Similar presentations are appropriate, and often very helpful, when students are more secure with their own research, but they are not a substitute for teaching introductory classes.

LITERARY MODEL

Although the above models do not present a very positive view of teaching, aspects of each of them probably exist in the work of most teachers, and there are many excellent teachers in colleges and universities. Most students have encountered at least a few such faculty members and have been inspired and moved by their work. What follows is a discussion of a literary model which attempts to inform practice by drawing parallels between the composition of teaching and the composition of literary works.

The Parallels of Literature and Teaching

Teaching shares many characteristics with literature. Both impose order on an often chaotic existence in an attempt to shape meaning and to provide personal space for human beings within that ordered existence; both engage persons and move them to become involved with problems they perceive as significant; and both provide a kind of aesthetic distancing by presenting the student or reader with opportunities to confront situations and try out solutions without being held accountable in the outside world for the consequences of those solutions. In the process, students or readers explore and create their own varied meanings within the virtual reality of the composition.

Teaching, like story, has traditions and enduring conventions that are rich in variety and vitality, as well as common elements of form which can be identified and discussed. In addition, all teaching is affected to some degree by its place and time—the "climate" in which it comes to be. Major emphasis in both content and form can be pointed to in the tradition of teaching, and although these overlap, there are certainly historical trends which can be distinguished. The discussion of the history of literary theory in Chapter One refers not only to what was taught at particular times, but also, to a lesser degree, to how that content was taught. Nonetheless, each teaching encounter is a unique composition which cannot be repeated because it is, as much as the encounter with story, an event in time; and the characters, the materials, and the relationships evolve, change, and disappear.

The uniqueness of individual teaching encounters makes it difficult to identify that which is generic and essential to all of teaching. For the purposes of this book, teaching can be said to exist in the sense that a literary work exists on paper, but only really comes alive when others become engaged with it. A faculty member creates a virtual reality for the purpose of confrontation, but it is only when the student encounters that virtual world, and enters into an engagement with the ideas, information, and activities of that world, that it becomes meaningful and useful. The actual physical classroom is not the product of teaching made visible, but a symbol for or container of that product, just as a book with its printed words on paper is merely a symbol of a world created by an author. It is the composition of the encounter even more than its content which most clearly communicates to students. In such a world, each student takes up residency and is made to feel at home as a unique maker-of-meaning in a world of many meanings, and is encouraged to extend personal meanings by bringing them in contact with shared fields of meaning.

The teacher, like an author, shapes the elements of the composition in order to intentionally exploit possibilities of ambiguity and to develop many interrelated levels of potential meanings. In teaching, one composes a design which orders the components of the created world to secure the balance and tensions necessary to enable students to break with their habitual ways of seeing, thinking, and behaving, and to give new embodiment and form to their feelings and perceptions. As an author shapes the overall structure of story and posits specific incidents of plot within that structure, such that each reader can create a personal story in the tensions between that presented story and the self, so a teacher composes a teaching design.

Neither teaching nor story were deliberately invented as an art form. Both are compositions formed experimentally and experientially long before they were labelled by those who observed them. In fact, they share a common origin in the storytelling of ancient societies. Thus, there is no original formula or design against which all works of teaching may be measured. The labels which have been devised to describe teaching technologies or methodologies are useful because they point to and bring clarity to existing examples of the work of teaching or to plans for work yet to be actualized. A faculty member, however, does not conform to the limits imposed by these labels any more than the creative writer does. Instead one works from them, using all that is known professionally as a teacher, and all the tacit, intuitive personal knowing to make choices as to when the established patterns and practices should be accepted, when rejected, and when modified. One of the things that separates the professional teacher from the gifted amateur is how knowledgeably such choices are made.

If education is, as John Dewey said, a "process of reconstruction and reconstitution of experience," teaching could be defined as the creation of the kind of education designed for the exercise of this process. It is the form of this reconstruction and reconstitution which allows students to bring their own personal knowing into contact with established fields of knowledge and to recognize wherein the context of each mind corresponds to a context of field. Each faculty member creates a world which, like story, is an autonomous and independently balanced unity existing as an expressive rendering of what it is to be alive in such a world at a given moment. This world, being teacher-made, is composed so as to bring about the reconstruction and reconstitution of experience.

Although the actual person-to-person encounter between student and faculty member is concerned primarily with the present moment, teaching always looks beyond the here and now to affirm in some way human potentialities for the future. In its narrowest sense, teaching is a closed construction leading all students in a single prescribed path to a predetermined destination so that they might know what some authority figure has determined they "should" know, or become what they "should" become. In its broadest sense, teaching is a multi-faceted design in which many ideas are contained, each related to all others, but in a relationship which is not fixed. Thus, each student can establish a personal position within the possibilities of that design, choose a particular course of action, make one's own private meaning, and assert the self in one's own dignity as a unique human being. In this case, the student is more concerned with personal destiny than with any one destination, with working toward possible outcomes rather than to specific objectives.

Teaching recognizes that the world is a world of many meanings but that each person must take up a personal meaning in that world. Human beings are thinking, feeling, intending beings, each of whom establishes a personal position among the collective meanings of the world and imposes an original perspective upon that world. Through the uniqueness of each person's perspective, both that person and the world are continually made anew. At the same time, each person is an intersubjective being whose personal meaning is shaped through interaction with the meanings of others in a social context. One can attain potential as a unique being only through respecting the same potential in all others and seeking a sense of harmony in the totality of all meanings. Thus, a faculty member composes forms in which the single mind can make its own authentic meaning, but can simultaneously hear other meanings in that world both as a member of the world community with its own part to play and as a critic of the whole. In this world of intentional existence, each person is at once author, main character, member of the cast, and critical audience. The intent of teaching is to provide a means of improving the creation, of rendering the characters more authentically, of getting the cast together, and of developing finer and more sympathetic means of criticism. Again, the parallels to literature are obvious.

Teaching is concerned with the acquisition and assembly of knowledge within the structures and modes of inquiry of particular disciplines, but it is also concerned with assemblages of knowledge to help students to a feeling of that knowledge as a part of their own knowing. The fact that knowledge must sometimes be reorganized, resynthesized, and even rehumanized by teachers to make it appropriate for and comprehensible to students is often overlooked, especially in higher education. The exploratory possibilities in teaching are not totally limited or predetermined by the perimeters of the particular discipline because students make their own meanings by accounting for themselves relative to the subject matter. The study of a particular discipline is often approached as one does the solution of a puzzle, that is, lacking order until all the parts are available and pieced together with additional knowledge causing a return to disorder, just as a new piece to be added to an apparently completed puzzle causes a rethinking of the total picture. On the other hand, teaching attempts to increase wonder and provoke mystery. Mystery is also a type of order but one which exists in the tension between knowledge and what will never be known. Thus, the more knowledge gained, the more intense the mystery. It is this sense of mystery and the excitement and the joy of investigation that encourages students to participate in a life-long pursuit of learning.

The Composition of Teaching

Teaching is a compositional act. It is a compositional act grounded in a field of meaning posited by a particular society, shared by professional teachers and enacted in a social setting with students. The act of teaching reflects the uniqueness of each person who composes it, but always within the deliberate, intentional, and limited field of meaning identified as teaching. A faculty member selects from available knowledge, materials, and technologies for use as elements to be shaped within the compositional form in ways that enable students to match their own personal knowing with defined fields of knowledge. As a compositional act, its proper means of study is criticism. Teaching may be criticized in terms of the appropriateness of the actual materials selected from the world to be posited in the teaching composition in terms of the virtual elements of that composition, that is, those factors in its semblance which are components of the total compositional form, or in terms of the craft of the teacher in attempting to realize that form.

As in our earlier discussion of literary texts, the made-world of the teacher's composition contains that person's unique meanings and experiences, but what it conveys does not necessarily correspond to that which is inherent in the composer's perception. Meanings may be suggested more than stated, which requires that each person who encounters them must, through active mental processes, imaginatively discover them for oneself. It is this mental activity or imaginative discovery which gives real generative power for students. Thus, the schooling composition, like a literary composition, may serve as a means of communication between composer and respondent, or it may exist independently of the teacher and allow students to interact with and bring personal meanings to various elements of that composition. As they do with story, students, due to the shape of their own personal knowing, may respond to different levels of meaning, perceive different insights, and become aware of different implications. The composition is intended to be a source of significance and satisfaction to all who enter into an engagement with it, by helping them to discover momentary order among chaos, substance in subject matter, and, perhaps even instances of aesthetic beauty within an often commonplace world.

Teaching about Literature

Figure 10 represents a view of students and teachers at the actual moment of teaching about literature. First, we must remind ourselves that none of us can really *teach* literature. We can only teach *about*

FIGURE 10

TEACHING ABOUT LITERATURE

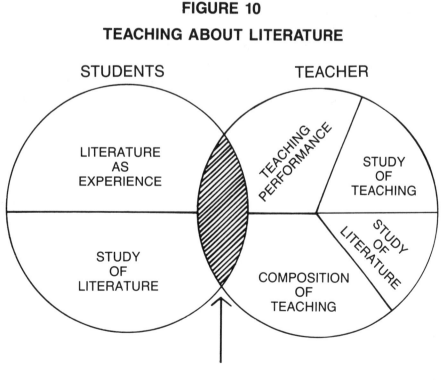

TEACHING ABOUT LITERATURE

literature. Literature itself must be experienced and, although a talented teacher can serve as a guide, introducer, cheerleader, or the like, the teacher can never actually *teach* someone else to experience literature. All of the many things we can teach students *about* literature, however, should have as their aim increased enjoyment of and appreciation of that literary experience which we cannot teach. We can teach about the history of the field, some specific works, selection tools, practical ways to share literature with young people, even some literary theory or research skills, but we cannot measurably influence students' experiencing of literary works.

Adult students ordinarily come to a children's literature course with a great deal of prior experience with literature and often with some formal literary study or previous coursework in children's literature itself. The teacher of children's literature certainly should have a rich background of literary experiences and scholarship, but that background may be a relatively small portion of the content of teaching, especially in the introductory or survey courses common in most colleges and universities. All that the teacher has experienced and studied, both about literature and about teaching, informs and determines what will be included in the teaching composition. During the actual classroom interaction, however, the teacher's attention is more often focused on the process than on the content of teaching. The teacher's composition of teaching is no more visible to students than students' experiences of literature are to the teacher. What is evident is the teacher's performance that is based both on the virtual composition and on the skillful use of the crafts of teaching.

Sources of Teaching Content

A teacher's literary knowledge is necessary for the composition of teaching but is mostly unseen in teaching performance. Each of the disciplines identified in Figure 11 contribute to the knowledge of literature, of teaching, and of audiences that become elements of the composition when teaching children's literature. Theory and research in these fields relate to and contribute to theory and research in the teaching of children's literature which, in turn, influence teaching performance. Obviously, the whole of each of the disciplines represented here cannot be contained within the boundaries of our work as teachers of children's literature. What a faculty member selects from the contributing disciplines depends upon one's own personal and professional background and current research interests, as well as both primary and secondary audiences for teaching. The primary audience is, of course, adult students in children's literature classes; but, especially in professional schools, one must remain cognizant of that secondary audience of young people and their caregivers with whom the primary audience will ultimately share this literature.

FIGURE 11

COMPONENTS OF THE TEACHING PROCESS

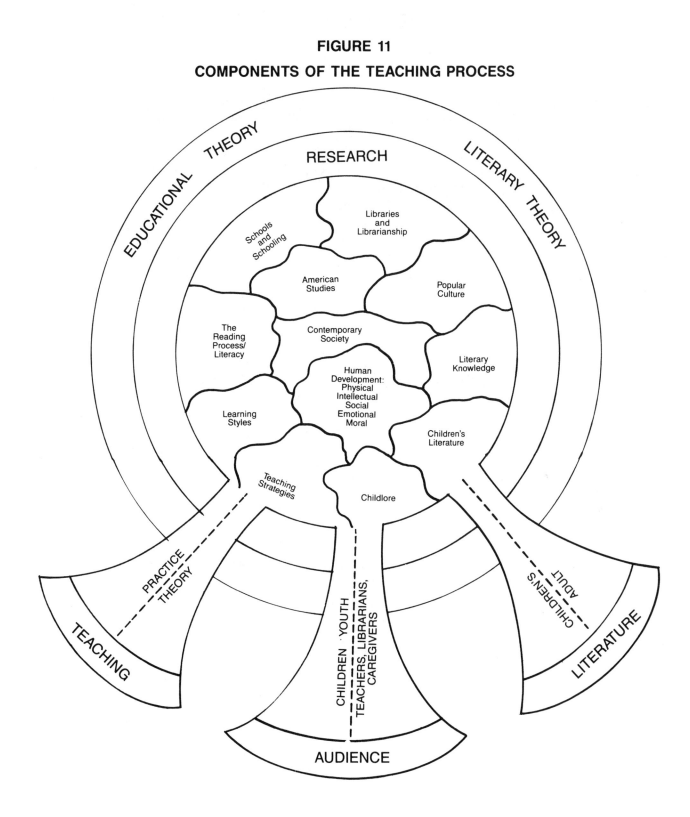

STAGES OF THE TEACHING COMPOSITION

The Preactive Stage: Ideal

Teaching might be thought of as consisting of knowledge, judgments and decisions related to each of the three basic stages represented in Figure 12. Knowledge and judgments are part of the preactive stages of teaching and help to determine the kind of decisions made in the interactive stage. The teacher as composer begins with a knowledge of literary content, of both primary and secondary audiences, and of the nature of the profession of teaching. Using this knowledge one can imagine an idealized composition which could result if all the resources, human and material, were always at optimal levels. This imagining of an ideal is a necessary first step in composing teaching and stands as a model for subsequent compositions based on more situation-specific judgments and decisions.

Obviously, our perceptions of literature determine how we teach it. If we are concerned primarily with the cultural heritage to be preserved and transmitted, literature may be thought of as literary artifacts and students as those who are expected to learn about and respect major works.[1] If we think of literature study as a means to some other end, such as literacy or moral practices, we select and exploit literature to that end and measure student skills or judge their moral development in response to literature. If

FIGURE 12

STAGES OF THE TEACHING COMPOSITION

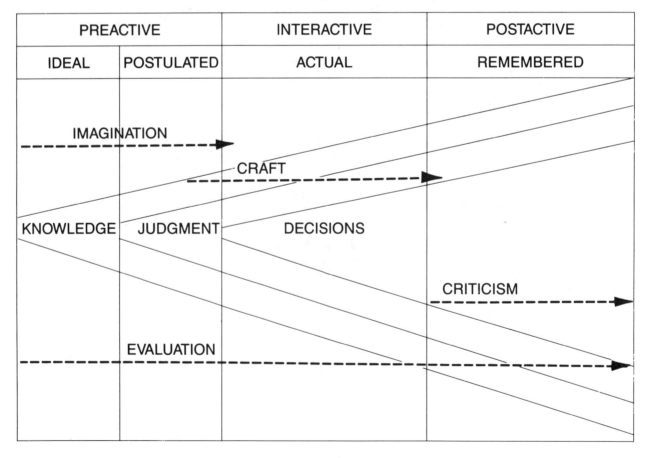

literature is thought of as representative of individual perceptions and expressions of the world, students may be expected to study key authors and their works over time. Of course, these perceptions of literature correspond to the mimetic, pragmatic, and expressive theories discussed in Chapter One.

Formalistic studies of literature as a body of knowledge may take any one of several approaches. A faculty member might focus on the chronology of literary history, which, in practice, may appear to be very close to the mimetic concern for cultural heritage, but differs in that it looks inward to the development of literary forms themselves rather than to the cultural bases of their origins. Another approach might be the study of literary types or genres and a third the relationship between reader and text which could concentrate on any point of that continuum between the two, from very subjective views of the reader to structuralist or linguistic views of texts. Teachers emphasizing reader-response theories share the expressionists' belief in literature as individual perceptions of the world, but shift the focus from the perceptions of authors to those of readers.

Some of the traditional patterns of teaching children's literature may either fit into or cut across these approaches. One of the most common practices is that of conducting the Grand Tour through children's literature via a standard text such as those by Huck (49) or Sutherland (94). These books are wonderful introductions to the field and contain a rich variety of information and resources, but that content needs to be selected, adapted, and interpreted within the context of the particular schooling composition. Another form of teaching this literature is based on the "great books" for children which might be organized to correspond to any or all of the four approaches identified in the previous paragraph. Thematic organizations of course content might also correspond to any of the four approaches, but they are most often related to sociological reflections of the world (mimesis) or to the psychological or developmental needs of readers (pragmatic). A closely related pragmatic means of organizing course content emphasizes applications—the selection and appropriate use of specific titles for reading instruction, for supplementing other subject areas, for storytelling, for bibliotherapy, or for values clarification.

Classes that emphasize formalistic studies of children's literature have traditionally concentrated on intratextual groupings of types or genres, or on innertextual analysis of literary elements. This focus on literary elements in children's literature has become a fairly common approach in recent years[2] and is helpful both to adult and child students in understanding that Reader-Text-Context triad for literary study as well as for an understanding of and appreciation for the writing process in which many students are also expected to participate. Unfortunately, however, the analysis of literary elements in children's story may have become too fashionable and too easy. Some teachers are substituting the study of those elements for the literary works themselves or are actually being destructive of students' experiences with those works by too early or too much emphasis on the elements.

Regardless of the overall approach taken in the first stage of the teaching composition, it is important to take time to imagine what the ideal teaching encounter might be. Without this image of the ideal we might be satisfied with less than our best.

The Preactive Stage: Postulated

A faculty member also uses personal and professional judgments, beliefs and expectations about students, about teaching, and about the classroom in which they interact to move from an ideal to a postulated composition of teaching. Figure 13 explores this in a diagrammatic form. We have already postulated that many adult students will have a certain amount of knowledge of and experience with children's literature. Also, it is reasonable to assume that an evening class of practicing professionals may be at less than their peak, both physically and intellectually, after a full day of work. Such expectations for a particular group of students, along with the teacher's more general professional judgment about educational methodologies and learning styles, combine with both theoretical and practical perceptions

FIGURE 13

RELATION OF THEORY TO PRACTICE IN TEACHING

		STAGES OF TEACHING			
COMPOSITION		PREACTIVE		INTERACTIVE	POSTACTIVE
		VIRTUAL		ACTUAL	VIRTUAL
	CLASSROOM	IDEAL	POSTULATED	ACTUAL	REMEMBERED
THEORETICAL BASE	DISCIPLINE				
	TEACHING				
	STUDENTS				

of the learning environment to compose the postulated teaching world. For instance, one might have a great deal of knowledge, based on years of research, about the types of physical, sociological, and psychological environments conducive to learning; but certain restrictions of the actual physical space of the classroom may make it difficult to act upon that knowledge. Information about the number of students enrolled combined with the type of furniture in the classroom or the adequacy of that room for media presentations are two very simple examples of the kinds of considerations which force teachers to modify their ideal images as they move from a virtual to an actual classroom encounter.

One's ideal knowledge of teaching and learning styles or of the nature of instruction may also have to be modified based on postulated teaching judgments. One faculty member, for instance, might be a superb lecturer who really wants to present content through that mode and is very successful at it, but recognizes that a two and one half-hour lecture, especially during the evening hours, may not result in the most alert or appreciative students. On the other hand, a teacher who is very effective in facilitating student learning through small group activities may find the two and one half-hour class session constraining for those not available on campus at other times.

The Preactive Stage: Articulation of Courses

The articulation of courses within the total curriculum is of primary consideration in the preactive stage of teaching. One must assume that students interested in children's literature and children's services will enroll in the whole constellation of courses in those areas. Therefore, it would be logical to design each of these courses in relation to all others. If there is a children's services in public libraries or programming course the teacher of the children's literature course would be less likely to spend time on programmatic activities with children. If there is a class for the history of children's literature, one would limit the amount of historical content in the regular children's literature course and so forth.

Many institutions have courses in both children's and young adult's literature — one in the fall and one in the spring semester — with many students enrolling in both courses. Having students return for a second semester of literary study should be an advantageous situation for teaching, and indeed it would be if all students enrolled in both courses and in the same sequence. In reality, first-time students are in the second class and are left behind if there is too much dependence on the content of the previous course. On the other hand, too much repetition of basic literary principles, considered essential for both courses, is neither fair nor educationally responsible for those who were enrolled in the earlier course. This kind of problem is common in higher education and is one faculty members must resolve in their own way.

The use of worksheets as discussed in Chapter 6 may be helpful in this situation. Worksheets used in the first class might be distributed as self-study sheets to new students in the second. These worksheets were intended for class use, however, and are not necessarily the most effective tools for self-study. Of course, the teacher might also meet with these students to help them catch up with the rest of the class. Not only is this very time consuming for both teacher and students, but also it would be unreasonable to require students to complete work for two courses when they enroll in just one. It is also possible that some students will take both courses but in the reverse order. The logical solution would seem to be to have the children's literature course a prerequisite for the young adult course. This is done in some institutions. The difficulty is that there are many students who work only with young adults, or even reference librarians in public libraries who have high school students as their youngest patrons, who cannot afford to take the prerequisite in an already overcrowded schedule. Ideally, there would be two sections of each of these courses each year, one for those who plan to take both and one for students who will take only one literature course.

The Interactive Stage

Both the ideal and the postulated teaching compositions may be set aside in the immediacy of the actual interactive teaching situation. The decisions made in the reality of that situation are often dependent upon that which could not have been predicted. A sick or disgruntled student, a faulty heating system, a broken projector, or even an exciting and stimulating digression may cause the teacher to take decisive actions that could not have been anticipated in either stage of the preactive teaching composition. Such decisions in response to situational variables maintain the flow of activities, pacing, grouping, the learning environment, and the development of content which makes each teaching encounter a unique and vital representative of the discipline of teaching.

THE PHYSICAL ENVIRONMENT

In elementary or secondary school classrooms which are normally the domain of a single teacher, that teacher's personality and teaching style may shape the physical space of a classroom environment and become a visual symbol of the vitality of the ideas, the skills, and the feelings expressed there. Those who teach in colleges and universities have only our offices as personal space; and, of course, some of our most significant teaching does take place there. The classrooms in which we teach are usually "ours" for only a few hours each week with many other persons and activities occupying them the remainder of the time. Because of this, there is often an unwritten law that no university teacher should attempt to personalize a classroom by such things as unique physical arrangements or any signs or symbols of a particular subject area. This, along with the longer intervals of time between teaching encounters, makes it extremely difficult to compose that virtual reality of schooling. But it can be done. Fortunate students had at least one teacher, perhaps even a teacher of children's literature, who turned a barren graduate school classroom into a busy and exciting world filled with ideas, insights, and a sense of wonder.

THE CRAFT OF TEACHING

Once the ideal and postulated teaching compositions have been imagined by the teacher, there is yet the difficulty of giving the composition a tangible form—one both symbolic and functional—to make it available for use by students. As in any virtual composition, the task of executing that design and transferring ideas, content, and feelings to perceptible form is one of crafting. It is the skilled use of the media and techniques of the teaching craft with which ideas are furnished with relevant materials and cognitive meanings are made aesthetically meaningful. In order to create the clearest images with the most impact, the teacher-craftsperson must shape media to perform at the utmost limits of their possibilities to compose a unified schooling design which will present many potentialities for use by students. Such mastery over craft is achieved gradually and requires the kind of study and practice which goes with the initiation into any discipline or art form. Although the creation of a compositional product often appears to be spontaneous and intuitive, it must be remembered that intuition produces more dross than fine work, and that to become a skilled composer one must first become thoroughly familiar with the materials and skills of the craft. Composition is learned indirectly through disciplined, often piecemeal, study of individual media and techniques and their possibilities for use. After "playing with" all the elements of the craft available for the composition and exploring their possibilities for use, the teacher must shape them so as to come to some merger of content and form. Putting together all appropriate media and techniques in a form which gives unity, meaning, and integrity to the composition requires the crafts of teaching.

The crafts of teaching are many, each worthy of study. The scientific and artistic forms of the disciplines which are the content of teaching are already crafted; but, in the compositional act of teaching, one must have enough knowledge of the craft of those various forms to be able to reorder them to make them available to students without violating the integrity of the original content. But teaching has its own form and its own elements of craft. One's selection and presentation of both content and form require skillful use of time, materials, facilities, and both curricular and personal language. The selection of classroom activities and student assignments requires well-crafted skills in structuring the learning environment, pacing, questioning, feedback, cuing and other teaching techniques which can be learned.

Structuring

Part of the structuring of the learning environment obviously takes place during the preactive stage of teaching as one plans activities and selects materials. The actual use of such plans and materials is often modified, however, according to variables in the interactive stage. What was assumed to be the optimal procedure or example just might not work in the actual situation, even if it has worked many times previously. Thus, the ability to recognize when and how to modify a plan or to substitute materials in presenting, reinforcing or verifying course content is vital to the craft of teaching. The faculty member who plans for student-directed or -negotiated learning activities rather than teacher-directed ones still has a form of structure in mind, but will probably have to be more flexible in rethinking possibilities for learning. This is especially true with adult students who may either go beyond expected boundaries or, on the contrary, resist assuming the responsibility for shaping the learning environment.

Pacing

Another craft of teaching that is difficult to master but relatively easy to observe in the actual teaching encounter is that of pacing. Good teaching has a rhythm to it that helps to keep participants actively involved, and the skilled teacher recognizes when to pick up or slow down the pace to maximize that involvement.

The Questioning Process

One of the most difficult elements of craft in the design and execution of any course is that of the questioning process as revealed in the syllabi itself, in class discussions, assignments, or in written examinations. Often a faculty member fails to think through the purpose of questioning techniques. Students should be stimulated intellectually by the questions asked, but they may also benefit from the example of the questioning process and be able to transfer questioning skill to their own work with children. Both adult and child students need ample opportunity to learn a questioning mode as they address problems and issues in their examination of literature. When things are too tight, too neat, or too orderly that natural process of speculation may be inhibited. *Memory and factual knowledge* may have to be tested at times. Faculty members should encourage students to recall facts, definitions, and observations; but, at the same time, both faculty and students should recognize the limits of those types of questions. When we ask the famous list of "who, what, where, when," we are only testing memory which is a lower order of thinking.

When we move to a next order we begin to access the *comprehension* of students; here we ask them to translate from one symbol system to another. The ability to describe, compare and contrast, and note likes and differences are tests of such comprehension. In children's literature this ability may be tested when we ask for comparisons among the books of a given author or among the books of various authors. This may be asked equally in relation to genres or to varying formats. We have often tested for *applicability* in practice by asking students to examine a problem and to select the best solution for that specific problem. This level of questioning requires that the student recognize and use thinking skills.

The next level of questioning is that of *analysis*, where we are often weak in our questioning mode. Here we want students to make inferences, find evidence to support a point of view, and identify causes or motivations. The analytical mind is essential to our work in children's literature, and we need to develop the types of questions to stimulate this level of thought. *Synthesis* requires additional talents from students by asking them to creatively think about an issue or a problem and to propose solutions. They must place themselves "at risk," stake out new territory, and rely on the workings of their own minds to respond to a question in this mode. The process can be enjoyable, even playful, but it can also be serious and scholarly, such as when one begins to explore a new theory of criticism that emerges from knowledge of the child, literary theory, and existing critical ideas. This kind of thought leads eventually to the highest level of response, *evaluation*, when the student is asked to judge and render opinions. The use of evaluative questions demonstrates an implicit as well as explicit respect for those enunciated ideas and opinions of students on the part of the teacher. If the teacher asks a student which set of illustrations are preferred, it is essential that the teacher is willing to accept the responses of students, provided that they are able to articulate the reasoning for their judgment.

Good questions help to set the intellectual atmosphere of the schooling composition and put ideas and information into context and perspective. They should be valued more for their ability to illuminate than to evaluate, and even more for raising additional questions than for answering existing ones. Too much of teaching is anti-intellectual in that the teacher predetermines both the questions and the answers in such a way that students can match the two with little real thinking. I have often thought that since the teacher is presumed to have the greater knowledge, that students should raise the greater number of questions and teachers be required to answer them. On the other hand, we should remember that it is far more difficult, and requires more knowledge, to raise good questions than to answer mediocre ones.

Of course, there are questions that confuse more than they clarify. Dual questions ask students to address more than one thing at a time. Frequently a student loses the focus of the question through this approach. Sometimes the faculty member has overlooked the fact that connections made in the teacher's mind are not necessarily in the mind of the student. It is unfair to penalize a student for answering a question in an inept fashion when the question was not clearly focused by the instructor. A dual question may cause an internal struggle for supremacy of ideas and, in that process, the student fails to get the question straight. For instance, a teacher may raise the following question: "Explore the development of characters in Judy Blume's work and explain how those characters reflect child problems in today's society." The student may be momentarily confused by what is being asked. Does the teacher want an exploration of character development in Judy Blume's books or does the teacher want an exploration of Blume and society. To try to elicit both responses to one question may disadvantage students and lead them to respond with an unacceptable answer.

"More questions" supply a portion of an answer, often in the form of a quotation, and expect students to add to what has been said. Often students are in the unhappy state of not knowing what the quote means, or not caring what it means, or, more likely, not perceiving the connection between the quote and what seems to be asked. For instance, a teacher might ask, "Given the statement by Frances Clark Sayers (below) how do you perceive the Disney phenomenon?":

> What I deplore about Mr. Disney is his tendency to take over a piece of work and make it his own without regard for the original author or to the original book.[3]

If students do not understand when and how Sayers said what she said and also do not understand the intent of the Disney empire, how do they add to that piece of information and answer the question appropriately?

Feedback

If questioning is an important aspect of the craft of teaching, so too is the process of providing feedback to students. The many years of studies of verbal interactions in elementary and secondary classrooms have paid particular attention to the language used to give positive, negative, or neutral feedback to students. Through these studies, teachers identified language that is receptive and supportive to be used even when responding to a wrong answer or to negative behavior. Such language is easily learned, but using appropriate language with clarity and variety in response to individual needs is a craft that requires much thought and practice. Non-verbal forms of feedback may be obvious or subtle, but they are often more powerfully perceived than verbal ones and are probably more difficult fo the teacher to master. Some non-verbal forms are personal mannerisms that may be either functional or dysfunctional in the classroom and require a sometimes painful self-examination for the improvement of teaching. Other non-verbal forms of feedback may be easily learned. Patterns of eye contact, for instance, are something most of us are not aware of in ourselves, but a consciousness of them may help to provide better feedback to students.

Cuing

All teachers use cues that alert students to certain aspects of the social or intellectual content of the classroom. Some of these may begin as personal mannerisms, but they can be identified and used more effectively, as well as enhanced by other means of cuing. For example, one teacher may, consciously or unconsciously, use the same words or a particular tone of voice to emphasize that what is to follow is of special importance. Another teacher may move to a particular place in the room or write on the blackboard to signify vital content. Still others might organize the total learning environment differently, use more repetition than usual, use a certain teaching strategy or type of material, or any of a number of other techniques to cue students to the fact that a portion of class content is of special importance. Each teacher combines personal and professional attributes and behaviors in developing a repertoire of well-crafted techniques to enhance the composition of teaching and help students respond more fully to that composition.

The Postactive Stage: Evaluation

Teaching may be planned with precise crafting to achieve desired ends or to transmit specific information, or it may use elements of craft more fluidly to encourage personal encounters with a subjectively experienced world. In either case, it will have certain definite characteristics and allow for only certain kinds of relationships and activities. In teaching, as in story, many different kinds of worlds are created, and it would be inappropriate to attempt to assign relative values to them. Each faculty member attempts to bring order and meaning to the often chaotic experiences of existence, but one does not necessarily seek order in the same way. Even among the most perceptive and knowledgeable teachers, there will be many different interpretations of what is going on in a particular classroom at a given time, and there will be many different kinds of activities which are valued as appropriate educational pursuits.

Attempts to identify and evaluate teaching in ways that can both contain useful ideas and generate new ones fail most often because they are too closely tied to the persons who can be observed when teaching is taking place. Ordinarily teaching is described either in terms of what the teacher does or of the responses of students to that behavior. A teacher is a person before that person is a member of a profession, and much of any teacher's observable behavior is uniquely personal rather than professional in nature. The professional question is not "What does the teacher do?" but "What is the work of teaching?" One does not pay a doctor for taking a pulse or looking at a throat, but for the knowledge of the practice of medicine in doing these things. Similarly, the act of teaching takes place more in the mind of the teacher than in overt behavior which might be observed and copied by others. In the teaching act, one makes deliberate choices, both personal and professional, from among many possible teaching behaviors; but it is always the act of knowledgeable choice within teaching boundaries rather than the behavior itself which is the work of teaching. Almost anyone can stand in front of a group of children and read a picture story book, but when the teacher of children's literature does this, what is important is the intent involved in the selection, presentation, and follow-up activities.

An even more common means of attempting to identify teaching through observations of persons is the reliance on the concept of learning. This approach to the study of teaching assumes that the basic function of teaching is to change the behavior of students and measure the effectiveness of teaching according to the amount of such change. The assumption that teaching is a deliberate attempt to promote certain learnings and that when other factors intrude to prevent such learnings the teaching fails has been a powerful one. For many years, the majority of educational writings accepted this premise and were content to define teaching in terms of something that happened to a learner. This definition, although true in part, diverts attention, and therefore responsibility, from the teacher to the student. Students may very well change their attitudes or behavior as a result of teaching, but knowing that does not help to identify what it is that happens in that interval of change—the space and time between what was and what now is. Neither does the measurement of change help to determine what, if anything, the teacher did to cause that change nor does it reveal whether that change was a part of the original intent of the teacher.

TECHNOLOGY AND TEACHING

Views of teaching emphasizing the primacy of the personal dimension developed historically over a period of time in which the scarcity of technological means of storing and processing information made it necessary for the teacher to personally remember much of society's knowledge and to transmit that knowledge to students. Modern technology releases both teachers and students from the necessity of storing information in memory and allows them to develop more efficient means of access to knowledge, thereby freeing teachers to give voice to the possibilities of that which is yet to be known. Thus, technology frees teachers to respond more humanely to the students they encounter.

Educational and communications research has provided faculty with many new teaching models and devices. In order to make effective use of these tools, a faculty member must study both their special characteristics and their limitations, and be able to use them smoothly and unobstrusively in the classroom. It must be remembered, however, that no one model, device, or method can serve all subject matters or all learning styles and that a variety of approaches to knowledge is generally more effective than any single one.

Thus, the image of the faculty member as a presenter of material is disappearing, and we find a new image of one assuming many different roles in education. Faculty might prepare students for a variety of presentations, guide the individual learning of each person, provide opportunities for the use of many diverse facilities, evaluate the kinds of information students are acquiring, and then repeat, adapt, and clarify material, guide class discussions, and ensure fuller participation for all students by helping them to find in what they have learned both its use and its personal significance. This may sound more like what goes on in an elementary school than in graduate education, but it should not be so. College and university students deserve the benefits of what has been learned through research in teaching strategies and educational technologies just as much as children do.

Used sensibly and humanely, technology can supplement the work of teaching and enhance its effectiveness. Rather than dehumanizing education to control persons as extensions of things, technology can provide unique opportunities to extend the power and the range of persons and to amplify the force of the faculty member's creative, human potential by freeing that teacher from classroom routines. When teachers conceive of the products of technology not as means to narrow ends, nor as ways to do their work for them, but as additional ways of reaching out to others and of gaining new meanings from them through more divergent opportunities for communication, technology will take its rightful place in our educational community, even perhaps in our teaching of children's literature.[4]

TEACHING STYLE

How a particular teacher uses knowledge and judgment to imagine the virtual reality of the preactive schooling composition and then makes decisions about the crafts of teaching in the interactive composition is often referred to as teaching style.

Teaching style is a multifaceted topic with qualities corresponding to the elements of both substance and craft and, at its best, with that melody, harmony, and proportion indicative of an aesthetic experience. In addition, the faculty member helps to maintain a rhythm in the environment which allows students to recognize and become involved in the polarities of existence. Students analyze and synthesize, withdraw and draw together, particularize and universalize, emerge and converge; they deal with things that are functional and beautiful, concrete and abstract, serious and humorous, structured and haphazard, predictable and unknown; they engage in situations which are active and inactive, loud and quiet, tension building and tension releasing; they work alone and in groups, with great intimacy and at great distances, out of choice and out of necessity, with direction and with none; and they use language which is formal and informal, emphatic and noncommittal, personal and objective, self-revealing and self-concealing. These rhythms are not just means of preparing students for a better or fuller life, or for a more competent professional performance in the future, but they are also attempts to find meaning in life for each as it is being lived now. That meaning may change, but the memory of it and of the process of meaning-making are tools which students take with them as they face new tasks in their personal and professional futures.

Criticism of Teaching

The composition that results from the kind of teaching style described above may be criticized in terms of its pervasive compositional elements as well as for precise elements of content or craftsmanship. A critic might ask such questions as:

1. Does the composition have both unity and variety, balance and harmony, coherence and flexibility?

2. Does it have a dynamic quality which encourages students to become involved in and make use of that composition?

3. Does it have both an uncluttered simplicity and the possibility of great depth?

4. Is it appropriately student-sized and shaped, that is, does it provide various points of entry, attachment, and use for those who enter into its world?

5. Is it significantly formed to be both functional and beautiful, that is, does it contain a sense of the spirit of the field, its knowledge, skills, and attitudes in a form that encourages students to think, to feel, to imagine, and to care.

None of these questions have simple answers if they are authentic ones, but then questions worth asking seldom do. Educators might learn much by using ideas from the various forms of aesthetic criticism to look at teaching, for if teaching is indeed a compositional form, an analysis of the elements of the craft of teaching, no matter how important, does not, in itself, measure either the value or the effect of education.

In teaching, as in other types of compositional work, there are certain recognizable traits or conventions. There is not only a unity within one particular composition, but also a unity among various works of teaching which enables one to identify such work and begin to make professional judgments about it. The first level of criticism of teaching attempts to sort out what is, in fact, acknowledged as teaching. This is not so much a matter of content as of form. New content is continually added to teaching compositions as demanded by changes in theory, research, practice, and new developments in technology. New teaching forms, however, develop more slowly by evolving or breaking off from existing forms.

The kind of criticism suggested above can be considered only in the immediacy of the classroom encounter and, in fact, is seldom attempted. Students may be able to answer some of these questions, at least in retrospect, but ordinarily both teacher and students are too caught up in the moments of teaching to make any attempt to analyze or evalute them. It is also extremely rare for an observer or evaluator to set foot in a college or university classroom. What is needed is a collegial approach to college and university teaching in which those who wish to improve the quality of teaching work together to develop their craft and to devise and put into practice means of criticizing teaching compositions in an intellectually and socially supportive environment.

Student Evaluation

Student evaluations of instructors are common in higher education, but often the instruments used to collect this data would be an embarrassment to anyone doing serious research, and the analysis of results, if done at all, is inadequate. Sometimes faculty members do not receive feedback from these evaluations. Evaluative forms which allow faculty members to indicate the relative importance of different objectives or types of content and to personalize at least a few of the questions could be very useful in a teacher's self-assessment and in overall program evaluation as well as for student use. We should remember, however, that the results of certain types of teaching are not necessarily obvious to or appreciated by students until long after actual classroom encounters when they realize their value in professional practice. Such instruments, combined with the kind of teaching criticism discussed above, would do much to help teachers improve their work.

SUMMARY

Adult students of children's literature deserve the very best teaching that we can provide. The theory of teaching presented in this chapter, along with a knowledge of literary theory and research, form the bases upon which skillful, well-crafted teaching performances are built. The intermediate step between knowledge and performance is best represented to others in that preactive teaching composition known as a syllabus which will be discussed in the chapter to follow.

NOTES

[1]The democratization of literary studies begun in the 1960s moved away from this approach, but recent works bemoaning young people's lack of cultural literacy may be influential in a new emphasis on "great books." The works which follow clearly demonstrate this: Allan Bloom, (1987). *The Closing of the American Mind.* (New York: Simon and Schuster); E. D. Hirsch. (1987). *Cultural Literacy: What Every American Needs to Know.* (Boston, MA: Houghton Mifflin); and Diane Ravitch and Chester Finn, Jr. (1987). *What Do Our 17-Year-Olds Know?* (New York: Harper & Row).

[2]See Kay Vandergrift. (1980). *Child and Story: The Literary Connection.* (New York: Neal Schuman); and Rebecca Lukens. (1986). *A Critical Handbook of Children's Literature.* (Glenview, IL: Scott, Foresman).

[3]Frances Clark Sayers and Charles M. Weisenberg. (December 1965). "Walt Disney Accused," *Horn Book.* 40: 602-611.

[4]Kay E. Vandergrift. (November 1988). "Hypermedia: Breaking the Tyranny of the Text," *School Library Journal.* 35: 30-35.

Development of Course Syllabi in Children's Literature

INTRODUCTION

This chapter includes a discussion of the design and development of syllabi and, thereby, the structuring of courses which reflects the knowledge of theory, research, and teaching discussed in previous chapters. It includes discussion of several of the problems that emerge in this development and suggests alternative tools and materials that might enhance a teaching/learning experience. Examples from course materials presented in Chapter Five are used to demonstrate how the justifications for teaching decisions are reflected in the syllabi distributed to students. Readers may wish to refer to specific syllabi as they read portions of this chapter. By following this decision-making process, teachers may reflect upon the process of making educational decisions that best fits their own priorities and the needs of their students, and may recognize some of the questions that might make the preactive process of teaching more rewarding. The intent is not to present these syllabi as models, but rather to analyze them and to consider the academic and professional judgments that were made in their preparation. In this way, readers are invited to participate in the kind of sharing among colleagues that all value so highly for the increased insight it brings to the work of teachers of children's literature.

If one divides teaching into preactive and interactive stages, it is without question the preactive in which teachers can exercise the most control, both intellectually and imaginatively, over their work. In the planning process, without the same limitations of time, or the distractions and the delights of the actual setting, or the people who inhabit that setting, a teacher can envision a deliberate, highly rational plan of action. At its best, this vision is a design rather than a more restrictive lesson plan, prepared lecture, or scheduled sequence of events. It is, in effect, a form of symbolic schooling in which one carefully considers the sources and the effects of alternative paths of teaching performance. This overall design may then be translated into a more detailed teaching plan.

In the actual flesh and blood, brick and mortar classroom, however, the spontaneous encounter with students and with ideas allows little time to keep any design or plan at the forefront of the mind, and the teacher frequently acts upon what "feels right" in the particular situation and setting. Of course, what feels right is learned; it is the result of previous thought and experience. Thus, it is to be expected that a beginning teacher would translate an overall teaching design into much more precise teaching plans than would one with years of experience. In the process of developing increased confidence in both the subject matter and one's own teaching ability, a teacher is released from the captivity of the course syllabus or the lesson plan without totally departing from it, allowing students greater mental space to approach the subject or targeted ideas in their own ways and from their own perspectives. This does not mean, however, that the experienced teacher can just "wing it." As some things become easier in the classroom, it may become increasingly difficult to bring fresh ideas and insights, as well as new approaches, into teaching. If the subject matter and our work as teachers do not continue to be exciting and intellectually challenging to us, we cannot expect to stimulate a real interest and a spirit of inquiry in our students. If a teacher conveys that there is nothing more to be known or done in a field, how can one expect students to want to become involved in that field? Thus, scholarship and research keep teaching alive.

The Syllabus As Accountability

The overall teaching design for most courses in colleges and universities is realized in a course syllabus. Since the 1960s, when accountability became more prominent as a key concept in education, syllabi have been more frequently required and more fully detailed. In some institutions, they are even perceived as quasi-legal documents or contracts identifying goals and objectives, content, assignments, and grading procedures. This demand for more detailed syllabi has had, for the most part, positive effects on post-secondary teaching. Teachers think through various aspects of their courses more carefully, and students enter classes with a clearer understanding of what is expected of them. When the syllabus represents a contractual relationship, however, it can have a detrimental, sometimes deadening, effect on teaching by forcing the teacher to adhere to the contract even when chasing down an elusive or a tangential idea might be more beneficial to students at that moment and more representative of scholarly activities. Another concern is that some teachers might be tempted to reduce course content to easily realized goals and objectives rather than risk failing to honor the contract. A syllabus should be a kind of spotlight which defines and illuminates the field of study by focusing and restricting content but not fixing it absolutely.

The Syllabus As Metaphor

Rather than a contract, or even an outline of content, one might find it useful to think of a syllabus metaphorically as a kind of kaleidoscopic container in which a teacher captures some aspects of course content, including a list of topics, suggested readings, and assignments. This capturing of some of the potential visions of the course represents the tentative determination of the intellectual, social, and perhaps even emotional, dialogue which might occur through the necessary and exciting juxtaposition of ideas. Like the patterns of a kaleidoscope, a teaching design is dynamic rather than fixed; it shifts and changes in response to action within and upon it. Important aspects of this metaphor are the sense of joy and the sense of potentiality which grow with alternative patterns that are created as a course is developed and taught. Thus, the experienced teacher may repeat some finely honed and polished examples, strategies, and perhaps even stories over the years; but these pieces come together in new patterns as the time, the situation, and the class composition change. The constant injection of new knowledge and new ideas also keeps the teaching design fresh and alive and brings new perspectives to established teaching practices. Thus, thinking of a syllabus as both a metaphor and a means of accountability reminds the teacher of the tension which always exists between that accountability and creativity in the act of teaching.

THE DESIGN PROCESS

In designing a syllabus it is essential that the teacher has a clear and rather precise image of course outcomes. Some teachers can immediately translate and articulate that image into goals and objectives. Others need a number of intermediary steps between image and objectives. Few would suggest that writing objectives for a course is an easy task. Numerous volumes are available to help teachers write them more precisely and to remind us to include all of the appropriate components, but most of these books and articles seem to assume a more logical thought process than that with which many of us normally begin.

Identifying the Content

In this author's preactive teaching, either as an individual or as a member of a team, the task of identifying content is begun by jotting down, in whatever words and whatever order they come to mind, all the ideas, items, or activities to be included in the course. This list of concerns for content of a given course might be labelled a shopping or "wish" list and is a reflection of an ideal image of the teaching composition. The intention here is to brain-storm in order to determine all of the things this specific course might do or might provide for students. It is obvious that any such list will vary in terms of the type and the significance of the items, as well as in relation to the specific interests of the teacher and the relation of this course to a total program of studies. Obviously, members of a team will differ somewhat not only in the items originally contributed to the list, but also in the ways each categorizes and values those items. The discussions resulting from these differences have provided some of the most stimulating professional dialogues. Why, for instance, out of the whole history of children's literature, should the only individual title to appear on the list in Figure 14 be the relatively little-used *In My Mother's House*?[1] What does that work symbolize for this particular teacher.

FIGURE 14

SAMPLE OF "WISH" LIST FOR COURSE IN THE HISTORY OF CHILDREN'S LITERATURE

- image of child in literature over time
- effects of industry/society and education on child and treatment of child
- what about traditional literature? Folk and Fairy Tales?
- trade and text books
- didactic nature of literature
- illustrators of note
- read the books of the period—not just *about* the books
- assess the research needs of scholars in this field
- tools for access to information
- visit rare book collections and stores
- "The Classics"?
- handle and read rare items
- facsimiles-need and use
- relation to child today—can we use this material?
- the relationship to the 20th century—what is to be included?
- should time be spent on items like Ann Nolan Clark's *In My Mother's House*?
- how to approach informational books?
- what portion of poetry should be included? Nursery rhymes?
- publishing/printing history
- toy books/moveable books

Even the most cursory look at this list reveals the unevenness of its contents; but the "neatness" of the printed page masks, to some extent, its tentative and disorderly nature. In reality such jottings are scribbled somewhat haphazardly on, around, between, and across the lines of a pad of paper. The freedom of *not* placing items neatly in a list, even a random list, seems to free the mind for more effective brainstorming. (Some may use a typewriter or word processor for note-taking, but the technology may make the content appear too "fixed" for this first stage of planning.) You will notice issues related to the broad social, educational, or literary context side-by-side with a very idiosyncratic interest in a particular title, but the very act of putting all these ideas on paper helps to bring to the surface tacit feelings for and understandings of the contents of such a course.

Categorizing the Content

The next step is to categorize the various items on the list and attempt to rationalize those categories and relate them more closely to teaching practices (see Figure 15).

FIGURE 15

SAMPLE OF "WISH" LIST CATEGORIZED

RARE MATERIALS
> handle and read rare items
> visit rare book collections and stores
> facsimiles-need and use

CHILD AND SOCIETY
> image of child in literature over time
> effects of industry/society and education on child
> treatment of the child
> relation to children today—can we use this material?
> should time be spent on items like Ann Nolan Clark's *In My Mother's House*?
> the relationship to the 20th century—what is to be included?

ACCESS
> assess the research needs of scholars in this field
> tools for access to information

CONTENT
> folktale/fairy tale traditions
> read the books of the period-not just *about* the books
> illustrators of note
> what portion should be devoted to poetry? nursery rhymes?

LITERARY CONCERNS
> didactic nature of literature
> how to approach informational books

Rationalizing the Content

A next logical step is to explain why some "wishes" are categorized in the pattern displayed in Figure 15 and to establish rationale for their inclusion in the course content at all. This step is accomplished below for a few of those items listed in the figure. It should be noted, however, that the list is but a small selection of a rather long and highly individualized one. It must be emphasized that this entire process is improved by working with a colleague to test notions and ideas as well as to determine directions to be taken. The arguments that ensue in such a dialogue are a natural means of selectivity and often lead to growth in both individuals. Of course, the face-to-face, mind-to-mind communication with a colleague in your own or a neighboring institution is ideal; but for those not fortunate enough to have this kind of contact, professional publications and conferences are essential means of maintaining vitality in teaching. Such an exchange might be an ideal topic for an online conference using BITNET to bring teachers of children's literature together.

RARE ITEMS: HANDLE AND READ RARE ITEMS

As scholars, students need to deal with primary sources as much as possible rather than be dependent upon selected and interpreted knowledge reflected in secondary sources. In addition, it is important to realize that literary works are also physical objects dependent upon the technologies available as well as upon the decisions made by printers, publishers, and booksellers at the time of their production. Since children have always been sensitive to the size, shape, "look," and "feel" of a book as well as its contents, it is important for students to handle the actual objects encountered by children over time. Finally, one gets a marvelous sense of child readers of times past upon opening a book to find names, rhymes, threats, notes, etc., inscribed in the archaic penmanship of a previous owner. Sometimes there are even little "gifts" of pressed leaves, flower petals, drawings of hand-made bookmarks from one who was a child generations ago. Obviously, this implies the availability of a collection of historical children's books. Since most collections are not easily accessible to students, I have built and lend my own collections of representative children's books from various time periods to those in my classes.

CHILD AND SOCIETY: IMAGE OF THE CHILD IN LITERATURE

Since children's literature is produced by adults for children, it reflects adult perceptions of what childhood was or "ought to be" at a particular time. Whether or not that literature was overtly didactic, and it often was, it reveals, at least to some extent, expectations of child behavior and relationships with adults. It also gives some indications of the social customs of childhood such as language, popular games and toys, school life, and even styles of dress. All of this information helps the contemporary student to see children and the literature created for them in a larger cultural context. Illustrations and other works of graphic artists of various periods are very helpful for their revelations of just such cultural information. It is also fascinating and informative to compare the images of childhood in children's books with those in adult books with child characters.

ACCESS: TOOLS FOR ACCESS TO INFORMATION

Work in any discipline requires scholarly rigor and some means of access to the established body of knowledge in that field, as well as a means of keeping up with new developments from other researchers and scholars. In the field of historical children's literature, it is particularly difficult to verify sources, and numerous bibliographies and reference tools may need to be consulted in order to be accurate in the identification of particular items. Collection development decisions and the appraisal of either individual items or entire collections are dependent upon knowledge gained from such tools.

MATERIALS: READ THE BOOKS OF THE PERIOD—NOT ABOUT THE BOOKS

Literary works themselves are dominant. Students need to make literary judgments about what is available to them to read rather than accept the judgments of others. While writing this, however, it became obvious that this consideration is not significantly different from that identified under "Rare Items" above. Since rare items are indeed materials, everything noted there can be moved to the Materials section. Identification of such repetitions and overlaps are important in the process of determining course content because they cause us to reflect upon and sometimes reevaluate our priorities.

LITERARY CONCERNS: HOW TO APPROACH INFORMATIONAL BOOKS

Informational books for children raise some interesting questions from the perspective of the history of bookmaking, as well as in the contexts of literature and the history of childhood. For instance: Were informational books given the same care and attention (or lack thereof) as imaginative works in respect to overall book design? Did illustrations accurately portray information? Did informational and imaginative works for children develop simultaneously and along the same lines? Was the division between informational and imaginative works made in the early history of children's book publishing or was that separation a later development? Were children's information books comparable in literary quality to story books? What were the major subject areas or categories of information presented in these books? What do the modes of presentation reveal about preceptions of children as learners? Should textbooks, which were often a primary source of reading material for children, be considered informational materials even though a large portion of their contents were stories and poetry?

If the above processes sound very time consuming, perhaps even ideal, they are and they should be. If we do not take time to imagine the ideal in our preactive planning, how can we hope to compose something worthwhile in the actual performance of teaching? It is too easy to accept a very narrow and restrictive view of our work, and to repeat the same year of teaching over and over again rather than infusing new life into a course each year. In so doing, we expect far more of our students than we expect of ourselves, a practice all too common and totally unworthy of the nature of teaching.

During this process of rationalization, it is possible to alter or realign items that seem to have differing levels of importance. It is also true that new ideas and ingredients surface at this time. For instance, what will we do about periodicals in the course discussed above? Such reconsiderations often lead to more arguments with oneself and, in turn, to perhaps better decisions. Along the way, some determination will need to be made about the levels of competence the teacher expects from students in the interaction with this content. In some instances, concern is focused upon the acquisition of specific skills or items of information while in others, a change in attitude or increased appreciation is more important.

Theoretical Unity

Decisions also have to be reached about the fundamental governing principles, or the underpinnings of the course that convey a sense of unity in approach to content. For instance, the literary works themselves are paramount in the course; an understanding of the child and of the schooling process is essential;

a competence in using the bibliographical apparatus is critical to professional work; materials from the first half of the twentieth century are to be included because a significant portion of the whole history of children's literature resides in this century; relationships to children in the 1990s are to be drawn. Implicit in all of this is the desire to educate students as decision-makers, as researchers and users of research, and as competent professionals with an increased ability to ask the right questions about the relevance of course content to their work.

TEACHING DECISIONS

Once all of the above has taken place, it is possible to integrate the various components and to explore the best alternatives for teaching. At this point, a matching of teaching modes to objectives occurs. During this process, the syllabus begins to take shape in terms of its external form and a new set of problems emerges. How is the student to be oriented to the course through this document? What structure should be imposed for this course that will permit the best possible use of student time? Are there advantages to requiring group work as well as individual effort? What materials and resources might the student use to best advantage? What kinds and types of assignments will provide the most positive, the most stimulating, the most challenging, and the most interesting experiences for the student? How do course assignments permit the instructor to evaluate student work fairly and effectively? How much and what kind of detail is needed in instructions for assignments in order to give the student sufficient awareness of teacher expectations?

Among the most difficult decisions for the instructor to make for courses in contemporary children's literature is whether to include all media within the course or to concentrate on books. This decision may change radically as one moves from the ideal, to the postulated, to the actual composition of teaching. One might ideally wish to represent all media equally but also know that students do not have equal access to media other than print. We can assign books for out-of-class readings, but films or videos may have to be seen in class time. Even if there is a place in the school where students may view these works on their own, many working students are not on campus for other than class hours. There is no question that media other than print have a place in such courses, but lack of time or resources often interferes. The nature of children's literature and the broad scope of materials and clientele that it reaches seems to indicate a need for an entire set of courses. One such course might be devoted to other media formats, or further breakdowns by age level or genre could provide the time required for their full integration with print.

Determination of Readings

One of the most difficult aspects of developing a syllabus is the determination of the readings to be assigned or suggested to the student. It is easy to err in giving either too much or too little. In the first instance, students may become frustrated or overwhelmed while, in the second, the concern for and depth of knowledge in the field may not be conveyed adequately. Is the intent to provide a broad overview or to offer the student a concentrated portion of essential readings? Should we require readings which confirm our own opinions or attempt to present diversity in perspective and conclusions?

Another difficult question arises in determining what children's books might be appropriate for students to read in a basic children's literature course. Is there a magic list of preferred required readings? Members of the Children's Literature Association have compiled a list of the canon of children's literature of which students should be aware. Teaching, however, should not be based only on the great books of the past. It is vitally important that students learn to evaluate new books as they become available. The use of some titles rather than others is determined by those which demonstrate the teaching goals selected.

If, for example, the intention is to explore the use of conventions from comics in picture story books, it would be logical to suggest that students examine the different uses of such conventions in Raymond Briggs's *Fungus the Bogeyman* and *The Snowman*, in James Stevenson's illustration of *Georgia Music*, and in Steven Kellogg's *Pecos Bill* as well as in the work of many other contemporary author/illustrators.[2] If the intention is to look at language and metaphor in children's literature, students might examine the work of Alan Garner or perhaps juxtapose the early and the later works of Dr. Seuss.

My students are required to read widely, select and be prepared to defend the inclusion of works that they believe demonstrate the particular literary points or topics being discussed. There is also need for discussion of a single title from time to time. The books selected to be read by the entire class are often determined by the nature of interests and attitudes of the students in the class as well as on current interests in the field of practice. Among the books used have been: *Amy's Eyes; Edgar Allan; Dicey's Song; Rain Makes Applesauce; Molly's Pilgrim; The Tricksters; Looking Out; Dr. Dredd's Wagon of Wonders; Z Was Zapped; Pigs from A to Z; Hey, Al; Owl Moon,* and *Gertrude's Child*.[3] No one book dominates; rather, books are selected for their ability to stimulate a variety of responses. Students are then encouraged to articulate their views, to go back to the text to substantiate those views in discussion with others, and try to synthesize the various responses of group members. Often it is elucidating to compare and contrast similar works. In dealing with children's biography, for instance, one might select a particular person such as Abe Lincoln, Ben Franklin, Marie Curie, or Amelia Earhart in order to demonstrate some basic biographical concerns and the various approaches to a single life in this genre.

Determination of Assignments

The inclusion of assignments in the syllabus focuses students' attention from the onset of the course and provides direction as well as a clear statement of expected work performance. The nature of assignments should be determined by the objectives of the course and reflect the best means of reaching those objectives. Some faculty members believe that graduate students should be able to design and execute their work without detailed instructions and suggest that such instructions are intellectually limiting. This is what I characterize as the "I will know it when I see it" philosophy. This view reflects a lack of clear, conscious, detailed decision-making on the part of the instructor. In a climate of increased educational and fiscal accountability, or indeed at any time, this type of behavior is irresponsible. If we cannot share with students the specifics of what we expect from them, how can they ensure satisfactory performance? The placement of a student in jeopardy is simply unethical, and certainly any competent and caring teacher should be able to design assignments which both provide direction and allow for creativity and personal shaping of content. The amount of detail for assignments in the History of Children's Literature syllabus, for instance, is appreciated by students and ensures a basic quality of work from all students without inhibiting those who go beyond the minimum required to do outstanding or innovative work. I truly believe that the selection and evaluation of assignments may reveal as much about the teacher as about the students in a course.

Probably the most common expression of a lack of thought about assignments is the classic use of examinations or the assignment of a term paper. This is not to indicate that either term papers or examinations are unacceptable modes of evaluation, but that they are often employed by an instructor without careful consideration of their purpose in the particular course. For example, questions to ask are: What is the purpose of a term paper? What does it seek to measure? How might the instructions for such a paper give the student the appropriate information to accomplish what is expected? Is a term paper intended to demonstrate that a student can select, read, analyze, and synthesize the literature of the discipline with some skill? Is it to show that the student can write in English with some evidence of style? Is it to develop a rationale for a service or a brief for a position to be taken? Is it to demonstrate the accuracy of bibliographical citations or organizational and logical arrangements of ideas? Creative ability? Original insights? Or is it simply busy work? Should term papers be designed with potential publication in mind? If so, how might this be best accomplished? If the intent of the teacher in assigning a term paper is to provide a frame of reference for students to help them make appropriate decisions about the practical application of course content, then this must be taken into account in the development of the requirements for a paper.

In one course students became fascinated by Robin McKinley's *The Blue Sword* and *The Hero and the Crown*.[4] From a rather simple, albeit exciting, discussion of these books, the students agreed to pursue a series of papers which would examine such questions as the possibility of preparing a geographical map of the land; an itemized chart of the changes in name with correlations to character alteration; the use of color as a metaphor throughout the stories; a comparison of language use as it is reflected in setting; the meaning and use of the "kelar"; the power and nature of the female protagonist. These are but a few of the papers, but in each instance the teacher discussed with the class or the individual what might be included and debated the need to include or exclude a contextual or conceptual frame in the paper. For example, in examining the feminist heroine, should the student examine feminist criticism and, if so, to what extent and for what specific purposes? As a teacher, the question in mind had to be: is the concentration on the text itself as the basis for analysis more significant than the literature surrounding the text? The nature of the dialogue that takes place with each student should hopefully increase that student's ability to see the logical progression of ideas as well as the personal growth in literary criticism they have achieved.

Examinations, on the other hand, may be used in a quite different manner. Often they become a means to measure the success of an instructional unit to evaluate how much factual information students retain or whether or not students are able to use the factual information in problem situations. It is also possible to have students explore or justify a thesis, perhaps controversial in nature, which in turn might require demonstration of specifically acquired knowledge or competence. It is difficult to determine both the nature and the intent of examinations, but they require careful consideration before we accept them as means to evaluate students. One of the most difficult aspects is to help students to prepare for examinations and execute study patterns that will permit concise and thoughtful answers. Sometimes we need to teach even graduate students that an important first step in taking an exam is the recognition of what is being asked and a quick mental assessment of the nature of an appropriate answer. The evaluator of an examination should be assured that a student has understood the question and has a logic in the response. Helping students develop test-taking skills may require a more precise analysis of the nature of the language we use in asking questions and some clarification for students of the differing levels of questioning.

An analysis of the assignments required of students in the syllabi which follow should reveal both recurring patterns reflecting a philosophical approach to the teaching of literature and unique assignments corresponding to specific course content. Different types of assignments within a sequence of courses also provide variety both to students who take several courses in that sequence and to the teacher who responds to those assignments.

In most of these syllabi, development of a set of questions based on readings and class activities was considered essential to help students focus attention on important critical concerns related to learning objectives. The use of a reading assignment log and accompanying personal conferences in several of the courses permits the professor to have a personal dialogue with the student on work completed. Such conferences reveal the nature and amount of work done for assignments and often reflect greater depth of student perceptions than those expressed in class. Such conferences also convey to students the importance placed on their own self-directed work for the course and ensure that they take this work seriously and complete an adequate amount.

Reviews As an Assignment

Since it is often true that children's literature courses, especially those in library schools, have focused on criteria for selection and used reviews as the means to study such criteria, it is important to think through whether or not writing reviews is an appropriate approach. The author doubts that anyone who teaches children's literature would say that reviews are as important as the literary works, but some design their courses in ways that seem to indicate that the reviews are valued at least as much, often more than, the original works. Students do need to learn to analyze published reviews, but reading reviews is no substitute for reading the works themselves.

The writing of critical reviews is also a part of professional practice and a valuable skill for students to acquire; however, this is a difficult skill to acquire and usually comes only after much practice and detailed critiques of early efforts. Writing of a series of reviews over the course of a semester permits the professor to analyze and assess the growth of a student as well as allowing for a cumulative grade reflecting that growth. This is an example, however, of what was considered a sound teaching decision that was unsuccessful in practice. Although extensive comments were written on each of a series of three reviews and each of the previous reviews were required to be submitted with the second and third part of the assignment so that growth could more adequately be evaluated, students still complained that they had to wait too long for a grade. It is sad that even graduate students feel a simple letter grade is to be desired over detailed written response; but it is understandable, especially since ultimately a letter grade must be assigned.

After several semesters of student unrest in reaction to this assignment, a letter grade was provided for each of the reviews in the series, but this effectively negated the intent of the assignment. Since many students require not only practice but also a great deal of help before they are able to write an adequate review, and students learn more from successes than from failures, many initial reviews were intentionally graded higher than they should have been. Overgrading may have avoided discouragement in the process of learning to write a review, but it also gave some students overrated perceptions of their abilities and thus reduced their incentive to improve. An attempt to keep the cumulative nature of the grading to indicate that the process was more important than the product also failed. Intellectually and philosophically, students were able to accept that of two sequences of letter grades, B-C-D or D-C-B, the latter showed growth and deserved a higher overall rating than the former. In the abstract, they even agreed that this was an appropriate way to evaluate a very diverse student population, some of whom had a great deal of experience with course content and others who had none. When it came down to individual cases, however, those who demonstrated consistent improvement were happy with the system, but others were not. The focus had shifted in the minds of the students from the process of learning to the process of grading (not even evaluation) and thus the assignment was dropped, somewhat reluctantly.

An alternative to the series of reviews is a combination of one longer critical review, one review similar to those in *School Library Journal*, one computer review similar to those in *Bookbrain* and *BookWhiz*, and one annotation for parents, all for the same work. The intent of this combination of reviews for parents, children, and professional colleagues is to encourage students to think carefully about various audiences of reviews and try to tailor their reviews to those very different audiences.

Syllabus As a Physical Object

Too often faculty members are insensitive to the syllabus as a physical object. Consideration of color, spacing, and format are important as is the quality of the typing and the actual presentation on the page. Such things as illustration may be useful to capture or highlight a specific set of points in a syllabus or to give a "feel" for the content. For example, in the worksheets developed for the History of Children's

Literature, the insertion of sample illustrations from books for children during the nineteenth century introduces students to materials ordinarily unknown to them. Quotations in a syllabus may serve as dividers of content, as a reinforcement of a direction or ideas within a unit, or simply as "thought provokers."

Color-coding course materials makes my organization easier and sometimes brightens my mood as well as the file cabinet. Students have reported that they appreciate color for the same reasons. Whenever possible, of course, try to match hue or tone to the content or the spirit of the course. Materials for the History of Children's Literature are almost always duplicated on a buff or salmon-colored paper with a somewhat "antiqued" look. Day-long institutes, on the other hand, may have a rainbow effect so that it is easier to control a variety of materials in an intensive work period. It's often far easier to locate the green sheets or the goldenrod page among a mass of materials than it is to identify each item by title.

Details such as punching holes in pages for insertions in noteboks or providing call numbers with references demonstrate the faculty member's concern for students as well as a valuing of their time and effort in completing course requirements. Of course, some students may not appreciate hole-punched paper and can be given a choice. Although some might prefer an alternative means of organizing their work, students could be asked to keep all their notes, reading logs, and other class materials in a notebook, or on a computer disk. These need not be graded, but I look them over at a final conference with each student near the end of the semester. Knowing that the instructor will see their work encourages some students to do more or to keep better records of what they have done. Former students have affirmed that the requirement to organize and contain all class materials as a unit makes it easier to retrieve and, therefore, more useful after graduation. It is especially important in a professional school to find ways to remind students that what they are studying should have some relationship to future practice.

Even placing call numbers on a bibliography or reading list serves as a subtle means of communicating that it is the thoughtful consideration of suggested works that is valued rather than the process of locating them. Library school students especially need this reinforcement because they are too often caught up in the kind of library instruction that focuses more on the location of resources than on their analysis and use.

The physical organization of the syllabus represents the intellectual organization of the course and gives students a sense of the mind set of the professor. Thus, even determinations of space and layout are important means to communicate with students. If the division of the syllabus is by units, questions might be included to help students focus attention or direct their readings. The purpose of such questions, like other aspects of the syllabus, is to enlarge the vision and perspective of the student and to suggest considerations that might lead to depth and breadth in the treatment of a subject.

NOTES

[1]Ann Nolan Clark. (1941). *In My Mother's House.* Illus. by Velino Herrara. (New York: Viking Press).

[2]Raymond Briggs. (1977). *Fungus the Bogeyman.* (London: Hamish Hamilton); Raymond Briggs. (1978). *The Snowman.* (New York: Random House); Helen V. Griffith. (1986). *Georgia Music.* Illus. by James Stevenson. (New York: Greenwillow Books); Steven Kellogg. (1986). *Pecos Bill.* (New York: William Morrow).

[3]Richard Kennedy. (1985). *Amy's Eyes.* (New York: Harper & Row); John Neufeld. (1968). *Edgar Allan.* (New York: S. G. Phillips); Cynthia Voigt. (1982). *Dicey's Song.* (New York: Atheneum); Julian Scheer. (1964). *Rain Makes Applesauce.* Illus. by Marvin Bileck. (New York: Holiday House); Barbara Cohen. (1983). *Molly's Pilgrim.* (New York: Lothrop, Lee & Shepard); Margaret Mahy. (1986). *The Tricksters.* (New York: Margaret K. McElderry Books); Victoria Boutis. (1988). *Looking Out.* (New York: Four

Winds Press); Bill Brittain. (1987). *Dr. Dredd's Wagon of Wonders.* (New York: Harper & Row); Chris Van Allsburg. (1987). *Z Was Zapped.* (Boston, MA: Houghton, Mifflin); Arthur Geisert. (1986). *Pigs from A to Z.* (Boston, MA: Houghton Mifflin); Arthur Yorinks. (1986). *Hey, Al.* Illus. by Richard Egielski. (New York: Farrar, Straus and Giroux); Jane Yolen. (1987). *Owl Moon.* Illus. by John Schoenherr. (New York: Philomel); Richard Hughes. (1966). *Gertrude's Child.* Illus. by Rick Schreiter, (New York: Harlin Quist); Richard Hughes. (1974). *Gertrude's Child.* Illus. by Nicole Claveloux. (New York: Harlin Quist).

[4]Robin McKinley. (1982). *The Blue Sword.* (New York: Greenwillow Books); Robin McKinley. (1984). *The Hero and the Crown.* (New York: Greenwillow Books).

Examples of Syllabi for Various Courses

INTRODUCTION

The syllabi in this chapter have grown and changed over the author's years of teaching and each has been used successfully with graduate students. All such syllabi are dynamic representations of the postulated composition of teaching and are intended to set a tone, capture the spirit of and share an enthusiasm for course content as well as set expectations for student participation. Although commonalities representative of the teacher's priorities and research activities are evident among these syllabi, they do vary somewhat in both approach and style. Readings are updated each year and other modifications are made to reflect current interests and materials and to help maintain a freshness and vitality in course content and in teaching.

DIVISIONS OF COURSE CONTENT

The "Critical Analysis of Materials for Children" syllabus is typical of the introductory courses taught in colleges and universities throughout the country in that it attempts to introduce and provide an overview of the field to those who may or may not take additional courses. It concentrates on print because that, along with the home television viewing assigned, is most accessible to a diverse student body that is not normally on campus beyond class hours. Some children's films are shared in class, but this takes a great deal of time in an already crowded schedule. Occasionally one arranges for film or video showings, game and toy exhibits, or a "media fair" demonstrating magazines, filmstrips, recordings, posters, teaching materials, and whatever else is available either before or after class. Most frequently, however, this course is taught at night (7:00-9:30) with most students rushing in after a full day's work, often having eaten their "dinner" in the car in the midst of a long, hectic commute. These students can neither arrive on campus before class nor stay beyond the normal hours.

The content represented by the "Critical Analysis of Materials for Children" syllabus has sometimes been divided into two courses. Content was divided either by the form of the materials (Print Materials for Children, Nonprint Materials for Children) or by the age of the intended audience (Literature for Young Children, Literature for Older Children). The first often works better from the practical considerations of providing the appropriate environment for and access to nonprint materials and the display technologies necessary for their use. The second seems to make more sense intellectually. The reality, however, is that, in most institutions, any courses in this area are electives, and students frequently have so many requirements that they cannot afford more than two such courses. Since many adults who work with children and literature also work with young adults, they prefer the packaging of content represented by the "Critical Analysis of Materials for Children" and "Materials for Young Adults" syllabi.

A more logical means of responding to the various concerns for these introductory literature courses might be the regular offering of three age level courses (Young Children, Older Children, Young Adults) with all students taking the middle course plus one of the others, depending upon their interests and job responsibilities. The primary difficulty with this solution is one of scheduling, particularly within a one-year program, both for students and for the faculty member who would probably teach all of these courses plus several others in the larger programs of which these literatures are a part. Another difficulty for the faculty member and the institution is that adding a third introductory level course might cut into the enrollments in the Storytelling course and in the more advanced courses in Aesthetic Criticism and the History of Children's Literature also presented in this chapter.

ARTICULATION AMONG COURSES

The content of these and similar courses obviously is dependent upon the articulation with other courses taught in the school or program. For example, there is relatively little concern with the practical problems of planning activities to bring children and literature together in these syllabi. Since these courses are taught in a library school, almost all students enrolled are also taking either the children's services course for public librarians or a curriculum course for school librarians. In addition, the management course for school and public librarians includes content relevant to the effective organization of services and programs. The emphasis on the literary aspects of these materials and the development of critical and evaluative skills evident in the syllabi which follow was also present when the author taught similar courses in a graduate school of education. In that context too, students were involved with other coursework related to activities and programs with young people. Those who teach in English, literature, popular culture, or American studies programs in which these courses are the only ones related to youth audiences may have to include more content relative to audience characteristics and more of the actual use of these materials with children or young adults.

The particular constellation of offerings in which these literature for youth courses are found also has very important implications for the scholarly endeavors of those who teach them. It is not unusual for faculty who specialize in literature for youth to also teach all of the related courses. Thus, while many of our colleagues teach multiple sections of the same one or two required courses plus another related to a particular topic or institutional setting, youth specialists often teach five or six different courses each year. This may offer variety and prevent the kind of "burnout" which comes from repetition, but it also adds the burden of trying to remain current in all of these areas while, at the same time, focusing on scholarly pursuits in the primary area of concern. The author's teaching, for instance, includes courses in both school libraries (either curriculum or management) and public library services for children and youth as well as a course each year related to adult materials or services. One such course is Adult Materials in Public Libraries which includes the history and current status of reader services and use studies in libraries, adult literacy materials and programs, other resources for adult users with special needs, and the evaluation and selection of all types of genre fiction for adults. Another is a general collection development course for all types of libraries. These teaching responsibilities require one to remain current in many areas, including that of technology which encompasses all types of library services and materials.

ADMINISTRATIVE DECISIONS

Administrative decisions, as well as the institutional setting, student needs, and the larger constellation of courses, determine what is taught. All of the sample syllabi represent semester-long, three-credit courses that are fairly general in content. This generality probably increases enrollment, but it also makes it difficult for advanced students to specialize or to pursue more in-depth work in a subset of the field. The author has often imagined but never actualized a total graduate level curriculum in children's literature. This curriculum might include courses on comparative literature for children to provide the much-needed international perspective, illustration and book design, and courses in various genres such as poetry, biography or informational books. There is certainly enough content to conduct semester long courses in these and virtually every other topic touched upon in the general introductory courses. More specialized courses need not, however, be thought of only in the normal administrative pattern. It has always seemed reasonable and possible to divide a normal fifteen-week, three-credit course into three five-session, one-credit courses. Thus, a student could enroll in one, two, or three short-term courses on, for instance, folklore, fantasy and science fiction. To date, however, my opportunities to teach this type of more focused content have been only in special institutes or workshops for continuing education, either in a one-day or a three-day period. A three-day institute such as the one discussed in Chapter 7 may contain the same number of class hours as one of these short courses, and there is greater opportunity for the development of a sense of challenge and colleagueship. On the other hand, some intellectual rigor may have to be sacrificed because students do not have the same intervals between classes to read and reflect on course content.

SAMPLE SYLLABI

The syllabi presented here then are representative more of what currently exists than of what might be. Increased dialogue among teachers of children's literature and a sharing of ideas and materials will undoubtedly lead to new and better course designs and syllabi.

THE CRITICAL ANALYSIS OF
MATERIALS FOR CHILDREN

1. *Course Description*

   Evaluation, selection, and use of both print and nonprint materials for children; impact of mass media on children in our society; analysis of attitudes, issues and values reflected in these media and their use in educational settings.

2. *Direction of Course Content*

   This course is designed to help students develop critical abilities in the evaluation of materials and to encourage them to look at children as both consumers and producers of all forms of media. Film and television will be the chief areas of concentration in the nonprint media.

3. *Competencies Addressed*

   Knowledge of—

   User characteristics and information needs, including developmental psychology and learning theory relating to reading, cross-cultural, ethnic, and other special needs.

   The varieties of materials for children, including publishing trends.

   Research relating to children and materials.

   Various genres of compositional forms and the characteristics of each.

   Various illustrative techniques and their effectiveness in relation to particular texts.

   Criteria for evaluating various types of media for children.

   Various elements of compositional forms and the use of these elements in print and non-print compositions.

   Professional materials about children's media.

   Intellectual freedom: ways to meet challenges to materials, policies, programs, etc.

   Skill In—

   Selection and evaluation of materials.

   The use of critical abilities in the discussion (both oral and written) of various media for children.

   Interpretation and evaluation of research relating to the group.

"... children's literature is 'literature *for* children' rather than literature *by* them. Accordingly it reflects not so much that reality of childhood as how adults perceive that reality. The type of literature a society or an age produces for its children is an excellent indicator of what that society perceives its children to be." —Eric A. Kimmel

4. *Nature of the Course/Resources for the Course*

This course is designed to permit the greatest possible dialogue and exchange of views. The sharing process will require you to bring a variety of materials to class in order to demonstrate points you wish to make.

You are expected to become familiar with a wide variety of resources *about* children's media although the major emphasis should be on the children's materials themselves. You might, for instance, look at particular works or genres in light of what Huck, Sutherland, Vandergrift, etc. have to say about them and compare and contrast what these and other authors have said about the same topic in children's literature.

The following book most clearly matches the content of this course and will give you some insight into the priorities and prejudices of the professor.

Vandergrift, Kay E. (1980). *Child and Story: The Literary Connection*. New York: Neal-Schuman Publishers, Inc. (reprinted in paperback 1986).

In addition, you will find it most helpful to examine the following journals on a regular basis:

1. *The Horn Book*

2. *Journal of Youth Studies in Libraries* (*Top of the News*)

3. *School Library Journal*

4. *Children's Literature Association Quarterly*

5. *Signal*

6. *Children's Literature in Education*

7. *Phaedrus*

8. *Children's Literature*

9. *Bulletin for the Center of Children's Books*

10. *The New Advocate*

11. *Booklist*

5. *Required Readings*

There is no single text for this course, although *Child and Story* may prove helpful throughout. Instead you will receive a general list of readings which should be used to acquire a basic knowledge about children's media. The instructor's master bibliography is available on computer so that students who wish to do so may download either the entire bibliography or various segments thereof. Titles pertinent to particular areas or topics will be identified in class. Worksheets will also be distributed throughout the semester to help you evaluate various types of materials discussed in class.

6. *Specific Required Readings Related to Topics and Assignments*

Arnheim, Rudolf. (1964). *Art and Visual Perception*. Berkeley, CA: Univerity of California Press.

Arts and Cognition. (1977). David Perkins and Barbara Leondar, Editors. Baltimore, MD: The Johns Hopkins University Press.

Association for Library Service to Children/Young Adult Services Division. (1980). *Selecting Materials for Children and Young Adults: A Bibliography of Bibliographies and Review Sources*. Chicago, IL: American Library Association.

Bader, Barbara. (1976). *American Picturebooks from Noah's Ark to the Beast Within*. New York: Macmillan.

Bettelheim, Bruno. (1975). *The Uses of Enchantment: The Meaning and Importance of Fairy Tales*. New York: Alfred Knopf.

"Biography for the Young Reader," (Autumn 1976). *Children's Literature in Education*. 22: 107-127.

Carlson, Ann D. (1985). *Early Childhood Literature Sharing Programs in Libraries*. Hamden, CT: Library Professional Publications.

Carr, Jo. (1982). *Beyond Fact: Nonfiction for Children and Young People*. Chicago, IL: American Library Association.

Dewey, John. (1930). *Construction and Criticism*. New York: Columbia University Press. (The first Davies Memorial Lecture).

Egoff, Sheila. (1981). *Thursday's Child*. Chicago, IL: American Library Association.

Fisher, Margery. (1972). *Matters of Fact*. New York: Crowell.

Frye, Northrop. (1964). *The Educated Imagination*. Bloomington, IN: Indiana University Press.

Gardner, Howard. (1973). *The Arts and Human Development*. New York: Wiley.

Higgins, James. (1970). *Beyond Words: Mystical Fancy in Children's Literature*. New York: Teachers College Press.

Hildick, Wallace. (1970). *Children and Fiction*. New York: World.

Inglis, Fred. (1981). *The Promise of Happiness: Values and Meaning in Children's Fiction*. Cambridge, England: Cambridge University Press.

Lacy, L. E. (1986). *Art and Design in Children's Picture Books: An Analysis of Caldecott Award-Winning Illustrations*. Chicago, IL: American Library Association.

Langer, Susanne K. (1953). *Feeling and Form*. New York: Charles Scribner's Sons.

_____. (1957). *Problems of Art*. New York: Charles Scribner's Sons.

Lukens, Rebecca. (1986). *A Critical Handbook of Children's Literature*. 3rd Edition. New York: Scott, Foresman & Co.

Parker, Elizabeth Ann. (1975). *Teaching the Reading of Fiction*. New York: Teachers College Press.

Protherough, Robert. (1983). *Developing Response to Fiction*. Milton Keynes, England: Open University Press.

Purves, Alan C. and Monson, Dianna L. (1984). *Experiencing Children's Literature*. Glenview, IL: Scott, Foresman & Co.

Rosenblatt, Louise M. (1981). *The Journey Itself*. The Leland B. Jacobs Lecture, 1981. New York: Friends of Leland B. Jacobs.

_____. (1976). *Literature As Exploration*. 3rd Edition. New York: Nobel & Noble Publishers. (First Published in 1938).

Ruthven, K. K. (1984). *Feminist Literary Studies: An Introduction*. Cambridge, England: Cambridge University Press.

Shulevitz, Uri. (1985). *Writing with Pictures: How to Write and Illustrate Children's Books*. New York: Watson-Guptill.

Sloan, Glenna Davis. (1984). *The Child As Critic: Teaching Literature in the Elementary School*. 2nd Edition. New York: Teachers College Press.

Smith, James Steel. (1967). "The Child and the Facts: Nonfiction for Children," in *A Critical Approach to Children's Literature*. New York: McGraw Hill.

Smith, Lillian. (1953). *The Unreluctant Years*. Chicago, IL: American Library Association.

Sutherland, Zena. (1986). *Children and Books*. 7th Edition. Chicago, IL: Scott, Foresman.

White, Mary Lou. (1976). *Children's Literature: Criticism and Response*. Columbus, OH: Charles E. Merrill.

7. *Overview of Course Content/Probe Questions*

Each of these topics may include discussion of both print and nonprint materials.

List of Topics to Be Covered:

    Literature in the Lives of Today's Children

    Illustrated Materials for Young Children

    Compositional Elements and Genres

    Modern Realistic Fiction

    Fanciful Fiction

    Historical and Regional Fiction

    Biography

    Informational Materials

    Poetry

A. *Literature in the Lives of Today's Children*:

— How important are books and reading in a media-saturated environment?

— How much influence can parents, teachers, and librarians expect to have on the reading and viewing habits of young people?

— Have the nature and concerns of childhood and adolescence changed so radically that materials produced prior to the 1960s no longer have any "relevance" for young people?

B. *Illustrated Materials for Young Children*:

— Are there distinctions between "picture books" and "picture story books" for young children?

— What are the distinctions among story, mood, concept, and everyday experience books for young children?

— How do concept books differ from informational books?

— How do illustrations create story? How do they add to or interact with verbal texts?

— Does the transformation from picture story book to film change the nature of that story? Does this differ depending upon the filming technique, i.e., iconographic as contrasted with animation or realistic footage?

C. *Compositional Elements and Genres*:

— What is a genre? Does the use of the term "genre" in children's literature differ from its use in relationship to works for adults?

— What are the literary motifs and archetypes?

— Are there particular elements within a genre which, by nature of that genre, tend to have special significance in that composition?

— Is it possible to examine the same elements and genre in film and television as in print?

D. *Modern Realistic Fiction*:

— What is the nature and extent of didacticism in modern realistic fiction for young people?

— Does modern realistic fiction for children and young people present alternative life styles and views of society?

— What is the basic distinction between a series and a chronicle as a literary form for children?

— What factors have influenced the recent increase in censorship in the public schools of this country?

— To what do you attribute the continual appeal of such series as Nancy Drew and the Hardy Boys?

E. *Fanciful Fiction*:

— How do you respond to the statement: "Those things that are most 'real' in life can best be conveyed through fancy."?

— Is it true that most fanciful literature appeals only to the talented or "special" reader?

— How does the creator of fanciful fiction make that fiction believable to readers and viewers?

F. *Regional and Historical Fiction*:

— What is the difference between regionalism and sectionalism in literature?

— Is it true that most historical fiction is highly romanticized?

— How accurate are the background details in the settings of historical fiction?

— Is historical fiction an appropriate means of explaining history to youngsters?

G. *Biography*:

— What degree of fictionalization, if any, is acceptable in biography for children and young people?

— Is it necessary for the characters of children's biography to be inspiring to or role models for readers?

— Is it true that children are not interested in most aspects of the adult lives of famous individuals?

H. *Informational Materials*:

— Should informational materials for children begin at the most basic level in the presentation of that information?

— Do adults involved in the production of children's materials make too many assumptions about the age or grade level at which young people will be interested and able to deal with specific informational topics?

— Do the majority of informational materials for children really reveal a respect for the child's ability to inquire and to know?

— What kinds of illustrations are used in informational books for children and how does each convey content?

I. *Poetry*:

— Is poetry the natural language of childhood?

— What do adults do to turn children away from poetry?

— Is popular or folk music a form of poetry?

— What kinds of poetry have the greatest appeal to youngsters?

— Is there such a thing as "visual poetry"?

8. *Assignments for the Course*

All students are required to complete assignments 1, 2, and 3 plus one assignment from Group A and one from Group B. In selecting your specific assignments, discuss your ideas with the professor, then decide upon and declare your topics to the class as early as possible so each of you can route appropriate materials to your colleagues throughout the semester. In turn, you will be expected to share the results of your work with others.

1. Participation in class discussions which demonstrate your knowledge of outside readings (both children's and professional materials) and thoughtful consideration of the probe questions included in the syllabus and on distributed worksheets.

2. Read as many books for children as possible. Watch as many children's TV shows as possible. Visit children's libraries, bookstores, toy shops, museums, exhibits, zoos, puppet shows, etc. Listen to/view as many other examples of children's media as possible. Observe children responding to media in the situations and settings above. Select and share books or other media with children whenever possible. Read professional monographs and journals in the field of children's media and reading. *Keep a log of all the above activities*. Schedule a conference with the professor during the last weeks of the semester to discuss your log.

3. Select one picture book and one book for older children from those provided by the professor and write a series of annotations, reviews, and critical evaluations of each. Your work should introduce these books to the following audiences:

Children: Begin with a "Teaser" of no more than two 40-character lines. Then prepare an annotation not to exceed ten 40-character lines (See the new ETS *BookWhiz* program for samples).

Parents: Very brief annotations to help parents and other caregivers select materials for children. (See *A Gift*, distributed in class).

Children's Librarians: *SLJ*'s reviews are the most widely read in our field, so study several issues of this journal for indications of style and content. Length should not exceed 250 words.

Students, Scholars, Critics of Children's Literature: This evaluation will allow you to look more critically at a particular work using criteria developed in class discussions, outside readings and worksheets distributed to students. (Sample papers will be available in class.)

GROUP A

1. In consultation with the professor, select a topic and plan a library or classroom *program* for children using both print and nonprint media. Be clear about the objectives of your program; keep a list of selection aids used for the identification of materials; provide for differing interest and ability levels of children; be specific about program activities and include some means of evaluation.

2. Select, in consultation with the professor, a particular area of the school curriculum or topic of interest to children and identify *materials* in a variety of media which support the informational needs of young people. Be very specific in the selection of your topic, keep a list of selection aids used, and verify whether or not each item is reviewed in the standard lists. (This does *not* mean that all items selected must be reviewed in the established reviewing media.) The number of items included is not as critical as your identification of the specific contributions of each one in relation to the topic selected.

3. Submit an annotated bibliography of materials selected on a particular topic and prepare the layout and content for a brochure, poster, or other publicity release highlighting the topic and specific items from your bibliography.

4. Organize a workshop for parents or teachers on the evaluation and selection of materials for children. Submit a detailed plan for the contents of this workshop. Include a budget, a list of materials to be used, copies of any handouts for the participants, appropriate advertisement copy for the workshop, and an evaluation form.

5. Identify a geographic/social area of the country or the world about which you have some degree of personal knowledge and evaluate the presentation of that place and its people in fiction and nonfiction materials for children. Examples: New York City in the 1970s, modern London, Pennsylvania Dutch country, etc.

6. Identify a historical figure about whom you can locate at least two biographies for children and compare the information in those biographies with other historical accounts of that person's life. Check such reference tools as encyclopedias, biographical dictionaries, textbooks, etc., for verification. You may also find references to this person in historical fiction or in the biographies of contemporaries which would be helpful in your analysis. Example: Deborah Sampson Gannett has been known as "the female soldier of the Revolution." In Rollins' collective biography *They Showed the Way*, she is included as a representative black citizen while in Cheney's *The Incredible Deborah*, she is portrayed as white.

7. Identify a particular incident or event in American history and evaluate its coverage in both historical fiction and in factual materials for children. Has this coverage changed over time? If so, how? Example: The evacuation and containment of Americans of Japanese origins during World War II—see Means' *The Moved-Outers* and Uchida's *Journey to Topaz*, as well as trade and textbooks for children discussing this period of our history.

GROUP B

1. Select a particular story from the folk or fairy tale tradition or other story that has been illustrated by a number of artists and examine at least four or five different visual interpretations of that work. Prepare a set of slides which compares and contrasts the various interpretations of the story to be used in a class presentation of your findings. (Arrange with the professor for class time for this assignment.) For your presentation, consider such questions as the following:

   — What are the differences among the textual interpretations of the story?

   — Are the different versions intended for different audiences?

   — How do these versions compare with the earliest available written form of the story?

   — What are the differences among the visual interpretations of the story?

   — Is the specific content of the story altered in any way by the illustrations? If so, how? (character, mood, plot, etc.?)

   — What is the relationship, if any, between illustrative technique and mood in story? Between color and mood?

   — How are the visual details of setting used in storytelling?

   — Is the number of illustrations and their placement in relation to the text appropriate to the story?

   — Do visual and verbal points of view correspond?

   — Is the format of the book as a physical object part of its affective statement as story?

2. Prepare a 15-20 minute book talk to be presented to the class. The topic of this book talk should be designed for youngsters of a particular age or interest group and should introduce them to materials they are unlikely to select on their own. (Arrange with the professor for class time for this assignment.)

3. Select a children's book that has been the target of some sort of censorship. Identify at least two specific incidents of the censoring of that title and the rationale for the censorship. Examine the reviews of this title and then prepare your own analysis of the case including:

   — critical review of the work's literary qualities;

   — consideration of the validity of the charges against the work; and

   — a decision as to how you would handle this work in your own school or public library or classroom.

4. Working from the list of compositional elements on the "Matrix of the Relationship of Key Compositional Elements to Genre" (Vandergrift, *Child and Story*, p. 137) select three to five examples of interesting, unique, or excellent use of each element in both words and pictures. You need not include all genres for every element, but various genres should be represented in the total project. The pictures may be drawn from available sources but should also include samples of your own photographic work for at least three of the six elements.

5. Prepare an interview schedule and interview at least two children (ages 8-13) to determine their reading/viewing habits and their preferences for books, magazines, television programs, motion pictures, etc. Read or view some of those materials yourself and write a brief analysis of them and their appeal to youngsters. If possible, discuss your own responses to these materials with the children who originally identified them for you.

6. Select a particular genre or type of material for children and write a paper on that topic. In order to do this, you should:

   A. Read about that genre in references dealing with both children's and adult literature.

   B. Identify key authors and/or titles in this genre for children.

   C. Use specific materials for children as examples in discussing characteristics of the genre.

   D. Relate your discussion of the genre to compositional elements and to critical criteria developed in this course.

MATERIALS FOR YOUNG ADULTS

Catalog Description

Evaluation and selection of materials based upon the biological, socio-cultural, psychological and developmental characteristics of young adults; guidance in their use, emphasizing attitudes, interests, problems, and opportunities of young adults in contemporary society.

Competencies Addressed

At the conclusion of the course it is expected that students will be able to:

1. Recognize the literary elements in story and apply critical judgments to selected literature.

2. Work with the literary theories of the Reader-Response school as well as those of the Feminist Critics.

3. Apply factual and interpretive information on adolescent psychology, growth and development, sociology, and popular culture in planning for materials and services for young adults.

4. Describe the historical development, current trends, and enduring characteristics of young adult literature.

5. Identify current reading, viewing, and listening interests of young adults and incorporate these findings into collection development and program planning.

6. Provide a variety of information services (e.g., information referral, crisis intervention counseling, online data bases) to meet the diverse needs of young adults.

7. Interpret current research on young adult reading, information needs, and library usage and apply it to selecting materials for young adults.

8. Select and use appropriate tools in collection building and user guidance; analyze and criticize the usefulness of the tools in terms of coverage, cost, and special features.

9. Devise and publicize pathfinders, book lists, displays, etc., which will ease access to collections and motivate use.

10. Develop a materials collection for young adults which includes all appropriate formats, using a broad range of selection sources.

Readings: (See "Vandergrift's Hundred," Young Adult Titles, p. 108)

Aiken, Joan. (1985). "Interpreting the Past," *Children's Literature in Education* Vol. 16, No. 2: 67-83.

Alpern, Mildred. (Winter 1982). "Cultural Views of Gender in Works of Art and Contemporary Advertisements: An Approach for the High School Classroom," *Women's Studies Quarterly* Vol. 10, No. 4: 16-19.

Anthony, Kathryn H. (Summer 1985). "The Shopping Mall: A Teenage Hangout," *Adolescence* Vol. 20, No. 78: 307-312.

Bemhabib, Seyla, and Drucilla Cornell. (1987). *Feminism As Critique: On the Politics of Gender*. Minneapolis, MN: University of Minnesota Press.

Black, Cheryl and Richard R. DeBlassie. (Summer 1985). "Adolescent Pregnancy: Contributing Factors, Consequences, Treatment, and Plausible Solution," *Adolescence* Vol. 20, No. 78: 281-290.

Bloom, Allan. (1987). *The Closing of the American Mind*. New York: Simon and Schuster.

Bodart, Joni. (1988). *Booktalk! 3*. 3rd Edition. New York: H. W. Wilson Co.

Carlsen, G. Robert. (1980). *Books and the Teen-Age Reader*. 2nd Edition. New York: Harper & Row.

Cline, Ruth, and William McBride. (1983). *A Guide to Literature for Young Adults*. Glenview, IL: Scott, Foresman and Co.

Collier, Christopher. (August 1982). "Criteria for Historical Fiction," *School Library Journal*. Vol. 28, No. 10: 32-33.

Crew, Hilary. (Spring 1987). "Blossom Culp and Her Ilk: The Independent Female in Richard Peck's YA Fiction," *Top of the News*. Vol. 43, No. 3: 297-301.

Crosby, Christina. (Summer 1984). "Stranger Than Truth: Feminist Literary Criticism and Speculation on Women," *Dalhousie Review* Vol. 64, No. 2: 247-259.

Culp, Mary Beth. (December 1985). "Literature's Influence on Young Adult Attitudes, Values, and Behaviors, 1975 and 1984," *English Journal* Vol. 74, No. 8: 31-35.

Dalsimer, Katherine. (1986). *Female Adolescence: Psychoanalytic Reflections of Works of Literature*. New Haven, CT: Yale University Press.

De Marr, Mary Jean and Jane S. Bakerman. (1986). *The Adolescent in the American Novel Since 1960*. New York: Ungar.

Donelson, Ken. (March 1985). "Almost 13 Years of Book Protests. Now What?" *School Library Journal*. Vol. 31, No. 7: 93-98.

_____. (August 1984). "And the Critics Say, 'Kids Don't Read Like They Use To'." *VOYA* Vol. 7, No. 3: 133-34.

Early, Margaret J. (March 1960). "Stages of Growth in Literary Appreciation," *English Journal*. Vol. 49: 161-67.

Edwards, Margaret A. (1974). *The Fair Garden and the Swarm of Beasts: The Library and the Young Adult*. Rev. Edition. New York: Hawthorn Books.

Epstein, Connie C. (February 1984). "The Well-Read College-Bound Student," *School Library Journal* Vol. 30, No. 6: 32-35.

Fish, Stanley. (1980). *Is There a Text in This Class?* Cambridge, MA: Harvard University Press.

Fisher, Margery. (1986). *The Bright Face of Danger: An Exploration of the Adventure Story*. Boston, MA: Horn Book.

Graff, Gerald, and Reginald Gibbons, Editors. (1985). *Criticism in the University*. Evanston, IL: Northwestern University Press.

Greene, Gayle, and Coppelia Kahn, Editors. (1985). *Making a Difference: Feminist Literary Criticism*. London: Methuen.

Gregory, Thomas West. (1978). *Adolescence in Literature*. New York: Longman.

_____. (1979). *Juvenile Delinquency in Literature*. New York: Longman.

Guy, Rosa. (Winter 1983). "All About Caring," *Top of the News* Vol. 39, No. 2: 192-196.

Hirsch, E. D. (1987). *Cultural Literacy: What Every American Needs to Know*. Boston, MA: Houghton Mifflin.

Howington, Judy. (October 1983). "A Pathfinder: Nuclear Freeze," *VOYA* Vol. 6, No. 4: 190-191 + .

Hubbard, Rita C. (Spring 1985). "Relationship Styles in Popular Romance Novels, 1950 to 1983," *Communication Quarterly* Vol. 33, No. 2: 113-125.

Hutchinson, Margaret. (November 1973). "Fifty Years of Young Adult Reading 1921-1971," *Top of the News* Vol. 30, No. 3: 24-53.

Iser, Wolfgang. (1978). *The Act of Reading: A Theory of Aesthetic Response*. Baltimore, MD: The Johns Hopkins University Press.

_____. (1974). *The Implied Reader*. Baltimore, MD: The Johns Hopkins University Press.

Jacobus, Mary. (1986). *Reading Woman: Essays in Feminist Criticism*. New York: Columbia University Press.

Jenkinson, Edward B. (1979). *Censors in the Classroom: The Mind Benders*. Carbondale, IL: Illinois University Press.

Kaplan, Justin. (1985). *Born to Trouble: One Hundred Years of Huckleberry Finn*. Washington, DC: Library of Congress.

Kaye, Marilyn. (Fall 1981). "The Young Adult Romance: Revival and Reaction," *Top of the News* Vol. 38, No. 1: 42-47.

Klein, Norma. (Summer 1981). "Thoughts on the Adolescent Novel," *Top of the News* Vol. 37, No. 4: 352-359.

Kohlberg, Larry, and Carol Gilligan. (1971). "The Adolescent As a Social Philosopher," *Daedalus* Vol. 4: 1051-1086.

Kundin, Susan G. (Summer 1985). "Romance Versus Reality: A Look at YA Romantic Fiction," *Top of the News* Vol. 41, No. 4: 361-368.

Lenz, Millicent, and Ramona M. Mahood, Compilers. (1980). *Young Adult Literature: Background and Criticism*. Chicago, IL: American Library Association.

LiBretto, Ellen V., Editor. (1983). *New Directions for Young Adult Services*. New York: R. R. Bowker Co.

Literature—News That Stays News. (1985). Urbana, IL: National Council of Teachers of English.

Mengers, Susan. (Spring 1989). "Self-Sacrifice or Self-Development? Choices Made by Characters in the Novels of Cynthia Voigt," *Journal of Youth Services in Libraries.* Vol. 2, No. 3: 250-255.

Miller, Nancy K. (1986). *The Poetics of Gender*. New York: Columbia University Press.

Mitchell, Judith. (June 1985). "A Cheer and a Half for Independence," *VOYA* Vol. 8, No. 2: 107-109+.

Newman, Joan. (Fall 1985). "Adolescents: Why They Can Be So Obnoxious," *Adolescence* Vol. 20, No. 79: 635-646.

Nilsen, Alleen Pace, and Kenneth L. Donelson. (1985). *Literature for Today's Young Adults*. 2nd Edition. Glenview, IL: Scott, Foresman and Co.

Office of Intellectual Freedom of the American Library Association. (1983). *Intellectual Freedom Manual*. 2nd Edition. Chicago, IL: American Library Association.

Peck, Richard. (Winter 1983). "The Invention of Adolescence and Other Thoughts on Youth," *Top of the News* Vol. 39, No. 2: 182-190.

Probst, Robert. (1984). *Adolescent Literature: Response and Analysis*. Columbus, OH: Charles Merrill.

Protherough, Robert. (1983). *Developing Response to Fiction*. Milton Keynes, England: Open University Press.

Purves, Alan C. (1972). *How Porcupines Make Love*. Lexington, MA: Xerox College Publishing.

Purves, Alan C., and Richard Beach. (1972). *Literature and the Reader: Research in Response to Literature, Reading Interests and the Teaching of Literature*. Urbana, IL: University of Illinois Press.

Radway, Janice. (Summer 1984). "Interpretive Communities and Variable Literacies: The Functions of Romance Reading," *Daedalus* Vol. 113, No. 3: 49-73.

Radway, Janice A. (1984). *Reading the Romance: Women, Patriarchy, and Popular Literature*. Chapel Hill, NC: University of North Carolina Press.

Radway, Janice A. (Spring 1983). "Women Read the Romance: The Interaction of Text and Context," *Feminist Studies*. Vol. 9, No. 1: 53-78.

Ramsdell, Kristin. (Winter 1983). "Young Adult Publishing: A Blossoming Market," *Top of the News*. Vol. 39, No. 2: 173-181.

Ravitch, Diane and Chester Finn, Jr. (1987). *What Do Our 17-Year-Olds Know?* New York: Harper & Row.

Reed, Arthea. (1984). *Reaching Adolescents: The Young Adult and the School*. New York: Holt, Rinehart & Winston.

Reid, Pamela Trotman and Dorothy Stenson Stephens. (March 1985). "The Roots of Future Occupations in Childhood: A Review of the Literature on Girls and Careers," *Youth & Society*. Vol. 16, No. 3: 267-288.

Rochman, Hazel. (1987). *Tales of Love and Terror*. Chicago, IL: American Library Association.

Rosenberg, Betty. (1986). *Genreflecting*. 2nd Edition. Littleton, CO: Libraries Unlimited.

Rosenblatt, Louise M. (1981). *The Journey Itself*. The Leland B. Jacobs Award Lecture, April 11, 1981. School of Library Service, Columbia University, New York. Published by The Friends of Leland B. Jacobs.

Rosenblatt, Louise M. (1983). *Literature As Exploration*. 3rd Edition. New York: Modern Language Association. (same as 1976 Noble & Noble edition)

Rosenblatt, Louise M. (1978). *The Reader the Text the Poem: The Transactional Theory of the Literary Work*. Carbondale, IL: Southern Illinois University Press.

Rosenblatt, Louise M. (February 1985). "Viewpoints: Transaction Versus Interaction—A Terminological Rescue Operation," *Research in the Teaching of English*. Vol. 19, No. 1: 96-107.

Ross, Catherine Sheldrick. (April 1985). "Young Adult Realism: Conventions, Narrators, and Readers," *Library Quarterly*. Vol. 55, No. 2: 174-191.

Rubin, Rhea. (Spring 1985). "Compiling Your Own Bibliography," *Collection Building*. Vol. 7, No. 1: 45-47.

Ruthvon, K. K. (1984). *Feminist Literary Studies: An Introduction*. Cambridge, England: Cambridge University Press.

Sarafino, Edward P., and James W. Armstrong. (1980). *Child and Adolescent Development*. Glenview, IL: Scott, Foresman.

Schwartz, Sheila. (1979). *Teaching Adolescent Literature: A Humanistic Approach*. Rochelle Park, NJ: Hayden Book Co.

Scott, Joseph W. (Winter 1983). "The Sentiments of Love and Aspirations for Marriage and Their Association With Teenage Sexual Activity and Pregnancy," *Adolescence*. Vol. 18: 889-98.

Searles, Patricia, and Janet Mickish. (1984). " 'A Thoroughbred Girl': Images of Female Gender Role in Turn-of-the-Century Mass Media," *Women's Studies*. Vol. 10, No. 3: 261-281.

Shaw, Peter. (Autumn 1988). "Feminist Literary Criticism," *The American Scholar*. 495-513.

Showalter, Elaine, Editor. (1985). *The New Feminist Criticism: Essays of Women, Literature & Theory*. New York: Pantheon Books.

Smith, Karen Patricia. (Winter 1986). "Claiming a Place in the Universe: The Portrayal of Minorities in Seven Works by Andre Norton," *Top of the News*. Vol. 42, No. 2: 165-172.

Spacks, Patricia Meyer. (1981). *The Adolescent Idea: Myths of Youth and the Adult Imagination*. New York: Basic Books.

_____. (Spring 1977). "Women's Stories, Women's Selves," *Hudson Review*. Vol. 30, No. 1: 29-46.

Strouse, Jeremiah, and Richard A. Fabes. (Summer 1985). "Formal Versus Informal Sources of Sex Education: Competing Forces in the Sexual Socialization of Adolescents," *Adolescence*. Vol. 20, No. 78: 251-263.

Suleiman, Susan R., Editor. (1980). *The Reader in the Text*. Princeton, NJ: Princeton University Press.

Sutton, Roger. (November 1982). "The Critical Myth: Realistic YA Novels," *School Library Journal*. Vol. 29, No. 3: 33-35.

Taubenheim, Barbara Weise. (March 1979). "Erikson's Psychosocial Theory Applied to Adolescent Fiction: A Means for Adolescent Self-Clarification," *Journal of Reading*. Vol. 22: 517-22.

Tompkins, Jane P., Editor. (1980). *Reader-Response Criticism: From Formalism to Post-Structuralism*. Baltimore, MD: The John Hopkins University Press.

Vandergrift, Kay. (Winter 1987). "Critical Thinking Misfired: Implication of Student Responses to *The Shooting Gallery*," *School Library Media Quarterly*. Vol. 15, No. 2: 86-91.

Varlejs, Jana, Editor. (1978). *Young Adult Literature in the Seventies: A Selection of Readings*. Metuchen, NJ: Scarecrow Press.

White, Barbara A. (1985). *Growing Up Female: Adolescent Girlhood in American Fiction*. Westport, CT: Greenwood Press.

Wigutoff, Sharon. (Winter 1982). "Junior Fiction: A Feminist Critique," *Top of the News*. Vol. 38, No. 2: 113-124.

Yolen, Jane. (Fall 1982). "Here There Be Dragons: Reflections on Fantasy and Science Fiction," *Top of the News*. Vol. 39, No. 1: 54-56.

MAJOR ASSIGNMENTS

Required of All Students

1. Read as many young adult books (see Vandergrift's Hundred) and magazines as possible and view motion pictures and television programs popular with this age group. Each student is required to maintain a log of all items read or viewed throughout the semester. Other than bibliographical information, the contents and form are at the discretion of the student. Although the professor will ask to see this log near the end of the semester, the primary purpose is to record information and reactions for your future use. Also include conversations with or interviews of young adults relating to their reading-viewing-listening habits and/or any other experiences that provided information about or insight into their media environment.

2. Write brief annotations for TEN of the titles on the Vandergrift's Hundred List. (Instructions given in class.)

3. Read at least one of the three 1987 studies of Education and culture (Bloom, Hirsch or Ravitch and Finn) that have been in the news in recent months and be prepared to discuss in class. Submit one page including the citation of the book read and brief notes concerning the relevance to the content of the course.

4. Keep a response journal as you read the books assigned for class discussion. (Instructions given in class.)

5. Select a topic that allows you to synthesize some of the work you have done in this course and write an article on that topic similar in style and length to those you have read in the professional journals in the field. For example, you may wish to write on the use of setting in historical novels, feminist ideals as revealed in language and metaphor used by a specific author, applications of reader-response criticism to a specific body of works, or an analysis of character in the work(s) of one author. (The Crew and Mengers articles in the bibliography began as an assignment in this course.)

6. Final Examination: A celebration of the work done during the semester, with presentations of projects and a sharing of work with all in the course. Organize yourselves into groups of four to five. Select an author of some significance whose work is read by young adults and prepare a brief oral presentation with appropriate handouts to be presented to the entire class. Consider not only the specific criticism of the work of this author but attempt to apply some of the literary theory read and discussed in class to that body of work. You will be given additional guidelines on time and format of this examination.

Alternative Assignments: Each student should select ONE assignment from this list of alternatives.

1. Develop a video tape or slide presentation that demonstrates the thesis explored in the article by Alpern (see Readings) and use any additional theories to enhance your position.

2. Prepare a teaching and/or a discussion guide for a particular work or group of works of young adult fiction. Identify the audience for whom this is intended and demonstrate your understanding of adolescent development and literary criticism in its preparation.

3. Develop a questionnaire or interview schedule to be used with young adults to determine their reading and viewing habits and preferences that incorporates the theories of reader-response criticism and/or feminist criticism. Do a pilot test of your instrument with at least one or two young people and revise as necessary before final submission.

4. Select two research reports/articles relating to the adolescent. Analyze these reports/articles in terms of the methodology and findings and indicate how the findings might prove useful to the professional working with young adults.

5. Develop a pathfinder for young adult use on a subject of importance to the adolescent. You may find the model given in the reading list (see Item by Howington) of some help. It is expected that you will include some local resources. (This assignment should be no more than four to six pages. The intent is brevity and format is critical.)

Note Regarding Assignments: Professionals rarely work in isolation. You are encouraged to discuss work in progress with each other, with colleagues in the field and with the professor.

Methods of Assessment

Grades will be determined on the following basis:

Log and Class Participation demonstrating knowledge of readings and thoughtful consideration of the content of this course: 15%

Annotations, Response Journal: 15%

Article: 30%

Alternative Assignment: 20%

Final Examination: 20%

Organization of the Course

The following topics will be included in this course. A more detailed schedule will be distributed in class.

Introduction and Overview of the Course.

The Adolescent and Society

Adolescent Problems and Concerns

Literary Structure and Reader-Response Critics

Literary Structure and Feminist Critics

Focus on the Work of Specific Authors in Light of the Above

Informational Works for Young Adults

Periodical Literature for Young Adults

Visual & Electronic Media and the Adolescent

Research Relating to the Adolescent

Review media and Bibliographical Tools Useful in Building Collections for Young Adults.

VANDERGRIFT'S HUNDRED:
READINGS IN YOUNG ADULT LITERATURE

This list, which changes each year, is a very small portion of the wealth of literature available to young adults. In most instances only one title per author is listed, even for those who have written a number of popular books for this age group. Many of the titles are in paperback, and almost all will be in public libraries. This list is intended to provide guidance for those unfamiliar with literature for young adults, but it is certainly not exhaustive. Read as many of these books as possible but, in addition, plan to add your favorites to a more expansive listing. V. C. Andrews and Stephen King are not represented here but remain among the most popular authors for young adults, and you should read at least one work by each.

1. Douglas Adams. *The Hitchhiker's Guide to the Galaxy.*

2. Richard Adams. *Watership Down.*

3. Maya Angelou. *I Know Why the Caged Bird Sings.*

4. Anonymous. *Go Ask Alice.*

5. Fran Arrick. *Tunnel Vision.*

6. James Baldwin. *If Beale Street Could Talk.*

7. Jay Bennett. *Say Hello to the Hitman.*

8. Judy Blume. *Forever.*

9. Nancy Bond. *Another Shore.*

10. Hal Borland. *When the Legends Die.*

11. Robin Brancato. *Sweet Bells Jangled Out of Time.*

12.   Sue Ellen Bridgers. *Home Before Dark.*

13.   Bruce Brooks. *The Moves Make the Man.*

14.   Bruce Brooks. *Midnight Hour Encores.*

15.   Eve Bunting. *If I Asked You, Would You Stay?*

16.   Sylvia Cassedy. *M. E. and Morton.*

17.   Aiden Chambers. *Dance on My Grave.*

18.   Alice Childress. *Rainbow Jordan.*

19.   Barbara Cohen. *Unicorns in the Rain.*

20.   Barbara Corcoran. *The Hideaway.*

21.   Robert Cormier. *The Chocolate War.*

22.   Robert Cormier. *Fade.*

23.   Chris Crutcher. *Running Loose.*

24.   Charlotte Culin. *Cages of Glass, Flowers of Time.*

25.   Peter Dickinson. *Eva.*

26.   Lois Duncan. *Killing Mr. Griffin.*

27.   Paula Fox. *The Moonlight Man.*

28.   Nancy Garden. *Annie on My Mind.*

29.   Bette Greene. *Summer of My German Soldier.*

30.   Judith Guest. *Ordinary People.*

31.   Rosa Guy. *And I Heard a Bird Sing.*

32.   Virginia Hamilton. *Sweet Whispers, Brother Rush.*

33.   Marilyn Harris. *Hatter Fox.*

34.   Torey Hayden. *The Sunflower Forest.*

35.   Jamake Highwater. *Anpao: An American Indian Odyssey.*

36.   S. E. Hinton. *The Outsiders.*

37.   Isabelle Holland. *Man Without a Face.*

38. Felice Holman. *Slake's Limbo.*

39. Irene Hunt. *The Lottery Rose.*

40. Norma Johnson. *Return to Morocco.*

41. Diana Wynne Jones. *Dogsbody.*

42. June Jordan. *His Own Where.*

43. M. E. Kerr. *Gentlehands.*

44. M. E. Kerr. *Night Kites.*

45. Daniel Keyes. *Flowers for Algernon.*

46. Norma Klein. *Going Backwards.*

47. Harper Lee. *To Kill a Mockingbird.*

48. Ursula Le Guin. *The Left Hand of Darkness.*

49. Sonia Levitin. *The Return.*

50. Myron Levoy. *Shadow Like a Leopard.*

51. Robert Lipsyte. *The Contender.*

52. Lois Lowry. *A Summer To Die.*

53. Patricia A. McKillip. *The Riddle Master of Hed.*

54. Robin McKinley. *Beauty.*

55. Robin McKinley. *The Hero and the Crown.*

56. Anne McCaffrey. *The Ship Who Sang.*

57. Michelle Magorian. *Good Night, Mr. Tom.*

58. Margaret Mahy. *Memory.*

59. Sharon Bell Mathis. *Listen for the Fig Tree.*

60. Harry Mazer. *When the Phone Rings.*

61. Louise Moeri. *The Girl Who Lived on the Ferris Wheel.*

62. Walter Dean Myers. *Fallen Angels.*

63. Walter Dean Myers. *Scorpions.*

64. Jean Lowery Nixon. *The Stalker.*

65. Robert O'Brien. *Z for Zachariah.*

66. Zibby Oneal. *A Formal Feeling.*

67. Pat O'Shea. *The Hounds of the Morrigan.*

68. Katherine Paterson. *Jacob Have I Loved.*

69. Gary Paulson. *Hatchet.*

70. Richard Peck. *Remembering the Good Times.*

71. Robert Newton Peck. *A Day No Pigs Would Die.*

72. Sylvia Plath. *The Bell Jar.*

73. Kin Platt. *The Boy Who Could Make Himself Disappear.*

74. Meredith Pierce. *Darkangel.*

75. Otfried Preussler. *The Satanic Mill.*

76. Philip Pullman. *The Ruby in the Smoke.*

77. Wilson Rawls. *Where the Red Fern Grows.*

78. Margaret I. Rostkowski. *After the Dancing Days.*

79. J. D. Salinger. *Catcher in the Rye.*

80. Danny Santiago. *Famous All Over Town.*

81. Pamela Sargent. *Earthseed.*

82. Ouida Sebestyen. *Words By Heart.*

83. Ruth Minsky Sender. *The Cage.*

84. William Sleator. *The House of Stairs.*

85. Todd Strasser. *Friends Till the End.*

86. Joyce Sweeney. *Center Line.*

87. Mildred D. Taylor. *Let the Circle Be Unbroken.*

88. Joyce Carol Thomas. *Marked By Fire.*

89. Joyce Thompson. *Conscience Place.*

90. Julian F. Thompson. *Grounding of Group 6.*

91. Cynthia Voigt. *Dicey's Song.*

92. Alice Walker. *The Color Purple.*

93. Jill Paton Walsh. *Fireweed.*

94. Barbara Wersba. *Carnival in My Mind.*

95. Robert Westall. *The Machine Gunners.*

96. Margaret Willey. *The Bigger Book of Lydia.*

97. Joan Vinge. *Psion.*

98. Jane Yolen. *Sister Light, Sister Dark.*

99. Paul Zindel. *The Pigman.*

100. Paul Zindel. *The Effects of Gamma Rays on Man-In-The-Moon Marigolds.*

STORYTELLING

Course Description

Examination of the art and practice of storytelling, exploration of the folk and fairy tale tradition as well as contemporary literature for oral narration. This course includes performance and the study of techniques in this art.

Objectives

Upon completion of this course the student will:

1. Prepare and use a variety of stories for presentation to an audience

2. Employ techniques of voice control to foster excellence in performance

3. Plan a range of programs for different audiences

4. Recognize the role and responsibility of the storyteller in society

Organization of the Course

Nature of Storytelling in Various Cultural Contexts

Role of the Storyteller in Society

Sources for Storytelling

Selection and Matching of Stories to Audiences

Story Structuring and Mapping

Variants and Versions in Folk and Fairy Tales

Poetry as a Storytelling Experience

Tall tales, Legends and Hero Tales

The work of Professional Storytellers: Ed Stivender, Donald Davis, Patrick Ball, Brother Blue, Alice Kane, Syd Lieberman, Jackie Torrence, Jay O'Callahan, and others.

Programming for Storytelling

Body Language, Voice Control, and Techniques

Use of Puppets and other objects

Storytelling Environments

"Storytelling is an art form through which a storyteller projects mental and emotional images to an audience using the spoken word, including sign language and gestures, carefully matching story content with audience needs and environment. The story sources reflect all literatures and cultures, fiction and nonfiction, for educational, recreational, historic, folkloric, entertainment and therapeutic purposes."

—National Association for the Preservation
and Perpetuation of Storytelling

Readings for the Course:
on Storytelling and Programming

Baker, Augusta, and Ellin Greene. (1987). *Storytelling: Art & Technique.* 2nd Edition. New York: R. R. Bowker.

Bauer, Caroline Feller. (1977). *Handbook for Storytellers.* Chicago, IL: American Library Association.

_____. (1985). *Celebrations.* New York: H. W. Wilson Company.

Breneman, Lucille N., and Bren Breneman. (1983). *Once Upon a Time: A Storytelling Handbook.* Chicago, IL: Nelson-Hall.

Bodart, Joni. (1988). *Booktalk!* 3rd Edition. New York: H. W. Wilson Company.

Chambers, Dewey. (1970). *Literature for Children: Storytelling and Creative Drama.* Dubuque, IA: Wm. C. Brown Co.

Champlin, Connie, and Nancy Renfro. (1985). *Storytelling with Puppets.* Chicago, IL: American Library Association.

Colwell, Eileen. (1980). *Storytelling.* Toronto, Canada: Bodley Head.

Davidson, H. R. Ellis. (1986). *Katherine Briggs: Storyteller.* Cambridge, England: Lutherworth Press.

Foster, Joanna. (1978). *How To Conduct Picture Book Programs: A Handbook.* Yonkers, NY: Westchester Library System.

Greene, Ellin, and George Shannon. (1986). *Storytelling: A Selected Annotated Bibliography.* New York: Garland.

Kimmel, Margaret Mary, and Elizabeth Segel. (1988). *For Reading Out Loud! A Guide to Sharing Books with Children.* 2nd Edition. New York: Delacorte.

Livo, Norma J., and Sandra A. Rietz. (1986). *Storytelling: Process and Practice.* Littleton, CO: Libraries Unlimited.

MacDonald, Margaret Read. (1982). *Storyteller's Sourcebook: A Subject, Title, and Motif Index to Folk-lore Collections for Children*. New York: Neal-Schuman Publishers, Inc. (Distributed by Gale Research).

_____. (1986). *Twenty Tellable Tales: Audience Participation Folktales for the Beginning Storyteller*. New York: H. W. Wilson Co.

Moore, Vardine. (1972). *Pre-School Story Hour*. 2nd Edition. Metuchen, NJ: Scarecrow Press.

Nichols, Judy. (1987). *Storytimes for Two-Year-Olds*. Chicago, IL: American Library Association.

Paulin, Mary Ann. (1982). *Creative Uses of Children's Literature*. Hamden, CT: Shoe String Press.

Pellowski, Anne. (1987). *The Family Story-Telling Handbook*. New York: Macmillan.

Pellowski, Anne. (1984). *The Story Vine: A Source Book of Unusual and Easy-To-Tell Stories from Around the World*. New York: Macmillan.

Pellowski, Anne. (1977). *The World of Storytelling*. New York: R. R. Bowker.

Peterson, Carolyn, and Brenny Hall. (1980). *Story Programs: A Source Book of Materials*. Metuchen, NJ: Scarecrow Press.

Sawyer, Ruth. (1962). *The Way of the Storyteller*. Revised Edition. New York: Viking Press.

Shedlock, Marie. (1952). *The Art of the Storyteller*. 3rd Edition. New York: Dover.

Sitarz, Paula G. (1987). *The Picture Book Story Hours from Birthdays to Bears*. Littleton, CO: Libraries Unlimited.

Tooze, Ruth. (1959). *Storytelling*. Englewood Cliffs, NJ: Prentice Hall.

Trelease, Jim. (1982). *The Read-Aloud Handbook*. New York: Penguin Books.

Wagner, Joseph Anthony. (1970). *Children's Literature Through Storytelling*. Dubuque, IA: Wm. C. Brown, Co.

Wilson, Jane B. (1979). *The Story Experience*. Metuchen, NJ: Scarecrow Press.

Ziskind, Sylvia. (1976). *Telling Stories to Children*. New York: H. W. Wilson, Co.

On Folklore and Fairy Tales

Adams, Jeff. (1986). *The Conspiracy of the Text: The Place of Narrative in the Development of Thought*. London: Routledge & Kegan Paul.

Arrowsmith, Nancy. (1977). *A Field Guide to the Little People*. New York: Hill and Wang.

Attebery, Brian. (1980). *The Fantasy Tradition in American Literature from Irving to Le Guin*. Bloomington, IN: Indiana University Press.

Bettelheim, Bruno. (1975). *The Uses of Enchantment: The Meaning of Fairy Tales*. New York: Alfred A. Knopf.

Beyond The Looking Glass: Extraordinary Works of Fairy Tale & Fantasy. (1974). Jonathan Cott, Editor. London: Hart-Davis, MacGibbon.

Blount, Margaret. (1974). *Animal Land: The Creatures of Children's Fiction*. New York: Avon.

Bottigheimer, Ruth B. (1987). *Grimms' Bad Girls and Bold Boys: The Moral and Social Vision of the Tales*. New Haven, CT: Yale University Press.

Bridges to Fantasy. (1982). George Slusser and Others, Editors. Cabondale, IL: Southern Illinois University.

Briggs, Katharine M. (1967). *The Fairies in Tradition and Literature*. London: Routledge & Kegan Paul.

Briggs, Katharine M. (1978). *The Vanishing People: Fairy Lore and Legends*. New York: Pantheon.

Brown, Carolyn S. (1987). *The Tall Tale in American Folklore and Literature*. Knoxville, TN: University of Tennessee.

Carter, Lin. (1973). *Imaginary Worlds*. New York: Ballantine Books.

Cinderella: A Casebook. (1983). Alan Dundes, Editor. New York: Wildman Press.

Clarkson, Atelia, and Gilbert Cross. (1980). *World Folktales: A Scribner Resource Collection*. New York: Scribner's and Sons.

Cook, Elizabeth. (1976). *The Ordinary and the Fabulous*. Cambridge, England: Cambridge University Press.

Cruikshank, George. (1910). *The Cruikshank Fairy-Book*. New York: Putnam's Sons.

de Camp, L. Sprague. (1976). *Literary Swordsmen and Sorcerers: The Makers of Heroic Fantasy*. Sauk City, WI: Arkham House.

Dorson, Richard M. (1968). *The British Folklorists: A History*. Chicago, IL: University of Chicago Press.

Dorson, Richard M. (1976). *Folklore and Fakelore: Essays Toward a Discipline of Folk Studies*. Cambridge, MA: Harvard University Press.

Dundes, Alan. (1965). *The Study of Folklore*. Englewood Cliffs, NJ: Prentice Hall.

Edwards, Malcolm, and Robert Holdstock. (1983). *Realms of Fantasy*. Garden City, NY: Doubleday.

Ellis, John M. (1983). *One Fairy Story Too Many: The Brothers Grimm and Their Tales*. Chicago, IL: University of Chicago Press.

Fables: From Incunabula to Modern Picture Books. (1966). Barbara Quinnam, Compiler. Washington, DC: Library of Congress.

Fairy Tales and Society: Illusion, Allusion and Paradigm. (1986). Ruth B. Bottigheimer, Editor. Philadelphia, PA: University of Pennsylvania Press.

Fine, Elizabeth C. (1985). *The Folklore Text: From Performance to Print.* Bloomington, IN: Indiana University Press.

Folk Literature and Children: An Annotated Bibliography of Secondary Materials. (1981). George Shannon, Compiler. Westport, CT: Greenwood Press.

Folklore and Folktales Around the World. (1972). Ruth Kearney Carlson, Editor. Newark, DE: International Reading Association.

Gose, Elliott B. (1985). *The World of the Irish Wonder Tale: An Introduction to the Study of Fairy Tales.* Buffalo, NY: University of Toronto Press.

Handbook of American Folklore. (1983). Richard M. Dorson, Editor. Bloomington, IN: Indiana University Press.

Hartland, Edwin Sidney. (1890). *The Science of Fairy Tales: An Inquiry Into Fairy Mythology.* New York: Frederick A. Stokes Co.

Irwin, William R. (1976). *The Game of the Impossible: A Rhetoric of Fantasy.* Urbana, IL: University of Illinois Press.

Kennard, Jean E. (1975). *Number and Nightmare: Forms of Fantasy in Contemporary Fiction.* Hamden, CT: Archon Books.

Krappe, Alexander H. (1964). *The Science of Folklore.* New York: Norton.

Kready, Laura. (1916). *A Study of Fairy Tales.* Boston, MA: Houghton Mifflin.

Krohn, Kaarle. (1971). *Folklore Methodology.* Austin, TX: American Folklore Society/University of Texas.

Le Guin, Ursula K. (1979). *The Language of the Night: Essays on Fantasy and Science Fiction.* New York: Perigee Books.

Lochhead, Marion. (1977). *The Renaissance of Wonder.* Edinburgh, Scotland: Canongate.

Luthi, Max. (1982). *The European Folktale: Form and Nature.* Trans. by John D. Niles. Bloomington, IN: Indiana University Press.

_____. (1984). *The Fairytale As Art Form and Portrait of Man.* Trans. by Jon Erickson. Bloomington, IN: Indiana University Press.

_____. (1976). *Once Upon A Time: On the Nature of Fairy Tales*. Trans. by Lee Chadeayne and Paul Gottwald. Bloomington, IN: Indiana University Press.

Macculloch, J. A. (1905). *The Childhood of Fiction: A Study of Folk Tales and Primitive Thought*. London: John Murray, Albermarle Street.

Mercatante, Anthony S. (1974). *Zoo of the Gods: Animals in Myth, Legend and Fable*. New York: Harper & Row.

Moore, Raylyn. (1974). *Wonderful Wizard, Marvelous Land*. Bowling Green, OH: Bowling Green University Popular Press.

Opie, Iona, and Peter Opie. (1974). *The Classic Fairy Tales*. London: Oxford University Press.

Pitcher, Evelyn G., and Ernst Prelinger. (1963). *Children Tell Stories: An Analysis of Fantasy*. New York: International Universities Press.

Propp, Vladimir. (1968). *Morphology of the Folktale*. Trans. by Laurence Scott. Austin, TX: University of Texas Press.

Propp, Valdimir. (1984). *Theory and History of Folklore*. Trans. by Ariadna Martin and Richard Martin. Minneapolis, MN: University of Minnesota Press.

Sale, Roger. (1978). *Fairy Tale and After*. Cambridge, MA: Harvard University Press.

Summerfield, Geoffrey. (1985). *Fantasy and Reason: Children's Literature in the Eighteenth Century*. Athens, GA: University of Georgia Press.

Sinfen, Ann. (1984). *In Defense of Fantasy: A Study of the Genre in English and American Literature Since 1945*. London: Routledge & Kegan Paul.

Thompson, Stith. (1977). *The Folktale*. Berkeley, CA: University of California Press. (reprint of 1946 edition).

Thomas, Katherine Elwes. (1930). *The Real Personages of Mother Goose*. Boston, MA: Lothrop, Lee & Shepard Co.

Tolkien, J. R. R. (1965). *Tree and Leaf*. New York: Houghton Mifflin.

Yolen, Jane. (1981). *Touch Magic: Fantasy, Faerie and Folklore in the Literature of Childhood*. New York: Philomel Books.

Zipes, Jack. (1979). *Breaking the Magic Spell: Radical Theories of Folk & Fairy Tales*. Austin, TX: University of Texas.

_____. (1986). *Don't Bet On the Prince: Contemporary Feminist Fairy Tales in North America and England*. New York: Methuen.

_____. (1983). *Fairy Tales and the Art of Subversion*. New York: Wildman Press.

_____. (1983). *The Trials and Tribulations of Little Red Riding Hood*. South Hadley, MA: J. F. Bergin Publishers.

Class Assignments

Storytelling Sampler: This is for your personal use in the future and should be designed with this practical use in mind. You must include photocopies of 10 stories you have selected; at least one must be a folktale, one a fairy tale and one a tall tale. Try to include short and longer tales. Include only those tales that you feel you will be able to tell. For each story included you must add a story structure and map. You may also include any relevant materials for yourself. You should examine variants and versions of the selected stories. Be sure that you have the story intact and that you have provided the source for your story. You are to maintain a complete listing of each story collection that you examine with notes on content. You must also include 10 poems that you have chosen as a part of your personal repertoire. In addition, you are to select something you can use as a ritual and design it as a part of the kit. You may also wish to design puppets and/or a stage, flannel board materials, or other materials to be used in the telling if this works for you. The intent is to have a notebook of stories that have been selected and analyzed by you so that story learning is made easier. It is also the beginning of a project that should be a continuous portion of your professional preparation.

Storytelling Practice: Each student will have the opportunity to practice stories, poems, fingerplays, and chants in class throughout the semester. Various forms of evaluation will be used.

Storytelling Celebration: Each student is required to prepare two stories and one poem for presentation to an audience. This presentation will be videotaped for critique. It is suggested that each student purchase a blank tape (VHS) to have a record for future analysis and demonstration.

Storytelling Context: Each student is expected to read within the range of materials identified in the syllabus and use this reading in discussions, particularly relating to folk and fairy tales.

Storytelling Programming: Each student is expected to prepare and present a plan for a storytelling program for a specific audience. It is expected that appropriate beginnings and closings will be discussed as well as the specific stories to be used.

Sample of Ritual Openings and Closings

“Under the Earth I Go.
On the oak leaf I stand.
I ride on the filly.
That was never foaled.
And I carry the dead in my hand.”

“I have learned … that the head does not hear anything until the heart has listened, and that what the heart knows today the head will understand tomorrow.”

“Snip, Snap, Snout, the tale’s run out.”

"If they haven't moved on, why they're still there!"

"And so they were married and lived happily together—may we live as happily and do as well!"

"Long ago and far away, over seven seas and seven mountains and across seven plains, there reigned a...."

"If it had been dark, it was darker now, and if the sound had been loud before, it was louder now, and more horrible, and nearer,...."

"Once on a time, long, long ago, when good people were scarcer, and enchantments more plentiful...."

"Once upon a time, and a very good time it was, though it was neither in my time nor in your time no in any one else's time, there was...."

"Once upon a time when pigs spoke rhyme, and monkeys chewed tobacco, and hens took snuff to make them tough, and ducks went quack, quack, quack!..."

Sample Chants

The grand Old Duke of York
He has ten thousand men,
He marched them up a very high hill
and he marched them down again.
And when he was up he was up
and when he was down he was down.
And when he was only halfway up
He was neither up nor down.

Each student will have copies of "The Lion Hunt" which will be worked on in class for use with children.

Poetry Used in Class

The following poems are among those to be used in class to demonstrate the power of poetry but also to give practice to voice tone and pacing. You will have copies of the poems in hand and are expected to make any appropriate notes on the page.

"The Goblin"—Rose Fyleman

"Galoshes"—Rhoda Bacmeister

"The Mysterious Cat"—Vachel Lindsay

"The Dream Keeper"—Langston Hughes

"Eensy, Weensy Spider"—Author Unknown

"Albert and the Lion"—Marriot Edgar

THE HISTORY OF CHILDREN'S LITERATURE

Course Description:

A historical overview of the literary content, illustration, social values, and publishing of children's literature, primarily in England and the United States. Consideration of scholarship and resources in the field.

Objectives of the Course:

The student, upon completion, will:

— Identify and describe the images of childhood as revealed in children's literature over time.

— Compare and contrast the images of childhood revealed in children's literature to those of philosophical, educational, and sociological theories over time.

— Demonstrate familiarity with major archetypes and motifs of traditional children's literature.

— Identify and describe characteristics of children's textbooks over time.

— Recognize and describe major media types of illustration and identify the most influential illustrators in the history of children's literature.

— Identify and discuss key authors and works in the history of children's literature.

— Identify and describe key publishers and publishing trends in the history of children's literature.

— Describe the nature and extent of early children's book reviewing.

— Analyze the role of the periodical in historical children's literature.

— Use various approaches to study and bibliographic access to historical children's literature.

— Relate the history of children's literature to professional library and educational activities in work with children and youth.

— Read (and enjoy!) a selection of historical children's literature.

Topics to Be Covered in the Course:

— The Beginnings of Children's Literature

— Developing Views of Childhood

— Bibliographic Access to the History of Children's Literature

— Early Textbooks

— Traditional Literature for Children

— Illustration in Children's Literature

— Children's Book Reviewing in America

— Periodicals for Children

— "The Classics"

— Facsimiles of Early Children's Books

— Series Books for Children

Field Visits:

Students are encouraged to explore, independently, historical collections of children's literature in Rutgers University Libraries and in other libraries. Columbia University Libraries, the New York Public Library, the Philadelphia Free Library, and the Morgan Library in New York City have extraordinary collections of historical children's literature.

There are a number of bookstores in the NYC/NJ area which deal extensively with rare children's books. Visits to these shops can be useful in your exposure to and knowledge of historical children's literature.(Check the NYT Book Review Section or check with the professor for specifics. Call in advance for permission and/or special arrangements.) Whether or not you are able to visit such bookstores, their catalogs are invaluable research tools in the history of children's literature.

Evaluation:

Evaluation will be based upon a combination of factors among which are the following:

— Submission of a reading and visitation log. (Instructions will be given in class.)

— Class participation that shows evidence of having completed class assignments and giving thoughtful consideration to the questions which follow in the next section. (The "seminar" nature of the course will provide ample opportunity for student participation.)

— Submission of worksheets on assigned readings and the completion of the workbook on bibliographic access. (Instructions to be given in class.)

— Class presentation and typed brief outline on selected illustrator.

— Class presentation of selected adult novel with child character.

— Model Research Portfolio.

Questions to Focus Inquiry for the Course:

It is expected that the student will bring specific and detailed information to bear on the questions listed in this section. Such information, although reflecting a synthesis on the part of the student, should, clearly derive from an analysis of, not only the literature itself, but also books about that literature. It is also expected that the student will use philosophical, educational, and sociological ideas to provide a conceptual and contextual base for his/her own ideas.

— Are the philosophical, educational, and sociological theories of childhood reflected in the literature for children? If so, how?

— How does the popular reading of children over the years relate to what scholars have said about the history of childhood and of children's literature?

— How much did early publishers influence the writing and illustrating of books for children?

— To what extent does the history of American children's literature reflect the ideals and attitudes of the American experience?

— How has the history of children's literature been related to the teaching of reading?

— To what extent were early textbooks avenues for recreation and entertainment for children?

— How has the reviewing process influenced what is made available to the child?

— How is the culture of childhood (family life, games, peer relationships) revealed in literature for children?

— What distinctions can be drawn between sentiment and sentimentality in the history of children's literature?

— How were minorities (religious, racial, sexual) treated in early children's literature?

Required Readings:

Aries, Philippe. (1962). *Centuries of Childhood: A Social History of Family Life*. New York: Knopf.

Bingham, Jane and Scholt, Grayce. (1980). *Fifteen Centuries of Children's Literature: An Annotated Chronology of British and American Works in Historical Context*. Westport, CT: Greenwood Press.

De Mause, Lloyd. (1974). *The History of Childhood*. New York: The Psychohistory Press.

Fraser, James. (October 1975). "Children's Literature Collections and Research Libraries," *Wilson Library Bulletin*. Volume 50, No. 2: 128-169.

Gottlieb, Robin. (1978). *Publishing Children's Books in America, 1919-1976: An Annotated Bibliography*. New York: The Children's Book Council.

Kelly, R. Gordon. (September 1963). "American Children's Literature: Historiographic Review," *American Literary Realism*. Volume 6: 89-107.

_____. (May 1974). "Literature and the Historian," *American Quarterly*. Volume 26: 141-159.

Kiefer, Monica. (1948). *American Children Through Their Books, 1700-1835*. Philadelphia, PA: University of Pennsylvania Press.

Lopez, M. D. (Winter 1974). "A Guide to the Interdisciplinary Literature of the History of Childhood," *History of Childhood Quarterly*. Volume I: 463-494.

Meigs, Cornelia, and others. (1969). *A Critical History of Children's Literature*. New York: Macmillan. (Note: If you use an earlier edition [1953] please be sure to read the following to identify errors and concerns: Walbridge, Erle. "A Critical History of Children's Literature Critically Considered," in *The Papers of the Bibliographical Society of America*. Volume XLVIII [second and third quarters, 1974]: 199-208, 263-267).

Richardson, Selma K., Editor. (1980). *Research About Nineteenth-Century Children and Books: Portrait Studies*. Urbana-Champaign, IL: Graduate School of Library Science, University of Illinois.

_____, Editor. (Spring 1979). "The Study and Collecting of Historical Children's Books," *Library Trends*. Volume 27, No. 4: 421-567.

Salway, Lance, Editor. (1976). *Research About Nineteenth-Century Writings on Books for Children*. London: Kestral Books.

Schiller, Justin G. (May 1974). "Magazines for Young America: The First Hundred Years of Juvenile Periodicals," *Columbia Library Columns*. Volume 23: 24-39.

Safford, Barbara Ripp, and Sharyl Smith. (1979). *Children's Literature: A Guide to Research Collections in the Columbia University Libraries*. New York: School of Library Service, Columbia University.

Sutton-Smith, B. (January 1970). "Psychology of Childlore: The Triviality Barrier," *Western Folklore*. Volume 29: 1.

Vandergrift, Kay E. (October 1986). "Collecting: Passion with a Purpose," *School Library Journal*. Vol. 33, No. 2: 91-95.

Vandergrift, Kay E., and Jane Anne Hannigan. (April 1985). "A Celebration of Tradition in Children's Literature," *School Library Journal*. Vol. 31, No. 8: 33-37.

Additional Readings That Provide Background and Explication:

Adams, Bess Porter. (1953). *About Books and Children*. New York: Holt, Rinehart & Winston.

Andrews, Siri, Editor. (1963). *The Hewins Lectures, 1947-62*. Boston, MA: The Horn Book.

Avery, Gillian E. (1975). *Childhood Patterns: A Study of the Heroes and Heroines of Children's Fiction, 1770-1950*. London: Hodder and Stoughton.

Baker, W. (Winter 1975). "Historical Meaning in Mother Goose: Nursery Rhymes Illustrative of English Society Before the Industrial Revolution. *Journal of Popular Culture*. Volume 9: 645-652.

Billman, Carol. (1986). *The Secrets of the Stratemeyer Syndicate: Nancy Drew, The Hardy Boys, and the Million Dollar Fiction Factory*. New York: The Unger Publishing Co.

Cable, Mary. (1975). *The Little Darlings: A History of Child Rearing in America*. New York: Charles Scribner's Sons.

Cadogan, Mary, and Craig, Patricia. (1976). *You're a Brick, Angela! A New Look at Girls' Fiction from 1839 to 1975*. London: Gollanez.

Carpenter, Charles. (1963). *History of American Schoolbooks*. Philadelphia, PA: University of Pennsylvania Press.

Cleverly, John, and Philips, D. C. (1986). *Visions of Childhood: Influential Models from Locke to Spock*. Revised Edition. New York: Teachers College Press.

Curtis, John Gould. (1929). "Saving the Infant Class from Hell," *Scribner's Magazine*. Volume 86: 564-570.

Darling, Richard L. (1968). *The Rise of Children's Book Reviewing in America, 1865-1881*. New York: R. R. Bowker Co.

Darton, Frederick J. Harvey. (1982). *Children's Books in England: Five Centuries of Social Life*. 3rd Edition. Revised by Brian Alderson. Cambridge, England: Cambridge University Press.

Feaver, William. (1977). *When We Were Young: Two Centuries of Children's Book Illustration*. London: Thames and Hudson.

Field, Mrs. E. M. (1968). *The Child and His Book*. Reprint. Detroit, MI: Singing Tree Press.

Gumuchian, Kirkor. (Summer 1941). "From Piety to Entertainment in Children's Books," *American Scholar*. Volume 10, No. 3: 337-350.

Halsey, Rosalie. (1969). *Forgotten Books of the American Nursery: A History of the Development of the American Story-Book*. Reprint. Detroit, MI: Singing Tree Press.

Kelly, R. Gordon. (1974). *Mother Was a Lady: Self and Society in Selected American Children's Periodicals 1865-1890*. Westport, CT: Greenwood Press.

Kolmer, E. (Winter 1976). "The McGuffey Readers: Exponents of American Classical Liberalism," *The Journal of General Education*. Volume 27: 309-316.

MacLeod, Anne Scott. (1975). *A Moral Tale: Children's Fiction and American Culture, 1820-1860*. Hamden, CT: Archon Books.

Rayward, W. Boyd. (October 1976). "What Shall They Read? A Historical Perspective," *Wilson Library Bulletin*. Volume 51: 146-162.

Targ, William, Editor. (1957). *Bibliophile in the Nursery: A Bookman's Treasury of Collectors' Lore on Old and Rare Children's Books*. Cleveland, OH: World.

Thwaite, Mary F. (1972). *From Primer to Pleasure in Reading: An Introduction to the History of Children's Books in England, From the Invention of Printing to 1914 with an Outline of Some Development in Other Countries*. 2nd Edition. London: Library Association.

Townsend, John Rowe. (1975). *Written For Children: An Outline of English-Language Children's Literature*. Revised Edition. Philadelphia, PA: Lippincott.

Tuer, Andrew W. (1897). *The History of the Horn Book*. New York: Charles Scribner's Sons.

————. (1899). *Pages and Pictures From Forgotten Children's Books*. London: Leadenhall Press.

Whalley, Joyce Irene. (1975). *Cobwebs to Catch Flies: Illustrated Books for the Nursery and Schoolroom 1700-1900*. Berkeley, CA: University of California Press.

Wooden, Warren W. (1986). *Children's Literature of the English Renaissance*. Lexington, KY: University Press of Kentucky.

Periodicals That May Prove Helpful in the Study of Historical Children's Literature:

Children's Literature. (Formerly *Children's Literature: the Great* Excluded.)

Children's Literature Association Quarterly

Children's Literature in Education

Horn Book Magazine

The Lion and the Unicorn

The New Advocate

Phaedrus: An International Annual Journal of Children's Literature Research

Signal: Approaches to Children's Books.

Bibliographical Resources in the Study of Historical Children's Literature:

Items for this aspect of the course are contained in the separate workbook to be distributed by the professor.

Assignments:

1. Discussion of the Classic Adult Novel: Read or reread a classic (or at least well-known) adult novel from among the titles listed. Think critically about the work from the singular point of view of how the

nature of the child and the condition of childhood are represented via the child character or characters. Communicate your impressions to the class in a brief (5 to 8 minute) presentation. *Do not recount the plot but rather discuss questions such as*:

— Is childhood characterized as a halcyonic or nightmarish period?

— Are there striking or subtle autobiographical references to the author's life?

— Is the child exceptional, proto-heroic or more in the normal range?

— Is the portrayal of the child character(s) predominantly external or internal?

— Is the view of childhood represented by the novel appropriate to the date of composition and/or to the fictional time setting?

— Does this work evoke comparison to or contrast with any children's book(s) of the same time period in its perception of the child and of childhood?

— Is the portrayal realistic for a child of the class, society, situation, and time?

List of Novels:

Jane Austin	*Pride and Prejudice*
James Baldwin	*Go Tell It on the Mountain*
William M. Campbell	*The Bad Seed*
Agatha Christie	*Crooked House*
Charles Dickens	*Hard Times*
	Oliver Twist
_____.	*Bleak House*
_____.	
James T. Farrell	*Young Lonigan* (in the trilogy *Studs Lonigan*)
William Golding	*Lord of the Flies*
Herman Hesse	*Demian*
Richard Hughes	*A High Wind in Jamaica*
Henry James	*The Turn of the Screw*
James Joyce	*A Portrait of the Artist As a Young Man*
Jerzy Kosinski	*The Painted Bird*
Harper Lee	*To Kill a Mockingbird*
Doris Lessing	*Memoirs of a Survivor*
Carson McCullers	*The Member of the Wedding*
Vladimir Nabokov	*Lolita*
Alan Paton	*Too Late the Phalarope*
Marcel Proust	*Swann's Way*
Francois Truffaut	*400 Blows*
_____.	*The Wild Child*

2. Facsimiles of Historical Children's Books: The objective of this assignment is twofold: 1) to permit you to read several facsimiles of early items since the originals are not easily available; and 2) to permit you to distinguish among the various types of facimiles and reproductions. Examine as many items as you are able to locate, particularly some of the new examples available from the museums, publishers, and special presses. Consider the recommendations listed below as well as those on page 525 of the Robertson and Stahlschmidt article. After consideration, do you agree with their position? *Read*: Robertson, Ina, and Stahlschmidt, Agnes. (Spring 1979). "Facsimiles of Historical Children's Books." *Library Trends*. Vol. 27, No. 4: 513-527.

" ... additional criteria are necessary to ensure the production of quality facsimiles. The following recommendations are therefore proposed:

A.   The reprint should include the original copy in its entirety, consisting of *all* pages on which printing appears, including any advertisements.

B.   In addition to full and exact reproduction of the original title page, the publisher should include a half-title page or colophon (or a target card for microforms), giving the name and location of the publisher of the facsimile and the year of publication of the facsimile.

C.   Book-form facsimiles should be the same size as the original. (Alteration in size may be desirable if it results in a manageable book, e.g., wider margins to facilitate rebinding and to allow the book to lie flat while being used.) The original size should be indicated in the reprint edition. If there has been reduction in size, the reduction ratio should be stated." — p. 525.

3. *Select and read* at least one collection from the list below and type a card with your name and the collection used, items read, etc., to submit to the professor. Prepare remarks for class as indicated by the professor.

Arnold, Arnold. (1969). *Pictures and Stories from Forgotten Children's Books*. New York: Dover Publications.

DeVries, Leonard. (1965). *Flowers of Delight*. New York: Pantheon Press.

_____. (1967). *Little Wide-Awake: An Anthology from Victorian Children's Books and Periodicals in the Collections of Anne and Fernand G. Renier*. Cleveland, OH: World.

Frye, Burton C., Editor. (1969). *A St. Nicholas Anthology: The Early Years*. New York: Meredith Press.

The Glorious Mother Goose. (1988). Selected by Cooper Edens. New York: Atheneum.

Haviland, Virginia, and Coughlan, Margaret, Editors. (1974). *Yankee Doodle's Literary Sampler; Being An Anthology of Diverse Works Published for the Edification and/or Entertainment of Young Readers in America Before 1900*. New York: Thomas Y. Crowell.

Our Old Nursery Rhymes. (1989). Illus. by Henriette Willebeek Le Mair. New York: Philomel. (reprint of 1911 edition)

Tail Feathers From Mother Goose. (1988). The Opie Rhyme Book. Boston, MA: Little, Brown and Co.

Temple, Nigel, Editor. (1970). *Seen and Not Heard: A Garland of Fancies for Victorian Children.* New York: The Dial Press.

Select and read as many of the following as you can manage:

Bonn, Franz. (1978). *The Children's Theatre.* (reproduction of 1878 edition) London and New York: Kestral Books.

Crane, Walter. (1956). *Mr. Michael Mouse Unfolds His Tale.* (reproduced from the original manuscript in the collection of Mrs. Catherine T. Patterson with permission of Yale University Library) New York: Merrimack Publishing Corp.

The Great Menagerie. (1979). (an antique adaptation of the 1884 edition) London and New York: Kestral Books.

The History of Little Fanny. (1830). London: S. and J. Fuller. (Reprint edition available from Green Tiger Press, La Jolla, California.)

Meggendorfer, Lothar. (1979). *A Doll's House: A Reproduction of the Antique 1890c. Pop-up Book.* New York: The Metropolitan Museum of Art.

_____. (1979). *International Circus.* (A reproduction of the 1887 Antique Pop-Up Book) London and New York: Kestral Books.

Newbery, John. (1967). *A Little Pretty Pocket-Book.* Introductory essay by M. F. Thwaite. New York: Harcourt, Brace & World.

Nister, Ernest. (1980). *Animal Tales.* (A reproduction from the Antique Book of 1894) New York: Collins.

_____. (1980). *Magic Windows.* (A reproduction of an antique revolving picture book of 1895) New York: Philomel Books.

A selection of titles of reproductions, without authorship identification or date of publication; most published by Merrimack Publishing Corp.:

The Book of Frogs and Mice

The Children's Omnibus

Doggie Pranks

The Last of the Mohicans

Miss Brownie: The Story of a Superior Mouse

Moving Picture Teddies

Railroad Story Book

Rip Van Winkle

2 Wonderful Animal Stories: The Dogs' Dinner Party and The Cats' Dinner Party

Turn Again, Turn Again!

Other titles may be added by the professor, however, all of the above titles are available from various department and bookstores such as Macy's, Daltons, etc. You may wish to purchase one for display and discussion with children. (They are almost all priced between $1.50 and $9.95).

You may also wish to contact The Green Tiger Press, 7458 La Jolla Blvd., La Jolla, California, 92037 in order to be on the mailing list. Green Tiger Press is the producer of some fine reproductions of illustrations from children's literature as well as posters, postal cards, etc. They have also produced a number of titles that are fine examples of book art.

3. *Read* a selection of works from the list which follows that includes both individual titles and series books. The professor will supply copies of many of the titles which must be cared for in a special manner as they are *original editions not replicas*. These items are from the personal collection of the professor.

Abbott, Jacob. (1854). *Rollo in Paris*. Boston, MA: W. J. Reynolds & Co.

Abbott, Jacob. (1857). *The Rollo Story Books/Rollo's Garden*. Boston, MA: Phillips, Sampson & Company.

Alger, Horatio, Jr. (n.d.). *Tony the Tramp or Right is Might*. New York: Hurst & Company.

Ewing, Juliana Horatia. (n.d.) *Lob-Lie-By-The-Fire, and Other Tales*. New York: A. L. Burt Company.

———. (1887). *The Story of a Short Life*. Boston, MA: Roberts Brothers.

Finley, Martha. (1867). *Elsie Dinsmore*. New York: Dodd, Mead Company. (Or any other title in series)

Goodrich, Samuel Griswold. (1863). *Tale of the Sea and Land*. By Peter Parley. New York: Sheldon & Co.

Hegan, Alice Caldwell. (1902). *Mrs. Wiggs of the Cabbage Patch*. New York: The Century Co., 1901c.

Henty, George Alfred. (n.d.) *For Name and Fame: or, Through Afghan Passes*. New York: A. L. Burt Company, (after 1902).

Jewett, John Howard. (1907). *Gyp At Home and Abroad*. New York: Frederick A. Stokes Company.

May, Sophie. (1865). *Fairy Book, Little Prudy Series*. Boston, MA: Lee and Shepard.

———. (1894). *Aunt Madge's Story; Little Prudy's Flyaway Series*. Boston, MA: Lee and Shepard.

Memoirs of a London Doll, Written by Herself. (1852). Edited by Mrs. Fairstar. Boston, MA: Ticknor, Reed and Fields.

Molesworth, Mary Louisa (Stewart). (189-). *Robin Redbreast; A Story for Girls*. New York: A. L. Burt Company.

Optic, Oliver. (1869). *Work and Win; or Noddy Newman on a Cruise*. Boston, MA: Lee and Shepard.

Pollard, Josephine. (1885). *Our Hero General U.S. Grant, When, Where and How He Fought, in Words of One Syllable with Eighty-Six Etchings by Edwin Forbes*. New York: McLoughlin Brothers.

Standish, Burt L. (1910). *Dick Merriwell's Fighting Chance or the Split in the Varsity*. New York: Street & Smith Company.

Wiggin, Kate Douglas. (1890). *The Birds' Christmas Carol*. Cambridge, MA: The Riverside Press.

Wiggin, Kate Douglas. (1912). *A Child's Journey With Dickens*. Boston and New York: Houghton Mifflin.

Yonge, Charlotte M. (1894). *The Cook and the Captive, or, Attalus the Hostage*. New York: Thomas Whittaker.

Yonge, Charlotte Mary. (1871). *Countess Kate, by the author of The heir of Redclyffe*. 3rd Edition. London: J. and C. Mozley, Masters and Son.

The professor may suggest an alternative title or author as need arises. It may also be feasible for the entire class to read the same book; if so, this will be announced. All books read for this section should be entered into the log.

4. Illustrator Fact Sheet: Select an illustrator from the list provided. Prepare a two to three page fact sheet for your colleagues containing the following:

— Personal Data

— Primary Techniques Used

— Basic Qualities of Work

— Major Works Illustrated

— Minor Works Illustrated

— Primary Sources of Information About this Person and his/her Work.

— If possible, include a photocopied example of work representative of the artist's style.

— In addition, bring to class the oldest, rarest, most unusual, or best exemplars of this person's work to share with others in a brief oral presentation. (Do not repeat what you are giving your classmates on paper!)

Please select and sign up for a particular illustrator to assure that each student is studying the work of a different individual.

List of Illustrators:

John Batten	(1871-1932)
Thomas Bewick	(1753-1828)
William Blake	(1757-1827)
Louis Boutet de Monvel	(1850-1913)
Leslie Brooke	(1862-1940)
Randolph Caldecott	(1846-1901)
Palmer Cox	(1840-1924)
Walter Crane	(1845-1915)
George Cruikshank	(1792-1878)
Edmund Dulac	(1882-1953)
Kate Greenaway	(1846-1901)
Arthur Hughes	(1832-1915)
Kay Nielsen	(1886-1957)
Maxfield Parrish	(1870-1966)
Beatrix Potter	(1866-1943)
Howard Pyle	(1853-1911)
Arthur Rackham	(1867-1939)
William Heath Robinson	(1872-1944)
Ernest Shepard	(1879-1976)
Jessie Wilcox Smith	(1863-1935)
Sir John Tenniel	(1820-1914)
N. C. Wyeth	(1882-1945)

The student should make every effort to examine at least one work illustrated by each of the artists named in the list. Again, the Green Tiger Press will be most useful in seeing the range of illustration.

List of Titles that May Prove Helpful in Examining Illustration:

Bader, Barbara. (1976). *American Picturebooks from Noah's Ark to the Beast Within*. New York: Macmillan.

Crane, Walter. (1979). *Of the Decorative Illustration of Books Old and New*. London: Bell & Hyman. (First published in 1896.)

Feaver, William. (1976). *When We Were Young: Two Centuries of Children's Book Illustration*. London: Gollanez.

Mahony, Bertha and others. (1947). *Illustrators of Children's Books 1744-1945*. Boston, MA: The Horn Book.

Ovenden, Graham, Editor. (1972). *The Illustrators of Alice in Wonderland and Through the Looking Glass*. London: Academy Editors.

Pitz, Henry C. (1963). *Illustrating Children's Books*. New York: Watson-Guptill.

Various editions of the *Horn Book* have been devoted to illustrators. For example, see the Arthur Rackham issue of May-June, 1940 and the Leslie Brooke issue of May-June 1941.

5. During the course it is important that you examine carefully some of the classic titles that have achieved importance in children's literature. These titles include those works that may still be read or suggested to children today. Please select and read as many as possible of the list given below:

Louisa M. Alcott	*Little Women*
Thomas B. Aldrich	*Story of a Bad Boy*
Helen Bannerman	*The Story of Little Black Sambo*
James Mathew Barrie	*Peter Pan*
L. Frank Baum	*The Wizard of Oz*
John Bennett	*Master Skylark*
France Hodgson Burnett	*The Secret Garden*
Carlo Collodi	*The Adventures of Pinocchio*
Susan Coolidge	*What Katy Did*
James Fenimore Cooper	*The Deerslayer*
Mary Mapes Dodge	*Hans Brinker, or, The Silver Skates*
Sir Arthur Conan Doyle	*The Adventures of Sherlock Holmes*
Alexander Dumas	*The Three Musketeers*
Kenneth Grahame	*The Wind in the Willows*
Lucretia Peabody Hale	*The Complete Peterkin Papers*
Joel Chandler Harris	*Uncle Remus*
Helen Hunt Jackson	*Ramona*
Charles Kingsley	*Water Babies*

Rudyard Kipling	*The Jungle Book*
Selma Lagerlof	*The Wonderful Adventures of Nils*
Sinclair Lewis	*Holiday House*
Hugh Lofting	*The Story of Doctor Dolittle*
George MacDonald	*At the Back of the North Wind*
Capt. Frederick Marryat	*The Children of the New Forest*
A. A. Milne	*Winnie-the-Pooh*
L. M. Montgomery	*Anne of Green Gables*
Edith Nesbit	*The Story of the Treasure Seekers*
James Otis	*Toby Tyler, or, Ten Weeks With a Circus*
Eleanor H. Porter	*Pollyana*
Beatrix Potter	*The Tale of Peter Rabbit*
Howard Pyle	*Otto of the Silver Hand*
Charles Reade	*The Cloister and the Hearth*
Laura Elizabeth Howe Richards	*Captain January*
John Ruskin	*The King of the Golden River*
Anna Sewell	*Black Beauty*
Margaret Sidney	*The Five Little Peppers and How They Grew*
Catherine Sinclair	*Holiday House*
Johanna Spyri	*Heidi*
Robert Louis Stevenson	*Treasure Island*
Frank R. Stockton	*The Bee-Man of Orn and Other Fanciful Tales*
Mark Twain	*The Prince and the Pauper*
Jules Verne	*Twenty Thousand Leagues Under the Sea*
Kate Douglas Wiggin	*Rebecca of Sunnybrook Farm*
Oscar Wilde	*The Happy Prince and Other Tales*

6. Traditional Literature: This will permit you the opportunity to read extensively in both fairy tale and folklore. At the same time, it will be useful for you to examine several books that focus on discussion of these genres. Select and read as many titles as possible during the course of the semester.

Bettelheim, Bruno. (1976). *The Uses of Enchantment: The Meaning and Importance of Fairy Tales*. New York: Knopf.

Briggs, Katherine M. (1967). *The Fairies in Tradition and Literature*. Chicago, IL: University of Chicago Press.

Cook, Elizabeth. (1969). *The Ordinary and the Fabulous: An Introduction to Myths, Legends and Fairy Tales for Teachers and Storytellers*. London: Cambridge University Press.

Thompson, Stith. (1946). *The Folktale*. New York: Dryden.

List of Folk and Fairy Tale Titles:

Grimm, Jakob Ludwig Karl and Grimm, Wilhelm Karl. (1944). *The Complete Grimm's Fairy Tales*. New York: Pantheon.

Jacobs, Joseph, Editor. (1891). *English Fairy Tales*. New York: Putnam.

Lang, Andrew, Editor. (1889). *The Blue Fairy Book*. London: Longmans. (Compare to new revisions.)

Opie, Iona and Opie, Peter. (1974). *The Classic Fairy Tales*. London: Oxford University Press.

7. Model Research Portfolio: An important aspect of the study of historical children's literature is the bibliographical control and access to relevant materials. In order to help you to familiarize yourself with this aspect of scholarship two assignments have been developed:

1. The Workbook for examination of resources in historical children's literature; and

2. A Simulation portfolio.

The Workbook will be distributed by the professor and you will be responsible for completing your annotations and comments, as well as sample pages by the end of the semester. You may wish to punch holes in your workbook and use a three-ring binder.

The Model Research Portfolio is, in part, a simulation exercise.

You are to assume that you are the librarian in a research library with a collection of historical children's literature. A scholar approaches you asking for assistance in locating information on a particular topic (see list of topics) which is tangential to his/her major research.

Your objective is to provide the first hours of direction to the scholar in order to permit the most efficient use of his/her time. Your scholar is eager to explore this topic but is anxious to efficiently synthesize and incorporate this information into his/her major work. In order to accomplish this, please follow the outline provided *but add* the touches that will make this portfolio exciting to use. (This might include format, design, packaging, illustrations, etc.) Remember that you are responsible to the user of the collection. For purposes of this simulation you are to assume that you have all the research tools available as well as a reasonable selection of primary and secondary materials.

Outline for the Model Research Portfolio:

—   Select the target item from the list below in consultation with the professor.

— Identify basic facts about the item selected; e.g., if a person, events of life, major/minor works, etc.

— Indicate access terms for the item.

— Select outstanding books and articles about this item; include a form of abstract.

— Reproduce one or more articles/chapters of books that might be deemed critical to understanding this item.

— Identify manuscript collections and other collections that might prove useful.

— Prepare a series of questions that might be asked about this item.

— Identify events of educational, historical, and sociological context that are important to recognize in relation to this item.

— Identify other items/names that are related to this topic.

— Indicate availability of appropriate works: facsimiles, reprints, microforms, etc.

— Identify particular problems concerning this item; e.g., censorship.

— Indicate if the item is in contemporary use with children.

— Indicate the printing history of item, if relevant.

— You may wish to place the item in the world of historical children's literature; indicate how important the item is. To whom? Why?

— Is there a relationship of the item to the media? e.g., film and television.

— Has the item a later history of production in other formats, such as dolls, toys, etc.?

— List the sources consulted.

List of Suggested Topics for the Research Portfolio: (Others may be substituted after consultation with the professor.)

Jacob Abbott

William Taylor Adams

Thomas Bailey Aldrich

American Sunday School Union

American Tract Society

Battledores

Boys of England

Edgar Rice Burroughs

Chatterbox

Lydia Maria Child

Maria Edgeworth

Edmund Evans

Julia Ewing

Samuel Goodrich

Goody Two Shoes

George Alfred Henty

Caroline M. Hewins

Lucy Larcum

Little Wide Awake

Mrs. Molesworth

Horace Scudder

Isaiah Thomas

Sarah Trimmer

Frederick Warne

Charlotte Yonge

AESTHETIC CRITICISM OF LITERATURE
FOR CHILDREN AND YOUTH

Course Description: Application of the principles of aesthetic criticism to the selection of literature for children and youth in relation to social values and approaches to the teaching of reading; analysis of research in the field of literature for children and youth.

Objectives of the Course:

The student, upon completion of this course will:

— Identify the commonalities and differences among various approaches to and types of literary criticism.

— Discuss the relationship between aesthetic criticism and the development of taste.

— Analyze and describe specific examples of critical theory, particularly indicating the application to literature for children and youth.

— Use critical theories in the analysis of materials for children and youth.

— Examine and discuss the relationship of the current emphasis on reader-response criticism to work with children and youth.

— Discuss and use various methodological approaches to research in literature for children and youth.

— Explore the relationship between aesthetic excellence and social issues in the selection of books for children and youth.

— Explore the relationship between the teaching of reading and the teaching of literature in American schools.

"A true critic ought to dwell rather upon excellencies than imperfections, to discover the concealed beauties of a writer, and communicate to the world such things as are worth their observation." — Joseph Addison in *The Spectator*, No. 291, February 2, 1712.

The course is divided into several units. Some beginning readings are identified for each unit; additional references are also listed and others will be mentioned during classes. Since this is an advanced class, it is assumed that students will already be familiar with the basic materials in children's literature and with a wide variety of both historical and contemporary books for children and young people. Throughout the semester, principles of aesthetic criticism will be applied to specific works for children and young people.

"An age that has no criticism is either an age in which art is immobile, hieratic, and confined to the reproduction of formal types, or an age that possesses no art at all." — Oscar Wilde in *The Critic As Artist*.

Unit One: Aesthetic Criticism

The purpose of this unit is to provide the opportunity to explore the commonalities and differences among various approaches to criticism. The student is expected to compare and contrast, in some detail, the various types of literary criticism. The questions that follow may prove useful in your thinking about this topic:

— What is criticism?

— How and to what degree have prominent approaches to critical theory corresponded to concurrent societal concerns and beliefs?

— Is what has been called "wise eclecticism" a valid approach to literary criticism or merely an excuse to ignore or eliminate critical theory?

— Must one understand literary genres and compositional elements in order to practice any form of literary criticism?

— What is the difference between reviewing and criticism?

— What is the relationship between aesthetic criticism and the development of taste?

— Is there a conflict between aesthetic excellence and social issues in book selection for children and youth?

"The practice of 'reviewing' ... in general has nothing in common with the art of criticism." — Henry James in *Criticism*.

Required Readings for Unit One:

Frye, Northrop. (1963). *The Educated Imagination*. Toronto, Canada: Canadian Broadcasting Co.

Kwant, Remy C. (1967). *Critique: Its Nature and Function*. Pittsburgh, PA: Duquesne University Press.

Suleiman, Susan, and Inge Crosman, Editors. (1980). *The Reader in the Text: Essays on Audience and Interpretation*. Princeton, NJ: Princeton University Press.

Tompkins, Jane P., Editor. (1980). *Reader-Response Criticism: From Formalism to Post-Structuralism*. Baltimore, MD: The John Hopkins University Press.

Wellek, Rene and Austin Warren. (1977). *Theory of Literature*. New Revised Edition. New York: Harcourt, Brace, Jovanovich.

White, Mary Lou. (1976). *Children's Literature: Criticism and Response*. Columbus, OH: Charles E. Merrill, Co.

Optional Readings for Unit One:

Bettelheim, Bruno. (1975). *The Uses of Enchantment: The Meaning of Fairy Tales*. New York: Alfred A. Knopf.

Crews, Frederick C. (1965). *The Pooh Perplex*. New York: E. P. Dutton.

Dewey, John. (1930). *Construction and Criticism*. New York: Columbia University Press. (The First Davies Memorial Lecture).

Forster, E. M. (1927). *Aspects of the Novel*. New York: Harcourt, Brace & World.

Graff, Gerald. (1979). *Literature Against Itself: Literary Ideas in Modern Society*. Chicago, IL: The University of Chicago Press.

Heins, Paul, Editor. (1977). *Crosscurrents of Criticism: Horn Book Essays 1968-1977*. Boston, MA: The Horn Book.

James, Henry. (1934). *The Art of the Novel: Critical Prefaces*. New York: Charles Scribner's Sons.

Langer, Susanne. (1957). *Problems of Art*. New York: Charles Scribner's Sons.

Lentricchia, Frank. (1980). *After the New Criticism*. Chicago, IL: The University of Chicago Press.

Phillips, Robert, Editor. (1972). *Aspects of Alice*. London: Victor Gollancz.

> "I am bound by my own definition of criticism: a disinterested endeavor to learn and propagate the best that is known and thought in the world." — Matthew Arnold in *Essays in Criticism*

Assignments Relating to One Unit:

Write a critical review of a children's book.

Steps in Writing a Critical Review

Since many of you are both graduate students and teachers, instructions for the preparation of a critical review have been prepared for both.

As A Student

1. Select a literary work that you enjoy and ask yourself "What do I like about this work?" "What is this work about?"

As A Teacher

1. Share with students a wide variety of literary works and encourage them to discuss those works in their own language. Ask questions such as "What is this work about?" "How does it differ from other works you have read?" "How is it similar to other works?"

2. Express what you like and/or dislike about this work in terms of literary elements, motifs, genres, etc.

2. Analyze student answers to #1 above to help them connect their responses to established structures of literary knowledge.

3. Decide how you can use standard organizational structures or critical theory in relating literary ideas to the work selected.

3. Remind students of organizational patterns such as cause/effect, comparison/contrast, etc. Ask "Why?" "For example?" "In comparison to what?"

4. Jot down or outline major aspects of your response in terms of one or more literary theses. These are often combinations of #1 and #2 above, i.e., character + motif = characterization in this work is made more striking because it breaks with traditional expectations. Example: the cowardly lion.

4. Help students formulate what they really want to say about this work. Make sure the focus is a literary one, *not* "I loved this story because it reminded me of the time I...."

5. Write a critical review of no more than six (6) pages and be prepared to give a brief summary of your analysis in class.

5. Remind students of the distinction between a review and a report and that the task of the reviewer is not just to *tell others of his/her opinions but to convince* them of the soundness of the critical judgment.

Unit Two: Literary Theorists

The purpose of this unit is to provide an opportunity for the student to examine the work of a number of critical theorists in order to see the significance and use of that work when applied to the area of literature for children and youth. Since Northrop Frye is one critic whose writings have included a consideration of children's literature and popular culture, he will serve as an exemplar. Louise Rosenblatt is another critic whose work has stimulated a great deal of interest in those concerned with children and youth. Her critical theory makes an interesting contrast to that of Frye. One of the intentions in this unit is to make use of a variety of theories in our examination of children's literature. The questions which follow may prove useful to individual students and to the class.

— How does Northrop Frye apply his critical theory to children's literature? How have others related his work to this body of literature?

— Identify what you consider to be the key elements in Frye's theories?

— Does Frye's concept of romance add to your perception of books for children and youth? If so, how?

— How applicable are interpretations of Frye's theories by such authors as Cawelti, Sloan, and Vandergrift?

— How does the work of Jung, Campbell, and Bettelheim relate to that of Frye and other archetypal critics?

— How does Rosenblatt distinguish between aesthetic and efferent reading?

— What are the implications of Rosenblatt's transactional theory of literature for those of us who work with children?

— How might research be structured to investigate reader-responses?

— Using Vandergrift's Model of Meaning-Making, what do you see as the role of the adult intermediary?

— The concept of the implied reader has been articulated through the work of a number of scholars. Explore the relationships, if any, among Rosenblatt, Wolfgang Iser, and Norman Holland.

— What applicability might *semiotica* and levels of meaning as articulated by Roland Barthes have for the study of literature for children and youth?

— What might you extrapolate from the works of George Lukacs, Gaston Bachelard, Frank Kermode, Elaine Showalter, and Ihab Hassan?

— It has been noted that feminist criticism is still unsure of a theory. Comment on this viewpoint.

— What key ideas might be derived from the works of Roland Barthes, Stanley Fish, David Bleich, Wayne Booth, Jonathan Culler, and E. D. Hirsch, Jr.?

"Art, like nature, is the subject of a systematic study, and has to be distinguished from the study itself, which is criticism. It is therefore impossible to 'learn literature'; one learns about it in a certain way, but what one learns, transitively, is the criticism of literature. Similarly, the difficulty often felt in 'teaching literature' arises from the fact that it cannot be done; the criticism of literature is all that can be directly taught." — Northrop Frye in "The Archetypes of Literature"

"There is a danger that literary texts may be used mainly as a medium for generating other activities. Hence the need to make sure that follow-up activities are such as to maintain connection with the lived-through evocation which is the poem or story." — Louise Rosenblatt in "What Facts Does This Poem Teach You?"

"Year after year as freshmen come into college, one finds that even the most verbally proficient of them, often those most intimately drawn to literature, have already acquired a hard veneer, a pseudoprofessional approach. They are anxious to have the correct labels—the right period, the biographical background, the correct evaluation. They read literary histories and biographies, critical essays, and then, if they have time, they read the works." — Louise Rosenblatt in "Acid Test in Teaching Literature" in *English Journal*. February, 1956, p. 71.

Required Readings for Unit Two:

Cawelti, John G. (Winter 1969). "The Concept of Formula in the Study of Popular Literature," *Journal of Popular Culture*. Volume III, No. 3: 381-390. also you might find chapters one and two in (1976). *Adventure, Mystery and Romance*. Chicago, IL: University of Chicago Press, helpful.

Denham, Robert D. (1978). *Northrop Frye and Critical Method*. University Park, PA: The Pennsylvania State University Press.

Frye, Northrop. (1956). *Anatomy of Criticism*. Princeton, NJ: Princeton University Press.

_____. (1972). *On Teaching Literature*. New York: Harcourt, Brace, Jovanovich.

Rosenblatt, Louise M. (1976). *Literature As Exploration*. 3rd Edition. New York: Nobel & Nobel Publishers.

_____. (1978). *The Reader, The Text, The Poem*. Carbondale, IL: Southern Illinois University Press.

Shaw, Peter. (Autumn 1988). "Feminist Literary Criticism: A Report from the Academy," *The American Scholar*. 495-513.

Sloan, Glenna Davis. (1975). *The Child As Critic*. New York: Teachers College Press.

Vandergrift, Kay E. (1980). *Child and Story: The Literary Connection*. New York: Neal-Schuman Publishers, Inc. (Reprinted in paperback in 1986)

_____. (Winter 1987). "Critical Thinking Misfired: Implications of Student Responses to The Shooting Gallery," *School Library Media Quarterly*. 15 (2): 86-91.

"It is commonplace that over the past fifteen years or so we have witnessed extraordinary transformation in literary theory and critical method. Those who hoped to keep quiet, sit it out, and wait for a return to normal must now suppose that they have lost their wager. We have, without question, had some sort of revolution, and are now suffering its aftermath. At one time it was possible for some to believe that utopia had arrived; solutions, ruthless, surgical, had been found to a whole set of problems; new philosophies and new politics of art contemptuously dismissed an ancient regime so blinkered and perverted as to mistake its ideology for objective truth. But since that time simplicity has departed; epochs have followed one another at the accelerated pace revolutions seem to induce; structuralism became post-structuralism before one knew it; new rivals entered the field, to be in their turn subjected to severe criticism; the certainties of 1966 became the anxieties of 1979. And by now we may perhaps say that the bandwagon is slowing down a bit; it is easier to climb aboard, or anyway to inspect the goods on offer and make a choice. There are signs, even, that the rifts between the parties are closing ...." — Frank Kermode in "Figures in the Carpet: On Recent Theories of Narrative Discourse" in *Comparative Criticism: A Yearbook*, Volume 2, E. S. Shaffer, Editor, p. 291.

Required On A Highly Selective Basis:

Because there will not be enough time during one course to complete reading of all of the works of these critics, a sharing process seems to be in order. The list which follows provides at least one title from the body of works of several theorists of significance. Obviously this list is but the beginning; each student is asked to provide additional information through the completion of the assignment for this unit.

"All classes, all human groups, have their narratives, enjoyment of which is very often shared by men with different, even opposing, cultural backgrounds. Caring nothing for the division between good and bad literature, narrative is international, transhistorical, transcultural: it is simply there, like life itself." — Roland Barthes in *Image, Music, Text*.

Bachelard, Gaston. (1969). *The Poetics of Space*. Trans. by Maria Jolas. Boston, MA: Beacon Press.

Bachelard, Gaston. (1969). *The Poetics of Reverie: Childhood, Language and the Cosmos*. Trans. by Daniel Russell. Boston, MA: Beacon Press.

Barthes, Roland. (1967). *Elements of Semiology*. Trans. by Annette Lavers and Colin Smith. London: Jonathan Cape, Ltd.

_____. (1977). *Image, Music, Text*. Trans. by Stephen Heath. New York: Hill and Wang.

_____. (1972). *Mythologies*. Trans. by Annette Lavers. New York: Hill and Wang.

Bleich, David. (1975). *Readings and Feelings: An Introduction to Subjective Criticism*. Urbana, IL: National Council of Teachers of English.

_____. (1978). *Subjective Criticism*. Baltimore, MD: The Johns Hopkins University Press.

Booth, Wayne. (1961). *The Rhetoric of Fiction*. Chicago, IL: The University of Chicago Press.

Culler, Jonathan. (1975). *Structuralist Poetics: Structuralism, Linguistics, and the Study of Literature*. Ithaca, NY: Cornell University Press.

Fish, Stanley E. (1980). *Is There a Text in This Class? The Authority of Interpretive Communities*. Cambridge, MA: Harvard University Press.

_____. (1967). *Surprised by Sin: The Reader in Paradise Lost*. New York: St. Martin's Press.

Hassan, Ihab. (1973). *Contemporary American Literature, 1945-1972*. New York: Frederick Ungar.

Hirsch, E. D. Jr. (1976). *The Aims of Interpretation*. Chicago, IL: The University of Chicago Press.

Holland, Norman. (1975). *The Dynamics of Literary Response*. New York: W. W. Norton.

_____. (1975). *5 Readers Reading*. New Haven, CT: Yale University Press.

Iser, Wolfgang. (1978). *The Act of Reading: A Theory of Aesthetic Response*. Baltimore, MD: The Johns Hopkins University Press.

_____. (1974). *The Implied Reader: Patterns of Communication in Prose Fiction from Bunyan to Beckett*. Baltimore, MD: The Johns Hopkins University Press.

Kermode, Frank. (1966). *The Sense of an Ending: Studies in the Theory of Fiction*. New York: Oxford University Press.

Lukacs, Georg. (1974). *Soul and Form*. Cambridge, MA: MIT Press, translated by Anna Bostock from the 1910 edition.

Mailloux, Steven. (1982). *Interpretive Conventions: The Reader in the Study of American Fiction*. Ithaca, NY: Cornell University Press.

Making A Difference: Feminist Literary Criticism. (1985). Gayle Greene and Coppelia Kahn, Editors. London: Methuen.

Martin, Wallace. (1986). *Recent Theories of Narrative.* Ithaca, NY: Cornell University Press.

Meese, Elizabeth. (1986). *Crossing the Double-Cross: The Practice of Feminist Criticism.* Chapel Hill, NC: University of North Carolina Press.

Miller, J. Hillis. (1982). *Fiction and Repetition: Seven English Novels.* Cambridge, MA: Harvard University Press.

Moi, Toril. (1985). *Sexual/Textual Politics: Feminist Literary Theory.* London: Methuen.

The New Feminist Criticism: Essays on Women, Literature & Theory. (1985). Elaine Showalter, Editor. New York: Pantheon Books.

Norris, Christopher. (1982). *Deconstruction: Theory and Practice.* New York: Methuen.

Northrop Frye in Modern Criticism. (1966). Murray Krieger, Editor. New York: Columbia University Press.

Novarr, David. (1986). *The Lines of Life: Theories of Biography, 1880-1970.* Lafayette, IN: Purdue University Press.

The Poetics of Gender. (1986). Nancy K. Miller, Editor. New York: Columbia University Press.

Pratt, Annis and others. (1981). *Archetypal Patterns in Women's Fiction.* Bloomington, IN: Indiana University Press.

Pratt, Mary Louise. (1977). *Toward a Speech Act Theory of Literary Discourse.* Bloomington, IN: Indiana University Press.

Psychoanalysis and the Literary Process. (1970). Frederick C. Crews, Editor. Berkeley, CA: University of California Press.

Psychoanalysis and the Question of the Text. (1978). Geoffrey Hartman, Editor. Baltimore, MD: The Johns Hopkins University Press.

The Reader in the Text: Essays on Audience and Interpretation. (1980). Susan Suleiman and Inge Crosman, Editors. Princeton, NJ: Princeton University Press.

Reader-Response Criticism: From Formalism to Post-Structuralism. (1980). Jane P. Tompkins, Editor. Baltimore, MD: The Johns Hopkins University Press.

The Representation of Women in Fiction. (1983). Carolyn G. Heilbrun and Margaret R. Higonnet, Editors. Baltimore, MD: The Johns Hopkins University Press.

Richards, I. A. (1935). *Practical Criticism: A Study of Literary Judgment.* New York: Harcourt Brace and Co.

_____. (1959). *Principles of Literary Criticism*. New York: Harcourt Brace and Co. (Originally published in 1924)

Rosenblatt, Louise M. (1981). *The Journey Itself*. The Leland B. Jacobs Lecture, 1981. New York: School of Library Service, Columbia University.

_____. (1976). *Literature As Exploration*. 3rd Edition. New York: Noble & Noble Publishers, Inc. (First published in 1938)

_____. (1978). *The Reader, The Text, The Poem*. Carbondale, IL: Southern Illinois University Press.

Russian Formalist Criticism: Four Essays. (1965). Lee T. Lemon and Marion J. Reis, Editors. Lincoln, NB: University of Nebraska Press.

Ruthven, K. K. (1984). *Feminist Literary Studies*. Cambridge, England: Cambridge University Press.

Said, Edward W. (1983). *The World, The Text, and the Critic*. Cambridge, MA: Harvard University Press.

Scholes, Robert and Robert Kellogg. (1966). *The Nature of Narrative*. Oxford, England: Oxford University Press.

Scholes, Robert. (1974). *Structuralism in Literature*. New Haven, CT: Yale University Press.

Silverman, Kaja. (1983). *The Subject of Semiotics*. New York: Oxford University Press.

Slatoff, Walter. (1970). *With Respect to Readers; Dimensions of Literary Response*. Ithaca, NY: Cornell University Press.

Spacks, Patricia Meyer. (1975). *The Female Imagination*. New York: Alfred A. Knopf.

Structuralism and Since. (1979). John Sturrock, Editor. New York: Oxford University Press.

The Structuralist Controversy: The Languages of Criticism and the Sciences of Man. (1972). Richard A. Macksey and Eugenio Donato, Editors. Baltimore, MD: The Johns Hopkins University Press.

Theory and Practice of Feminist Literary Criticism. (1982). Gabriela Mora and Karen S. Van Hooft, Editors. Ypsilanti, MI: Bilingual Press.

Todorov, Tzvetan. (1975). *The Fantastic: A Structural Approach to a Literary Genre*. Ithaca, NY: Cornell University Press.

Todorov, Tzvetan. (1977). *The Poetics of Prose*. Ithaca, NY: Cornell University Press. (First Published in French in 1971)

Todorov, Tzvetan. (1982). *Theories of the Symbol*. Trans. by C. Porter. Ithaca, NY: Cornell University Press.

Tolstoy, Leo N. (1953). *What Is Art?* Trans. by Aylmer Maude. New York: Bobbs-Merrill.

Weldon, Fay. (1984). *Letters To Alice: On First Reading Jane Austen*. New York: Harcourt Brace Jovanovich.

Wellek, Rene and Austin Warren. (1977). *Theory of Literature*. New Revised Edition. New York: Harcourt Brace Jovanovich.

Wellek, Rene. (1982). *The Attack on Literature and Other Essays*. Chapel Hill, NC: University of North Carolina Press.

Wicker, Brian. (1975). *The Story-Shaped World*. Notre Dame, IN: University of Notre Dame Press.

Wilson, Anne Deidre. (1976). *Traditional Romance and Tale: How Stories Mean*. Cambridge, England: Rowman & Littlefield.

Wimsatt, William K. (1965). *Hateful Contraries: Studies in Literature and Criticism*. Lexington, KY: University of Kentucky Press.

_____. (1954). *The Verbal Icon: Studies in the Meaning of Poetry*. Lexington, KY: University of Kentucky Press.

Assignments Relating to Unit Two:

1. Students will complete the assignment entitled "Critical Analysis of the Work of a Particular Author of Stories for Children and Youth" in three distinct phases over a three-week period as described below:

   A.   Select the author whose work you will analyze and submit his/her name to the instructor for approval. It is obvious that the author selected must have a body of work for children and youth.

   B.   Submit in typed form (or computer output) your plan for this analysis including:

      1.   The name of the author

      2.   The titles of the specific works of that author to be analyzed and your reasons for selecting those titles.

      3.   A series of from five to ten literary questions you are going to respond to which will demonstrate your understanding of some of the approaches to and the theories of literary criticism.

      4.   A list of the critical works you have read which were useful to you in developing your questions. It might be useful to list the critical sources from which the question was derived immediately following that question.

   C.   Submit your analysis of the works of the selected author based on the questions submitted previously.

NOTE: The second phase of this assignment is at least as significant as the final paper in revealing your knowledge of the contents of this course. It is through the skillful and sensitive asking of questions that the critic unveils that which is of aesthetic value.

2. Students are expected to select (*as an individual if necessary, but preferably in a group of two to three students*) a literary theorist from the list below. A sharing process is operative in this instance and each student or group is to prepare items for distribution; show and tell; demonstration; etc. Each presentation should include the following:

A.   a brief paragraph of background information on the person selected

B.   a list of works by and about your critic which you have read and recommend (include monographs, journal articles, criticism: pro and con); a list of additional works identified or recommended by others or in reviews

C.   a synthesis of the critical theory with supporting documentation including quotations and/or page references

D.   at least two or three examples of the application of this person's theory or a segment of that theory to literature for children and youth

E.   a diagram and/or chart of the work of the literary theorist you have selected that demonstrates your synthesis of that theory or any aspect thereof.

The list of theorists that you may select from follows:

Wolfgang Iser	Ihab Hassan
Roland Barthes	Stanley E. Fish
Elaine Showalter	David Bleich
Gaston Bachelard	Wayne C. Booth
Norman Holland	Jonathan Culler
Georg Lukacs	Frank Kermode
E. D. Hirsch, Jr.	Ivan Todorev
Toril Moi	Elizabeth Meese

One of the benefits of this assignment is the dialogue that should take place among the team and between the team and the class. This is particularly important in developing the synthesis and in the application to books for children and youth. Part of the joy of criticism and critical explorations is the argument and defenses we make for our varying opinions. Needless to say, parts C, D, and E are the most important for this assignment.

"The primary understanding of any work of literature has to be based on the assumption of its unity. However mistaken such an assumption may eventually prove to be, nothing can be done unless we start it as a heuristic principle. Further, every effort should be directed toward understanding the whole of what we read, as though it were all on the same level of achievement. The critic may meet something that puzzles him, like, say, Mercutio's speech on Queen Mab in *Romeo and Juliet*, and feel that it does not fit. This means either that Shakespeare was a slapdash dramatist or that the critic's conception of the play is inadequate. The odds in favor of the latter conclusion are overwhelming; consequently he would do well to try to arrive at some understanding of the relevance of the puzzling episode. Even if the best he can do for the time being is a far-fetched or obviously rationalized explanation, that is still his sanest and soundest procedure. The process of academic criticism begins, then, with reading a poem through to the end, suspending value-judgments while doing so. Once the end is reached, we can see the whole design of the work as a unity." — Northrop Frye in *The Aims and Methods of Scholarship in Modern Languages and Literature*, edited by James Thorpe.

Unit Three: Research in Literature for Children and Youth

The purpose of this unit is to provide opportunity for the student to examine a number of research studies and to discuss various methodological approaches to research in literature for children and youth. The questions that follow may prove helpful:

— How does one distinguish between research or scholarly studies in literature for children and youth and popular works in the field? What are the values of each?

— What approaches to research in literature for children and youth have been most commonly used? (Identify areas, trends, patterns, and methodological approaches.)

— What is the relationship between the structure of research methodology and the nature of criticism?

— How would you determine priorities in research in literature for children and youth?

— In the design of a schematic for research purposes, what are some of the problems and dangers?

"We have not even evolved a theory of criticism which can distinguish the genuine from the useless in scholarship itself. This distinction is left to the common sense of the scholar, which is usually but by no means invariably the best place to leave it." — Northrop Frye in "The Developing Imagination"

"It is one of the hateful characteristics of a degenerate age, that the idle world will not let the worker alone, accept his offering of work, and appraise it for itself, but must insist upon turning him inside out, and knowing all about him, and really troubling itself a great deal more about his little peculiarities and personal pursuits, than his abiding work. I wish we knew nothing of Carlyle but his writings; I am thankful we know so little of Chaucer and Shakespeare ... I have persistently refused to answer the whole buzzing swarm of biographers, saying simply, 'I am a nobody—if you have anything to say about the Dictionary, there it is at your will—but treat me as a solar myth, or an echo, or an irrational quantity, or ignore me altogether.' It was unfortunately not practical to edit the dictionary anonymously, else I should have done so ... it is extremely annoying to me to see the Dictionary referred to as Murray's English Dictionary." — James A. H. Murray, quoted in *Caught in the Web of Words*, p. 2.

Required Readings for Unit Three:

The student should examine and read *Phaedrus: An International Annual of Children's Literature Research*. It is important to check all volumes of this journal/annual.

Applebee, Arthur N. (1978). *The Child's Concept of Story*. Chicago, IL: University of Chicago Press.

Favat, F. Andre. (1977). *Child and Tale: The Origins of Interest*. Urbana, IL: National Council of Teachers of English, No. 19 Research Report.

Kelly, R. Gordon. (1974). *Mother Was a Lady: Self and Society in Selected American Children's Periodicals, 1865-1890*. Westport, CT: Greenwood Press.

Monson, Dianne L. and Bette J. Peltola, Comp. (1976). *Research in Children's Literature: An Annotated Bibliography*. Newark, DE: International Reading Association.

Protherough, Robert. (1983). *Developing Responses to Fiction*. Milton Keynes, England: Open University Press.

Optional Readings for Unit Three:

Kelly, R. Gordon. (Spring 1973). "American Children's Literature: An Historiographical Review," *American Literary Realism*. Volume 6, No. 2: 89-107.

Nye, Russell B. (1966). "The Juvenile Approach to American Culture, 1870-1930," *New Voices in American Studies*. Edited by Ray E. Browne. Lafayette, IN: Purdue University Press.

Assignments Relating to Unit Three:

1. Students are expected to prepare their analysis of Favat and Kelly for class discussion. Each student is expected to address the question of how Favat and Kelly demonstrate research competence. In addition, they are expected to categorize the various research methodologies and content emphases observed in reviewing Monson and the various issues of *Phaedrus*.

"Conceptions of literature and the humanities both reflect and shape our conceptions of humanness and our views of man in society. Most theories of the nature of literature are more or less concealed theories of the nature of men and of the good society. In this sense, literary thinking is inseparable from moral and social thinking." — Gerald Graff. *Literature Against Itself*, p. 1.

Unit Four: Book Selection and Reading

The purpose of this unit is to provide the opportunity for the student to examine various approaches to the teaching of reading and relate these approaches to book selection for children and youth. The questions which follow may prove useful:

— What are the basic approaches to the teaching of reading? How do these influence book selection?

— To what extent is book selection influenced by social concerns and values?

— Is there a conflict between aesthetic excellence and societal issues in book selection for children and youth?

Required Readings for Unit Four:

Gerhardt, Lillian N. (1980). "Bias, Prejudice and the Growing '-ISM' Schism," in *Excellence in School Media Programs*. Chicago, IL: American Library Association, pp. 23-31.

Hansen, Jane. (1987). *When Writers Read*. Portsmith, NH: Heineman.

Jennings, Frank. (1965). *This Is Reading*. New York: Teachers College Press.

Johnson, Katie. (1987). *Doing Words: Using the Creative Power of Children's Personal Images to Teach Reading and Writing*. Boston, MA: Houghton Mifflin.

Kohl, Herbert. (1973). *Reading, How To*. New York: E. P. Dutton.

Moffett, James. (1988). *Storm in the Mountains: A Case Study of Censorship, Conflict, and Consciousness*. Carbondale, IL: Southern Illinois University Press.

Smith, Frank. (1971). *Understanding Reading: A Psycholinguistic Analysis of Reading and Learning to Read*. New York: Holt, Rinehart & Winston.

Vandergrift, Kay E. (1988). "Whole Language, Literacy and the School Library Media Center," in *School Library Media Annual—1988*. Edited by Jane Bandy Smith. Englewood, CO: Libraries Unlimited.

"The critical sense is so far from frequent that it is absolutely rare, and the possession of the cluster of qualities that minister to it is one of the highest distinctions.... In this light one sees the critic as the real helper of the artist, a torch-bearing outrider, the interpreter, the brother.... Just in proportion as he is sentient and restless, just in proportion as he reacts and reciprocates and penetrates, is the critic a valuable instrument." — Henry James in *Criticism*.

Assignment Relating to Unit Four:

Class discussions will focus on specific titles as "case studies" in an attempt to combine our study of critical theory with the practical concerns of finding the best possible literature and making it accessible to young readers. No written assignment required.

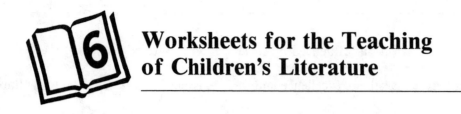 **Worksheets for the Teaching of Children's Literature**

INTRODUCTION

The worksheets included at the end of this chapter are used primarily to help students focus on appropriate content either in classroom activities or as they complete assignments for a course. Some of them are merely frames of reference (often actual frames or containers) which students may use to organize the ideas and materials they extract from required readings or assignments. Figure 16 is an example of this type of worksheet and is intended to help students select key ideas from the often difficult reading of adult literary theory.

FIGURE 16

LITERARY CRITICISM AND THE TEACHING OF CHILDREN'S LITERATURE

CRITIC OR SCHOOL	EMPHASIS OF APPROACH	VIEW OF READER	CONCEPT OF TEXT	READER–TEXT RELATIONSHIP	CONCEPT OF MEANING	LEARNING MODE	ROLE OF ADULT INTERMEDIARY	INTERACTIVE STRATEGIES

WORKSHEETS: ILLUSTRATION

Figure 17, on the other hand, contains the author's notes on the elements to be considered in the critique of a picture story book. The nonlinear representation on the page just "seems right" and apparently serves as a visual reminder to students that story must be both experienced and evaluated as a holistic

FIGURE 17

PICTURE STORY BOOKS
COMPOSITIONAL ELEMENTS

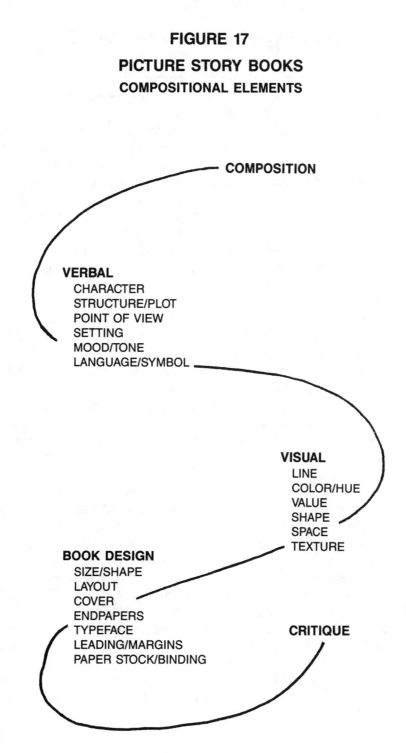

COMPOSITION

VERBAL
CHARACTER
STRUCTURE/PLOT
POINT OF VIEW
SETTING
MOOD/TONE
LANGUAGE/SYMBOL

VISUAL
LINE
COLOR/HUE
VALUE
SHAPE
SPACE
TEXTURE

BOOK DESIGN
SIZE/SHAPE
LAYOUT
COVER
ENDPAPERS
TYPEFACE
LEADING/MARGINS
PAPER STOCK/BINDING

CRITIQUE

aesthetic composition rather than as a series of discrete elements. The spacing on the page allows students to add their own notes to the diagram if they wish to do so. Many of the worksheets which follow are just more obvious and more linear forms for note-taking, and are sometimes presented as a series of questions. Often figures from an earlier work *Child and Story* are used as tools for exploring various books or literary ideas.

WORKSHEETS: STRUCTURES

Many other worksheets, however, are "tighter" in content; that is, they present more organized and complete content for students to reflect upon. Worksheet 1 presents an overview of and a frame of reference for much of the content of the beginning of a course and provides an outline for students to fill in as they move through the semester. In some instances, the statements on worksheets are intended to provoke class discussion or to encourage students to locate evidence to support an idea or opinion either in support of or contrary to the one presented. Both types of worksheets are useful in liberating class members from that syndrome of graduate students which seems to infect them with the compulsion to write down everything the teacher says. In other instances, students are told that these sheets contain the teacher's synthesis of what is known about the topic under discussion, which should be more accurate than an oral presentation and any notes they might take from that. This enables the class to focus discussion on points of special interest or of confusion and challenge each other to go beyond what is on the page. Of course, a belief in the need for classroom discussion to stimulate learning is evident both in the content of these worksheets and in their use.

Very few of the worksheets are "stand alone" learning materials. For instance, Figure 17 presented earlier accompanies a slide show and Worksheet 14, on "Point of View," is used with a series of examples that demonstrate the comparison with camera angles. Although the worksheet and the focus of the class discussion is on books for older children, visual representations of point of view in picture books are often used to reinforce understanding of this literary element. *Two Bad Ants* by Chris Van Allsburg is the latest of his books that lend themselves to this type of examination.[1] The point of view of the ants dominates the entire book, but it is the ants looking up at the wall of the house and the illustration of the man drinking the coffee that best demonstrate this element. This may be contrasted with Arthur Yorinks and Richard Egielski's *Sid & Sol* in which the point of view is that of a normal-sized human being looking up at a giant.[2] It is with the examination of many books, followed by much discussion, that students begin to appreciate the various uses of this element of story.

Worksheets 2 and 3 are used most often as the basis for one or more classes. It is exciting to watch students discuss specific examples of "colorful, tongue-tickling words" drawn from the books they select such as Caron Cohen's *Whiffle Squeek*[3] and Steven Kellogg's *Pecos Bill*.[4] "Predicting outcomes" has led to some powerful interchanges and disagreements about how predictable a story should be. We might begin with the obvious predictability of a "Once upon a time" story, move to the more realistic expectations for most modern "protagonist with a problem" stories, and then to stories that end with a twist or a surprise such as the old favorite *The Camel Who Took a Walk*.[5] A more interesting or exciting class discussion might result from the use of a work such as *Where The Wild Geese Go* by Meredith Ann Pierce.[6] Most readers are not able to predict where Pierce is going within this story since, as in her *The Darkangel*[7] she tends to mix many traditional motifs and patterns. For many Truzjka is too weak a character to dominate her story and merely moves from one myth-like encounter to another without the credibility necessary for reader involvement. The metamorphic scene in which she begins to turn into a bird could be compared to the similar scene in *Hey, Al*.[8] In *Hey, Al* readers are cheering the characters on; but in *Where the Wild Geese Go*, it's just one more confusing incident.

Many of the worksheets relate the literature to children by asking the student to think in relation to the audience that will read or hear the book or view the film. These may consider audience characteristics (Worksheets 3 and 6) or activities (Worksheets 7, 8, and 19). On the other hand, Worksheet 21 provides an outline of literary criticism which permits an exploration of a variety of theories and relates them to specific children's books. A quotation from an adult Western novel is used to stimulate a discussion of transactional theories of literature. A character in Louis L'Amour's *Ride The River*[9] describes her reading in a way which reinforces the belief in the relationship of reader responses and critical thinking skills.

"From memory?" "Of course. We Sacketts all have good memories...." "Someone says 'George Washington,' and right away you think of Mount Vernon, of 1776, of John Adams and Thomas Jefferson, Valley Forge and all that, and each one of those things tips you off to another set of memories." ... "as youngsters we were taught not just to learn something but to learn something else that went with it. Pa, he used to say that no memory is ever alone, it's at the end of a trail of memories, a dozen trails that each have their own associations...."[10]

Intellectually exciting fun-filled classes have also been built around the use of theories of feminist criticism to examine such works as *Mighty Mountain and the Three Strong Women*.[11]

WORKSHEETS: POETRY

Since poetry is a favorite of the author's and a genre often neglected by those who work with children, some class time is devoted to introducing classic collections from *Poems of Childhood,*[12] to *Sing-Song,*[13] to *Reflections on a Gift of Watermelon Pickle.*[14] Newer collections like *Sing A Song of Popcorn,*[15] *Cats Are Cats*[16] and *You Be Good & I'll Be Night*[17] also demonstrate the points outlined on Worksheet 11. The relationship of illustration to poetry is clearly seen in some of these works and in the newer interpretation of older poems like *The Cremation of Sam McGee*.[18]

WORKSHEETS: HISTORY OF CHILDREN'S LITERATURE

The worksheets designed for the "History of Children's Literature" demonstrate the author's belief in the need for tools as means for students to control their experiences with the bibliographical apparatus of this field (Worksheet 22.) They provide a reasonable approach to investigation and assure the student of accomplishment at the completion of an assignment. Since many historical source materials are themselves rare, their introduction serves as the basis of one class presentation, but it is made clear that the presentation is merely an introduction to the full range of resources and to the complexity of scholarly work in the field. Students are then expected to complete information on the worksheets during the remainder of the semester. Worksheets 23 and 27 are provided to help students with their analysis of other types of materials examined for this course. Often students design their own worksheets to control and record their analysis of materials. Figure 18 is an example of a Probe Sheet created by students to focus their analysis of historical children's books.

FIGURE 18

PROBE SHEET

1. FORMAT:
   a. Size
   b. Margins
   c. Number of Pages
   d. Index
   e. Typeface
   f. Frontispiece
   g. Illustrations
   h. Table of Contents
   i. Other

2. PURPOSE OF THE WORK:

3. CONTENT OF THE WORK SUMMARIZED:

4. STYLE USED WITHIN THE WORK:
   a. Vocabulary
   b. Poetry
   c. Didactic tone
   d. Sexist
   e. Religious
   f. Other

5. SPECIAL FEATURES:

In many instances, students also photocopied sample title pages or typical pages from the text and attached these to the appropriate worksheet. Students using Figure 19 are concerned with the kinds or types of cultural or historical information contained in children's informational books.

FIGURE 19

CULTURAL CONTEXT FORM

1. Dates of Coverage:

2. Bibliographical Style:

3. What is the approach to the period:
   a. Thematic
   b. Chronological
   c. Geographical
   d. Biographical
   e. Political

4. Examples of Cultural Placement:

5. Examples of historical evidence:

Regardless of the particular aspects of a work highlighted, such forms serve only as a means of control so that examination and note-taking are more rigorous and more focused. Obviously some students prefer their personal eclectic methods for accomplishing the same objective rather than using a pre-established form, and this is acceptable. Even in such instances, however, a general worksheet may be helpful in focusing attention on particular aspects of the items being examined.

SUMMARY

Although some of the worksheets which follow obviously relate to a particular course and syllabus, others might be used in more than one course or situation, depending upon the previous knowledge and experiences of students and on the articulation of various courses within a program. Ordinarily they are used for class activities, but some might be distributed to individuals who need to add to or refresh knowledge expected as a prerequisite for the content of a particular course.

NOTES

[1]Chris Van Allsburg. (1988). *Two Bad Ants*. (Boston, MA: Houghton Mifflin).

[2]Arthur Yorinks. (1977). *Sid & Sol*. Illus. by Richard Egielski. (New York: Farrar, Straus & Giroux).

[3]Caron Lee Cohen. (1987). *Whiffle Squeek*. (New York: Dodd, Mead).

[4]Steven Kellogg. (1986). *Pecos Bill*. (New York: Wm. Morrow).

[5]Jack Tworkov. (1951). *The Camel Who Took A Walk*. (New York: E. P. Dutton).

[6]Meredith Ann Pierce. (1988). *Where the Wild Geese Go*. (New York: E. P. Dutton).

[7]Meredith Ann Pierce. (1982). *The Darkangel*. (New York: Atlantic Monthly).

[8]Arthur Yorinks. (1986). *Hey, Al*. Illus. by Richard Egielski. (New York: Farrar, Straus & Giroux).

[9]Louis L'Amour. (1983). *Ride the River*. (New York: Bantam Books).

[10]Louis L'Amour. pp. 110-111.

[11]Irene Hedlund. (1984). *Mighty Mountain and the Three Strong Women*. Translated from Danish by Judith Elkin. (London: A & C Black).

[12]Eugene Field. (1904). *Poems of Childhood*. (New York: Charles Scribner's Sons).

[13]Christina G. Rossetti. (1924). *Sing-Song*. (New York: Macmillan).

[14]*Reflections on a Gift of Watermelon Pickle ... And Other Modern Verse*. (1966). Compiled by Stephen Dunning and others. (New York: Lothrop, Lee & Shepard).

[15]*Sing a Song of Popcorn: Every Child's Book of Poems.* (1988). Compiled by Beatrice Schenk de Regniers and others. Illus. by Marcia Brown and others. (New York: Scholastic).

[16]Nancy Larrick. (1988). *Cats Are Cats.* Illus. by Ed Young. (New York: Philomel).

[17]Eve Merriam. (1988). *You Be Good & I'll Be Night.* (New York: Wm. Morrow).

[18]Robert W. Service. (1987). *The Cremation of Sam McGee.* Illus. by Ted Harrison. (New York: Greenwillow Books).

LIST OF WORKSHEETS FOR DISCUSSION

1. The Literary Experience for Children (Nondiscursive Literature)

2. Content of Picture Story Books

3. Critical Abilities Necessary for the Enjoyment of Story

4. Some Keys to Literary Excellence

5. Fictional Composition

6. Overview of Some Key Comprehension Abilities for Reading Fiction

7. Sharing Literary Experiences with Children

8. Asking Literary Questions: Primary Grades

9. Biography for Children

10. Informational Books for Children

11. Criteria for Selecting Poetry for Young Children

12. Compositional Elements: Character

13. Compositional Elements: Structure/Plot

14. Compositional Elements: Point of View

15. Compositional Elements: Setting

16. Compositional Elements: Mood/Tone

17. Compositional Elements: Language/Symbol

18. Story/Mood/Concept/Reasoning/Everyday Exprience Books for Young Children

19. Asking Literary Questions: Intermediate Grades

20. Comparison of Science and Fiction

21. Approaches/Types/Functions in Criticism

22. Probe Sheet

23. Historical Readers/Textbooks

24. Fairy Tales

25. Children's Classics

26. Format and Illustration in Children's Picture Books

27. Historical Periodicals for Children

28. Folk Literature for Children: An Inquiry

29. Illustrator as Storyteller

30. Thinking about Illustration

31. Fantasy

32. Pathfinder Instructions for Informational Materials

33. Things to Think about in Genre Fiction

34. Literary Motifs

35. Horror and the Occult

36. Romance

37. Sagas and Chronicles

38. Science Fiction

39. An Exploration of *The Hobbit* and the *Lord of the Rings* Trilogy

40. Instructions for a Bibliographic Essay

41. Fun Project

42. Story Pattern

43. Mythology and Folklore

44. Critical Thinking

45. David Macaulay and His Work

WORKSHEETS FOR DISCUSSION: NUMBER ONE

Worksheets for Discussion in Children's Literature: #1—The Literary Experience for Children (Nondiscursive Literature)

THE LITERARY EXPERIENCE FOR CHILDREN (NON-DISCURSIVE LITERATURE)

1.

Presuppositions:

Literature deals with some aspect of the human condition.

Literature attempts to come symbolically or metaphorically to some revelation or testament of life.

Literature is thought about feeling.

Literature is an aesthetic ordering of some components of existence to compose a complete story world.

Each reader recreates literature to make it uniquely his or her own.

Components: (Progressive levels of understanding)

Entertainment is the prime purpose of all literature.

Books do not entertain people; people entertain books.

People may be willing to entertain what they do not "like." Entertain in a spirit of playfulness to escape or put in time. Entertain in a spirit of exultation for a "spiritual" uplift or a "good cry".

Enjoyment in its literary use, asks not "Did you like it?" but "Did it get and hold your attention?" or "Was it *aesthetically* satisfying as a literary experience?

Literature is an exploration of life and living, a chance to try life on for size as a confirmation, an illumination, or an extension of life experiences.

The life of literature is in its *language*.

Beauty in literature is a combination of qualities which exults the human mind or spirit. It may be "tragic" or "pretty".

Literature is an authentic and essential *way of knowing*, an aesthetic knowing through feeling.

2.

Approach may be:
Realistic
Romantic
Fanciful

Made manifest at:
The narrative level—
  What is said?
  (Engagement)

The interpretive level—
  Does it ring true?
  (Involvement)

The transcendent or residual level—Is there a residue of meaning or truth?
  (Evocation)

In a mode of:

Comedy-Heroic powers: equal to those of ordinary man/woman. Incongruity of character in relation to situation, society, or self.

Romance-Heroic powers: greater than ordinary and often greater than that of his/her environment. Exaggerated characters and adventures.

Tragedy-Heroic powers: somewhat greater than ordinary man/woman but not superhuman. Man/woman overcome by his/her environment. Close association of character with fate, courage in the face of the inevitable.

Irony-Heroic powers: less than those of ordinary man/woman, the victim of his/her environment and of circumstances.

3.

By means of:
- Word: choice of language to affect reader
- Aesthetic ordering of a constellation of conditions of existence to focus and order experience.
- Craftsmanship: Means of embodying aesthetic meaning in appropriate form.
- Imagination: Imposition of a unique and personally-imagined world view on the above.

With appropriate ordering of content:

Literary Genre or Types

Traditional tales: Riddles, Chants, Jokes, Folk Tales, Myths Legends, Fables, Fairy Tales, Tall Tales

Modern Stories: Comedy, Romance, Tragedy, Irony
Poetry
Drama
Short Stories

Themes (Examples: Courage, Getting Along with Others, Conflict and Crisis, Freedom and Responsibility)

Literary Motifs

Major:
Journey, Quest, Good vs. Evil, Test, Triumph of Underdog, Rags to Riches, Loss-Recovery

Minor:
Rescue, Triangle, Talisman, Mysterious Birth, Scapegoat, Defiance of Rules, Tempting of Fate, Twist, Heedless Mocking of Power, Transformation or Exchange, Magic Numbers (3, 7), Dream as Omen or Portent

4.

Comparison—Contrast

Fiction— Nonfiction
Realism— Fancy
Prose— Poetry
Books— Periodicals
Beautifully Bound—Paperback
Old— New
Action— Mood
Humorous— Serious
Popular— Precious
Familiar— Unfamiliar
Comedy— Tragedy
Romance— Irony

Content Types

Historical Fiction
Regional Fiction
Everyday Experience
Fancy (Fairy Tales, Modern Fancy)
Sociological Stories (Intergroup Stories, Childlife in Other Cultures)
Animal Stories
Mystery
Sports
Science Fiction
War Stories
Family Chronicles
Personification of Machines

5.

WORKSHEETS FOR DISCUSSION: NUMBER TWO

Worksheets for Discussion in Children's Literature: #2—
Content of Picture Story Books

CONTENT OF PICTURE STORY BOOKS

In plot development, some chief characteristics of picture story books may be:

The plot centers in one main sequence of events with little or no sub-plot.

One main character, or a group of characters acting with oneness, with whom it is easy to identify holds the attention of the young reader throughout the story.

The plot is so structured that the young reader is able to anticipate to some degree the outcome of the events included.

Once a mood of realism or romance or fancy is established, that basic tone does not shift. The child is thus quickly oriented in his or her expectations for the content.

Much direct conversation or a conversational tone is commonly used.

Elaboration of detail is related more closely to its intimate psychological significance in the story than to its general importance in life.

Colorful, tongue-tickling words, neatly-turned phrases and refrains that are quickly memorized may be an integral part of many stories for children. Young children, however, also appreciate the down-to-earth and the commonplace as a confirmation of their own experience.

Story climaxes are simple, natural, and satisfying rather than theatrical, overstimulating, or melodramatic.

Either a boy or a girl here is acceptable to young children. Specific details rather than vague generalizations appeal to the young child.

6.

WORKSHEETS FOR DISCUSSION: NUMBER THREE

Worksheets for Discussion in Children's Literature: #3—
Critical Abilities Necessary for the Enjoyment of Story

CRITICAL ABILITIES NECESSARY FOR THE ENJOYMENT OF STORY

Distinguishing Various Modes of Story

Following a Narrative Sequence

Recognizing Patterns of Organization

Recreating Character

Noting and Recalling Significant Detail

Making Inferences and Comprehending Implied Meanings

Predicting Outcomes

Detecting Clues to Mood and Tone

Perceiving Author's Perspective and Point of View

Recognizing and Responding to Literary Devices

Comprehending Symbol and Extended Metaphor

7.

WORKSHEETS FOR DISCUSSION: NUMBER FOUR

Worksheets for Discussion in Children's Literature: #4— Some Keys to Literary Excellence

SOME KEYS TO LITERARY EXCELLENCE

Unity (Constructional development of the whole)

Variety (Contrast-Complexity)

Harmony (Coordination and enhancement of the whole)

Balance (Proportion between elements of the whole)

Functionality (Good design; achievement in the product of the promise of the ideas and the form)

Craftsmanship (Execution of design; control of medium; finesse in execution)

Depth (Succeeding levels of depth: narrative, interpretive, transcendent or residual)

Universality (Feeling of being in and of humankind)

Authenticity (An internal, believable "world view")

Validity (Agreement between what a work appears to be and what it is; true either to life or to its own fancy)

Simplicity (No extraneous parts: "lean" but not "barren," looks effortless and uncluttered, but more than just a framework)

Beauty (Containment of feeling in suitable form; compositional complementation of Spirit, Idea, and Language)

8.

WORKSHEETS FOR DISCUSSION: NUMBER FIVE

Worksheets for Discussion in Children's Literature: #5— Fictional Composition

FICTIONAL COMPOSITION

An author makes his/her literary statement.

The author's literary statement is his/her metaphorical composition of his/her subjectively experienced world.

The author, as fiction writer, makes his/her literary statement in story form.

Story form is the creation of a universe that is but never *was*.

The author makes his/her fictional literary statement by aesthetically ordering some components of existence.

Those components of existence can be ordered fancifully or realistically.

To do this aesthetic ordering, the author develops thought about feeling.

This thought about feeling draws on his/her consciousness and subconsciousness.

The author uses what he/she knows cognitively and intuitively.

The author's thought about feeling relies on the material and non-material culture within his/her ken.

The material culture is used for feeling one with the created reality in the story.

9.

The non-material culture pervades the story as beliefs, values, ideas, and symbols.

The author composes story from material already experienced and from material consciously sought out for this particular creative endeavor.

The author orders his/her creation in terms of what, in his/her judgment, will give the reader the clearest images with the most powerful impact.

The author creates fictional characters, situations, and actions that can be looked at critically at the narrative level, the interpretive level, the residual or transcendent or world view level. In other words:

What does the writer say?

In terms of what the writer posits, do the characters and their actions and reactions ring true?

Is there a residue of meaning or "truth" in what is said?

The tests of the fiction writer's success in making his/her literary statement are:

Is it thinkable? Imaginable?

Does it evoke response?

Is it feelingful?

Is it believable?

Is it significantly formed?

10.

WORKSHEETS FOR DISCUSSION: NUMBER SIX

Worksheets for Discussion in Children's Literature: #6—Overview of Some Key Comprehension Abilities for Reading Fiction

OVERVIEW OF SOME KEY COMPREHENSION ABILITIES FOR READING FICTION

At the Verbal Level:
Initial Comprehension Abilities

Understanding word denotations

Understanding word connotations

Selecting appropriate meaning from words with multiple meanings

Understanding foreign terms, idiomatic expressions, etc.

Recognizing protagonist and antagonist

Following a sequence of events

Understanding chronological time elements

More Subtle Comprehension Abilities

Noting significant details

Understanding uses of figurative language

Noting author's voice

Understanding unusual or complex phraseology

Recognizing direct author statements about actions and reactions of characters

At the Interpretive Level:
Initial Comprehension Abilities

Understanding setting (place, time)

Comprehending story problem, complications, and resolution

Understanding key character attributes and changes

Recognizing realism or fancy as approaches to story

Noting mood and tone

Recognizing pivotal incidents or happenings

Predicting outcomes

Recognizing modes of story (comedy, romance, tragedy, irony)

11.

More Advanced Comprehension Abilities

Recognizing dynamic and static characters
Understanding revealed characterization
Understanding psychological time elements
Recognizing romance as an approach to story
Understanding symbols—their relationships to main ideas or character development
Noting possible foreshadowing
Recognizing literary allusions
Recognizing caricatures

At the Critical Level:

Story Import

Understanding limits of the story world
Understanding stylistic structure
Assessing validity of writer's assumptions
Sensing story's world view
Relating present story to previously read stories with regard to content and/or form
Recognizing stereotypes and literary archetypes

Story Impact

Detecting author's intent in story
Recognizing story perspective
Comprehending sentiment versus sentimentality
Recognizing uses of writing craftsmanship
Detecting over-statement and under-statement
Recognizing consistencies or inconsistencies among elements of story form

12.

WORKSHEETS FOR DISCUSSION: NUMBER SEVEN

Worksheets for Discussion in Children's Literature: #7—Sharing Literary Experiences with Children

SHARING LITERARY EXPERIENCES WITH CHILDREN

Children's responses to literature may take any one of a variety of forms, most of which are far more "in tune" with the literary experience than the kind of "back talk" too often demanded by teachers. A child's play-acting, sometimes many days after the sharing of a story, or even that moment of secure silence following the close of a favorite book may be the best means one has for expressing what has gone before.

Following are some of the ways the other arts have been used to share literary experiences.

Language Arts:

Listening— Story hour, book discussions, tapes, recordings, radio programs

Speaking— Storytelling, reading aloud, oral book reviews and book talks, choral speaking, group discussions, progressive stories, word games, personal experiences related to literature, poetry happenings. As much and as many kinds as kids can handle. (Relate forms, conventions, themes, ideas, characters, etc.)

Reading—

Writing— Book reviews, descriptions of favorite characters or incidents from books, sequels to stories, imaginary diary, letters or newspaper reports related to books, letters to authors, correspondence with children of other schools, class magazine or book, original compositions in story, verse, or play form, personal reading records and recommendations.

13.

Dramatics—
Creative dramatics, formal plays, pantomime, shadow plays, marionettes, puppet plays.

Graphic Arts—
Illustrations for stories, bookplate designs, bookmarks or book jackets; displays, exhibits and bulletin boards; chalk talks; roller movies; story maps; story mobiles; Kamishibai; diorama; felt characters; puppet (hand, glove, stick, finger silhouette, sock, bottle, towel tube, spool, paper cups, paperbags, paper mache, pipe cleaner) peep shows; book binding; jigsaw puzzles; posters; stage settings; marionettes.

Music and Dance—Folk songs and dances as literature; interpretation of print literature through music and dance, poetry rhythm bands, and poetry set to music, children's original compositions set to music or dance; storytelling with musical accompaniment.

Film—
Silent and sound film records of most of the above; film as literature; corresponding moods, structures or characters on film.

Contributing Factors:

Adequate reading skills
Adequate and varied material resources
Environment
Time and place for personal reading
Emphasis on literature as literature
Opportunity to share literary experiences
Lively, attractive visual environment
Using other media as springboards to literature

14.

Evaluation:
Concerned with appreciation and enjoyment
Concerned with understandings more than information—Cannot be tested
Does it sharpen our observations and perceptions?
Does it develop our emotional sensitivity?
Does it extend our acquaintance with life?
On personal level—Cooperative work with children to help them become more critical of their own perception of literary forms and meanings.

15.

WORKSHEETS FOR DISCUSSION: NUMBER EIGHT

Worksheets for Discussion in Children's Literature: #8—Asking Literary Questions: Primary Grades

ASKING LITERARY QUESTIONS: PRIMARY GRADES

"Literary" questions are those that take the child into the story's form and structure. They take the child back into what has been read or heard rather than into a discussion that is peripheral. The latter type of discussion sometimes has its place: "Have you ever had an experience like this?", etc., but it is not as helpful in developing critical and appreciative readers of story as the questions that discuss content in terms of the story's form and structure. Literary questions effectively test comprehension of detail, of interrelationships of character and incident; they also test the child's ability to make inferences and judgments based upon what has been read.

EXAMPLES:

How soon did you know if this story was "believe" or "make-believe"?

How did you know?

Who is the main character in this story? (Whom is the story about?)

What kind of a character is he/she? How do you know this? Would a real person act like this character does? Why or why not? How do the other characters feel toward him/her? How do you know this?

Do the animals (any non-humans characters) in this story behave like real people? In what way?

Could _____ (one event) have happened after _____ (another event)? Why or why not?

Were any parts of this story especially funny, sad, etc.? Which ones? What made them this way?

Are there any words in this story that sound like the things they represent? That sound funny or unusual? That are fun to say?

How did you suspect how this story would end? What clues did the author give you?

Do you think the illustrations go with the story? Why or why not?

Is this (story or character) like any other (story or character) you have heard or read before? In what way? In what ways are they different?

Do you think the title is a good one for this story? Why or why not?

WORKSHEETS FOR DISCUSSION: NUMBER NINE

17.

Worksheets for Discussion in Children's Literature: #9—
Biography for Children

BIOGRAPHY FOR CHILDREN

Biographies as history should be authentic, reasonably objective, and verifiable.

The prose style in biography should be beautiful to read and appropriate to the subject matter and mood of the story.

Biographies should avoid "typing" characters.

Biographies for children should be true as they go, though they probably will differ from adult biographies in that they present only as complete a picture of the character as a child can comprehend.

Biographies for children include accounts of the appealing, personal details of the character's appearance and behavior, particularly those that deal with the character's childhood.

In biographies for children, the central character should emerge as an integrated human being, in spite of contradictions, with purposes, drives, and direction of energies that give unity and significance to living.

In biographies for children it seems legitimate to cast known facts about an episode into actual dialogue, to interpret the thoughts of the characters, and to reconstruct small "daily happenings."

Good biography not only acquaints the reader with significant information about real people but also recreates the times and conditions in which they lived.

Biography for children has inspirational values in that it deals with themes and thoughts that encourage and enlighten the reader. But good biography does not moralize.

Biography for children is ordinarily sympathetic to the main character presented.

18.

In good biography for children, the author tries to let the life of the person being written about stand on its own, as free from direct judgments and opinions by the writer as is possible.

Biography for children may be either individual biography, about one main character, or collective biography, which includes several lives.

Biography for children should keep a good balance of action and ideas.

19.

WORKSHEETS FOR DISCUSSION: NUMBER TEN

Worksheets for Discussion in Children's Literature: #10— Informational Books for Children

INFORMATIONAL BOOKS FOR CHILDREN

Are accurate and authentic in fact and feeling.

Are free from gross over-simplifications, over-generalizations, or anthropomorphism.

Respect children's abilities to comprehend.

Are free from sole dependence on the age of the reader.

Are doors to further searching for knowledge.

Give children big ideas to weigh and ponder.

Extend sympathies, deepen insights, encourage sound scholarship.

Are so developed that print and other forms of symbolization complement each other.

Relate content to child life and living.

Present knowledge as developing and integrative rather than static, final, or piece-meal.

Are clearly and precisely written.

Are delightful and original in their composition.

Are organized for ease in locating and understanding information.

20.

WORKSHEETS FOR DISCUSSION: NUMBER ELEVEN

Worksheets for Discussion in Children's Literature: #11— Criteria for Selecting Poetry for Young Children

CRITERIA FOR SELECTING POETRY FOR YOUNG CHILDREN

In selecting poems for young children, one will want to be sure it is quite good poetry—that is, poetry which

Possesses truly poetic content.

Is the meaning an aesthetic meaning rather than a matter of ordinary discourse?

Is the total conception fresh and unhackneyed?

Is the imagery feelingfully graphic?

Uses words appropriate to the meaning to be felt.

Is there the feel of precise sensory impressions?

Is the poem free from too difficult figurative or allusive language?

Do the word combinations have freshness and originality?

Are the images, deductions, observations presented in child-like (but not childish) language?

Has delightful melody and movement.

Is the sound appropriate to the poetic content?

Does the sound of the lines come unaffectedly and smoothly from the reader's lips?

Is the rhythmic pattern in keeping with the poetic content?

Is the movement of the poem integral in the mood and meaning?

Are the rhymings seemingly natural and unforced even if they are funny or unexpected?

21.

WORKSHEETS FOR DISCUSSION: NUMBER TWELVE

Worksheets for Discussion in Children's Literature: #12—Compositional Elements—Character

COMPOSITIONAL ELEMENTS: CHARACTER

In identifying and criticizing characterizations, students should . . .

a) Distinguish between character description and character revelation in a variety of media.

b) Recognize means of revealing character in a variety of media.

c) Develop criteria for assessing characterization in a variety of media.

d) Recognize and discuss the role of characterization in the total composition within various media.

e) Define and identify in various media and genre the following terms:

    Major character
    Minor character
    Round character
    Flat character
    Dynamic character
    Static character
    Protagonist
    Antagonist
    Character foil
    Archetype
    Stereotype

22.

WORKSHEETS FOR DISCUSSION: NUMBER THIRTEEN

Worksheets for Discussion in Children's Literature: #13—Compositional Elements—Structure/Plot

COMPOSITIONAL ELEMENTS: STRUCTURE/PLOT

Structure: the nondiscursive ordering or the organization of an aesthetic composition as influenced by its plot (in fiction) or main idea (in exposition); a metaphor implying that the work is, both topically and affectively, a connected and unified whole.

Narration: the orderly progression of a relationship among incidents in a composition.

Plot: the discursive ordering or the casually related sequence of events showing characters in action.

In recognizing and evaluating structure and plot in various forms of media for children, students should . . .

a) Recognize both conventional and experimental structures and cite examples of each.

b) Identify narrative forms other than plot and cite examples of each.

c) Identify the most common patterns of plot development and the components of each, citing examples from works for children.

d) Identify the most common kinds of conflict in plot, citing examples of each.

e) Define and identify in works for children the following terms:

    Foreshadowing
    Flashback
    Episodic
    Stream of Consciousness
    Motif

f) Identify and explain Northrop Frye's classification of plots.

23.

WORKSHEETS FOR DISCUSSION: NUMBER FOURTEEN

Worksheets for Discussion in Children's Literature: #14— Compositional Elements—Point of View

COMPOSITIONAL ELEMENTS: POINT OF VIEW

Point of view is the position from which the object, scene or action is viewed in a composition—the relationship of the narrator to the mind of the character or of the photographer to his/her subject.

One may think of the various types of point of view as:

I. *Looking On*
A. *Objective*: Third person narration; narrator outside story revealing nothing from inside the minds of characters except indirectly; reports behavior and speech leaving reader or viewer to make inferences from them.
B. *Omniscient*: Third person narrator outside the story; knows all and tells all.

II. *Looking Through a Character's Eyes** *Subjective*: First person narration; the narrator as character tells his/her thoughts and feelings.

III. *Looking Over the Character's Shoulder** A. *Limited Objective*: Third person narrator outside story stays with a particular character; all else is described as if seen by that character.
B. *Limited Omniscient*: Third person narrator outside story stays with a particular character and tells what that character thinks and feels.

24.

In recognizing and evaluating various points of view in different media, students should . . .
a) Identify the advantages and limitations of first person narration.
b) Identify ways in which point of view influences characterization and plot.
c) Identify and explain the relationship between viewpoint on the screen and point of view in print.

*One should distinguish whether the character in Types II & III is a major participant in or an observer of the primary action of the story.

25.

WORKSHEETS FOR DISCUSSION: NUMBER FIFTEEN

Worksheets for Discussion in Children's Literature: #15—Compositional Elements—Setting

COMPOSITIONAL ELEMENTS: SETTING

Time: Chronological—Past, Present, Future
Psychological—Fast, Slow

Place: Verifiable (Actual)
Constructed (Realistic, Romantic or Fanciful)

In identifying and criticizing characterization, students should . . .

a) Identify specific works in which setting is revealed through the dialect, vocabulary, or levels of usage in the language of the character.

b) Recognize that setting may be established immediately and directly or revealed gradually and indirectly.

c) Recognize the restrictions that setting imposes on character and plot development.

d) Identify specific works in which mood or atmosphere is produced by the setting.

e) Identify specific works in which the relationship between character and setting is a means of expressing theme.

f) Recognize the relationship between changes in setting and episodes in plot.

g) Recognize that setting may either place limitations on or open up possibilities for human action.

h) Recognize that actual times or places may affect reader/viewer expectations for action, character's behavior and attitudes.

i) Identify specific works in which pacing influences mood.

26.

WORKSHEETS FOR DISCUSSION: NUMBER SIXTEEN

Worksheets for Discussion in Children's Literature: #16—Compositional Elements—Mood/Tone

COMPOSITIONAL ELEMENTS: MOOD/TONE

Tone: Attitudes toward compositional content or attitudes toward readers (Example: cynical, sympathetic, satirical, etc.)

Mood: Overall tone which prevails; establishes limits of composed world (Example: adventurous, serious, humorous, etc.)

In identifying and criticizing mood and tone, students should . . . .

a) Recognize when mood is of major importance to a composition.

b) Identify works in which mood is created by particular sounds or rhythms.

c) Identify specific works or types of works for children which demonstrate respect for young readers through tone.

27.

WORKSHEETS FOR DISCUSSION: NUMBER SEVENTEEN

Worksheets for Discussion in Children's Literature: #17— Compositional Elements—Language/Symbol

COMPOSITIONAL ELEMENTS: LANGUAGE/SYMBOL

Language in a compositional form may be either literal or metaphorical.

Symbols in artistic composition:

1) are both literal and figurative, that is, they are objects or deeds that seem to stand for more than their literal meaning.
2) carry their meaning in a single element.
3) have many meanings.

In identifying and criticizing language and symbol, students should . . .

a) Identify specific works in which language plays a primary role in establishing mood.
b) Distinguish between symbol as used in allegorical works and in other aesthetic compositions.
c) Identify specific works in which symbolic meanings are stated explicitly within the composition and those in which the symbols are implicit.
d) Identify specific works in which symbolic meaning is something contained within the composition and those which are outside or beyond the work.

28.

WORKSHEETS FOR DISCUSSION: NUMBER EIGHTEEN

Worksheets for Discussion in Children's Literature: #18— Story/Mood/Concept/Reasoning/Everyday Experience Books for Young Children

STORY/MOOD/CONCEPT/REASONING/EVERYDAY EXPERIENCE BOOKS FOR YOUNG CHILDREN

AUTHOR	TITLE	STORY/MOOD/ CONCEPT/REASONING/ EVERYDAY EXPERIENCE
Barton	Trucks	
Berger	When The Sun Rose	
Brown	Four Fur Feet	
Brown	The Dead Bird	
Bubney	A Kiss Is Round	
Caldwell	Excuses, Excuses	
Carlstrom	Jesse Bear, What Will You Wear?	
Charlip & Moore	Hooray for Me	
Cohen	Three Yellow Dogs	
Emberley	Ed Emberley's ABC	
Ets	Gilberto and the Wind	
Garelick	Where Does the Butterfly Go When It Rains	
Geisert	Pigs From A to Z	
Hoban	Shapes, Shapes, Shapes	
Howard	When I'm Sleepy	
Jonas	Where Can It Be?	
Lexau	That's Good, That's Bad	
Lloyd	The Sneeze	
Schlein	Heavy Is the Hippopotamus	
Skofield	Nightdances	
Thaler	Moonkey	
Titherington	Pumpkin, Pumpkin	
Williams	Cherries and Cherry Pits	
Wolcott	The Dragon and the Wild Fandango	
Ziefert	Bear Gets Dressed	

29.

DEFINE AND LIST SOME OF THE CHARACTERISTICS OF EACH OF THE GENRE

STORY:

MOOD:

CONCEPT:

REASONING:

EVERYDAY EXPERIENCE:

30.

WORKSHEETS FOR DISCUSSION: NUMBER NINETEEN

Worksheets for Discussion in Children's Literature: #19—
Asking Literary Questions: Intermediate Grades

ASKING LITERARY QUESTIONS: INTERMEDIATE GRADES

"Literary" questions are those that take the child into the story's form and structure. They take him back into what he has read or heard rather than out into discussion that is peripheral. The latter type of discussion sometimes has its place: "Would you have behaved as the hare did?" "Have you ever had an experience like this?" etc. but it is not as helpful in developing critical and appreciative readers of story as the question which discusses content in terms of the story's form and structure. Literary questions effectively test comprehension of detail, of interrelationships of character and incident; they also test the child's ability to make inferences and judgments based upon what he has read.

EXAMPLES OF LITERARY QUESTIONS

1. What is this story about? (Responses may be in terms of character, plot, theme, etc. and should help students focus on the most important literary elements in a particular story.)
2. What idea or ideas does this story make you think about? How does the author get you to think about this?
3. Do any particular feelings come across in this story? Does the story actually make you feel in a certain way or does it make you think about what it is to feel that way? How does the author accomplish this? (This is intended to help students become more aware of the distinctions between literary and "real life" experiences.)

31.

4. Is there one character you know more about than any of the others? If so, who is this character and what kind of a person is he? How does the author reveal this character to you? (Description, dialogue, his behavior, other characters' reactions to him?) What words would you use to describe the main character's feeling in this book?

5. Are there other characters who are important to the story? Who are they? Why are they important?

6. Are all the characters the same at the end of the story as they were at the beginning? If not, how and why are they different?

7. Is there a lot of action in the story? How is the plot arranged? (Chronological order, individual incidents, flashback, etc.) Does it all fit together and relate to one main idea?

8. Did the story end as you expected it to? How did the author prepare you for the ending?

9. Suppose we thought of a different ending for the story. How would the rest of the story have to be changed for the new ending?

10. What does the author do to get the story going? Suppose that incident were changed or removed, how would the rest of the story be changed?

11. Suppose the order of events were changed? What would happen to the story? Would it be a new story or no story at all?

12. Where does the story take place? Could it have taken place in another place? In another time?

13. Does the story as a whole create any particular mood? If so, what is this mood and how does the author establish it?

14. Is there anything that seems to make this particular author's work unique? If so, what?

15. Did you notice any particular patterns in the form of this book? If you are reading this book in more than one sitting, are there natural points at which to break off your reading? If so, what are these?

32.

16. Were there any clues that the author built into the story which helped you to anticipate the outcome? If so, what were they? Did you think these clues were important bits of information when you first read them?

17. What signs and signals indicate that a story will be fanciful rather than realistic? Funny rather than serious?

18. Does the story language seem natural for the intent of the story and for the various speakers?

19. Who is the "teller" of the story? If the teller is one of the characters in the story, how is the story different from one that is related by a narrator who is not a character in the story?

20. Every writer creates a make-believe world and peoples it with characters. Even when the world is far different from your own, how does the author make the story seem possible or probable?

33.

WORKSHEETS FOR DISCUSSION: NUMBER TWENTY

Worksheets for Discussion in Children's Literature: #20—
Comparison of Science and Fiction

COMPARISON OF SCIENCE AND FICTION

SCIENCE	FICTION
Facts & Ideas	Images & Feelings
Objective	Subjective
Denotative	Connotative
Literal	Literary
Explanation	Narrative
Observation	Insight
Concepts	Percepts
Discourse	Nondiscourse
Logical	Inferential
Puzzle	Design
Belief "that"	Belief "in"
Verifiable	Believable
Information	Entertainment
Educated Mind	Educated Imagination

34.

WORKSHEETS FOR DISCUSSION: NUMBER TWENTY-ONE

Worksheets for Discussion in Children's Literature: #21—
Approaches/Types/Functions in Criticism

APPROACHES/TYPES/FUNCTIONS IN CRITICISM

Basic Approaches to Criticism:
1. Mimetic
2. Pragmatic
3. Expressive
4. Objective/Formal

Functions of Criticism:
1. Technical
2. Social/Journalistic
3. Practical
4. Theoretical

Types of Criticism:
1. Impressionistic
2. Genre
3. Textual
4. Historical
5. Sociological
6. Biographical
7. Comparative
8. Judicial
9. Scientific
10. Psychological
11. Archetypal
12. Mythic
13. Ethical
14. Existential
15. Moral
16. Phenomenological
17. Marxist
18. Freudian
19. Structuralist
20. Post-Structuralist
21. Deconstructionist
22. Transactional
23. Feminist
24. Reader Response

35.

WORKSHEETS FOR DISCUSSION: NUMBER TWENTY-TWO

Worksheets for Discussion in Children's Literature: #22—
Probe Sheet

PROBE SHEET

Author

    Type of Book

    c. Date

Title

Publishing Information

Authority

Other Works

Publishing History

1. Format
    a. Size
    b. Margins
    c. No. of pages
    d. Index
    e. Type Style(s)
    f. Table of Contents
    g. Frontispiece
    h. Illustrations
    i. Other

36.

2. Purpose

3. Contents

4. Style
    a. Vocabulary
    b. Poetry
    c. Sexist
    d. Didactic
    e. Religious
    f. Other

5. Special Features

37.

WORKSHEETS FOR DISCUSSION: NUMBER TWENTY-THREE

Worksheets for Discussion in Children's Literature: #23—Historical Textbooks/Readers

HISTORICAL READERS/TEXTBOOKS:

1. What virtues are stressed for the child to emulate?

2. What vices are children warned against?

3. Cite some examples of virtues and vices from texts examined.

4. What is the nature of the religious content?

5. What is the perception of the child conveyed through these books?

38.

6. What is the nature of the illustration and how is it related to the text?

7. What is the nature of the emphasis on elocution?

8. To what extent is reiteration a characteristic of the textbooks?

9. What is the nature of the vocabulary?

10. How was poetry used in the textbook reader?

39.

WORKSHEETS FOR DISCUSSION: NUMBER TWENTY-FOUR

Worksheets for Discussion in Children's Literature: #24—Fairy Tales

FAIRY TALES

1. Which fairy tales seem most appropriate for reading aloud to children today?

2. Select a standard tale and examine as many versions and variants as you can find. Does the tale change radically over time? How does the tale actually change? How do differing illustrations influence the interpretation of the tale?

3. How is language used as an important factor in the telling of tales? Do you feel that it is critical?

4. What collections of fairy tales would you recommend to children?

40.

5. What fairy tales would you suggest to anyone interested in storytelling?

6. Are the Lang and Jacobs editions viable today? (See Brian Alderson's work)

WORKSHEETS FOR DISCUSSION: NUMBER TWENTY-FIVE

41.

Worksheets for Discussion in Children's Literature: #25—Children's Classics

CHILDREN'S CLASSICS

1. Are these "good stories"? Why or why not?

2. Are they "dated"? If so, in what ways? (social concerns, morality, language, etc.)

3. Are they didactic? Sentimental?

4. Are they of value for today's children? Why or why not?

42.

5. Should some classics be read aloud to children? Which ones?

6. How might a teacher or librarian encourage children to enjoy classics?

43.

WORKSHEETS FOR DISCUSSION: NUMBER TWENTY-SIX

Worksheets for Discussion in Children's Literature: #26— Format and Illustration in Children's Picture Books

FORMAT AND ILLUSTRATION IN CHILDREN'S PICTURE BOOKS

- For each of the items below, list specific examples which demonstrate the point you wish to make.
- You may wish to bring a few examples to class to share with others.

1. How can the size and shape of a book contribute to its impact?

2. Name some illustrators who make use of unusual techniques or special effects in book design.

3. What are "toy books"?

4. How can endpapers support the message or the mood of a book?

44.

5. What different patterns of relationship between text and illustration can be seen in the physical layout of the pages of picture books?

6. Give examples of various degrees of complexity in illustration. Is there any relationship between complexity and the artistic medium?

7. What, if any, is the relation of technique to mood in illustration?

8. How is motion revealed in illustration?

9. How is humor conveyed in illustration?

10. Identify picture books which might demonstrate representational, abstract and impressionistic styles of art work.

45.

11. Identify stereotypical aspects of illustration in picture books.

12. Give examples of books in which the illustrator's knowledge of history, culture, art, architecture, etc., add dimension to the work.

13. Identify realistic, romantic and fanciful elements in illustration of picture books.

14. Give examples of illustrations in which subtle visual details require the viewer to study the page in order to discover them.

• Bring to class as many examples of different illustrations of *Snow White*, *Beauty and the Beast*, *Puss in Boots*, and *Cinderella* as you can find.

• Bring examples of different types of illustrations of mice and pigs in children's picture books.

46.

WORKSHEETS FOR DISCUSSION: NUMBER TWENTY-SEVEN

Worksheets for Discussion in Children's Literature: #27—Historical Periodicals for Children

HISTORICAL PERIODICALS FOR CHILDREN

ANALYSIS OF PERIODICALS:

Name:

Date:

Publisher:

Editor:

Contents: No. of Items   Column Inches

Fiction:

Traditional Works:

Original Works:

Serials:

Other:

Nonfiction:

Current Events/News Coverage:

Documentary/Travel:

Biography:

Sports:

Other:

47.

Poetry:

Columns:

Letters:

Games/Puzzles:

Reader Contributions:

Illustration:

Advertisements:

Other:

Sample Analysis of Specific Fictional Work in Periodical:

Author:

Title:

Length:

Genre:

Characters:

    Number: Major   Minor

    Human:

    Animal:

    Age:

    Sex:

    Race:

48.

Setting:

    Unspecified:

    Specified:

    U.S.:

    England:

    Other:

    Urban:

    Rural:

    Suburban:

Importance to the story?

Mood/Tone:

    Overall Mood:

    Attitude toward the Reader:

    Attitude toward the Material:

Language:

    Vocabulary:

    Reading Level:

WORKSHEETS FOR DISCUSSION: NUMBER TWENTY-EIGHT

*Worksheets for Discussion in Children's Literature: #28—
Folk Literature for Children; An Inquiry*

FOLK LITERATURE FOR CHILDREN: AN INQUIRY

Please take a few minutes to think about these questions to help focus your attention on the topic of folklore and fairy tales in a child's life and literature.

1. Are there folk and/or fairy characters or tales that were important to you in your own childhood? If so, can you remember how and why they assumed importance in your life? If not, do you know why not? Do you think you were unusual in this respect?

2. Were you exposed to a wide range of folk literature as a child? If so, who shared this literature with you?

3. Do you recall any examples of folk or fairy tale from your childhood that frightened you?

4. How important are folk and fairy tales to today's children? How much should we (as parents, teachers, librarians, etc.) do to encourage the child's appreciation of such stories?

5. Are there any dangers in a child's belief in fairy tales?

6. Is there such a thing as "creative violence," that is, violence that helps to resolve rather than heighten fears and tensions? Is this the violence of the fairy tales?

7. Do you really believe that many of the favorite fairy tales deal with oedipal conflicts and sexuality?

8. Who are the mythical heroes for today's children? Where do they come from?

9. If folktales were the television of a printless society, is television now the folk literature of our media-saturated society?

10. Give at least two descriptors for each of the following: Stepmother, Godmother, Prince, Princess, Mother, Fox, Youngest Son, Hare, Castle, Forest, Sword, Spell and Fairy. Who are some of the other recurring characters of folk literature?

51.

WORKSHEETS FOR DISCUSSION: NUMBER TWENTY-NINE

Worksheets for Discussion in Children's Literature: #29—
Illustrator As Storyteller

ILLUSTRATOR AS STORYTELLER

I. Wordless Picture Books
II. Story as interaction of Illustrations and Text
III. Picture Story Books
A. Illustration as Confirmation of Text
B. Illustration as Extension of Text
1. Illumination of Character
2. Variations of Plot
   a. Addition of Detail
   b. Addition of Subplots or Parallel Plots
3. Variations of Settings
   a. Addition of Detail
   b. Alternative Settings
4. Variations of Point of View
5. Variations of Mood and Tone
IV. Illustrated Books
V. Decorated Books

52.

WORKSHEETS FOR DISCUSSION: NUMBER THIRTY

Worksheets for Discussion in Children's Literature: #30—
Thinking About Illustration

THINKING ABOUT ILLUSTRATION

The following quotations may be useful in stimulating your thoughts about illustration in children's books.

"This illustrator's career [Van Allsburg] in sculpture was evident to one child, who remarked after long study that a picture in *Jumanji* looked like 'a photograph of clay people'; indeed for centuries the monochromatic gray paintings called grisaille were intended to look like sculpture from a distance."

—Lacy (1986) p. 112.

"Is there rhythm of line, of movement, of shape and mass in the drawings, and are these rhythms suitable to that of the story? If the text has sweep, do the pictures move likewise? Are the drawings so slick and photographically perfect that they were dead before we had a chance to look at them?"

—M. Brown (1986) p. 11.

"In fact, pictures by themselves convey little. Just as our understanding of language depends on our knowledge of the grammar that gives it shape, our understanding of pictures depends on our knowledge of the conventions they operate by."

—*Image and Maker.* (1984) p. 1.

"Perhaps there is a problem with that word 'illustrator.' It sounds as if someone is trying to enhance something that is already there. Actually Fritz Eichenberg's work does not so much 'enhance' as it 'embodies' a text. The word of the text is made flesh, as it is in the work of Rembrandt and Holbein and Durer."

—Eichenberg (1979) Introduction p. 13.

53.

"The main function of illustration is to illuminate text, to throw light on words. In fact, illustration in medieval books is called illumination and the term illustration derives from the Latin verb meaning 'to light up,' 'to illuminate.'"

—Shulevitz (1985) p. 120.

"It can justifiably be asserted that the pictorial material in children's books reaches a degree of intricacy and reflects an abundance of individual styles far beyond what can be found in accompanying text. Therefore, it offers more to and demands more of the child's mind."

—Schwarcz (1975) p. 2.

54.

WORKSHEETS FOR DISCUSSION: NUMBER THIRTY-ONE

Worksheets for Discussion in Children's Literature: #31
—Fantasy

FANTASY

1. Discuss how shape-shifting is used in the writings of LeGuin, Cooper and Murphy. (Please bring specific passages to class.)

2. Compare and contrast Tolkien's and C. S. Lewis' views on fantasy as represented by the excerpts from their work distributed in class.

3. Use the above concepts in your analysis of different types of modern fantasy for children.

4. Discuss the testing of the protagonist in the writings of Robin McKinley or Madeleine L'Engle.

5. Explore how the "Choose Your Own Adventure" books either conform to or depart from the traditions of fantasy.

55.

6. Are the microcomputer software fantasy games really fantasy?

7. Trace the use of the dragon as a fantasy character for children over time. Has the power of the dragon in literature shifted from the forces of evil to the forces of good?

8. Where do the Dragons of Pern fit into the above context. How are they like and unlike the dragons in Jane Yolen's and Shirley Murphy's works?

9. Bring to class examples of three different uses of foreshadowing in fantasy.

10. How important is the mapping of place in the trilogies or series of fantasy works by a single author?

56.

WORKSHEETS FOR DISCUSSION: NUMBER THIRTY-TWO

Worksheets for Discussion in Young Adult Literature: #32—Pathfinder Instructions for Informational Materials

PATHFINDER INSTRUCTIONS FOR INFORMATIONAL MATERIALS

Prepare a pathfinder on a topic approved by the instructor and one that meets potential needs of young adult library users. You may specify the setting, the situation and the particular group of users in any reasonable fashion for the completion of this assignment.

A pathfinder differs from a bibliography in that it does not necessarily contain a fairly complete list of sources on a topic. Rather it serves as a guide (thus, a pathfinder) for the user to find his/her own specific information on a topic. It provides enough basic resources to get the user started and may even help him/her plan a strategy for further study and research. As such, it *might* include:

• Sources for an Introduction to the Topic (Perhaps an encyclopedia or basic text)
• Subject Headings (LC & Sears) & Classification Numbers (LC & Dewey)
• Alternative approaches to the topic
• Specialized reference sources
• Bibliographies
• Texts
• Review Sources
• Abstracting & Indexing Services (Including data bases)
• Journals
• Media other than print
• Special materials for specialized users (large print books, books for blind, etc.)
• Organizations and/or Associations
• Representative listings of most useful items

57.

Where appropriate, specify how each item included relates to the topic. Also, remember that you are helping a young adult select materials that will ultimately effect his/her personal and/or schooling life. Your approach to the selection and development of a topic for this pathfinder will, to some extent at least, reveal your priorities and understanding of the needs of the young adult users you have identified.

Your work will be evaluated *not* on the basis of its length or the number of citations but rather as evidence of your judgment as a partner in the lifelong learning process. The actual packaging of your product is a factor in evaluation. Thus, the determination of *how* you will present your pathfinder is critical.

58.

WORKSHEETS FOR DISCUSSION: NUMBER THIRTY-THREE

Worksheets for Discussion in Young Adult Literature: #33—Things to Think About in Genre Fiction

THINGS TO THINK ABOUT IN GENRE FICTION

1. What is "genre fiction"?

2. What are the different types of genre fiction?

3. Do these various types of genre fiction have more in common than in contrast?

4. Are there mythic elements evident in genre fiction? Explain.

5. What do we mean by "literary conventions"? Cite examples from genre fiction.

6. How are these genre represented on contemporary television?

7. Genre fiction is often where adult and young adult readers meet. What are the possibilities and the problems that result from this meeting for those of us who work with young adults?

59.

60.

WORKSHEETS FOR DISCUSSION: NUMBER THIRTY-FOUR

Worksheets for Discussion in Young Adult Literature: #34—Literary Motifs

LITERARY MOTIFS

The study of motifs is common in the traditional literature and even in stories for younger children. Identify and explore the use of these motifs in contemporary realism for young adults.

PRIMARY MOTIFS

— Good vs. Evil
— The Quest
— The Journey
— The Test
— Rags to Riches
— Loss / Recovery
— Triumph of the Underdog

SECONDARY MOTIFS

— The Rescue
— The Triangle
— Heedless Mocking of Power, Tempting of Fates
— Defiance of Rules
— Use of Magic Numbers (three, seven)
— The Twist
— The Talisman
— The Transformation, Exchange
— The Scapegoat
— Mysterious Birth
— The Dream as Omen or Portent

61.

WORKSHEETS FOR DISCUSSION: NUMBER THIRTY-FIVE

Worksheets for Discussion in Young Adult Literature: #35
—Horror and the Occult

HORROR AND THE OCCULT

1. What is the explanation for increased interest in horror reflected in the popularity of works of Stephen King, V. C. Andrews and others?

2. To what extent is horror a reflection of interest in the occult? Does this genre of reading easily move a reader to an increased interest in satanism?

3. What are the conventions of horror?

4. Why do some people associate gypsies and freaks with horror and is this justified?

5. Is evil the dominant characteristic of the horror story?

62.

6. To what extent is the horror story connected with folklore?

7. What is the role of astrology, parapsychology and other future-telling approaches in this literature?

8. Identify examples of horror and satinism in the music of young adults.

9. Does the association with horror and the occult in literature help young adults deal with the horrors in their own lives, serve as a release valve for their own horrific impulses or encourage them to act out the content of this literature?

10. Although horror and the occult are generally considered to be lesser forms of literature, there have been and continue to be many cross-overs from this genre to classic or at least recognized literary contributions. Identify examples.

63.

WORKSHEETS FOR DISCUSSION: NUMBER THIRTY-SIX

Worksheets for Discussion in Young Adult Literature: #36—Romance

ROMANCE

1. To what extent are the book jackets or covers important to the choice of the specific book in this genre?

2. What would you determine to be the characteristics of a romance novel? How do they differ from those of the more realistic problem novel?

3. It is said that romances are read by "little old ladies in pure white tennis shoes"—indicating a desire for books without sordid and/or detailed sexual encounters. Do you think this is true for young adults and how do you distinguish which books meet such a need?

4. What are the commonalities and differences among and within the various young adult romance series? Use specific examples to support your arguments.

64.

5. What is importance of adult romance writers such as Whitney, Stewart and Holt to young adult readers?

6. What do we mean by the "ripped bodice" novel? Are these a part of young adult literature or popular with young adult readers?

7. What do you derive from reading Radway's work that is applicable to young adult literature?

8. Do young adult males read romance novels?

9. Use the work of a particular theorist of feminist criticism to evaluate both romance novels themselves and their role in the developing feminist consciousness.

65.

WORKSHEET FOR DISCUSSION: NUMBER THIRTY-SEVEN

Worksheets for Discussion in Young Adult Literature: #37—Sagas and Chronicles

SAGAS AND CHRONICLES

1. What is the appeal of sagas and chronicles?

2. Identify and give examples of support for your position on the importance of setting in such novels.

3. It has been said that nationalism is a fundamental element in the saga and/or chronicle. Provide evidence to support or negate such a thesis.

4. Land ownership is a fundamental concern to humans. How does this form of genre deal with the rise and fall of families in relation to land ownership?

5. Linkages to historic events and achievements are often made in these works. Provide examples for sharing with the group.

66.

WORKSHEETS FOR DISCUSSION: NUMBER THIRTY-EIGHT

Worksheets for Discussion in Young Adult Literature: #38—Science Fiction

SCIENCE FICTION

1. What are some of the major motifs in science fiction?

2. Select any representational sample of titles in science fiction and be ready to discuss how they contribute to your perception of the genre. The titles might be by authors such as those appearing on your reading list.

3. Describe the nature and extent of reference materials in science fiction?

4. Why and how are the technological elements stressed in many sci-fi movies?

5. What might explain the importance of the Starship Enterprise, Darth Vader, Yoda and HAL?

67.

6. What are some of the variations and conventions in science fiction?

7. How would you describe the role of woman in sci-fi? Has there been any change?

8. Discuss science fiction as social criticism.

68.

WORKSHEETS FOR DISCUSSION: NUMBER THIRTY-NINE

Worksheets for Discussion in Young Adult Literature: #39—An Exploration of The Hobbit and the Lord of the Rings Trilogy

AN EXPLORATION OF THE HOBBIT AND THE *LORD OF THE RINGS* TRILOGY

How would you describe your overall response to reading Tolkien? How did these stories make you feel? What did they make you think about? What made them interesting to you?

Which literary element or elements were most important in these stories?

How does Tolkien create his fanciful world and make the impossible real through his selection of details?

Is the author's point of view revealed through the creation of his fanciful characters? If so, provide examples.

How is humor conveyed and used in these stories?

Does Tolkien's use of subplots help you to follow the main development of the stories or does it detract?

How do character names and personal idiosyncrasies reveal the personalities and motives of those characters?

Are the characters described or revealed? Do we know them through their actions, thoughts, or dialogue?

Does the dialogue appear to be natural to the characters? How much dialogue is used and what do characters talk about?

Is dialogue used primarily to reveal character, to emphasize events, to create mood, to establish setting, or to initiate action?

69. Choose another author of fantasy and adapt the above in order to compare and contrast.

Will these questions also work in the analysis and evaluation of realistic works? Give examples.

70.

WORKSHEETS FOR DISCUSSION: NUMBER FORTY

Worksheets for Discussion in Young Adult Literature: #40—Instructions for a Bibliographic Essay

INSTRUCTIONS FOR A BIBLIOGRAPHIC ESSAY

A bibliographic essay may take many forms and even a casual examination of the literature demonstrates this. For the purpose of this assignment, however, it would be most useful to model your essay on the attached examples. Your choice of topic should be approved by me and should be something of interest to you.

I suggest that topics such as: selecting a college, gardening, cooking, sewing, crafts, physical fitness, AIDS, death and dying, sports are appropriate starting points; that is, such informational topics are ordinarily more easily accomplished. It would be possible to select a subset within these groups that in itself has a variety of collection possibilities. For example, gardening might be approached by selecting a topic on roses or annuals or trees or ground covers. Recall that the narrower the topic the more problems you may have, so don't go too far in that direction. It is obvious from analysis of the examples that a form of classification was used by the authors in discussing their collections. The bibliographic essay on Vietnam is more complex, perhaps because it deals with imaginative rather than informational materials. It is important that you examine these examples and make use of similar devices in your essay. Remember that a bibliographic essay is neither an annotated list nor a bibliography. It will require that you develop a grasp on the selected field quickly and efficiently and then prepare an informative and readable guide to the literature of that field for others. Such bibliographic essays may, in this era of personal computers and desktop publishing, be, if not a substitute for, at least an alternative to traditional bibliographies for library patrons.

71.

Examples of Bibliographical Essays:

Carol Boyle. "Building the Canine Literature Collection," *Library Journal Special Report #6* pp. 35-39.

Edward K. Eckert and William J. Searle. (January 1987). "Creative Literature of the Vietnam War: A Selected Bibliography," *Choice* 24: 725-735.

72.

WORKSHEETS FOR DISCUSSION NUMBER FORTY-ONE

Worksheets for Discussion in Children's Literature: #41— Fun Project

FUN PROJECT

ASSUMPTION: A large portion of literature devoured by young children is presented in the form of TV commercials.

PROJECT: Categorize these commercials according to the broad, generally accepted categories of children's literature and compare their effectiveness in those groups with other types of literature (books, magazines, records, comics, radio, movies, regular TV programs) and among themselves.

ANTICIPATED OUTCOMES: They probably rank high!

73.

WORKSHEETS FOR DISCUSSION NUMBER FORTY-TWO

Worksheets for Discussion in Children's Literature: #42—Story Pattern

STORY PATTERN

1. Character is given instructions to do something
2. Character does not do what he/she is told to do
3. Character is saved from being punished for disobeying

(*The Tale of Peter Rabbit* and *Two Bad Ants* are probably good examples of this pattern.)

Can you think of other stories that use this pattern?
— a fairy tale
— a folktale
— an animal story
— a modern story about a boy or girl

Have you ever used this pattern in writing your own story?

74.

WORKSHEETS FOR DISCUSSION: NUMBER FORTY-THREE

Worksheets for Discussion in Children's Literature: #43—Mythology and Folklore

MYTHOLOGY AND FOLKLORE

Mythology: Myth is to be defined as a complex of stories—some no doubt fact, and some fantasy—which, for various reasons, human beings regard as demonstrations of the inner meaning of the universe and of human life. Myth is quite different from philosophy in the sense of abstract concepts—consisting of vivid, sensually intelligible narratives, images, rites, ceremonies, and symbols.

—Alan Watts. *Myth and Ritual in Christianity*

Myth is NOT a statement of fact clothed in obscure language (historic theory)

Myth is NOT a fanciful or speculative explanation of natural phenomenon (nature myth).

BUT Myth is a narrative linked with a rite or ritual; myths closely associated with rites become scripture; others become folklore.

There are basic kinds of myth:

1. Creation myths that explain the origins of the universe.
2. Exemplary or hero myths that show a model of behavior through the portrayal of a hero.
3. Nature myths that account for the operations of the physical environment.

Please refer to Joseph Campbell. (1988). *The Power of Myth.* With Bill Moyers. New York: Doubleday. (or use the video)

For example:

"Moyers: I came to understand from reading your books—the *Masks of God* or *The Hero With a Thousand Faces*, for example—that what human beings have in common is revealed in myths. Myths are stories of our search through the ages for truth, for meaning, for significance. . . . Campbell: People say that what we're all seeking is a meaning for life. I don't think that's what we're really seeking. I think what we're seeking is the experience of being alive . . . myths are clues to the spiritual potentialities of the human life."—p. 5.

Folklore: Folklore contains many of the same elements of mythology as an explanation of reality, as a guide to exemplary behavior, and as a statement of the nature of things. Folklore, however, does not involve such deep-seated and religious fervor as mythology. Folklore is mythology translated into literature.

We will use the following books in our discussion as well as any others you may wish to share.

Mordicai Gerstein. (1987). *Mountains of Tibet.* New York: Harper & Row.

Deborah Nourse Lattimore. (1987). *The Flame of Peace: A Tale of the Aztecs.* New York: Harper & Row.

Virginia Hamilton. (1988). *In the Beginning.* Illus. by Barry Moser. New York Harcourt Brace Jovanovich.

The Naked Bear: Folktales of the Iroquois. (1987). John Bierhorst, Editor. Illus. by Dick Zimmer. New York: Wm. Morrow.

Jamake Highwater. (1984). *Legend Days.* New York: Harper & Row. (1985); *Ceremony of Innocence.* New York: Harper & Row; (1986). *I Wear the Morning Star.* New York: Harper & Row.

75.

WORKSHEETS FOR DISCUSSION: NUMBER FORTY-FOUR

Worksheets for Discussion in Young Adult Literature: #44 —Critical Thinking

CRITICAL THINKING

The following items will be presented during class and followed by a time interval for team analysis.

"The Shooting Gallery" (1970). SIM Productions. (Weston Woods Studios.)

and

Kay E. Vandergrift. (Winter 1987). "Critical Thinking Misfired: Implications of Student Responses to *The Shooting Gallery,*" *School Library Media Quarterly.* 15: 86-91.

Given this film, and the article that discusses responses to the film, prepare a discussion guide or plan a program for sharing this film with young people. The objective is to sharpen perception of a visual medium, to increase appreciation of visual forms, to increase understanding of the grammar of film and to work towards the development of critical thinking skills.

Using what you have learned in the above activities, repeat the process with the film *Jabberwocky.* (1973). SIM Productions. (Weston Woods Studios.)

76.

77.

WORKSHEETS FOR DISCUSSION: NUMBER FORTY-FIVE

Worksheets for Discussion of Children's Literature: #45
—David Macaulay and his work

DAVID MACAULAY AND HIS WORK

Team A:

David Macaulay. (1985). *Cathedral: The Story of Its Construction*. Unicorn Projects, Inc. Distributed by Dorest Video. (VHS, 57.57 minutes/color.)

David Macaulay. (1973). *Cathedral*. Boston, MA: Houghton Mifflin.

Team B:

David Macaulay. (1983). *Castle*. Unicorn Projects, Inc. Distributed by Dorest Video. (VHS, 57.18 minutes/color.)

David Macaulay. (1977). *Castle*. Boston, MA: Houghton Mifflin.

Using the materials provided, each team is to work on the questions below and share their findings with the entire class.

1. Are the book and the video different or essentially the same?

2. Since the video production is in color and the book in black and white, what differences emerge?

3. Do the animated stories on the imaginary cathedral or on the castle add or interfere with the content?

78.

4. What differences could you list between book and video where *informational content is discussed?*

5. What visual images are the strongest in each medium? Why?

6. Identify those things that are better explored in one medium rather than another.

7. Do you believe that children will be able to transfer this information to places not included in either video or book?

At the end of our analysis the following items might be useful to add to our total evaluation of the work of David Macaulay.

David Macaulay in His Studio. VHS Videotape, 25 minutes. Houghton Mifflin Author and Artist Videotape Series. Boston, MA: Houghton Mifflin.

David Macaulay. (1988). *The Way Things Work*. Boston, MA: Houghton Mifflin.

David Macaulay. (1974). *City: A Story of Roman Planning & Construction*. Boston, MA: Houghton Mifflin.

David Macaulay. (1975). *Pyramid*. Boston, MA: Houghton Mifflin.

David Macaulay. (1983). *Mill*. Boston, MA: Houghton Mifflin.

David Macaulay. (1980). *Unbuilding*. Boston, MA: Houghton Mifflin.

David Macaulay. (1976). *The Underground*. Boston, MA: Houghton Mifflin.

 **Continuing Education in Children's Literature**

INTRODUCTION

Part of the task of teaching, perhaps the most important part, is conveying to students that the subject matter is both important and continuing to grow. Just as there is almost never a single book that contains all there is to know about a topic, no one course can adequately prepare those who will work with children and literature. Such courses serve as introductions to the field by providing a general outline of the territory, identifying some key landmarks, and mapping out potential paths that students might travel on their own. Even two or three courses in the field cannot provide access to all that is currently known about children's literature. What these courses can do is whet the appetite for further study.

Professional Associations and Reading

Further study, of course, does not necessarily mean formal courses of instruction in a college or university setting. One of the best forms of continuing education is through active involvement in professional associations. Reading the professional journals of these associations informs one about current theory, research, and practice in children's literature, but it is far more helpful to attend professional meetings in order to engage in a dialogue with those who have similar interests and concerns. The problem is that children's literature is a field of study that exists in a number of different disciplines, and the articulation and communication among them leaves much to be desired.

Professional reading must go in a variety of directions beginning with children's literature itself. The number of journals in the field has grown rapidly in the last two decades. This growth provides more information to the professional but it also makes it more difficult to keep up with current reading and research. The problem is compounded because much of the writing about children's literature is found in the journals of the International Reading Association, National Council of Teachers of English, Modern Language Association, and Popular Culture Association as well as in general publications and in the journals of publishing and the book trade. For instance, it was through reading the *English Journal* that some fascinating work with computers and literature was discovered.[1] Some of these software programs will be translated to children's literature in order to provide an alternative learning experience for students. *Book Research Quarterly* has also had some stimulating articles about children's books in recent issues.

Continuing Education for Teachers
of Children's Literature

One must recognize that teachers of children's literature also face the need for continued scholarly work in their discipline. Almost every conference, seminar, colloquium, workshop, and institute offered, and there are many, is open to anyone who applies. Thus, the audience is mixed between those who have a limited background and those who have a strong and sophisticated knowledge of the field. One approach that might address this imbalance is to bring together those with similar levels of sophistication to address questions and issues for research, teaching, and writing. Some attempt is made to do this at the Children's Literature Association meetings, but opportunities for intense discussions and exchanges are almost non-existent. A group within the Association of Library Service to Children (ALSC) called the Teachers of Children's Literature Section and a similar group in the International Reading Association (IRA) also attempts to provide a forum for discussion, but for the most part these efforts have failed to be as helpful as anticipated. On the occasions the author attended such meetings, they have been dominated by those who are new to teaching, often totally new to the field, and are just discovering many of the authors, titles, and ideas that have long been well-known to experienced teachers. The new and enthusiastic look at established work may be refreshing but it does not necessarily foster growth either as a teacher or a scholar for one who has much experience in the field. Other meetings seemed to be a version of the "Sitting at the Feet" model of teaching in which an especially well-known person in the field was urged to expound on a particular topic.

More experienced teachers of children's literature need increased opportunities for serious, and more sustained, exchange of ideas. For example, it would be fascinating for a group of teachers to discuss illustration and the use of slides with Gertrude Herman who writes the column for *Horn Book* entitled "A Picture Is Worth Several Hundred Words."[2] She generally explores the use of one picture and dwells on it with intensity; this author, on the other hand, most often focuses on an entire work by using close-ups of portions of an illustration as well as comparison of works that address the same subject. For instance, the author uses a contrast of presentations of Beauty and the Beast, Snow White, or even a specific animal such as a lion or a mouse to demonstrate alternate visual interpretations of the same text. Both approaches present the viewer with a world of information and detail. If a forum could be provided to discuss how and why such teaching choices are made with input from resource people in art and illustration, teachers would undoubtedly profit from the exchange.

Another reasonable approach would be the establishment of an online bulletin board for teachers of children's literature. This might be effected through BITNET, to which most university faculty have access, or through similar types of networks. Those in library schools might use ALANET as an alternative. This would increase communication and the exchange of ideas and might lead to more cooperative ventures. Most teachers of literature are anxious to know what books are being read in other courses, and even the simple exchange of reading lists, assignments, and the like might be a useful beginning of a more in-depth sharing of interests and ideas.

It would be helpful to have a centralized exchange system for sharing materials developed by individuals while keeping the monetary costs reasonable. The exchange would be open to all and might consist of content developed by faculty in various media such as slides, worksheets, transparencies, videos, films, and computer software that have been tested and used with students in children's literature programs. One institution may have better facilities for developing software while another may have greater resources for television and film. It is unfortunate not to share with other teachers of children's literature those teaching tools that might increase the competence of the students we teach. This concept of an exchange network might be similar to a paperback exchange in a public library in which those who are willing to share their own work are free to take from that contributed by others.

Seminars and Colloquia

The Children's Literature Center of the Library of Congress, under the leadership of Sybille Jagusch, has sponsored a number of seminars that have brought individuals from all over the country together in Washington to share a day devoted to a specific issue in children's literature.[3] Such activities are opportunities to focus on topics of significance and to visit the collection in the Library of Congress as well as to share and discuss mutual concerns with other experienced scholars in the field. Of course, these are infrequent and invitational, so they can not totally meet the need for a scholarly exchange. They may, however, serve as a model for a series of such meetings in various locations. Colloquia are potentially among the most useful means of professional development, particularly if we could begin to bring together faculty from various disciplines such as literature, education, and sociology to share their research interests.

An online colloquium among teachers of children's literature could also prove helpful, particularly if focused on a specific issue rather than on a general discussion. For instance, one concern is the desire to use a large number of books that are not easily available in the United States as well as those titles that have passed into history as forgotten works. The author has used *Rabbit Island*[4] and *na-ni*[5] because they permit one to make important points in teaching, but students sometimes are frustrated when they are unable to find these works in most libraries. Another question to raise in such an exchange would be the issue of multiple works of an author. Are students ready and able to make a sound judgment about Robert Cormier, M. E. Kerr, Cynthia Voigt, or Jane Yolen without reading multiple works? If not, how can we ever allow enough time in one young adult literature class to deal with major writers in the field. The author's solution to this problem has been the group assignment spelled out in the young adult syllabus in Chapter 5, but this is not a totally satisfactory resolution. Those involved in doctoral dissertations, would especially value the opportunity to exchange views about research studies with colleagues through both forms of colloquia.

Workshops and Institutes

Many of us remember the plenitude of the sixties, when monies for workshops and institutes were readily available. Sadly, that time is gone. We now must look to state resources and individual institutions for support. Institutes are useful to accommodate topics that can be explored in short time spans. They allow faculty members to concentrate their attention on a particular topic and share more information and ideas than would be possible within the time limits of a more general class. For example, topics such as folk literature, fantasy, science fiction, heroism, illustration of a particular artist, or feminism in children's literature all are valid topics for such efforts. Institutes or workshops designed for teachers of children's literature should also set admission requirements, such as education, professional experience, and publication. We might use a technique similar to one employed by the One-on-One Conference which is devoted to writing for children.[6] In this conference all who are accepted must provide evidence of their writing along with the application process. Only those with both a serious commitment and quality level work are accepted. Of course, the problem is that such institutes or workshops will not draw the large numbers of attendees that come for more general children's literature programs and authors' speeches. Therefore, although they may be more profitable educationally, they are not as remunerative and thus less likely to be supported by the institution. For many years, it has been the author's desire to plan a retreat in which experienced teachers of children's literature would go off somewhere, away from the normal distractions of their institutions, to share ideas, techniques, questions, and insights.

Two institutes which the author conducted within the past few years may serve as examples of some of the difficulties and the delights of this form of teaching. The first was a one-day session on "Metaphor and Metacognition". This institute met an immediate need for professional development and brought speakers together to examine the relationship between literature and critical thinking. Although the institute was very successful in many ways, there were also many things that would now be done differently. First, participants would be asked to do a great deal more work in advance. Although their knowledge of children's literature was generally high, many seemed to have only scattered and very uneven understanding of the work that has been done on critical thinking. Of course, some of the shortcoming might have been resolved by sending out appropriate materials far enough in advance of the institute so that those who attended would have the opportunity to come focused and prepared. Part of the problem was institutional and financial. Costs of photocopying and mailing had to come from the fees collected by enrollees; and by the time enough people signed up for the institute, it was too late to send out the materials. This led to the second change that would be made. So many speakers were scheduled during the day that there was too little opportunity for participants to follow up and try to relate the information and ideas shared within a smaller forum. A third, and interrelated, change has to do with the selection of speakers. In order to ensure attendance, an author whose works are fine literature and lend themselves to work with critical thinking was invited to speak. Certainly the presence of the author encouraged a few more people to attend; but, in some ways, the interest in his background and in getting him to autograph books detracted from the focus of the institute.

The case study of an institute on heroism which follows describes the design and execution of another program. It provides a plan and many of the materials used in the institute as well as information about the students who participated.

SHORT-TERM INSTITUTE — HEROISM

Focus of the Institute

"Enter a universe where brave souls still venture forth to battle the powers of darkness in strange and hostile worlds. Explore a sphere where small, quiet heroes prevail against the more subtle enemies within their own hearts. Come and uncover these heroic figures inside the pages of children's books and rediscover your own innocent sense of heroism." These were the words with which an intense three-Saturday seminar on heroism in children's literature was introduced on the brochure which described it. As an educator, it was a challenge to examine the concept of heroism and, after considerable study and dialogue, to analyze the nature and extent of heroism in today's children's literature. One question that acted as a driving force in the design of this seminar was whether children of the 1980s could be enticed by the heroic and develop the critical skills to grow in their knowledge of heroism in society and in their own lives.

Student Population for the Institute

One of the interesting aspects of this Saturday series was the sense of community developed in the group. Although a large number of teachers and librarians participated, there were also reading specialists, psychologists, family counsellors, parents, and writers. Some were graduate students taking the seminar for credit while others were participating for inservice education or more general personal interest. Although this wonderful diversity in the seminar was enriching, it did lead to additional teaching problems; 1) the size of the group (50 students) presented difficulty in providing the involvement that is present in smaller groups; 2) the participants' backgrounds in children's literature were unequal and thus common reference points were not readily available; and 3) the literary knowledge of participants was also very different and necessitated some basic explanations in order to assist those less knowledgeable which brought redundancy to others.

Environmental Aspects

The fact that the course met from 9:00-5:00 on Saturdays, a long day at the end of a busy week of work for most participants, necessitated a greater than usual range of materials and activities to vary the pacing, tone, and the required energy level. In contrast to a rather traditional time and hour distribution, this all-day seminar required additional environmental aspects to help mold the group cohesively. Coffee, food, opportunities for different types of interaction, and a generally informal atmosphere were essential to the overall warmth that was achieved. This kind of environment is typical of many workshops and institutes and is intended to make everyone delighted to be there and eager to share in the learning process.

The multi-layered design of this course led to a positive response from the participants and significant growth in the understanding of the literary qualities implicit in the term "heroism". This integration of staff, materials, and environment was critical to the overall success of the seminar. Although the course was primarily taught by a team of two, at least one outside expert joined the team during each of the three sessions. Materials for distribution were designed in advance, but new items were provided from week to week as the need was indicated. The folders of materials distributed to students at the first class were decorated with illustrations from early children's books, and all items were color-coded for attractiveness and ease of retrieval. The schedules, booklists, worksheets, and activity or assignment sheets were heavily illustrated (using clip-art books and etchings from old children's books) which aroused a great deal of interest and seemed to encourage students to enter into both the spirit and the events of our days together.

Costs of the Institute

Institutes can be designed to work in the continuing education or professional development units of most universities. Thus, some costs are carried by these units. An institute such as the one described can be implemented for approximately twenty-five hundred dollars. Obviously, some variation in costs would be expected because of the location of the institution in relation to the availability of speakers.

Questionnaire on the Concept of the Heroic

Drawing upon the experience of the participants and their recall of the heroic in their own lives was an essential factor in our plan. A questionnaire (see Figure 20) was used near the beginning of the first session to encourage recall and to increase consideration of qualities and attributes associated with the concept of the heroic. Although, in one segment of this instrument, students were asked which item in each of a number of pairs they considered to be more heroic (a ruby or a diamond, a rose or a lily, silk or velvet), the answers were not as important as the mental process encouraged through such thinking. Asking participants to consider whether they and the children with whom they work consider certain

(Text continues on page 208.)

FIGURE 20

HEROISM IN CHILDREN'S LITERATURE

AN INQUIRY

INSTRUCTIONS:

Please take a few minutes to respond to this brief inquiry to help focus your attention on the topic of heroism in child life and literature.

1. Who were the heroic characters from your own childhood?

   ____ Real people (Private or public figures?)

   ____ Book characters

   ____ Radio/TV/Movie heroes/heroines

   ____ Other _____

   ____ I can't remember any

2. Do you remember any *particular* heroes/heroines from your child-hood? If so, please indicate.

   _____

   _____

   _____

3. What do you think are the chief characteristics of heroic characters for children?

   _____

   _____

   _____

FIGURE 20 *Continued*

4. Of the terms that are paired in the lists below which term in each pair is more accurately a reflection of your view of heroism:

courage or bravery _____

inner strife or quietude _____

seeker of right or seeker of wisdom _____

male or female _____

task oriented or quest oriented _____

noble or gallant _____

self-sacrifice or nobility of purpose _____

visionary or leader _____

mortal or divine _____

5. Can you remember an example of a "PLACE" in a novel that seemed essential to the heroic qualities that occur? Please indicate.

_____

_____

_____

6. Of the pairs below, which do you consider most heroic?

lion or lamb _____

falcon or crow _____

rabbit or fox _____

gold or silver _____

ruby or diamond _____

rose or lily _____

FIGURE 20 *Continued*

English or Irish _____

silk or velvet _____

blue or red _____

clouds or stars _____

green or brown _____

castle or house _____

7. Do you recall any examples of heroic quests from your reading as a child?

_____

_____

8. Do you think the following persons are heroic and do you believe that children think so?

NAME OF PERSON	YOUR RESPONSE	CHILD
King Arthur _____		
Darth Vader _____		
Indiana Jones _____		
Robin Hood _____		
Johnny Tremain _____		
Joan of Arc _____		
Abraham Lincoln _____		
Helen Keller _____		
Aeneas _____		
Anne Frank _____		

FIGURE 20 *Continued*

9. Examine your answers in the previous question and try to determine if there are any commonalities in the way you reached your decisions.

_____

_____

_____

10. Please describe a heroic act, either real or imaginary?

_____

_____

11. How important are heroes or heroines to children and how much should we do to encourage their appreciation of such heroism? Are there any dangers in a child's belief in heroes/heroines?

_____

_____

figures to be heroic was another question that seemed to be fruitful. For example, were King Arthur, Joan of Arc, Darth Vader, and Indiana Jones all heroic? Do adults and young people have differing perceptions of who and what is heroic? This series of questions encouraged a growth in articulation of ideas on the concept of the nature of heroism. This was followed by a class-wide discussion of what makes someone heroic.

The heroic image as identified by students included a lengthy list of attributes that served as a focal point for subsequent discussion. For example, both internal and external manifestations of honor, bravery, courage, wisdom, and loyalty were explored in various works for children. Debate over changes in the concept of the heroic emerged and the sharing of views led to resolution of at least some of the different perceptions. The majority of participants believed, however, that children need strong exposure to heroic images in their literary encounters and some opportunity and means to explore the nature of heroic qualities.

Focus Questions to Guide Reading

A set of questions was prepared to accompany the reading lists of children's books to help students focus their attention on questions of heroism as they read a variety of works. These questions (see Figure 21) are simply catalyst ideas that, it was hoped, would trigger additional trains of thought in the readers.

FIGURE 21
FOCAL QUESTIONS FOR THE SEMINAR

1. Who is the hero/heroine and how is heroism revealed in the story?
2. Does the hero/heroine have any special qualities or gifts?
3. Is there a heroic quest?
4. How is the hero/heroine tested?
5. Is the challenge truly difficult for this particular hero/heroine?
6. Does the hero/heroine have protection? If so, who or what provides it?
7. Is point of view instrumental in conveying the spirit of the heroic?
8. Does setting have a major or minor role in the portrayal of the heroic?
9. To what extent do the illustrations contribute to our sense of the heroic?
10. Is the hero/heroine engaged in a classic struggle between good and evil or in a more "everyday conflict?"
11. What makes the hero/heroine truly heroic?
12. Are the heroic characters of children's stories akin to the tragic, the comic and/or the folk heroes/heroines of adult literature?

"Championing" a Book

Two major reading lists were developed as a focal point for the course. Figure 22 includes the children's books used as assigned reading from which each student chose a title to "champion" throughout the course. As the designated "champion" of a particular work, the student was expected to bring the work to the attention of the class when justified as an example of points being discussed. From time to time individuals were asked to speak about their selected works and to share their views on the literary development of the heroic in those works. Although each student selected a specific title, it was clear that they were expected to read as many of the suggested works as possible.

FIGURE 22

HEROISM IN CHILDREN'S LITERATURE

REQUIRED READINGS

Please read as many of the following titles as you can before the course begins. If you have already read the title indicated, it would be useful to re-read it, or at least re-think it, with the concept of heroism in mind. The folk and fairy tales, in particular, are merely representative of the vast range of traditional literature available. Other collections or versions of individual tales may be substituted.

CHILDREN'S BOOKS: A SAMPLING OF THE HEROIC

Alcott, Louisa May. *Little Women.* (any edition)

Armstrong, William H. (1969). *Sounder.* New York: Harper & Row.

Bang, Molly. (1983). *Dawn.* New York: William Morrow.

Boutet de Monvel, Louis Maurice. (1980). *Joan of Arc.* Facsimile of the original 1896 French Edition. New York: Viking Press.

Burnford, Sheila. (1961). *The Incredible Journey.* Boston, MA: Little Brown.

Carroll, Lewis. *Alice in Wonderland.* (any edition)

Childress, Alice. (1973). *A Hero Ain't Nothin' but a Sandwich.* New York: Coward.

Cleaver, Vera and Bill Cleaver. (1969). *Where the Lilies Bloom.* Philadelphia, PA: Lippincott.

Cooper, Susan. (1973). *The Dark Is Rising.* New York: Atheneum.

Cormier, Robert. (1979). *After the First Death.* New York: Pantheon.

Cormier, Robert. (1974). *The Chocolate War.* New York: Pantheon.

Dalgliesh, Alice. (1954). *The Courage of Sarah Noble.* New York: Charles Scribner's Sons.

Deveaux, Alexis. (1973). *na-ni.* New York: Harper & Row.

Favorite Tales From Grimm. (1982). Illustrated by Mercer Mayer. New York: Four Winds Press.

Forbes, Esther. (1943). *Johnny Tremain.* Boston, MA: Houghton-Mifflin.

Fritz, Jean. (1983). *The Double Life of Pocahontas.* New York: Putnam.

Garcia, Ann O'Neal. (1982). *Spirit on the Wall.* New York: Holiday House.

George, Jean. (1972). *Julie of the Wolves.* New York: Harper & Row.

Gramatky, Hardie. (1939). *Little Toot.* New York: Putnam.

Highwater, Jamake. (1977). *Anpao: An American Indian Odyssey.* Philadelphia, PA: Lippincott.

Holm, Ann. (1965). *North to Freedom.* New York: Harcourt.

FIGURE 22 *Continued*

Hunter, Mollie. (1983). *The Knight of the Golden Plain.* New York: Harper & Row.

Hyman, Trina Schart. (1983). *Little Red Riding Hood.* New York: Holiday.

Keats, Ezra Jack. (1965). *John Henry: An American Legend.* New York: Pantheon.

Knight, Eric. (1940). *Lassie Come Home.* New York: Holt.

Langford, Sondra Gordon. (1983). *Red Bird of Ireland.* New York: Atheneum.

Leaf, Munro. (1936). *The Story of Ferdinand.* New York: Viking Press.

LeGuin, Ursula. (1968). *The Wizard of Earthsea.* Oakland, CA: Parnassas.

L'Engle, Madeleine. (1962). *A Wrinkle in Time.* New York: Farrar.

McKinley, Robin. (1978). *Beauty.* New York: Harper & Row.

McKinley, Robin. (1982). *The Blue Sword.* New York: Greenwillow.

Mayer, Marianna. (1978). *Beauty and the Beast.* Illustrated by Mercer Mayer. New York: Four Winds Press.

Michael Hague's Favourite Hans Christian Andersen Fairy Tales. (1981). New York: Holt.

Namioka, Lensey. (1980). *Valley of the Broken Cherry Trees.* New York: Delacorte.

O'Brien, Robert C. (1971). *Mrs. Frisby and the Rats of NIMH.* New York: Atheneum.

Potter, Beatrix. (1902). *The Tale of Peter Rabbit.* New York: Warne.

Sendak, Maurice. (1981). *Outside Over There.* New York: Harper & Row.

Sperry, Armstrong. (1940). *Call It Courage.* New York: Macmillan.

Steig, William. (1976). *Abel's Island.* New York: Farrar.

Steig, William. (1982). *Doctor De Soto.* New York: Farrar.

Steiner, Jorg. (1978). *Rabbit Island.* New York: Harcourt.

Tolkein, J.R.R. (1938). *The Hobbit.* Boston: Houghton Mifflin.

Turkle, Brinton. (1965). *Obadiah the Bold.* New York: Viking Press.

Voight, Cynthia. (1982). *Dicey's Song.* New York: Atheneum.

Weik, Mary Hays. (1966). *The Jazz Man.* New York: Atheneum.

Weil, Lisl. (1983). *I, Christopher Columbus.* New York: Atheneum.

Wojciechowski, Maia. (1964). *Shadow of the Bull.* New York: Atheneum.

Yashima, Taro. (1955). *Crow Boy.* New York: Viking Press.

Yep, Laurence. (1977). *Child of the Owl.* New York: Harper & Row.

Zemach, Harve. (1969). *The Judge.* New York: Farrar.

Teaching Materials

Figure 23 includes general material on children's literature and literary criticism as well as specialized titles on heroism. This list, along with the previous one, proved useful as the course progressed and students agreed that the titles would be even more useful to them in the future as they continued to increase their competence in the area of heroism. Additional materials developed for the course included pertinent excerpts from Propp, Raglan, Campbell, Lewis, and others. These were text excerpts that helped guide students in their consideration of various means for examining literary works. Although all students were asked to read the works of these theorists/critics, many did not have the time to study them as carefully as we all would have liked. Thus, it seemed imperative to extract a few constructs that would demonstrate the use of their individual theories as well as permit the comparison of interpretations. Elements of story and literary motifs were discussed and examined in a variety of stories. Several shorter works were shared to provide some common reference points for class discussion. *A Knight of the Golden Plain* by Mollie Hunter and *The Seven Ravens* by Felix Hoffman were read aloud and then became the basis for exploring some general ideas about the nature of the heroic and points of reference in discussing other works.

The Voyage of Prince Fuji: An Analysis

The Voyage of Prince Fuji by Jenny Thorne was one work that evoked a great deal of discussion and involvement and led to a range of views, most strongly that of feminism, in the analysis. The book was read aloud and then, using photocopies for specific references, small groups explored its meaning with heated discussions taking place among each of the groups. What became obvious was the skirting of literary ideas and concerns in favor of a focus on feminism as a cultural attitude. It was clear that more time would have to be given in future planning to treatment of visual imagery and illustration as a means of interpretation of story. After this session, it was decided that a written response to the discussion should be distributed at the next class to alert students to additional means of criticism that had not been adequately discussed in class. (Figure 24 contains a portion of this response, indicating a recognition of the need to concentrate on literary aspects and not lose sight of the work as a whole.)

Terms and Definitions

An introduction to the historic roots of heroism led to a set of documents on these roots which was essentially an explanation of terms and definitions of fairy tale, folklore, tall tales, Mabinogion, chivalry, and so forth. Although these terms were defined from a group of standard texts, it seemed unnecessary to provide an elaborate and scholarly documentation for each item. The educational objective in this instance, was to alert students to the rich resources and the amount of investigation necessary to yield an accurate and fruitful literary reference.

(Text continues on page 216.)

FIGURE 23

HEROISM IN CHILDREN'S LITERATURE

GENERAL READINGS ABOUT CHILDREN'S LITERATURE

(There are literally hundreds of books on this topic. The first two listed are excellent general introductions often used as textbooks for children's literature classes. The third will give you some insight into the concerns of the course coordinator.)

Huck, Charlotte. (1979). *Children's Literature in the Elementary School.* 3rd Edition. New York: Holt, Rinehart & Winston.

Sutherland, Zena and Others. (1986). *Children and Books.* 7th Edition. Glenview, IL: Scott, Foresman Co.

Vandergrift, Kay E. (1980). *Child and Story: The Literary Connection.* New York: Neal-Schuman Publishers. (Reprinted in paperback in 1986.)

READINGS ABOUT HEROISM

Blackborn, William, Editor. (Fall 1983). "Adventure," *Children's Literature Association Quarterly.* Vol. 8, No. 3: 7–31.

Browne, Ray and Others. (1972). *Heroes of Popular Culture.* Bowling Green, OH: Bowling Green University Press.

Brownstein, Rachel. (1982). *Becoming a Heroine: Readings About Women in Novels.* New York: Viking Press.

Campbell, Joseph. (1968). *The Hero With a Thousand Faces.* 2nd Edition, Bollingen Series. Princeton, NJ: Princeton University Press.

Campbell, Joseph. (1972). *Myths to Live By.* New York: Viking Press.

Fishwick, Marshall. (1954). *American Heroes: Myth and Reality.* Washington, DC: Public Affairs Press. (Reprint 1975 by Greenwood Press.)

Fishwick, Marshall. (1969). *The Hero, American Style.* New York: David McKay.

Heilbrun, Carolyn. (Winter 1965). "Woman As Hero," *Texas Quarterly.* 132–141.

Hook, Sidney. (1943). *The Hero in History.* New York: John Day Co. (Reprint in 1955 by Beacon Press.)

Howarth, Patrick. (1973). *Play Up and Play the Game: The Heroes of Popular Fiction.* London: Methuen.

Hunter, Mollie. (April 1983). "A Need for Heroes," *The Horn Book.* Vol. LIX, No. 2: 146–154. (Text reprint supplied by Harper & Row for the course.)

FIGURE 23 *Continued*

Lehman, B. H. (1928). *Carlyle's Theory of the Hero: Its Sources, Development, History, and Influence on Carlyle's Work.* New York: AMS Press.

Levy, G. R. *The Sword from the Rock: An Investigation into the Origins of Epic Literature and the Development of the Hero.* New York: Grove Press, 1953. (Reprint 1977 by Greenwood Press.)

Lubin, Harold, Editor. (1968). *Heroes and Anti-Heroes: A Reader in Depth.* San Francisco, CA: Chandler Publishing Co.

Pearson, Carol and Katherine Pope. (1981). *The Female Hero in American and British Literature.* New York: R. R. Bowker Co.

Raglan, Fitzroy Richard Somerset 4th Baron. (1936). *The Hero.* London: Methuen. (Reprint in 1975 by Greenwood Press.)

Wecter, Dixon. (1941). *The Hero in America: A Chronicle of Hero-Worship.* New York: Charles Scribner's Sons.

Wilson, James D. (1982). *The Romantic Heroic Ideal.* Baton Rouge, LA: Louisiana State University Press.

Zweig, Paul. (1974). *The Adventurer.* New York: Basic Books. (Reprint 1981 by Princeton University Press.)

READINGS IN LITERARY CRITICISM

Bleich, David. (1975). *Readings and Feelings: An Introduction to Subjective Criticism.* Urbana, IL: National Council of Teachers of English.

Booth, Wayne C. (1979). *Critical Understanding: The Powers and Limits of Pluralism.* Chicago, IL: University of Chicago Press.

Culler, Jonathan. (1975). *Structuralist Poetics: Structuralism, Linguistics, and the Study of Literature.* Ithaca, NY: Cornell University Press.

Forster, E. M. (1927). *Aspects of the Novel.* New York: Harcourt, Brace & World.

Frye, Northrop. (1957). *Anatomy of Criticism.* Princeton, NJ: Princeton University Press.

Frye, Northrop. (1980). *Criticism As Education.* The Leland B. Jacobs Lecture, 1979. New York: School of Library Service, Columbia University. (Distributed in class.)

Frye, Northrop. (1964). *The Educated Imagination.* Bloomington, IN: Indiana University Press.

Graff, Gerald. (1979). *Literature Against Itself: Literary Ideas in Modern Society.* Chicago, IL: University of Chicago Press.

Hartman, Geoffrey. (1980). *Criticism in the Wilderness.* New Haven, CT: Yale University Press.

FIGURE 23 *Continued*

Iser, Wolfgang. (1979). *The Act of Reading: A Theory of Aesthetic Response.* Baltimore, MD: The Johns Hopkins University Press.

Lentricchia, Frank. (1980). *After the New Criticism.* Chicago, IL: University of Chicago Press.

Propp, Vladimir. (1968). *Morphology of the Folktale.* Translated by Louis A. Wagner. Austin, TX: University of Texas Press. (First published in 1928; First English translation in 1958.)

Rosenblatt, Louise M. (1981). *The Journey Itself.* The Leland B. Jacobs Lecture, 1981. New York: School of Library Service, Columbia University. (Distributed in the course.)

Rosenblatt, Louise M. (1976). *Literature As Exploration.* 3rd Edition. New York: Noble & Noble Publishers Inc. (First published in 1938.)

Rosenblatt, Louise M. (1978). *The Reader, The Text, The Poem.* Carbondale, IL: Southern Illinois University Press.

Suleiman, Susan and Inge Crosman, Editors. (1980). *The Reader in the Text: Essays on Audience and Interpretation.* Princeton, NJ: Princeton University Press.

Todorov, Tzvetan. (1982). *Symbolism and Interpretation.* Translated by Catherine Porter. Ithaca, NY: Cornell University Press.

Tompkins, Jane P., Editor. (1980). *Reader–Response Criticism: From Formalism to Post-Structuralism.* Baltimore, MD: The Johns Hopkins University Press.

Wellek, Rene and Austin Warren. (1977). *Theory of Literature.* New Revised Edition. New York: Harcourt, Brace Jovanovich. (First published in 1949.)

Young, Robert, Editor. (1981). *Untying the Text: A Post-Structuralist Reader.* Boston, MA: Routledge & Kegan Paul.

FIGURE 24

SOME COMMENTARY ON *THE VOYAGE OF PRINCE FUJI*

In thinking through our class discussion of the *The Voyage of Prince Fuji,* some ideas and questions seemed worth sharing with all of you. In essence, the sociological and cultural context of the work was emphasized. Our concerns seemed to focus on discussion of the feminist overtones and their meaning. We did not come to grips with the aesthetic qualities of the book, either literary or artistic. It was clear that many in the room liked *Fuji,* but none of us got around to describing why we perceived it as a "good story." Among the questions that we did not address were:

1. Does the character of Prince Fuji change? If so, how? What, if any, heroic qualities does he exhibit?
2. How does setting and its changes influence the composition of the story?
3. Does Fuji alter his quest because of his experiences?
4. Does the book really rely on the illustrations to carry the story?
5. Is the wife the true protagonist of the story? If we believe that this is so, what evidence supports this opinion? Does she have heroic qualities?
6. Does the author use language in any special way to convey the sense of the heroic to readers?
7. Did you perceive a flippant tone in the telling of this story? Is that tone a catering to the times? (Recall how Hunter did something similar in *The Knight of the Golden Plain?*)
8. Do the language and the illustrations complement each other? Are they consistent?
9. From whose point of view is the story told? Is it the same point of view as the pictures?
10. Does the device of the Kufu bird increase the involvement of the reader in the life of Fuji? If so, how?
11. For those of you who assume that the wife is creating the adventures in a tapestry, why do you think she chose to place these adventures before us? What evidence from the work supports these opinions?
12. Is the final statement in the book indicative of the wife's belief that when Fuji returns he will not have been changed from the adventurer he is, that she perceives no growth in the man?
13. To what extent is the format of the page and the type of illustration consonant with a traditional view of a tapestry?

FIGURE 24 *Continued*

14. To what extent does this work depart from the traditional and yet invoke the traditional?

15. If one uses the examples of parallels to the *Odyssey* does the author really seek to retell that tale—or to add a new dimension to the tale? Is she successful?

16. How is the plot structured in this story—can we identify the plot elements and indicate how the story unfolds?

17. Did the professor's enthusiasm place you in a mind set that predetermined support of the work? Do we remember Prince Fuji because we spent time discussing it or because Prince Fuji is worth remembering?

18. Is this work realistic, romantic, or fanciful?

19. Is it aesthetically sound?

20. Is it believable as a work of art?

21. Did you enjoy it?

These are just a few of the many additional questions about *The Voyage of Prince Fuji* which might be considered in a more literary evaluation of the work. The last one should be both first and last; all the rest are ways of getting at the reasons behind that answer.

Thorne, Jenny. (1980). *The Voyage of Prince Fuji.* London: Macmillan.

Special Presentations by Guest Speakers

Additional speakers brought a specific vision to the course ranging from exploration of the power of grandiose language to the tracing of heroic change in British fantasy over two centuries. One guest speaker had the group almost in tears with his reading of passages from the death of Robin Hood and subsequently laughing with his delightful rendering of segments of *Huckleberry Finn*. The insights provided through the use of a wide range of titles by this speaker to demonstrate the heroic in person and animal was exceptionally effective. Another guest explored heroism with insightful comments on the relationship of societal and educational events in the real child's world to what was addressed in the fantasy world. Her use of the Hobbit map as a means for demonstrating the quest, and how each test was dealt with proved very exciting to the group.

Assignments

Various assignments of the institute, Figure 25, were designed to enable students to test their competence and development in dealing with course topics, but there were some distinct problems based on the structure of a three-day course. Students could not give sufficient time to a set of projects during the allocated time frame, and those with a more limited range of experience were at a special disadvantage in attempting to complete their work within this time constraint. Some assignments could realistically be tied to personal time commitments, but students seeking graduate credits also had to be able to perform at that level. Those taking the institute for three credits generally turned their final assignment in at the end of the semester, many weeks after the completion of the institute. It was easier for most student-practitioners to prepare a practical project with or for children than to deal in the literary or scholarly

FIGURE 25

ASSIGNMENTS

GENERAL INSTRUCTIONS

The course is dependent on the participation of all members exchanging their views. Each student should read all, or at least as many as possible, of the children's books on the yellow list. It is hoped that each student will read at least some portion of the items listed in the literary bibliography provided.

Each student will be the champion of a given title from our list of children's books and will be expected to bring that work to our attention in order to make appropriate points in the dialogue.

SPECIFIC INSTRUCTIONS FOR CREDIT

Those taking the course for one credit should select one assignment from the following list. Those taking the course for two credits should select two assignments and those taking the course for three credits select three assignments. One point students have the option of submitting their work either (date inserted) or (date inserted). Both two and three point students have one assignment due on each of those days. The third point project may be submitted any time prior to (date inserted).

LIST OF PROJECTS

1. Select an element of story, such as setting or point of view, and provide specific examples of the element in relation to the heroic as it is revealed in at least six stories.
2. Devise your own list of characteristics of a heroic act and analyze at least six books using that list.
3. Determine a list of components of a quest and then trace the actions of at least three protagonists in relation to those components.
4. Compare and contrast at least three books with different settings to determine how time and place influence the way heroic events emerge.
5. Select any author from our list and explore all of the works of that author to determine how the heroic is revealed in each.
6. Select a specific book for analysis and explore it in terms of how the language conveys heroism.
7. Using some of the concerns of the feminist critics, explore the concept of heroism in at least two works of children's fiction.

FIGURE 25 *Continued*

8. Develop a program for children (you determine the age or grade span) that concentrates on the development of literary abilities in the child through exploration of the heroic.
9. Develop a microcomputer program that would permit children to explore characteristics of the heroic.
10. Write a paper on one of the topics: (A) The Quiet Hero in Picture Story Books for Children or (B) The Use of Symbol in the Hero Story for Children.
11. Prepare a "workbook" for students which would help them trace the roots of literary heroism from mythology to modern fiction.
12. Prepare a videotape with a group of children which explores characteristics of a hero/heroine.
13. Using a data file, set up a database that permits a child to select a program of reading on heroism.
14. Select at least eight illustrated books for young children and analyze the ways in which heroic ideas and elements are presented visually. (These need not be books from the yellow list.)
15. Write a critical review of three children's books from the yellow list, analyzing first general literary criteria and then specific aspects of the treatment of the heroic.
16. Negotiate your own assignment with the Professor.

mode. One improvement in this aspect of the course would be conferences with students to elicit personal goals that could be matched with course requirements prior to their choice of assignments. Again, this was difficult given both the time constraints and the number of students enrolled.

Gains of the Institute

Overall, what was gained? By the end of our three days together, it had become clear that our perceptions of heroism had changed in some major ways. All participants seemed to accept that the heroic in literature does not have to be "beyond the ordinary" or subject to grandiose language or actions. Certain writers are still using language to convey the extraordinary beauty of heroic qualities such as in *Legend Days* by Jamake Highwater, the first of the Ghost Horse Cycle. The reading aloud of passages from this work clearly demonstrated the power of rhythm and tone in a work and led to some perceptive analysis of these literary elements. The quest as a series of tests and an opportunity to see the character revealed as a hero/heroine proved to be as important in modern realism as in traditional tales. Essentially, the aesthetic nature of story dominated for almost all, and we came to a deeper realization that it is the entire work that must be addressed. Is the story good? Did it have the power to affect us? Did we enjoy it? These are after all the fundamental questions. Frye and Rosenblatt offered, along with Iser and Barthes, theories with which to examine the works and our responses to them; and these all proved helpful in increasing the ability of the students to see more aesthetically into the work. Recognition came that the questions of great significance included: How may children be encouraged to recognize the heroic? What can the professional who encounters the child reader do to encourage a swifter and stronger sense of the heroic?

Throughout the seminar extended discussion occurred as participants championed their assigned book. In addition, we, as instructors, used a variety of additional titles to demonstrate patterns and aspects of the heroic. Although it was relatively easy to use the Propp schema or that of Campbell with a traditional tale, it became increasingly difficult to use them with realistic stories. What did emerge, however, was a sense of and a sensitivity to honor as a characteristic of literary heroes. The integrity of the character became important to students, as did the factors influencing choices made and the acceptance of responsibility for the results of those choices.

One fascinating aspect of the course was the increased interest in the role of feminism, both as a theoretical construct and as a school of criticism. Exploration of this aspect of the literature was only begun, but certainly it was obvious that the seminar group was alert to this issue and clearly determined to address it. Lively discussion of heroines in stories and the need to have them do even more was encountered. Harry in *The Blue Sword* became a source for enlivened discussion as did the stay-at-home wife of Fuji.

Another particularly insightful aspect of the seminar was the discussion with an author whose characters are examples of the heroic. Robin McKinley visited and answered a number of questions posed by the class. It would take more time and a great deal of insight to have a thoroughly productive exchange between an author and a group of students, but this was useful to our participants as a beginning glimpse. One thing that is clear is that serious inquiry into the work of an author is exceedingly difficult and often impossible through personal exchange in such a situation.

Thus, a voyage was begun in the course; the quest was to explore and relish a concept of the heroic. Many dangers were met and overcome, and all participants grew in their perceptions of that concept and in their abilities to share their views in a literary context. The journey is over, but the experiences shared will remain a part of us all. The distance travelled was but the beginning of another voyage and another quest.

FUTURE DIRECTIONS

The professional community has always accepted that one or two courses would be sufficient education for anyone who wishes to work with children and literature. But what has clearly emerged over the past decades is a type of professional who seeks to both write and do research in this area in order to increase performance on the job. Increasingly, the children's literature and children's services community is demanding a greater share of the curriculum in order to meet the needs of its clientele. The time has come for at least a few institutions to respond to these needs and to offer programs of sufficient caliber and depth to attract the scholarly attention necessary to draw students and to survive in the university community. Both regular courses and a variety of forms of continuing education are essential if all of us in the community of concern for children's literature, whether we work with adult students or with children, are to share and thus increase that concern.

NOTES

[1]Software development work done by Kemp on *Idealog,* by Schwartz on *Seen* and by Spitzer on *Invent* are described in Frank Madden. (October 1988). "Literature Software," *English Journal.* 77: 75-76.

[2]Gertrude Herman contributes a column for *The Horn Book* entitled "A Picture Is Worth Several Hundred Words," see, for example, *The Horn Book* September/October 1988: 656-657.

[3]For a summary of one such seminar see: Kay E. Vandergrift and Jane Anne Hannigan. (April 1985). "A Celebration of Tradition in Children's Literature," *School Library Journal*. 31: 33-37.

[4]Jorg Steiner. (1978). *Rabbit Island*. Illus. by Jorg Muller and Trans. by Ann Conrad Lammers. (New York: Harcourt, Brace Jovanovich).

[5]Alexis Deveaux. (1973). *na-ni*. (New York: Harper & Row).

[6]An Annual Conference sponsored by the Rutgers Universtiy Advisory Council on Children's Literature in which those actively pursuing a career as authors or illustrators of books for young readers meet individually with established authors, illustrators, or editors in the field.

Selected Bibliography of Children's Literature

This bibliography is designed primarily for use in various courses dealing with literature for children and youth. It could also serve as a core list of monographs as foundation readings for any scholar or researcher in the field of children's literature. With few exceptions, the list excludes journal articles, dissertations, selection tools, review media, and foreign language materials. Any serious scholar in this area would go beyond what is presented here, and the young professional practitioner is encouraged to continue adding materials to the list for many years ahead. General works on literary criticism included in the various course syllabi are contained in a separate literary bibliography following this one. The list is organized into broad subject classifications according to their use in various classes. These categories are not mutually exclusive, so that a reader may need to check more than one category. For instance, works on major illustrators of children's books may be found both under "Picture Books and Illustration" and under "Studies of Authors and Illustrators." As organized, this might be considered a "browsing" list, please check the index to locate a specific title. Main entry rules are used in accordance with AACR 2.

GENERAL WORKS, TEXTS, CRITICISM, AND COLLECTIONS OF ARTICLES

1. Adams, Jeff. (1986). *The Conspiracy of the Text: The Place of Narrative in the Development of Thought*. London: Routledge & Kegan Paul.

2. *Aspects of Alice*. (1971). Robert Phillips, Editor. Harmondsworth, Middlesex, England: Penguin Books.

3. Anderson, William, and Patrick Groff. (1972). *A New Look at Children's Literature*. Belmont, CA: Wadsworth.

4. Ashley, L. F. (1970). *Children's Reading and the 1970's*. Toronto: McClellan and Stewart.

5. Bauer, Caroline Feller. (1983). *This Way to Books*. New York: H. W. Wilson Co.

6. Bechtel, Louise S. (1969). *Books in Search of Children: Speeches and Essays*. New York: Macmillan.

7. *The Best of the Best*. (1976). Walter Scherf, Editor. Federal Republic of Germany: Verlag Dokumentation.

8. Burke, Eileen M. (1986). *Early Childhood Literature: For Love of Child and Book*. Boston, MA: Allyn and Bacon.

9. Butler, Francelia. (1977). *Sharing Literature with Children: A Thematic Anthology*. New York: David McKay Co.

10. Cameron, Eleanor. (1969). *The Green and Burning Tree: On the Writing and Enjoyment of Children's Books*. Boston, MA: Little, Brown and Co.

11. Cass, Joan E. (1967). *Literature and the Young Child.* London: Longmans, Green & Co., Ltd.

12. *Celebrating Children's Books.* (1981). Betsy Hearne and Marilyn Kaye, Editors. New York: Lothrop, Lee and Shepard.

13. Chambers, Aidan. (1983). *Introducing Books to Children.* 2nd Edition. Boston, MA: Horn Book.

14. _____. (1969). *The Reluctant Reader.* New York: Pergamon Press.

15. _____. (1985). *Booktalk: Occasional Writing on Literature and Children.* New York: Harper & Row.

16. Chambers, Dewey. (1971). *Children's Literature in the Curriculum.* Chicago, IL: Rand McNally.

17. *Children and Literature.* (1970). Hane H. Catterson, Editor. Newark, DE: International Reading Association.

18. *Children and Literature: Views and Reviews.* (1973). Virginia Haviland, Editor. Glenview, IL: Scott, Foresman.

19. *Children and Their Literature: A Readings Book.* (1983). Jill May, Editor. West Lafayette, IN: Children's Literature Publications.

20. *Children, Books, and Reading.* (1964). Helen Huus, Editor. (Perspective in Reading #3). Newark, DE: International Reading Association.

21. *Children's Literature in the Reading Program.* (1987). Bernice E. Cullinan, Editor. Newark, DE: International Reading Association.

22. *Children's Literature—Old and New.* (1964). Virginia M. Reid, Editor. Champaign, IL: National Council of Teachers of English.

23. *The Cool Web: The Pattern of Children's Reading.* (1978). Margaret Meek, Aidan Warlow, and Griselda Barton, Editors. New York: Atheneum.

24. Cott, Jonathan. (1983). *Pipers at the Gates of Dawn: The Wisdom of Children's Literature.* New York: Random House.

25. *A Critical Approach to Children's Literature.* (1967). Sara Innis Fenwick, Editor. Chicago, IL: University of Chicago Press.

26. *Crosscurrents of Criticism: Horn Book Essays 1968-1977.* (1977). Paul Heins, Editor. Boston, MA: Horn Book.

27. Cullinan, Bernice E. (1989). *Literature and the Child.* 2nd Edition. New York: Harcourt Brace Jovanovich.

28. Dalsimer, Katherine. (1986). *Female Adolescence: Psychoanalytic Reflections on Literature.* New Haven, CT: Yale University Press.

29. De Marr, Mary Jean, and Jane Bakerman. (1986). *The Adolescent in the American Novel since 1960.* New York: Ungar.

30. Egoff, Sheila. (1981). *Thursday's Child.* Chicago, IL: American Library Association.

31. _____. (1979). *One Ocean Touching: Papers from the First Pacific RIM Conference on Children's Literature.* Metuchen, NJ: Scarecrow Press.

32. Emig, Janet. (1983). *The Web of Meaning.* Upper Montclair, NJ: Boynton/Cook Publishers.

33. Field, Carolyn. (1987). *Values in Selected Children's Books of Fiction and Fantasy.* Hamden, CT: Library Professional Publications.

34. Fisher, Margery. (1986). *The Bright Face of Danger.* Boston, MA: Horn Book.

35. _____. (1962). *Intent upon Reading.* New York: Franklin Watts.

36. Fox, Geoff, and others. (1976). *Writers, Critics and Children's Articles from Children's Literature in Education.* New York: Agathon Press.

37. Frank, Josette. (1960). *Your Child's Reading Today.* Garden City, NY: Doubleday.

38. Frey, Charles, and John Griffith. (1987). *The Literary Heritage of Childhood: An Appraisal of Children's Classics in the Western Tradition*. Hamden, CT: Greenwood Press.

39. *Frontiers of Library Service to Youth*. (1979). Essays Honoring Frances E. Henne. New York: School of Library Service, Columbia University.

40. Georgiou, Constantine. (1969). *Children and Their Literature*. Englewood Cliffs, NJ: Prentice Hall.

41. Glazer, Joan I., and Gurney Williams III. (1979). *Introduction to Children's Literature*. New York: McGraw-Hill.

42. Gerhardt, Lillian. (1977). *Issues in Children's Book Selection*. New York: R. R. Bowker.

43. Harrison, Barbara, and Gregory Maguire. (1987). *Innocence and Experience: Essays and Conversations on Children's Literature*. New York: Morrow.

44. Hazard, Paul. (1960). *Books, Children and Men*. 4th Edition. Boston, MA: Horn Book.

45. Heath, Peter. (1974). *The Philosopher's Alice*. New York: St. Martin's Press.

46. Hildick, Wallace. (1970). *Children and Fiction*. New York: World.

47. Hollowell, Lillian. (1966). *A Book of Children's Literature*. New York: Holt.

48. *A Horn Book Sampler*. (1959). Norma Fryatt, Editor. Boston, MA: Horn Book.

49. Huck, Charlotte. (1976). *Children's Literature in the Elementary School*. 3rd Edition. New York: Holt, Rinehart and Winston.

50. Hopkins, Lee Bennett. (1987). *Pass the Poetry, Please!* Revised Edition. New York: Harper & Row.

51. Huus, Helen. (1968). *Evaluating Books for Children and Young People*. (Perspective in Reading #4). Newark, DE: International Reading Association.

52. Inglis, Fred. (1981). *The Promise of Happiness: Values and Meaning in Children's Fiction*. Cambridge, England: Cambridge University Press.

53. Jan, Isabelle. (1973). *On Children's Literature*. Translated by Catherine Storr. London: Allen Lane.

54. Kingston, Carolyn T. (1974). *The Tragic Mode in Children's Literature*. New York: Teachers College Press.

55. Kircher, Clara J. (1966). *Behavior Patterns in Children's Books: A Bibliography*. Washington, DC: Catholic University of America Press.

56. Kujoth, Jean Spealman. (1973). *Best-Selling Children's Books*. Metuchen, NJ: Scarecrow Press.

57. Lewis, C. S. (1966). *Of Other Worlds: Essays & Stories*. New York: Harcourt, Brace and World.

58. _____. (1961). *An Experiment in Criticism*. Cambridge, England: Cambridge University Press.

59. Lickteig, Mary J. (1975). *Introduction to Children's Literature*. Columbus, OH: Charles E. Merrill Co.

60. *Literature with Children*. (1972). Monroe D. Cohen, Editor. Washington, DC: Association of Childhood Education International.

61. *Literature with Children*. (1961). Margaret Rasmussen, Editor. Washington, DC: Association for Childhood Education International.

62. Livingston, Myra Cohn. (1984). *The Child as Poet: Myth or Reality?* Boston, MA: Horn Book.

63. Lonsdale, Bernard J., and Helen K. Mackintosh. (1973). *Children Experience Literature*. New York: Random House.

64. Lukens, Rebecca. (1986). *A Critical Handbook of Children's Literature*. 3rd Edition. Glenview, IL: Scott, Foresman.

65. Murrow, Casey. (1971). *Children Come First*. New York: American Heritage Press.

66. Nelson, Mary Ann. (1972). *A Comparative Anthology of Children's Literature*. New York: Holt, Rinehart and Winston.

67. *Only Connect: Readings on Children's Literature*. (1980). Sheila Egoff, Editor. 2nd Edition. Toronto, Canada: Oxford University Press.

68. *Only the Best Is Good Enough*. (1985). Margaret Fearn, Editor. London: Rossendale.

69. *Opening Texts: Psychoanalysis and the Culture of the Child*. (1985). Joseph H. Smith and William Kerrigan, Editors. Baltimore, MD: The Johns Hopkins University Press.

70. Parker, Elizabeth Ann. (1969). *Teaching the Reading of Fiction*. New York: Teachers College Press.

71. Protherough, Robert. (1983). *Developing Response to Fiction*. Milton Keynes, England: Open University Press.

72. Purves, Alan, and Dianne L. Monson. (1984). *Experiencing Children's Literature*. Glenview, IL: Scott, Foresman.

73. Ray, Sheila G. (1972). *Children's Fiction: A Handbook for Librarians*. 2nd Edition. Leicester, England: Brockhampton Press.

74. *Reaching Children and Young People through Literature*. (1971). Helen W. Painter, Editor. Newark, DE: International Reading Association.

75. *Reading, Children's Books and Our Pluralistic Society*. (1972). Harold Tanyzer and Jean Karl, Editors. Newark, DE: International Reading Association.

76. *Readings about Children's Literature*. (1966). Evelyn Rose Robinson, Editor. New York: David McKay Co.

77. Rees, David. (1980). *Marble in the Water*. Boston, MA: Horn Book.

78. _____. (1984). *Painted Desert, Green Shade: Essays on Contemporary Writers of Fiction for Children and Young Adults*. Boston, MA: Horn Book.

79. Rose, Jacqueline. (1984). *The Case of Peter Pan or the Impossibility of Children's Fiction*. London: Macmillan Ltd.

80. Rudman, Masha K. (1984). *Children's Literature: An Issues Approach*. 2nd Edition. New York: Longman.

81. Sebesta, Sam, and William J. Iverson. (1975). *Literature for Thursday's Child*. Chicago, IL: Science Research Associates.

82. Shavit, Zohar. (1986). *Poetics of Children's Literature*. Athens, GA: University of Georgia Press.

83. *The Signal Approach to Children's Books*. (1981). Nancy Chambers, Editor. Harmondsworth, Middlesex, England: Kestral Books. (Distributed by Scarecrow Press).

84. *Signposts to Criticism of Children's Literature*. (1983). Robert Bator, Editor. Chicago, IL: American Library Association.

85. Sims, Rudina. (1982). *Shadow and Substance: Afro-American Experience in Contemporary Children's Fiction*. Urbana, IL: National Council of Teachers of English.

86. Sloan, Glenna Davis. (1975). *The Child as Critic*. New York: Teachers College Press.

87. Smith, James A., and Dorothy M. Park. (1977). *Word Music and Word Magic: Children's Literature Methods*. Boston, MA: Allyn and Bacon.

88. Smith, James Steel. (1967). *A Critical Approach to Children's Literature*. New York: McGraw-Hill.

89. Smith, Lillian. (1953). *The Unreluctant Years*. Chicago, IL: American Library Association.

90. *Society & Children's Literature*. (1978). James Fraser, Editor. Boston, MA: David R. Godine.

91. Spain, Frances Lander. (1960). *The Contents of the Basket and Other Papers on Children's Books and Reading*. New York: The New York Public Library.

92. Stewig, John W., and Sam Sebesta. (1978). *Using Literature in the Elementary Classroom*. Urbana, IL: National Council of Teachers of English.

93.   Stott, J. C. (1984). *Children's Literature from A to Z: A Guide for Parents and Teachers.* New York: McGraw-Hill.

94.   Sutherland, Zena. (1986). *Children and Books.* 7th Edition. Chicago, IL: Scott, Foresman.

95.   *Suitable for Children? Controversies in Children's Literature.* (1976). Nicolas Tucker, Editor. Sussex County, England; Sussex University Press.

96.   *Touchstones: Reflections on the Best in Children's Literature. Volume I.* (1985). Perry Nodelman, Editor. West Lafayette, IN: Children's Literature Association.

97.   *Touchstones: Reflections on the Best in Children's Literature. Volume II.* (1987). Perry Nodelman, Editor. West Lafayette, IN: Children's Literature Association.

98.   Tooze, Ruth. (1957). *Your Children Want to Read.* Englewood Cliffs, NJ: Prentice Hall.

99.   Tucker, Nicolas. (1981). *The Child and the Book: A Psychological and Literary Exploration.* Cambridge, England: Cambridge University Press.

100. Turow, Joseph. (1978). *Getting Books to Children.* Chicago, IL: American Library Association.

101. *Using Literature with Young Children.* (1965). Leland B. Jacobs, Editor. New York: Teachers College Press.

102. Vandergrift, Kay E. (1980). *Child and Story: The Literary Connection.* New York: Neal Schuman Publishers, Inc. (Reprinted in paperback in 1986).

103. *Webs and Wardrobes: Humanist and Religious World Views in Children's Literature.* (1987). Joseph O'Beirne Milner and Lucy Milner, Editors. Lanham, MD: University Press of America.

104. White, Mary Lou. (1976). *Children's Literature: Criticism and Response.* Columbus, OH: Charles M. Merrill, Co.

PICTURE BOOKS AND ILLUSTRATION

105. Alderson, Brian. (1986). *Sing a Song for Sixpence.* Cambridge, England: Cambridge University Press, in association with the British Library.

106. Allen, Douglas, and Douglas Allen, Jr. (1972). *N. C. Wyeth: The Collected Paintings, Illustrations, and Murals.* New York: Bonanza Books.

107. *The Art of Leo & Diane Dillon.* (1981). Byron Preiss, Editor. New York: Ballantine Books.

108. *The Art of Nancy Ekholm Burkert.* (1977). David Larkin, Editor. New York: Harper & Row.

109. Bader, Barbara. (1976). *American Picturebooks from Noah's Ark to the Beast Within.* New York: Macmillan.

110. Barr, John. (1986). *Illustrated Children's Books.* London: The British Library.

111. Blackburn, Henry. (1969). *Randolph Caldecott: A Personal Memoir of His Early Art Career.* Detroit, MI: Singing Tree Press. (Reprint of 1886 edition).

112. Blount, Margaret. (1975). *Animal Land: The Creatures of Children's Fiction.* New York: William Morrow.

113. Brown, Marcia. (1986). *Lotus Seeds: Children, Pictures, and Books.* New York: Charles Scribner's Sons.

114. Cianciolo, Patricia. (1976). *Illustrations in Children's Books.* 2nd Edition. Dubuque, IA: Wm. C. Brown Co.

115. _____. (1973). *Picture Books for Children.* Chicago, IL: American Library Association.

116. Crago, Maureen, and Hugh Crago. (1983). *Prelude to Literacy.* Carbondale, IL: Southern Illinois University Press.

117. Davis, Mary Gould. (1946). *Randolph Caldecott, 1846-1886.* Philadelphia, PA: Lippincott.

118. *1800 Woodcuts by Thomas Bewick and His School.* (1962). New York: Dover Books.

119. Engen, Rodney. (1981). *Kate Greenaway: A Biography*. New York: Schocken Books.

120. _____. (1976). *Kate Greenaway*. London: Academy Editions.

121. _____. (1976). *Randolph Caldecott: Lord of the Nursery*. London: Oresko Books.

122. _____. (1975). *Walter Crane as a Book Illustrator*. New York: St. Martin's Press.

123. *The Fantastic Paintings of Charles & William Heath Robinson*. (1976). David Larkin, Editor. Toronto, Canada: Peacock Press/Bantam Book.

124. Feaver, William. (1977). *When We Were Young: Two Centuries of Children's Book Illustration*. New York: Holt, Rinehart and Winston.

125. Gettings, Fred. (1975). *Arthur Rackham*. New York: Macmillan.

126. *Graphis*. (July 1975). No. 177 (Volume 3). (On children's book illustration).

127. Hands, Nancy. (1986). *Illustrating Children's Books: A Guide to Drawing, Printing, and Publishing*. New York: Prentice Hall Press.

128. Hamilton, Charles. (1987). *The Illustrated Letter*. New York: Universe Books.

129. Hancher, Michael. (1985). *The Tenniel Illustrations to the Alice Books*. Columbus, OH: Ohio State University Press.

130. Holme, Bryan. (1976). *The Kate Greenaway Book*. New York: Viking Press.

131. Hudson, Derek. (1960). *Arthur Rackham: His Life and Work*. London: Heinemann.

132. Hurlimann, Bettina. (1968). *Picture-Book World*. New York: Oxford University Press.

133. *Image & Maker: An Annual Dedicated to the Consideration of Book Illustration*. (1984). Harold Darling and Peter Neumeyer, Editors. La Jolla, CA: Green Tiger Press.

134. *The Illustrators of Alice*. (1972). Graham Ovenden, Editor. New York: St. Martin's Press.

135. *Illustrators of Children's Books, 1744-1945*. (1947). Bertha E. Mahony and others, Editors. Boston, MA: Horn Book.

136. *Illustrators of Children's Books, 1946-1956*. (1958). Ruth Hill Viguers and others, Editors. Boston, MA: Horn Book.

137. *Illustrators of Children's Books, 1957-1966*. (1968). Lee Kingman and others, Editors. Boston, MA: Horn Book.

138. *Illustrators of Children's Books, 1967-1976*. (1978). Lee Kingman and others, Editors. Boston, MA: Horn Book.

139. Kilborn, Richard. (1986). *Multi-Media Melting Pot: Marketing When the Wind Blows*. London: Comedia Publishing Group.

140. Klemin, Diana. (1966). *The Art of Art for Children's Books*. New York: Clarkson N. Potter, Inc.

141. _____. (1970). *The Illustrated Book: Its Art and Craft*. New York: Clarkson N. Potter, Inc.

142. Lacy, L. E. (1986). *Art and Design in Children's Picture Books; An Analysis of Caldecott Award-Winning Illustrations*. Chicago, IL: American Library Association.

143. Lanes, Selma G. (1980). *The Art of Maurice Sendak*. New York: Harry N. Abrams.

144. *Robert Lawson, Illustrator*. (1972). Introduction and Comment by Helen L. Jones. Boston, MA: Little, Brown and Co.

145. Lima, Carolyn W. (1986). *A to Zoo: Subject Access to Children's Picture Books*. 2nd Edition. New York: R. R. Bowker.

146. MacCann, Donnarae, and Olga Richard. (1973). *The Child's First Books: A Critical Study of Pictures and Text*. New York: H. W. Wilson Co.

147. Mellinger, Bonne E. (1932). *Children's Interests in Pictures*. New York: Teachers College Press.

148. Meyer, Susan E. (1983). *A Treasury of Great Children's Book Illustrators*. New York: Harry A. Abrams.

149. Noakes, Vivien. (1986). *Edward Lear: 1812-1888*. New York: Harry N. Abrams.

150. Pitz, Henry C. (1963). *Illustrating Children's Books*. New York: Watson-Guptill.

151. _____. (1963). *A Treasury of American Book Illustration*. New York: American Studio Books.

152. Polette, Nancy. (1981). *Picture Books for Gifted Programs*. Metuchen, NJ: Scarecrow Press.

153. Poltarnees, Welleran. (1972). *All Mirrors Are Magic Mirrors: Reflections on Pictures Found in Children's Books*. La Jolla, CA: Green Tiger Press.

154. *Howard Pyle*. (1975). Toronto, Canada: Peacock Press/Bantam Books.

155. *Arthur Rackham's Book of Pictures: With an Introduction by Sir Arthur Quiller-Couch*. (1979). New York: Avenel Books.

156. *Paul Rand: A Designer's Art*. (1985). New Haven, CT: Yale University Press.

157. *The Randolph Caldecott Treasury*. (1978). Elizabeth T. Billington, Editor. New York: Warne.

158. Ryder, John. (1960). *Artists of a Certain Line: A Selection of Illustrators for Children's Books*. London: Bodley Head.

159. Schwarcz, Joseph H. (1982). *Ways of the Illustrator: Visual Communication in Children's Literature*. Chicago, IL: American Library Association.

160. Schnessel, S. Michael. (1977). *Jessie Wilcox Smith*. New York: Crowell.

161. Shulevitz, Uri. (1985). *Writing with Pictures: How to Write and Illustrate Children's Books*. New York: Watson-Guptill.

162. Spencer, Isobel. (1975). *Walter Crane*. London: Studio Vista.

163. Tanchis, Aldo. (1987). *Bruno Munari: Design as Art*. Cambridge, MA: The MIT Press.

164. Taylor, Judy. (1987). *That Naughty Rabbit: Beatrix Potter and Peter Rabbit*. London: Warne.

165. Tudor, Bethany. (1979). *Drawn from New England: Tasha Tudor*. Cleveland, OH: Collins.

166. *The Unique World of Mitsumasa Anno: Selected Works (1968-1977)*. (1980). New York: Philomel Books.

167. Ward, Martha Eads. (1985). *Photography in Books for Young People*. Metuchen, NJ: Scarecrow Press.

168. *The Wood and the Graver: The Work of Fritz Eichenberg*. (1977). New York: Clarkson N. Potter.

169. *The Works of E. H. Shepard*. (1979). Rawle Knox, Editor. New York: Schocken Books.

170. *Yours Pictorially: Illustrated Letters of Randolph Caldecott*. (1976). Michael Hutchins, Editor. London: Warne.

STORYTELLING

171. Baker, Augusta and Ellin Greene. (1987). *Storytelling: Art & Technique*. 2nd Edition. New York: R. R. Bowker.

172. Bauer, Caroline Feller. (1977). *Handbook for Storytellers*. Chicago, IL: American Library Association.

173. Breneman, Lucille N. and Bren Breneman. (1983). *Once upon a Time: A Storytelling Handbook*. Chicago, IL: Nelson-Hall.

174. Chambers, Dewey. (1970). *Literature for Children: Storytelling and Creative Drama*. Dubuque, IA: Wm. C. Brown Co.

175. Davidson, H. R. Ellis. (1986). *Katherine Briggs: Storyteller*. Cambridge, England: Lutherworth Press.

176. Greene, Ellin, and George Shannon. (1986). *Storytelling: A Selected Annotated Bibliography*. New York: Garland.

177.   Kimmel, Margaret Mary, and Elizabeth Segel. (1988). *For Reading Out Loud! A Guide to Sharing Books with Children*. 2nd Edition. New York: Delacorte.

178.   Livo, Norma J., and Sandra A. Rietz. (1986). *Storytelling: Process and Practice*. Littleton, CO: Libraries Unlimited.

179.   MacDonald, Margaret Read. (1986). *Twenty Tellable Tales: Audience Participation Folktales for the Beginning Storyteller*. New York: H. W. Wilson Co.

180.   _____. (1982). *Storyteller's Sourcebook: A Subject, Title, and Motif Index to Folklore Collections for Children*. New York: Neal-Schuman Publishers, Inc. (Distributed by Gale Research).

181.   Nichols, Judy. (1987). *Storytimes for Two-Year-Olds*. Chicago, IL: American Library Association.

182.   Pellowski, Anne. (1987). *The Family Story-Telling Handbook*. New York: Macmillan.

183.   Sawyer, Ruth. (1962). *The Way of the Storyteller*. Revised Edition. New York: Viking Press.

184.   Shedlock, Marie. (1952). *The Art of the Storyteller*. 3rd Edition. New York: Dover.

185.   Tooze, Ruth. (1959). *Storytelling*. Englewood Cliffs, NJ: Prentice Hall.

186.   Trelease, Jim. (1982). *The Read-Aloud Handbook*. New York: Penguin Books.

187.   Wagner, Joseph Anthony. (1970). *Children's Literature through Storytelling*. Dubuque, IA: Wm. C. Brown Co.

188.   Wilson, Jane B. (1979). *The Story Experience*. Metuchen, NJ: Scarecrow Press.

189.   Ziskind, Sylvia. (1976). *Telling Stories to Children*. New York: H. W. Wilson Co.

FANTASY, FOLKLORE AND SCIENCE FICTION

190.   Adams, Jeff. (1986). *The Conspiracy of the Text: The Place of Narrative in the Development of Thought*. London: Routledge & Kegan Paul.

191.   Antczak, Janice. (1985). *Science Fiction: The Mythos of a New Romance*. New York: Neal-Schuman Publishers, Inc.

192.   Aquino, John. (1977). *Fantasy in Literature*. Washington, DC: National Educational Association.

193.   Arrowsmith, Nancy. (1977). *A Field Guide to the Little People*. New York: Hill and Wang.

194.   Asimov, Isaac. (1981). *Asimov on Science Fiction*. Garden City, NY: Doubleday.

195.   Attebery, Brian. (1980). *The Fantasy Tradition in American Literature from Irving to Le Guin*. Bloomington, IN: Indiana University Press.

196.   Bergsten, Staffan. (1978). *Mary Poppins and Myth*. Stockholm, Sweden: Almgvist and Wiksell International.

197.   Bettelheim, Bruno. (1975). *The Uses of Enchantment: The Meaning of Fairy Tales*. New York: Alfred A. Knopf.

198.   *Beyond the Looking Glass: Extraordinary Works of Fairy Tale & Fantasy*. (1974). Jonathan Cott, Editor. London: Hart-Davis, MacGibbon.

199.   Blount, Margaret. (1974). *Animal Land: The Creatures of Children's Fiction*. New York: Avon.

200.   Bottigheimer, Ruth B. (1987). *Grimms' Bad Girls and Bold Boys: The Moral and Social Vision of the Tales*. New Haven, CT: Yale University Press.

201.   *Bridges to Fantasy*. (1982). George E. Slusser and others, Editors. Carbondale, IL: Southern Illinois University.

202.   *Bridges to Science Fiction*. (1980). George E. Slusser and others, Editors. Carbondale, IL: Southern Illinois University Press.

203. Briggs, Katharine M. (1967). *The Fairies in Tradition and Literature*. London: Routledge & Kegan Paul.

204. _____. (1978). *The Vanishing People: Fairy Lore and Legends*. New York: Pantheon.

205. Brown, Carolyn S. (1987). *The Tall Tale in American Folklore and Literature*. Knoxville, TN: University of Tennessee.

206. Butler, Francelia. (1989). *Skipping around the World: The Ritual Nature of Folk Rhymes*. Hamden, CT: Library Professional Publications.

207. Carter, Lin. (1973). *Imaginary Worlds*. New York: Ballantine Books.

208. _____. (1969). *Tolkien: A Look behind the Lord of the Rings*. New York: Ballantine Books.

209. *Cinderella: A Casebook*. (1983). Alan Dundes, Editor. New York: Wildman Press.

210. Cook, Elizabeth. (1976). *The Ordinary and the Fabulous*. Cambridge, England: Cambridge University Press.

211. *The Craft of Science Fiction*. (1976). Reginald Bretnor, Editor. New York: Barnes & Noble.

212. Cruikshank, George. (1910). *The Cruikshank Fairy-Book*. New York: Putnam's Sons.

213. de Camp, L. Sprague. (1976). *Literary Swordsmen and Sorcerers: The Makers of Heroic Fantasy*. Sauk City, WI: Arkham House.

214. Dorson, Richard M. (1968). *The British Folklorists: A History*. Chicago, IL: University of Chicago Press.

215. _____. (1976). *Folklore and Fakelore: Essays toward a Discipline of Folk Studies*. Cambridge, MA: Harvard University Press.

216. Dundes, Alan. (1965). *The Study of Folklore*. Englewood Cliffs, NJ: Prentice Hall.

217. Edwards, Malcolm, and Robert Holdstock. (1983). *Realms of Fantasy*. Garden City, NY: Doubleday.

218. Egoff, Shiela A. (1988). *Worlds Within: Children's Fantasy from the Middle Ages to Today*. Chicago, IL: American Library Association.

219. Ellis, John M. (1983). *One Fairy Story Too Many: The Brothers Grimm and Their Tales*. Chicago, IL: University of Chicago Press.

220. *Fables: From Incunabula to Modern Picture Books*. (1966). Barbara Quinnam, Compiler. Washington, DC: Library of Congress.

221. *Fairy Tales and Society: Illusion, Allusion and Paradigm*. (1986). Ruth B. Bottigheimer, Editor. Philadelphia, PA: University of Pennsylvania Press.

222. Fine, Elizabeth C. (1985). *The Folklore Text: From Performance to Print*. Bloomington, IN: Indiana University Press.

223. *Folk Literature and Children: An Annotated Bibliography of Secondary Materials*. (1981). George Shannon, Compiler. Westport, CT: Greenwood Press.

224. *Folklore and Folktales around the World*. (1972). Ruth Kearney Carlson, Editor. Newark, DE: International Reading Association.

225. Ford, Paul F. (1980). *Companion to Narnia: A Complete, Illustrated Guide to the Themes, Characters and Events of C. S. Lewis's Imaginary World*. San Francisco, CA: Harper & Row.

226. Gibson, Evan K. (1980). *C. S. Lewis: Spinner of Tales*. Grand Rapids, MI: Christian University Press.

227. Gose, Elliott B. (1985). *The World of the Irish Wonder Tale: An Introduction to the Study of Fairy Tales*. Buffalo, NY: University of Toronto Press.

228. *Handbook of American Folklore*. (1983). Richard M. Dorson, Editor. Bloomington, IN: Indiana University Press.

229. Hartland, Edwin Sidney. (1890). *The Science of Fairy Tales: An Inquiry into Fairy Mythology*. New York: Frederick A. Stokes Co.

230. Hartwell, David. (1984). *Age of Wonders: Exploring the World of Science Fiction*. New York: Walker and Co.

231. Higgins, James E. (1970). *Beyond Words: Mystical Fancy in Children's Literature*. New York: Teachers College Press.

232. Hooper, Walter. (1979). *The Narnian Chronicles of C. S. Lewis: Past Watchful Dragons*. New York: Collier Books.

233. Irwin, William R. (1976). *The Game of the Impossible: A Rhetoric of Fantasy*. Urbana, IL: University of Illinois Press.

234. Karkainen, Paul A. (1979). *Narnia Explored*. Old Tappan, NJ: Fleming H. Revell Co.

235. Kennard, Jean E. (1975). *Number and Nightmare: Forms of Fantasy in Contemporary Fiction*. Hamden, CT: Archon Books.

236. Krappe, Alexander H. (1964). *The Science of Folklore*. New York: Norton.

237. Kready, Laura. (1916). *A Study of Fairy Tales*. Boston, MA: Houghton Mifflin.

238. Krohn, Kaarle. (1971). *Folklore Methodology*. Austin, TX: American Folklore Society/University of Texas.

239. Le Guin, Ursula K. (1979). *The Language of the Night: Essays on Fantasy and Science Fiction*. New York: Perigee Books.

240. *Light on C. S. Lewis*. (1965). Jocelyn Gibb, Editor. New York: Harcourt Brace Jovanovich.

241. Lindskoog, Kathryn. (1973). *The Lion of Judah in Never-Never Land: The Theology of C. S. Lewis Expressed in His Fantasies for Children*. Grand Rapids, MI: William Eerdmans Publishing.

242. Lochhead, Marion. (1977). *The Renaissance of Wonder*. Edinburgh, Scotland: Canongate.

243. Luthi, Max. (1982). *The European Folktale: Form and Nature*. Translated by John D. Niles. Bloomington, IN: Indiana University Press.

244. _____. (1984). *The Fairytale as Art Form and Portrait of Man*. Translated by Jon Erickson. Bloomington, IN: Indiana University Press.

245. _____. (1976). *Once upon a Time: On the Nature of Fairy Tales*. Translated by Lee Chadeayne and Paul Gottwald. Bloomington, IN: Indiana University Press.

246. Macculloch, J. A. (1905). *The Childhood of Fiction: A Study of Folk Tales and Primitive Thought*. London: John Murray, Albermarle Street.

247. Mercatante, Anthony S. (1974). *Zoo of the Gods: Animals in Myth, Legend and Fable*. New York: Harper & Row.

248. Moore, Raylyn. (1974). *Wonderful Wizard, Marvelous Land*. Bowling Green, OH: Bowling Green University Popular Press.

249. *Myth, Allegory, and Gospel; an Interpretation of J. R. R. Tolkien, C. S. Lewis, G. K. Chesterton, Charles Williams*. (1974). John Warwick Montgomery, Editor. Minneapolis, MN: Bethany Fellowship.

250. Opie, Iona, and Peter Opie. (1974). *The Classic Fairy Tales*. London: Oxford University Press.

251. Pflieger, Pat. (1984). *A Reference Guide to Modern Fantasy for Children*. Westport, CT: Greenwood Press.

252. Pitcher, Evelyn G., and Ernst Prelinger. (1963). *Children Tell Stories: An Analysis of Fantasy*. New York: International Universities Press.

253. Propp, Vladimir. (1968). *Morphology of the Folktale*. Translated by Laurence Scott. Austin, TX: University of Texas Press.

254. _____. (1984). *Theory and History of Folklore*. Translated by Ariadna Martin and Richard Martin. Minneapolis, MN: University of Minnesota Press.

255. Purtill, Richard. (1974). *Lord of the Elves and Eldils: Fantasy and Philosophy of C. S. Lewis and J. R. R. Tolkien*. Grand Rapids, MI: Zondervan Publishing.

256. Rabin, Eric S. (1976). *The Fantastic in Literature*. Princeton, NJ: Princeton University Press.

257. Sale, Roger. (1978). *Fairy Tale and After*. Cambridge, MA: Harvard University Press.

258. Sammons, Martha C. (1979). *A Guide through Narnia*. Wheaton, IL: Harold Shaw Publishers.

259. Schakel, Peter J. (1979). *Reading with the Heart: The Way Into Narnia*. Grand Rapids, MI: William Eerdmans Publishing.

260. Scholes, Robert, and Eric Rabin. (1977). *Science Fiction: History, Science, Vision*. London: Oxford University Press.

261. Scholes, Robert. (1975). *Structural Fabulation: An Essay on Fiction of the Future*. Notre Dame, IN: University of Notre Dame Press.

262. *Science Fiction: A Critical Guide*. (1979). Patrick Parrinder, Editor. London: Longman.

263. Summerfield, Geoffrey. (1985). *Fantasy and Reason: Children's Literature in the Eighteenth Century*. Athens, GA: University of Georgia Press.

264. Sinfen, Ann. (1984). *In Defense of Fantasy: A Study of the Genre in English and American Literature since 1945*. London: Routledge & Kegan Paul.

265. Thompson, Stith. (1977). *The Folktale*. Berkeley, CA: University of California Press. (Reprint of 1946 edition).

266. Thomas, Katherine Elwes. (1930). *The Real Personages of Mother Goose*. Boston, MA: Lothrop, Lee & Shepard Co.

267. Tolkien, J. R. R. (1965). *Tree and Leaf*. New York: Houghton Mifflin.

268. Waggoner, Diana. (1978). *The Hills of Faraway: A Guide to Fantasy*. New York: Atheneum.

269. Walsh, Chad. (1979). *The Literary Legacy of C. S. Lewis*. New York: Harcourt Brace Jovanovich.

270. Wendland, Albert. (1985). *Science, Myth, and the Fictional Creation of Alien Worlds*. Ann Arbor, MI: UMI Press.

271. Yolen, Jane. (1981). *Touch Magic: Fantasy, Faerie and Folklore in the Literature of Childhood*. New York: Philomel Books.

272. Zipes, Jack. (1979). *Breaking the Magic Spell: Radical Theories of Folk & Fairy Tales*. Austin, TX: University of Texas.

273. _____. (1986). *Don't Bet on the Prince: Contemporary Feminist Fairy Tales in North America and England*. New York: Methuen.

274. _____. (1983). *Fairy Tales and the Art of Subversion*. New York: Wildman Press.

275. _____. (1983). *The Trials and Tribulations of Little Red Riding Hood*. South Hadley, MA: J. F. Bergin Publishers.

INFORMATIONAL BOOKS

276. *Beyond Fact: Nonfiction for Children and Young People*. (1982). Jo Carr, Compiler. Chicago, IL: American Library Association.

277. Fisher, Margery. (1972). *Matters of Fact*. New York: Thomas Crowell.

278. *Portraits: Biography and Autobiography in the Secondary School*. (1985). Margaret Fleming and Jo McGinnis, Editors. Urbana, IL: National Council of Teachers of English.

STUDIES OF AUTHORS AND ILLUSTRATORS

279. Arnott, Anne. (1975). *The Secret Country of C. S. Lewis*. Grand Rapids, MI: William B. Eerdmans Publishing.

280. *The Art of Beatrix Potter*. (1955). London: Warne.

281. Bergsten, Staffan. (1978). *Mary Poppins and Myth*. Stockholm, Sweden: Almqvist & Wiksell International.

282. Bingham, Jane M. (1988). *Writers for Children: Critical Studies of Major Authors since the Seventeenth Century*. New York: Charles Scribner's.

283. Birkin, Andrew. (1979). *J. M. Barrie and the Lost Boys: The Love Story that Gave Birth to Peter Pan*. New York: Clarkson N. Potter.

284. Boston, L. M. (1973). *Memory in a House*. New York: Macmillan.

285. _____. (1979). *Perverse and Foolish: A Memoir of Childhood and Youth*. New York: Atheneum.

286. Brooke, Henry. (1982). *Leslie Brooke and Johnny Crow*. London: Frederick Warne.

287. Bucknall, Barbara J. (1981). *Ursula K. Le Guin*. New York: Frederick Ungar.

288. Burnett, Frances Hodgson. (1893). *The One I Knew the Best of All*. New York: Charles Scribner's Sons.

289. Campbell, Patricia J. (1985). *Presenting Robert Cormier*. (Twayne's United States Author Series.) Boston, MA: Twayne/G. K. Hall.

290. Carpenter, Humphrey. (1979). *The Inklings: C. S. Lewis, J. R. R. Tolkien, Charles Williams, and Their Friends*. Boston, MA: Houghton Mifflin.

291. Clark, Anne. (1979). *Lewis Carroll: A Biography*. New York: Schocken Books.

292. Cleary, Beverly. (1988). *A Girl from Yamhill: A Memoir*. New York: Morrow.

293. Coatsworth, Elizabeth. (1976). *Personal Geography: Almost an Autobiography*. Brattleboro, VT: The Stephen Greene Press.

294. Cummins, Roger W. (1973). *Humorous but Wholesome, A History of Palmer Cox and the Brownies*. Watkins Glen, NY: Century House.

295. Cutt, M. Nancy. (1974). *Mrs. Sherwood and Her Books for Children*. London: Oxford University Press.

296. Daly, Jay. (1987). *Presenting S. E. Hinton*. (Twayne's United States Author Series.) Boston, MA: Twayne/G. K. Hall.

297. Davies, Hunter. (1988). *Beatrix Potter's Lakeland*. London: Warne.

298. De Angeli, Marguerite. (1971). *Butter at the Old Price: The Autobiography of Marguerite De Angeli*. Garden City, NY: Doubleday.

299. Duncan, Lois. (1982). *Chapters: My Growth as a Writer*. Boston, MA: Little Brown.

300. *The Early Dreaming: Australian Children's Authors and Childhood*. (1980). Michael Dugan, Compiler. Milton, Queensland, Australia: The Jacaranda Press.

301. Forman, Jack Jacob. (1988). *Presenting Paul Zindel*. (Twayne's United States Author Series.) Boston, MA: Twayne/G. K. Hall.

302. French, Warren. (1988). *J. D. Salinger, Revisited*. (Twayne's United States Author Series.) Boston, MA: Twayne/G. K. Hall.

303. Gag, Wanda. (1984). *Growing Pains*. St. Paul, MN: Minnesota Historical Society Press. (Reprint of 1940 edition).

304. *Good Writers for Young Readers*. (1977). Dennis Butts, Editor. St. Albans, England: Hart Davis Educational.

305. Green, Roger Lancelyn. (1965). *Tellers of Tales*. Revised Edition. London: E. Ward.

306. Green, Roger Lancelyn and Walter Hooper. (1974). *C. S. Lewis: A Biography*. New York: Harcourt Brace Jovanovich.

307. Grotta-Kurska, Daniel. (1976). *J. R. R. Tolkien: Architect of Middle Earth*. Philadelphia, PA: Running Press.

308. Hoffman, Miriam, and Eva Samuels. (1972). *Authors and Illustrators of Children's Books: Writings on Their Lives and Works*. New York: R. R. Bowker.

309. Holtze, Sally Holmes. (1987). *Presenting Norma Fox Mazer*. (Twayne's United States Author Series.) Boston, MA: Twayne/G. K. Hall.

310. Hopkins, Lee Bennett. (1969). *Books Are by People*. New York: Citation Press.

311. Hoyt, Edwin P. (1974). *Horatio's Boys: The Life and Works of Horatio Alger, Jr.* Radnor, PA: Chilton Books.

312. Hyman, Trina Schart. (1981). *Self-Portrait: Trina Schart Hyman*. Reading, MA: Addison-Wesley.

313. Johnson, Judith A. (1985). *J. R. R. Tolkien: Six Decades of Criticism*. Westport, CT: Greenwood Press.

314. Jones, Cornelia, and Olivia R. Way. (1976). *British Children's Authors*. Chicago, IL: American Library Association.

315. Kerr, M. E. (1983). *Me, me, me, me, me: Not a Novel*. New York: Harper & Row.

316. *Rudyard Kipling "O Beloved Kids": Rudyard Kipling's Letters to His Children*. (1983). San Diego, CA: Harcourt Brace Jovanovich.

317. Kresh, Paul. (1979). *Isaac Bashevis Singer: The Magician of West 86th Street*. New York: Dial Press.

318. Kuznets, Lois R. (1987). *Kenneth Grahame*. (Twayne's English Authors.) Boston, MA: Twayne/G. K. Hall.

319. Lane, Margaret. (1968). *The Tale of Beatrix Potter: A Biography*. New York: Warne.

320. _____. (1978). *The Magic Years of Beatrix Potter*. London: Warne.

321. *C. S. Lewis, An Annotated Checklist of Writings about Him and His Works*. (1974). Joe R. Christopher and Joan K Ostlin, Compilers. Kent, OH: Kent State University Press.

322. *C. S. Lewis Letters to Children*. (1985). Lyle W. Dorsett and Majories Lamp Mead, Editors. New York: Macmillan.

323. Lewis, C. S. (1955). *Surprised by Joy*. London: Collins, Fontana Books.

324. Linder, Leslie. (1971). *A History of the Writings of Beatrix Potter*. London: Warne.

325. Little, Jean. (1988). *Little by Little: A Writer's Education*. New York: Viking Kestral.

326. MacDonald, Ruth. (1986). *Beatrix Potter*. (Twayne's United States Author Series.) Boston, MA: Twayne/G. K. Hall.

327. _____. (1988). *Dr. Seuss*. (Twayne's United States Author Series.) Boston, MA: Twayne/G. K. Hall.

328. _____. (1983). *Louisa May Alcott*. (Twayne's United States Author Series.) Boston, MA: Twayne/G. K. Hall.

329. Mare, Margaret, and Alicia C. Percival. (1948). *Victorian Best-seller: The World of Charlotte M. Yonge*. London: George G. Harrap & Co. LTD.

330. Meltzer, Milton. (1965). *Tongue of Flame: The Life of Lydia Maria Child*. New York: Thomas Crowell.

331. _____. (1988). *Starting from Home: A Writer's Beginning*. New York: Viking Kestral.

332. Milne, A. A. (1939). *Autobiography*. New York: E. P. Dutton.

333. Milne, Christopher. (1974). *The Enchanted Places*. New York: E. P. Dutton.

334. Moore, Doris Langley. (1966). *E. Nesbit: A Biography*. Philadelphia, PA: Chilton Books.

335. Nesbit, Elizabeth. (1988). *Long Ago When I Was Young*. New York: Dial.

336. Nilsen, Allen Pace. (1986). *Presenting M. E. Kerr*. (Twayne's United States Author Series.) Boston, MA: Twayne/G. K. Hall.

337. Norris, Jerrie. (1988). *Presenting Rosa Guy.* (Twayne's United States Author Series.) Boston, MA: Twayne/G. K. Hall.

338. *Once upon a Time: The Fairy Tale World of Arthur Rackham.* (1972). Margery Darrell, Compiler. New York: Viking Press.

339. Philip, Neil. (1981). *A Fine Anger: A Critical Introduction to the Work of Alan Garner.* New York: Philomel Books.

340. Phy, Allene Stuart. (1988). *Presenting Norma Klein.* (Twayne's United States Author Series.) Boston, MA: Twayne/G. K. Hall.

341. Pitz, Henry C. (1975). *Howard Pyle: Writer, Illustrator, Founder of the Brandywine School.* New York: Clarkson N. Potter.

342. *Beatrix Potter, 1866-1943: The Artist and Her World.* (1987). Judy Taylor and others, Editors. London: Warne/National Trust.

343. *Beatrix Potter's Americans: Selected Letters.* (1982). Jane Crowell Morse, Editor. Boston, MA: Horn Book.

344. Pudney, John. (1976). *Lewis Carroll and His World.* New York: Charles Scribner's Sons.

345. Ray, Sheila. (1982). *The Blyton Phenomenon: The Controversy Surrounding the World's Most Successful Children's Writer.* London: Andre Deutsch.

346. *Readers as Writers.* (1988). Compiled by Association for Library Service to Children. Chicago, IL: American Library Association.

347. Reef, Pat Davidson. (1987). *Dahlov Ipcar: Artist.* Maine Art Series for Young Readers. Falmouth, ME: The Kennebec River Press.

348. *The Reminiscences of Edmund Evans.* (1967). Ruari McLean, Editor. London: Oxford University Press.

349. Sayers, Frances Clark. (1972). *Anne Carroll Moore.* New York: Atheneum.

350. Sendak, Maurice. (1988). *Caldecott & Co.: Notes on Books & Pictures.* New York: Farrar, Straus and Giroux.

351. Slusser, George Edgar. (1976). *The Farthest Shores of Ursula K. Le Guin.* San Bernadino, CA: Borgo Press.

352. Smaridge, Norah. (1973). *Famous Authors-Illustrators for Young People.* New York: Dodd, Mead and Co.

353. Spaeth, Janet. (1987). *Laura Ingalls Wilder.* (Twayne's United States Author Series.) Boston, MA: Twayne/G. K. Hall.

354. Southhall, Ivan. (1975). *A Journey of Discovery.* Harmondsworth, Middlesex, England: Kestral Books.

355. Thwaite, Ann. (1974). *Waiting for the Party: The Life of Frances Hodgson Burnett 1849-1924.* New York: Charles Scribner's Sons.

356. Thwaite, Ann. (1980). *A Piece of Parkin.* Illus. by Glenys Ambrus. London: Andre Deutsch.

357. Townsend, John Rowe. (1971). *A Sense of Story.* Philadelphia, PA: Lippincott.

358. _____. (1979). *A Sounding of Storytellers: New and Revised Essays on Contemporary Writers for Children.* Philadelphia, PA: Lippincott.

359. *Ursula K. Le Guin.* (1979). Joseph D. Olander and Martin Harry Greenberg, Editors. New York: Taplinger.

360. White, Gabriel. (1979). *Edward Ardizzone: Artist and Illustrator.* New York: Schocken Books.

361. Wintle, Justin, and Emma Fisher. (1974). *The Pied Pipers, Interviews with the Influential Creators of Children's Literature.* New York: Paddington Press, Ltd.

362. *Writers for Children: Critical Studies of Major Authors since the Seventeenth Century.* (1988). New York: Charles Scribner's Sons.

363. Zemach, Margot. (1980). *Self-Portrait: Margot Zemach.* Reading, MA: Addison-Wesley.

364. Zochert, Donald. (1976). *Laura: The Life of Laura Ingalls Wilder.* New York: Avon.

WRITING FOR CHILDREN

365. Aiken, Joan. (1982). *The Way to Write for Children.* New York: St. Martin's Press.

366. Bulla, Clyde Robert. (1985). *A Grain of Wheat: A Writer Begins.* Boston, MA: David R. Godine.

367. Colby, Jean Poindexter. (1967). *Writing, Illustrating and Editing Children's Books.* New York: Hastings House.

368. Hunter, Mollie. (1975). *Talent Is Not Enough: Mollie Hunter Writing for Children.* New York: Harper & Row.

369. Karl, Jean. (1970). *From Childhood to Childhood: Children's Books and Their Creators.* New York: John Day.

370. L'Engle, Madeleine. (1972). *A Circle of Quiet.* New York: Farrar, Straus & Giroux.

371. _____. (1985). *Trailing Clouds of Glory: Spiritual Values in Children's Books.* Philadelphia, PA: Westminster Press.

372. Lewis, Claudia. (1981). *Writing for Young Children.* Garden City, NY: Doubleday.

373. Lowery, Joan. (1977). *Writing Mysteries for Young People.* Boston, MA: The Writer.

374. O'Hara, Mary. (1954). *Novel-in-the-Making.* New York: David McKay Co.

375. *The Openhearted Audience: Ten Authors Talk about Writing for Children.* (1980). Edited by Virginia Haviland. Washington, DC: Library of Congress.

376. Paterson, Katherine. (1981). *Gates of Excellence.* New York: Elsevier/Nelson Books.

377. Roberts, Ellen E. (1986). *The Children's Picture Book: How to Write It, How to Sell It.* Cincinnati, OH: Writer's Digest Books.

378. _____. (1986). *Nonfiction for Children: How to Write It, How to Sell It.* Cincinnati, OH: Writer's Digest Books.

379. Robinson, Mabel L. (1923). *A Course in Juvenile Story Writing and in the Study of Juvenile Literature.* New York: Columbia University.

380. Robinson, Mabel L. (1922). *Juvenile Story Writing.* New York: E. P. Dutton.

381. Roginski, James W. (1985). *Behind the Covers: Interviews with Authors and Illustrators of Books for Children and Young Adults.* Littleton, CO: Libraries Unlimited.

382. Southall, Ivan. (1975). *A Journey of Discovery: On Writing for Children.* Harmondsworth, Middlesex, England: Kestral Books.

383. *The Thorny Paradise: Writers on Writing for Children.* (1975). Edward Blishen, Editor. Harmondsworth, Middlesex, England: Kestral Books.

384. Whitney, Phyllis A. (1976). *Writing Juvenile Stories and Novels.* Boston, MA: The Writer.

385. Wilson, Barbara Ker. (1960). *Writing for Children.* New York: Franklin Watts.

386. Yolen, Jane. (1976). *Writing Books for Children.* Boston, MA: The Writer.

PERSONAL ACCOUNTS AND REMINISCENCES

387. Bodger, Joan. (1965). *How the Heather Looks.* New York: Viking Press.

388. Butler, Dorothy. (1980). *Cushla and Her Books.* Boston, MA: Horn Book.

389. Cullinan, Bernice, and M. Jerry Weiss. (1980). *Books I Read When I Was Young.* New York: Avon Books.

390. Duff, Annis. (1944). *Bequest of Wings.* New York: Viking Press.

391. _____. (1955). *Longer Flight.* New York: Viking Press.

392. Eaton, Anne T. (1940). *Reading with Children.* New York: Viking Press.

393. _____. (1957). *Treasure for the Taking.* Revised Edition. New York: Viking Press.

394. Fenner, Phyllis. (1957). *The Proof of the Pudding.* New York: John Day.

395. Hewins, Caroline M. (1926). *A Mid-Century Child and Her Books.* New York: Macmillan.

396. Lanes, Selma G. (1971). *Down the Rabbit Hole: Adventures and Misadventures in the Realm of Children's Literature.* New York: Atheneum.

397. Lepman, Jella. (1969). *A Bridge of Children's Books.* Leicester, England: Brockhampton Press.

398. Moore, Anne Carroll. (1961). *My Roads to Childhood.* Boston, MA: Horn Book.

399. Moore, Annie E. (1934). *Literature Old and New for Children.* Boston, MA: Houghton Mifflin.

400. Moss, Elaine. (1986). *Part of the Pattern: A Personal Journey through the World of Children's Books, 1960-1985.* New York: Greenwillow Books.

401. *Reflections on Literature for Children.* (1984). Francelia Butler and Richard Rotert, Editors. Hamden, CT: Shoestring Library Professional Publications.

402. Sayers, Frances Clarke. (1965). *Summoned by Books.* New York: Viking Press.

403. *Something Shared: Children and Books.* (1959). Phyllis Fenner, Editor. New York: John Day.

404. *That Eager Zest.* (1961). Frances Walsh, Editor. Philadelphia, PA: Lippincott.

405. *Triumphs of the Spirit in Children's Literature.* (1986). Francelia Butler and Richard Rotert, Editors. Hamden, CT: Shoestring Library Professional Publications.

406. Viguers, Ruth Hill. (1964). *Margin for Surprise.* Boston, MA: Little, Brown & Co.

407. White, Dorothy Neal. (1954). *About Books for Children.* New York: Oxford University Press.

408. _____. (1954). *Books before Five.* New York: Oxford University Press.

HISTORY OF CHILDREN'S LITERATURE

409. Avery, Gillian. (1975). *Childhood's Pattern: A Study of the Heroes and Heroines of Children's Fiction 1770-1950.* London: Hodder and Stoughton.

410. Bennett, Peter. (1979). *The Illustrated Child.* New York: G. P. Putnam's Sons.

411. Bett, Henry. (1924). *Nursery Rhymes and Tales: Their Origin and History.* London: Methuen.

412. Billman, Carol. (1986). *The Secret of the Stratemeyer Syndicate: Nancy Drew, the Hardy Boys and the Million Dollar Fiction Factory.* New York: Frederick Ungar.

413. Bingham, Jane. (1980). *Fifteen Centuries of Children's Literature.* Westport, CT: Greenwood Press.

414. Blanck, Jacob Nathaniel. (1975). *Peter Parley to Penrod.* New York: R. R. Bowker.

415. Brant, Sandra, and Elissa Cullman. (1980). *Small Folk: A Celebration of Childhood in America.* New York: E. P. Dutton in Association with the Museum of American Folk Art.

416. Bratton, J. S. (1981). *The Impact of Victorian Children's Fiction.* Totowa, NJ: Barnes & Noble Imports.

417. Cadogan, Mary, and Patricia Craig. (1978). *Women and Children First.* London: Gollancz.

418. _____. (1976). *You're a Brick, Angela! A New Look at Girl's Fiction from 1839-1975.* London: Gollancz.

419. Carpenter, Humphrey. (1985). *Secret Gardens: A Study of the Golden Age of Children's Literature.* Boston, MA: Houghton Mifflin.

420. Carpenter, Humphrey, and Mari Prichard. (1984). *The Oxford Companion to Children's Literature.* Oxford, England: Oxford University Press.

421. *Children's Books.* (1976). Virginia Haviland, Editor. Washington, DC: Library of Congress.

422. Craig, Patricia, and Mary Cadogan. (1981). *The Lady Investigates.* New York: St. Martin's Press.

423. Crane, Walter. (1979). *Of the Decorative Illustration of Books Old and New.* London: Bell & Hylan. (Reprint of 1896 edition).

424. *A Critical History of Children's Literature.* (1969). Cornelia Meigs and others, Editors. Revised Edition. New York: Macmillan.

425. Crouch, Marcus. (1972). *The Nesbit Tradition: The Children's Novel in England, 1945-1970.* Totowa, NJ: Rowman & Littlefield.

426. _____. (1962). *Treasure Seekers and Borrowers: Children's Books in England.* London: The Library Association.

427. Culff, Robert. (1969). *The World of Toys.* London: Hamlyn.

428. Darling, Richard L. (1968). *The Rise of Children's Book Reviewing in America, 1865-1881.* New York: R. R. Bowker.

429. Darton, Frederick Joseph. (1982). *Children's Books in England; Five Centuries of Social Life.* 3rd Edition. Revised by Brian Alderson. Cambridge, England: Cambridge University Press.

430. Drotner, Kirsten. (1988). *English Children and Their Magazines, 1751-1945.* New Haven, CT: Yale University Press.

431. Egoff, Sheila A. (1951). *Children's Periodicals of the Nineteenth Century: A Survey and Bibliography.* London: Library Association.

432. _____. (1975). *The Republic of Childhood: A Critical Study of Canadian Children's Literature.* 2nd Edition. London: Oxford University Press.

433. Ellis, Alec. (1968). *A History of Children's Reading and Literature.* Oxford, England: Pergamon Press.

434. Eyre, Frank. (1973). *British Children's Books in the Twentieth Century.* New York: E. P. Dutton.

435. Field, Elinor Whitney. (1969). *Horn Book Reflections: On Children's Books and Reading.* Boston, MA: Horn Book.

436. Fitzgerald, Frances. (1979). *America Revisited: History Schoolbooks in the Twentieth Century.* Boston, MA: Little Brown and Co.

437. Folmsbee, Beulah. (1942). *Little History of the Horn-Book.* Boston, MA: Horn Book.

438. Gillespie, Margaret C. (1970). *Literature for Children: History and Trends.* Dubuque, IA: Wm. C. Brown Co.

439. Goldstone, Bette P. (1984). *Lessons to Be Learned: A Study of Eighteenth-Century English Didactic Children's Literature.* New York: Peter Lang Publishers.

440. Gottlieb, Robin. (1978). *Publishing Children's Books in America, 1910-1976: An Annotated Bibliography.* New York: The Children's Book Council.

441. Greenleaf, Barbara Kaye. (1978). *Children through the Ages: A History of Childhood.* New York: McGraw Hill.

442. Gumuchian et Cie. (1931). *Les Livres de L'Enfance du XVe au XIXe Siecle.* 2 volumes. Paris, France: En vente a la Librairie Gumuchian & Cie.

443. Haining, Peter. (1979). *Movable Books*. London: New English Library Ltd.

444. *A Harvest of Russian Children's Literature*. (1967). Miriam Morton, Compiler. Berkeley, CA: University of California Press.

445. Hearn, Michael Patrick. (1973). *The Annotated Wizard of Oz*. New York: Clarkson N. Potter.

446. *The History of Childhood*. (1974). Lloyd DeMause, Editor. New York: Psychohistory Press.

447. *The House of Warne*. (1965). Arthur King and A. F. Stuart, Editors. London: Warne.

448. Hurlimann, Bettina. (1968). *Three Centuries of Children's Books in Europe*. Cleveland, OH: World.

449. Jordan, Alice M. (1948). *From Rollo to Tom Sawyer and Other Papers*. Boston, MA: Horn Book.

450. Kelly, R. Gordon. (1974). *Mother Was a Lady; Self and Society in Selected American Children's Periodicals, 1865-1890*. Westport, CT: Greenwood Press.

451. Kensinger, Faye Riter. (1987). *Children of the Series and How They Grew, Or a Century of Heroines and Heroes, Romantic, Comic, Moral*. Bowling Green, OH: Bowling Green University Press.

452. Kiefer, Monica. (1948). *American Children through Their Books 1700-1835*. Philadelphia, PA: University of Pennsylvania Press.

453. Lystead, Mary H. (1980). *From Dr. Mather to Dr. Seuss*. Cambridge, MA: Schenkman Publishing Co.

454. MacKay, James. (1976). *Childhood Antiques*. New York: Taplinger Publishing Co.

455. MacLeod, Anne Scott. (1975). *A Moral Tale: Children's Fiction and American Culture—1820-1860*. Hamden, CT: Archon Books.

456. McClinton, Katharine Morrison. (1970). *Antiques of American Childhood*. New York: Bramhall House.

457. McCulloch, Lou W. (1979). *Children's Books of the 19th Century*. Des Moines, IA: Wallace-Homestead Book Co.

458. Metzner, Seymour. (1966). *American History in Juvenile Books*. New York: H. W. Wilson Co.

459. Muir, Percival Horace. (1954). *English Children's Books, 1600-1900*. London: Batsford.

460. Patterson, Sylvia W. (1971). *Rousseau's Emile and Early Children's Literature*. Metuchen, NJ: Scarecrow Press.

461. *A Peculiar Gift: Nineteenth Century Writings on Books for Children*. (1976). Lance Salway, Editor. London: Kestral Books.

462. Pellowski, Anne. (1967). *The World of Children's Literature*. New York: R. R. Bowker.

463. Pickard, P. M. (1961). *If I Could a Tale Unfold: Violence, Horror, and Sensationalism in Stories for Children*. London: Tavistock Press/Humanities Press.

464. Praeger, Arthur. (1971). *Rascals at Large or the Clue of Old Nostalgia*. Garden City: NY: Doubleday.

465. Rose, Jacqueline. (1984). *The Case of Peter Pan or the Impossibility of Children's Fiction*. London: Macmillan LTD.

466. Rosenbach, Abraham S. W. (1933). *Early American Children's Books: With Bibliographical Description of the Books in His Private Collection*. Portland, ME: Southworth Press.

467. Schatzki, Walter. (1941). *Old and Rare Children's Books*. (Catalogue No. 1). New York: Walter Schatzki.

468. Schorsch, Anita. (1979). *Images of Childhood: An Illustrated Social History*. New York: Mayflower Books.

469. *A Sense of History. Papers Presented at the School of Librarianship, University of New South Wales, May, 1974*. (1975). Margaret Trask, Editor. Kensington, Australia: The University of New South Wales.

470.   Sloane, William. (1955). *Children's Books in England & America in the Seventeenth Century: A History and Checklist, Together with the Young Christian's Library, the First Printed Catalog of Books for Children.* New York: Kings Crown Press, Columbia University.

471.   Smith, Dora V. (1963). *Fifty Years of Children's Books: 1910-1960.* Champaign, IL: National Council of Teachers of English.

472.   Smith, Elva S. (1980). *Elva S. Smith's The History of Children's Literature.* Revised by Margaret Hodges and Susan Steinfirst. Chicago, IL: American Library Association.

473.   *Stratemeyer Pseudonyms and Series Books.* (1982). Deidre Johnson, Compiler. Westport, CT: Greenwood Press.

474.   "The Study and Collecting of Historical Children's Books," (Spring 1979). Edited by Selma K. Richardson. *Library Trends.* Volume 27, No. 4: 421-567.

475.   Summerfield, G. (1985). *Fantasy and Reason: Children's Literature in the Eighteenth Century.* Athens, GA: University of Georgia Press.

476.   Targ, William. (1957). *Bibliophile in the Nursery.* Cleveland, OH: World.

477.   Thwaite, Mary Florence. (1963). *From Primer to Pleasure in Reading.* Boston, MA: Horn Book.

478.   Tiedt, Iris M. (1979). *Exploring Books with Children.* Boston, MA: Houghton Mifflin.

479.   Townsend, John Rowe. (1987). *Written for Children: An Outline of English Language Children's Literature.* 3rd Revised Edition. New York: Lippincott.

480.   Vandergrift, Kay E. (October 1986). "Collecting: Passion With a Purpose," *School Library Journal.* Vol. 33: 91-95.

481.   Vandergrift, Kay E., and Jane Anne Hannigan. (April 1985). "A Celebration of Tradition in Children's Literature," *School Library Journal.* Vol. 31: 33-37.

482.   *Victorian Color Picture Books.* (1983). Jonathan Cott, Editor. New York: Stonehill/Chelsea House.

483.   Welch, D'Alte A. (1972). *A Bibliography of American Children's Books Printed Prior to 1821.* Worcester, MA: American Antiquarian Society.

484.   Whalley, Joyce Irene. (1974). *Cobwebs to Catch Flies.* Berkeley, CA: University of California Press.

485.   Wighton, Rosemary. (1963). *Early Australian Children's Literature.* Melbourne, Australia: Landsdowne Press.

486.   *The Wizard of Oz.* (1983). Michael Patrick Hearn, Editor. The Critical Heritage Series. New York: Schocken Books.

487.   Wooden, Warren W. (1986). *Children's Literature of the English Renaissance.* Jeanie Watson, Editor. Lexington, KY: University of Kentucky Press.

RESEARCH IN CHILDREN'S LITERATURE

488.   Applebee, Arthur N. (1978). *The Child's Concept of Story.* Chicago, IL: University of Chicago Press.

489.   Cooper, Charles R. (1972). *Measuring Growth in Appreciation of Literature.* (Reading Information Series: Where Do We Go?) Newark, DE: International Reading Association.

490.   Crago, Maureen, and Hugh Crago. (1983). *Prelude to Literacy: A Preschool Child's Encounter with Picture and Story.* Carbondale, IL: Southern Illinois University Press.

491.   Favat, Andre F. (1977). *Child and Tale: The Origins of Interest.* Research Report #19 NCTE. Urbana, IL: National Council of Teachers of English.

492.   Goldsmith, Evelyn. (1984). *Research into Illustration: An Approach and a Review.* Cambridge, England: Cambridge University Press.

493. Kamenetsky, Christa. (1984). *Children's Literature in Hitler's Germany*. Athens, OH: Ohio University Press.

494. Lukenbill, J. Bernard, and Sharon Lee Stewart. (1988). *Youth Literature: An Inter-disciplinary, Annotated Guide to North American Dissertation Research, 1930-1985*. New York: Garland Publishing.

495. Orvig, Mary, and others. (1975). *Catalog of the Reference Collection of the Swedish Institute for Children's Literature*. 2nd Edition. Stockholm, Sweden: Institute for Children's Literature.

496. Protherough, Robert. (1983). *Developing Response to Fiction*. Milton Keynes, England: Open University Press.

497. *Research in Children's Literature: An Annotated Bibliography*. (1976). Dianne Monson and Bette J. Peltola, Compilers. Newark, DE: International Reading Association.

498. *Response to Literature*. (1968). James R. Squire, Editor. Champaign, IL: National Council of Teachers of English.

499. Roberts, Patricia L. (1976). *The Female Image in the Caldecott Medal Award Books*. Stockton, CA: Bureau of Educational Research and Field Service, School of Education, University of the Pacific.

REFERENCE IN CHILDREN'S LITERATURE

500. Adamson, Lynda G. (1987). *A Reference Guide to Historical Fiction for Children and Young Adults*. Westport, CT: Greenwood Press.

501. *American Childhood: A Research Guide and Historical Handbook*. (1985). Joseph M. Hawes and N. Ray Hiner, Editors. Westport, CT: Greenwood Press.

502. *American Writers for Children, 1900-1960*. (1983). John Cech, Editor. Dictionary of Literary Biography. Vol. 22. Detroit, MI: Bruccoli Clark Books.

503. *American Writers for Children before 1900*. (1985). Glenn Estes, Editor. Dictionary of Literary Biography. Vol 42. Detroit, MI: Bruccoli Clark Books.

504. *American Writers for Children since 1960: Fiction*. (1986). Glenn Estes, Editor. Dictionary of Literary Biography. Vol. 52. Detroit, MI: Bruccoli Clark Books.

505. *American Writers for Children since 1960: Poets, Illustrators and Non-Fiction Authors*. (1987). Glenn Estes, Editor. Vol. 61. Detroit, MI: Bruccoli Clark Books.

506. *Anatomy of Wonder*. (1987). Neil Barron, Editor. 3rd Edition. New York: R. R. Bowker.

507. *Bibliography of the Little Golden Books*. (1987). Dolores Blythe Jones, Compiler. New York: Greenwood Press.

508. *Children's Periodicals of the United States*. (1984). R. Gordon Kelly, Editor. Westport, CT: Greenwood Press.

509. Ellis, Alec. (1973). *How to Find Out about Children's Literature*. Oxford, England: Pergamon Press.

510. *Fantasy Literature for Children and Young Adults*. (1988). Ruth Nadelman Lynn. 3rd Edition. New York: R. R. Bowker.

511. Fisher, Margery. (1975). *Who's Who in Children's Literature; A Treasury of the Familiar Characters of Childhood*. London: Weidenfeld & Nicholson.

512. *Folk Literature and Children: An Annotated Bibliography of Secondary Materials*. (1981). George Shannon, Compiler. Westport, CT: Greenwood Press.

513. *Girls Series Books: A Checklist of Hardback Books Published 1900-1975*. (1978). Minneapolis, MN: Children's Literature Research Collections, University of Minnesota Libraries.

514. Haviland, Virginia. (1966). *Children's Literature: A Guide to Reference Resources*. Washington, DC: Library of Congress.

515. Haviland, Virginia, and others. (1972). *Children's Literature: A Guide to Reference Resources: First Supplement*. Washington, DC: Library of Congress.

516. _____. (1977). *Children's Literature: A Guide to Reference Resources. Second Supplement.* Washington, DC: Library of Congress.

517. Helbig, Alethea, and Agnes Perkins. (1985). *Dictionary of American Children's Fiction, 1859-1959.* Westport, CT: Greenwood Press.

518. _____. (1986). *Dictionary of American Children's Fiction, 1960-1984: Recent Books of Recognized Merit.* New York: Greenwood Press.

519. Hendrickson, Linnea. (1987). *Children's Literature: A Guide to the Criticism.* Boston, MA: G. K. Hall.

520. *The Junior Book of Authors.* (1951). Stanley Kunitz and Howard Haycraft, Editors. 2nd Edition. New York: H. W. Wilson Co.

521. *More Junior Authors.* (1963). Muriel Fuller, Editor. New York: H. W. Wilson Co.

522. Pettus, Eloise S. (1985). *Master Index to Summaries of Children's Books.* Metuchen, NJ: Scarecrow Press.

523. Pfleiger, Pat, and Helen Hill. (1984). *A Reference Guide to Modern Fantasy for Children.* Westport, CT: Greenwood Press.

524. Rahn, Suzanne. (1981). *Children's Literature: An Annotated Bibliography of the History and Criticism.* New York: Garland.

525. Rovin, Jeff. (1985). *The Encyclopedia of Superheroes.* New York: Facts on File Publications.

526. *Sequences: An Annotated Guide to Children's Fiction in Series.* (1985). Susan Roman, Editor. Chicago, IL: American Library Association.

527. *Something about the Author Autobiography Series.* (1986). Adele Sarkissian, Editor. Volume 1. Detroit, MI: Gale Research Co.

528. *The Who's Who of Children's Literature.* (1969). Brian Doyle, Editor. New York: Schocken Books.

SPECIAL COLLECTIONS: CATALOGS

529. *An American Sampler: Children's Books from the Kerlan Collection of the University of Minnesota.* (1985). Minneapolis, MN: University of Minnesota.

530. *A Child's Garden of Delights: Pictures, Poems, and Stories for Children.* (1987). From the collections of The New York Public Library. New York: Harry N. Abrams.

531. Cobb, Edith. (1977). *The Ecology of Imagination in Childhood.* New York: Columbia University Press.

532. *Guide to Children's Libraries and Literature Outside the United States.* (1982). Amy Kellman, Compiler. Chicago, IL: American Library Association.

533. *The Illustrator as Storyteller: Caldecott Medal and Honor Books: 1938-1984.* (1984). Minneapolis, MN: University Art Museum/University of Minnesota.

534. *The Kerlan Collection: Manuscripts and Illustrations.* (1985). Karen Hoyle and staff, Compilers. Minneapolis, MN: University of Minnesota Libraries.

535. The Pierpont Morgan Library. (1975). *Early Children's Books and Their Illustrators.* New York: The Pierpont Morgan Library.

536. Quayle, Eric. (1971). *The Collector's Book of Children's Books.* New York: Clarkson Potter.

537. Rosenbach, Abraham. (1933). *Early American Children's Books with Bibliographical Descriptions of Books in His Private Collection.* Portland, ME: Southworth Press. (Reprinted in 1966, New York: Kraus).

538. Toronto Public Library. Osborne Collection. (1958). *The Osborne Collection of Early Children's Books, 1566-1910, Volume One.* Toronto, Canada: Toronto Public Library.

539. _____. (1975). *The Osborne Collection of Early Children's Books, 1476-1910, Volume Two.* Toronto, Canada: Toronto Public Library.

540. *Special Collections in Children's Literature.* (1982). Carolyn Field, Editor. Chicago, IL: American Library Association.

541. United States Library of Congress. Rare Book Division. (1975). *Children's Books in the Rare Book Division of the Library of Congress.* Totowa, NJ: Rowman & Littlefield. (2 volumes).

542. Welch, D'Alte A. (1972). *A Bibliography of American Children's Books Printed Prior to 1821.* Worcester, MA: American Antiquarian Society.

SELECTION AND LIBRARY APPLICATIONS

543. Adamson, Lynda G. (1987). *A Reference Guide to Historical Fiction for Children and Young People.* Westport, CT: Greenwood Press.

544. Association for Library Service to Children. (1980). *Selecting Materials for Children and Young Adults.* Chicago, IL: American Library Association.

545. Bauer, Carolyn Feller. (1983). *This Way to Books.* New York: H. W. Wilson Co.

546. *The Best in Children's Books: The University of Chicago Guide to Children's Literature, 1966-1972.* (1973). Zena Sutherland, Compiler. Chicago, IL: University of Chicago Press.

547. *The Best in Children's Books: The University of Chicago Guide to Children's Literature, 1979-1984.* (1986). Zena Sutherland, Compiler. Chicago, IL: University of Chicago Press.

548. *The Black American in Books for Children: Reading in Racism.* (1985). Donnarae MacCann, Compiler. 2nd Edition. Metuchen, NJ: Scarecrow Press.

549. *BookWhiz.* (1987). Princeton, NJ: Educational Testing Service. (Computer Disk).

550. Bracken, Jeanne. (1979). *Books for Today's Children.* New York: Feminist Press.

551. Carlson, Ann D. (1985). *Early Childhood Literature Sharing Programs in Libraries.* Hamden, CT: Library Professional Publications.

552. Carlson, Ruth Kearney. (1972). *Emerging Humanity: Multi-Ethnic Literature for Children and Adolescents.* Dubuque, IA: Wm. C. Brown Co.

553. _____. (1976). *Literature for Children: Enrichment Ideas.* 2nd Edition. Dubuque, IA: Wm. C. Brown Co.

554. *Children's Novels and the Movies.* (1983). Douglas Street, Editor. New York: Frederick Ungar.

555. Cleaver, Betty, and others. (1986). *Creating Connections: Books, Kits, and Games for Children: A Sourcebook.* New York: Garland.

556. Coody, Betty. (1983). *Using Literature with Young Children.* Dubuque, IA: Wm. C. Brown.

557. De Jovine, F. Anthony. (1971). *The Young Hero in American Fiction.* New York: Appleton-Century.

558. *Developing Active Readers: Ideas for Parents, Teachers, and Librarians.* (1979). Dianne L. Monson and DayAnn K. McClenathan, Editors. Newark, DE: International Reading Association.

559. Ettlinger, John R. (1987). *Choosing Books for Young People: A Guide to Criticism and Bibliography.* Chicago, IL: American Library Association.

560. Fader, Daniel N., and Elton B. McNeil. (1977). *Hooked on Books: Programs and Proof.* New York: Berley Publishing.

561. Fisher, Margery. (1986). *Classics for Children and Young People: A Signal Guide Book.* England: Thimble Press.

562. Greene, Ellin, and Madalynne Schoenfeld. (1972). *A Multimedia Approach to Children's Literature.* Chicago, IL: American Library Association.

563. Gross, Jacquelyn. (1986). *Make Your Child a Lifelong Reader.* Los Angeles, CA: Jeremy P. Tarcher, Inc.

564. Hass, E. A. (1987). *Bookbrain.* Phoenix, AZ: Oryx Press. (Computer Disk).

565. Hearne, Betsy. (1981). *Choosing Books for Children: A Commonsense Guide.* New York: Delacorte Press.

566. Hill, Janet. (1973). *Children Are People.* London: Hamish Hamilton Children's Books, Ltd.

567. Hotchkiss, Jeanette. (1972). *European Historical Fiction and Biography for Children and Young People.* 2nd Edition. Metuchen, NJ: Scarecrow Press.

568. Howard, Elizabeth F. (1988). *America as Story: Historical Fiction for Secondary Schools.* Chicago, IL: American Library Association.

569. Kemp, Fred. (1987). *Idealog.* English Department, Computer Research Laboratory. Austin, TX: University of Texas. (Computer Disk).

570. Kies, Cosette. (1987). *Supernatural Fiction for Teens.* Littleton, CO: Libraries Unlimited.

571. Kobrin, Beverly. (1988). *Eyeopeners! How to Choose and Use Children's Books about Real People, Places, and Things.* New York: Viking.

572. Larrick, Nancy. (1975). *A Parent's Guide to Children's Reading.* 4th Edition. Garden City, NY: Doubleday.

573. _____. (1966). *A Teacher's Guide to Children's Books.* Columbus, OH: Charles Merrill Co.

574. Laughlin, Mildred Knight, and Letty S. Watt. (1986). *Developing Learning Skills through Children's Literature: An Idea Book for K-5 Classrooms and Libraries.* Phoenix, AZ: Oryx Press.

575. *Learning to Love Literature: Preschool through Grade 3.* (1981). Linda L. Lamme, Editor. Urbana, IL: National Council of Teachers of English.

576. Leif, Irving P. (1977). *Children's Literature: A Historical and Contemporary Bibliography.* Troy, New York: The Whitson Publishing Co.

577. *Library Services for Hispanic Children: A Guide for Public and School Libraries.* (1987). Phoenix, AZ: Oryx Press.

578. MacCann, Donnarae, and Gloria Woodard. (1977). *Cultural Conformity in Books for Children.* Metuchen, NJ: Scarecrow Press.

579. Mahoney, Ellen, and Leah Wilcox. (1985). *Ready, Set, Read: Best Books to Prepare Preschoolers.* Metuchen, NJ: Scarecrow Press.

580. Marshall, Margaret Richardson. (1986). *Handicapped Children and Books.* Wetherby, West Yorkshire, England: British Library.

581. Martin, John Henry, and Ardy Friedberg. (1986). *Writing to Read: A Parents' Guide to the New Early Learning Program for Young Children.* New York: Warner Books.

582. Mason, Bobbie Ann. (1975). *The Girl Sleuth: A Feminist Guide.* New York: Feminist Press.

583. McCracken, Robert A., and Marlene J. McCracken. (1986). *Stories, Songs, and Poetry to Teach Reading and Writing: Literacy through Language.* Chicago, IL: American Library Association.

584. Melton, David. (1986). *How to Capture Live Authors and Bring Them to Your School.* Kansas City, MO: Landmark Editions.

585. Moss, Joy F. (1984). *Focus Units in Literature: A Handbook for Elementary School Teachers.* Urbana, IL: National Council of Teachers of English.

586. Paulin, Mary Ann. (1982). *Creative Uses of Children's Literature.* Hamden, CT: Shoestring Press.

587. *Periodicals for School Libraries.* (1977). Selma K. Richardson, Editor. 2nd Edition. Chicago, IL: American Library Association.

588. Petty, Walter T., and Mary Gowen. (1967). *Slithery Snakes and Other Aids to Children's Writing.* New York: Appleton-Century-Crofts.

589. Reasoner, Charles F. (1977). *Releasing Children to Literature.* Revised Edition. New York: Dell.

590. _____. (1975). *When Children Read.* New York: Dell.

591. _____. (1972). *Where the Readers Are.* New York: Dell.

592. Richardson, Selma K. (1983). *Magazines for Children: A Guide for Parents, Teachers and Librarians.* Chicago, IL: American Library Association.

593. Rochman, Hazel. (1987). *Tales of Love and Terror: Booktalking the Classics, Old and New.* Chicago, IL: American Library Association.

594. Rosenberg, Judith K., and Kenyon C. Rosenberg. (1972). *Young People's Literature in Series: Fiction.* Littleton, CO: Libraries Unlimited.

595. _____. (1973). *Young People's Literature in Series: Publishers' and Non-Fiction Series.* Littleton, CO: Libraries Unlimited.

596. Rossi, Mary Jane Mangini. (1982). *Read to Me! Teach Me!.* New York: American Baby Books.

597. Schwartz, Helen. (1987). *Seen.* Department of English. Pittsburgh, PA: Carnegie Mellon University. (Computer Disk).

598. Sebesta, Sam L. (1968). *Ivory, Apes, and Peacocks: The Literature Point of View.* Newark, DE: International Reading Association.

599. *Sources of Good Books and Magazines for Children.* (1970). Winifred Ladley, Compiler. Newark, DE: International Reading Association.

600. Terry, Ann. (1974). *Children's Poetry Preferences: A National Survey of Upper Elementary Grades.* (Research Reports, NCTE, No. 16). Urbana, IL: National Council of Teachers of English.

601. Vandergrift, Kay E. (1979). *The Teaching Role of the School Media Specialist.* Chicago, IL: American Library Association.

602. West, Mark I. (1988). *Trust Your Children: Voices against Censorship in Children's Literature.* New York: Neal Schuman Publishers.

603. Whitehead, Robert. (1968). *Children's Literature: Strategies of Teaching.* Englewood Cliffs, NJ: Prentice Hall.

AWARDS IN CHILDREN'S LITERATURE

604. *Caldecott Medal Books, 1938-1957.* (1957). Bertha E. Mahoney Miller and Eleanor Whitney Field, Editors. Boston, MA: Horn Book.

605. Children's Book Council, New York. (1975). *Children's Books: Awards and Prizes.* New York: Children's Book Council.

606. Helbig, Alethea K., and Agnes Regan Perkins. (1985). *Dictionary of American Children's Fiction, 1859-1959: Books of Recognized Merit.* Westport, CT: Greenwood Press.

607. Library Association. (1967). *Chosen for Children: An Account of the Books Awarded the Library Association Carnegie Medal, 1936-1965.* London: Library Association.

608. *Newbery Medal Books, 1922-1955.* (1955). Bertha E. Mahony Miller and Eleanor Field, Editors. Boston, MA: Horn Book.

609. *Newbery and Caldecott Medal Books, 1956-1965.* (1965). Lee Kingman, Editor. Boston, MA: Horn Book.

610. *Newbery and Caldecott Medal Books, 1966-1975.* (1975). Lee Kingman, Editor. Boston, MA: Horn Book.

611. *Newbery and Caldecott Medal Books, 1976-1985.* (1986). Lee Kingman, Editor. Boston, MA: Horn Book.

612. *Newbery and Caldecott Medalists and Honor Book Winners: Bibliographies and Resource Material through 1977.* (1982). Jim Roginski, Compiler. Littleton, CO: Libraries Unlimited.

613. Peterson, Linda K., and Marilyn L. Solt. (1982). *Newbery and Caldecott Medal and Honor Books: An Annotated Bibliography.* Boston, MA: G. K. Hall.

614. Smith, Irene. (1957). *History of the Newbery and Caldecott Medals.* New York: Viking Press.

Selected Bibliography of Literary Criticism

This selection, drawn primarily from my personal collection, reflects my interest in various areas of literary criticism. Feminist criticism, reader-response criticism, and general narrative theory are the strongest emphases in this bibliography.

615. Abrams, Meyer Howard. (1953). *The Mirror and the Lamp: Romantic Theory and the Critical Tradition*. New York: Oxford University Press.

616. Aristotle. (1961). *Poetics*. Translated by S. H. Butcher and Introduction by Francis Fergusson. New York: Hill and Wang.

617. *Arts and Cognition*. (1977). David Perkins and Barbara Leondar, Editors. Baltimore, MD: The Johns Hopkins University Press.

618. *Aspects of Alice*. (1972). Robert Phillips, Editor. London: Victor Gollancz.

619. *Aspects of Narrative*. (1971). J. Hillis Miller, Editor. New York: Columbia University Press.

620. Auerbach, Eric. (1953). *Mimesis: The Representation of Reality in Western Literature*. Translated by Willard R. Trask. Princeton University Press. (First Published 1946).

621. Auerbach, Nina. (1978). *Communities of Women, An Idea in Fiction*. Cambridge, MA: Harvard University Press.

622. Bachelard, Gaston. (1969). *The Poetics of Space*. Translated by Maria Jolas. Boston, MA: Beacon Press.

623. _____. (1969). *The Poetics of Reverie: Childhood, Language and the Cosmos*. Translated by Daniel Russell. Boston, MA: Beacon Press.

624. Barthes, Roland. (1972). *Critical Essays*. Translated by Richard Howard. Evanston, IL: University of Illinois Press.

625. _____. (1967). *Elements of Semiology*. Translated by Annette Lavers and Colin Smith. London: Jonathan Cape, Ltd.

626. _____. (1977). *Image, Music, Text*. Translated by Stephen Heath. New York: Hill and Wang.

627. _____. (1972). *Mythologies*. Translated by Annette Lavers. New York: Hill and Wang.

628. _____. (1975). *The Pleasure of the Text*. Translated by Richard Miller. New York: Hill and Wang.

629. _____. (1975). *S/Z*. Translated by Richard Miller. New York: Hill and Wang.

630. Baym, Nina. (1978). *Women's Fiction: A Guide to Novels by and about Women in America, 1830-1860*. Ithaca, NY: Cornell University Press.

631. Beardsley, Monroe C. (1981). *Aesthetics: Problems in the Philosophy of Criticism*. 2nd Edition. Indianapolis, IN: Hackett Publishers.

632. Bernikow, Louise. (1980). *Among Women*. New York: Harper & Row.

633. Blackmur, R. P. (1935). *The Double Agent: Essays in Craft and Elucidation*. New York: Arrow.

634. Bleich, David. (1975). *Readings and Feelings: An Introduction to Subjective Criticism*. Urbana, IL: National Council of Teachers of English.

635. _____. (1978). *Subjective Criticism*. Baltimore, MD: The Johns Hopkins University Press.

636. Bloom, Harold. (1973). *The Anxiety of Influence*. New York: Oxford University Press.

637. _____. (1982). *The Breaking of Vessels*. Chicago, IL: University of Chicago Press.

638. Bloom, Harold and others. (1979). *Deconstruction & Criticism*. New York: Continuum Publishing.

639. Booth, Wayne C. (1979). *Critical Understanding: The Powers and Limits of Pluralism*. Chicago, IL: University of Chicago Press.

640. _____. (1961). *The Rhetoric of Fiction*. Chicago, IL: University of Chicago Press.

641. Borklund, Elmer. (1977). *Contemporary Literary Critics*. London: St. James Press.

642. Brewer, Derek. (1980). *Symbolic Stories: Traditional Narratives of the Family Drama in English Literature*. Cambridge, England: D. S. Brewer, Rowman & Littlefield.

643. Brown, Cheryl, and Karen Olsen. (1978). *Feminist Criticism: Essays on Theory, Poetry and Prose*. Metuchen, NJ: Scarecrow Press.

644. Brooks, Cleanth, and Robert Penn Warren. (1943). *Understanding Fiction*. New York: Crofts.

645. Brownstein, Rachel. (1982). *Becoming a Heroine: Reading about Women in Novels*. New York: Viking Press.

646. Bruss, Elizabeth W. (1982). *Beautiful Theories: The Spectacle of Discourse in Contemporary Criticism*. Baltimore, MD: The Johns Hopkins University Press.

647. Burke, Kenneth. (1973). *The Philosophy of Literary Form*. 3rd Edition. Berkeley, CA: University of California Press.

648. Cain, William E. (1984). *The Crisis in Criticism: Theory, Literature, and Reform in English Studies*. Baltimore, MD: The Johns Hopkins University Press.

649. Carroll, David. (1982). *The Subject in Question: The Languages of Theory and the Strategies of Fiction*. Chicago, IL: University of Chicago Press.

650. Cassirer, Ernst. (1953). *Philosophy of Symbolic Form*. Translated by Ralph Manheim. New Haven, CT: Yale University Press.

651. Chatman, Seymour. (1978). *Story and Discourse: Narrative Structure in Fiction and Film*. Ithaca, NY: Cornell University Press.

652. Christian, Barbara. (1985). *Black Feminist Criticism: Perspectives on Black Women Writers*. New York: Pergamon Press.

653. *Clio's Consciousness Raised*. (1974). Mary S. Hartman and Lois Banner, Editors. New York: Harper & Row.

654. Coles, Robert. (1989). *The Call of Stories: Teaching and the Moral Imagination*. Boston, MA: Houghton Mifflin.

655. *Comparative Criticism: A Yearbook*. (1980). Elinor Shaffer, Editor. Cambridge, England: Cambridge University Press.

656. Crane, R. S. (1952). *Critics and Criticism*. Chicago, IL: Chicago University Press.

657. Crews, Frederick C. (1963). *The Pooh Perplex*. New York: E. P. Dutton.

658. *Criticism in the University*. (1985). Gerald Graff and Reginald Gibbons, Editors. Evanston, IL: Northwestern University Press.

659. Culler, Jonathan. (1982). *On Deconstruction: Theory and Criticism after Structuralism*. Ithaca, NY: Cornell University Press.

660. _____. (1980). *The Pursuit of Signs: Semiotics, Literature, Deconstruction*. Ithaca, NY: Cornell University Press.

661. _____. (1975). *Structuralist Poetics: Structuralism, Linguistics, and the Study of Literature*. Ithaca, NY: Cornell University Press.

662. Denham, Robert D. (1978). *Northrop Frye and Critical Method*. University Park, PA: The Pennsylvania State University Press.

663. De Man, Paul. (1971). *Blindness and Insight*. New York: Oxford University Press.

664. Derrida, Jacques. (1974). *Of Grammatology*. Translated by Gayatri Chakravorty Spivak. Baltimore, MD: The Johns Hopkins University Press.

665. Dalsimer, Katherine. (1986). *Female Adolescence: Psychoanalytic Reflections on Literature*. New Haven, CT: Yale University Press.

666. Dewey, John. (1930). *Construction and Criticism*. New York: Columbia University Press. (The First Davies Memorial Lecture).

667. Dillon, George. (1978). *Language Processing and the Reading of Literature: Toward a Model of Comprehension*. Bloomington, IN: Indiana University Press.

668. *Directions for Criticism: Structuralism and Its Alternatives*. (1977). Murray Krieger and L. S. Dembo, Editors. Madison, WI: University of Wisconsin Press.

669. Douglas, Ann. (1977). *The Feminization of American Culture*. New York: Alfred A. Knopf.

670. Dubois, Ellen Carol and others. (1987). *Feminist Scholarship: Kindling in the Groves of Academe*. Urbana, IL: University of Illinois Press.

671. Eagleton, Terry. (1983). *Literary Theory: An Introduction*. Minneapolis, MN: University of Minnesota Press.

672. _____. (1976). *Marxism and Literary Criticism*. Berkeley, CA: University of California Press.

673. Eco, Umberto. (1979). *The Role of the Reader: Explorations in the Semiotics of Texts*. Bloomington, IN: Indiana University Press.

674. _____. (1976). *A Theory of Semiotics*. Bloomington, IN: Indiana University Press.

675. Eliot, T. S. (1965). *To Criticize the Critic*. London: Faber & Faber.

676. _____. (1933). *The Use of Poetry and the Use of Criticism*. London: Faber & Faber.

677. Ellis, John M. (1974). *The Theory of Literary Criticism: A Logical Analysis*. Berkeley, CA: University of California Press.

678. Empson, William. (1947). *Seven Types of Ambiguity*. 2nd Edition. London: Chatto and Windus.

679. Fekete, John. (1977). *The Critical Twilight*. London: Routledge & Kegan Paul.

680. *Feminism as Critique*. (1987). Seyla Benhabib and Drucilla Cornell, Editors. Minneapolis, MN: University of Minnesota Press.

681. *Feminist Collage: Educating Women in the Visual Arts*. (1979). Judy Loeb, Editor. New York: Teachers College Press.

682. *Feminist Criticism and Social Change: Sex, Class and Race in Literature and Culture*. (1986). Judith Newton and Deborah Rosenfelt, Editors. London: Methuen.

683. Fetterley, Judith. (1979). *The Resisting Reader: A Feminist Approach to American Fiction*. Bloomington, IN: Indiana University Press.

684. Fish, Stanley E. (1980). *Is There a Text in This Class? The Authority of Interpretive Communities*. Cambridge, MA: Harvard University Press.

685. _____. (1972). *Self-Consuming Artifacts: The Experience of Seventeenth Century Literature*. Berkeley, CA: University of California Press.

686. _____. (1967). *Surprised by Sin: The Reader in Paradise Lost*. New York: St. Martin's Press.

687. Fokkema, D. W., and Elrud Kunne-Ibsch. (1977). *Theories of Literature in the Twentieth Century*. London: Christopher Hurst.

688. *For Alma Mater: Theory and Practice in Feminist Scholarship*. (1985). Paula Treichlar and others, Editors. Urbana, IL: University of Illinois Press.

689. Forster, E. M. (1927). *Aspects of the Novel*. New York: Harcourt Brace & World.

690. Frye, Northrop. (1956). *Anatomy of Criticism*. Princeton, NJ: Princeton University Press.

691. _____. (1980). *Criticism as Education*. The Leland B. Jacobs Lecture, 1979. New York: School of Library Service, Columbia University.

692. _____. (1964). *The Educated Imagination*. Bloomington, IN: Indiana University Press.

693. _____. (1963). *Fables of Identity: Studies in Poetic Mythology*. New York: Harcourt Brace & World.

694. _____. (1972). *On Teaching Literature*. New York: Harcourt Brace Jovanovich.

695. _____. (1976). *The Secular Scripture: A Study of the Structure of Romance*. Cambridge, MA: Harvard University Press.

696. Gadamer, Hans-George. (1975). *Truth and Method*. London: Sheed & Ward. (First published in 1960).

697. Gardner, John. (1973). *The Arts and Human Development*. New York: Wiley.

698. _____. (1978). *On Moral Fiction*. New York: Basic Books.

699. *Gender and Reading: Essays on Readers, Texts, and Contexts*. (1986). Elizabeth Flynn and Patrocinio Schweikart, Editors. Baltimore, MD: The Johns Hopkins University Press.

700. Genette, Gerald. (1979). *Narrative Discourse: An Essay on Method*. Translated by Jane E. Lewin. Ithaca, NY: Cornell University Press.

701. Gibson, Eleanor J., and Harry Gibson. (1975). *The Psychology of Reading*. Cambridge, MA: The MIT Press.

702. Gilbert, Sandra, and Susan Gubar. (1979). *The Madwoman in the Attic*. New Haven, CT: Yale University Press.

703. Goodheart, Eugene. (1979). *The Failure of Criticism*. Cambridge, MA: Harvard University Press.

704. Goodman, Kenneth S. (1968). *The Psycholinguistic Nature of the Reading Process*. Detroit, MI: Wayne State University Press.

705. Graff, Gerald. (1979). *Literature against Itself: Literary Ideas in Modern Society*. Chicago, IL: University of Chicago Press.

706. Gribble, James. (1983). *Literary Education: A Revaluation*. Cambridge, England: Cambridge University Press.

707. Hall, Nigel. (1987). *The Emergence of Literacy*. Portsmouth, NH: Heinemann Educational Books.

708. *Handbook of Discourse Analysis*. (1985). Volume 4: Discourse Analysis in Society. Teun A. Van Dijk, Editor. London: Academic Press.

709. Hartman, Geoffrey. (1970). *Beyond Formalism: Literary Essays 1958-1970*. New Haven, CT: Yale University Press.

710. _____. (1980). *Criticism in the Wilderness*. New Haven, CT: Yale University Press.

711. _____. (1975). *The Fate of Reading and Other Essays*. Chicago, IL: University of Chicago Press.

712. _____. (1982). *Saving the Text: Literature/Derrida/Philosophy*. Baltimore, MD: The Johns Hopkins University Press.

713. Hassan, Ihab. (1973). *Contemporary American Literature, 1945-1972*. New York: Frederick Ungar.

714. _____. (1975). *Paracriticism: Seven Speculations of the Time*. Chicago, IL: University of Illinois Press.

715. _____. (1980). *The Right Promethean Fire: Imagination, Science and Cultural Change*. Urbana, IL: University of Illinois Press.

716. Hawkes, Terence. (1977). *Structuralism and Semiotics*. Berkeley, CA: University of California Press.

717. Heilbrun, Carolyn G. (1973). *Toward a Recognition of Androgyny*. New York: Alfred A. Knopf. (First published in 1964).

718. Hernadi, Paul. (1972). *Beyond Genre: New Directions in Literary Classification*. Ithaca, NY: Cornell University Press.

719. Hirsch, E. D., Jr. (1976). *The Aims of Interpretation*. Chicago, IL: University of Chicago Press.

720. _____. (1967). *Validity of Interpretation*. New Haven, CT: Yale University Press.

721. Hochman, Baruch. (1985). *Character in Literature*. Ithaca, NY: Cornell University Press.

722. Holland, Norman. (1968). *The Dynamics of Literary Response*. New York: Oxford University Press.

723. _____. (1975). *5 Readers Reading*. New Haven, CT: Yale University Press.

724. _____. (1973). *Poems in Persons: An Introduction to the Psychoanalysis of Literature*. New York: Norton.

725. *The Horizon of Literature*. (1982). Paul Hernadi, Editor. Lincoln, NB: University of Nebraska Press.

726. *How Porcupines Make Love: Notes on a Response-Centered Curriculum*. (1972). Alan C. Purves, Editor. Lexington, MA: Xerox Publishing Co.

727. Howard, Roy J. (1982). *Three Faces of Hermeneutics: An Introduction to Current Theories of Understanding*. Berkeley, CA: University of California Press.

728. Hyman, Stanley Edgar. (1955). *The Armed Vision: A Study in the Methods of Modern Literary Criticism*. 2nd Edition. New York: Alfred A. Knopf.

729. *In Search of Literary Theory*. (1972). Morton B. Bloomfield, Editor. Ithaca, NY: Cornell University Press.

730. Ingarden, Roman. (1973). *The Literary Work of Art: An Investigation on the Borderline of Ontology, Logic, and the Theory of Literature*. Evanston, IL: Northwestern University Press.

731. *Interpretation of Narrative*. (1978). Mario J. Valdes and Owen J. Miller, Editors. Toronto, Canada: University of Toronto Press.

732. Irwin, W. R. (1976). *The Game of the Impossible: A Rhetoric of Fantasy*. Urbana, IL: University of Illinois Press.

733. Iser, Wolfgang. (1979). *The Act of Reading: A Theory of Aesthetic Response*. Baltimore, MD: The Johns Hopkins University Press.

734. _____. (1974). *The Implied Reader: Patterns of Communication in Prose Fiction from Bunyan to Beckett*. Baltimore, MD: The Johns Hopkins University Press.

735. Jackson, Rosemary. (1981). *Fantasy: The Literature of Subversion*. London: Methuen.

736. Jacobus, Mary. (1986). *Reading Woman: Essays in Feminist Criticism*. New York: Columbia University Press.

737. James, Henry. (1934). *The Art of the Novel: Critical Prefaces*. New York: Charles Scribner's Sons.

738. Jameson, Fredric. (1972). *The Prison House of Language*. Princeton, NJ: Princeton University Press.

739. Jauss, Hans R. (1982). *Towards an Aesthetic of Reception*. Minneapolis, MN: University of Minnesota Press.

740. Kaplan, Cora. (1987). *Sea Changes: Essays on Culture and Feminism*. New York: Verso/Methuen. (Distributed by Schocken).

741. Kermode, Frank. (1979). *The Genesis of Secrecy: On the Interpretation of Narrative*. Cambridge, MA: Harvard University Press.

742. _____. (1966). *The Sense of an Ending: Studies in the Theory of Fiction*. New York: Oxford University Press.

743. Kolody, Annette. (1975). *The Lay of the Land*. Chapel Hill, NC: University of North Carolina Press.

744. Krieger, Murray. (1976). *Theory of Criticism: A Tradition and Its System*. Baltimore, MD: The Johns Hopkins University Press.

745. Kwant, Remy C. (1967). *Critique: Its Nature and Function*. Pittsburgh, PA: Duquesne University Press.

746. Langer, Susanne. (1953). *Feeling and Form*. New York: Charles Scribner's Sons.

747. _____. (1942). *Philosophy in a New Key*. Cambridge, MA: Harvard University Press.

748. _____. (1957). *Problems of Art*. New York: Charles Scribner's Sons.

749. Le Guin, Ursula K. (1989). *Dancing at the Edge of the World*. New York: Grove Press.

750. _____. (1982). *The Language of the Night: Essays on Fantasy and Science Fiction*. New York: Berkley Books.

751. Leitch, Thomas M. (1986). *What Stories Are: Narrative Theory and Interpretation*. University Park, PA: Pennsylvania State University Press.

752. Leitch, Vincent B. (1982). *Deconstructive Criticism: An Advanced Introduction and Survey*. New York: Columbia University Press.

753. Lentricchia, Frank. (1980). *After the New Criticism*. Chicago, IL: University of Chicago Press.

754. Lesser, Simon O. (1957). *Fiction and the Unconscious*. Boston, MA: Vintage.

755. Levi-Strauss, Claude. (1963). *Structural Anthropology*. Translated by Claire Jacobson and Brooke Grungfest Schoepf. New York: Basic Books.

756. Lewis, C. S. (1964). *The Discarded Image*. Cambridge, England: Cambridge University Press.

757. *Literature and Learning*. (1978). Elizabeth Grudgeon and Peter Walden, Editors. London: Ward Lock Educational.

758. *Literary Criticism and Myth*. (1980). Joseph P. Strelka, Editor. University Park, PA: Pennsylvania State University Press.

759. *Literary Theory in the English Classroom*. (1981). Raymond E. Fitch, Editor. Athens, OH: The Southeastern Ohio Council of Teachers of English.

760. Lubbock, Percy. (1921). *The Craft of Fiction*. New York: Viking Press.

761. Lukacs, Georg. (1963). *The Historical Novel*. Translated by Hannah and Stanley Mitchell. Boston, MA: Beacon Press. (First published in 1937).

762. _____. (1974). *Soul and Form*. Translated by Anna Bostock from the 1910 edition. Cambridge, MA: The MIT Press.

763. _____. (1971). *The Theory of the Novel*. Translated by Anna Bostock from the 1920 edition. Cambridge, MA: The MIT Press.

764. Lund, Nancy, and Judith F. Duchan. (1988). *Assessing Children's Language in Naturalistic Contexts*. Revised Edition. Englewood Cliffs, NJ: Prentice Hall.

765. Mailloux, Steven. (1982). *Interpretive Conventions: The Reader in the Study of American Fiction*. Ithaca, NY: Cornell University Press.

766. *Making a Difference: Feminist Literary Criticism*. (1985). Gayle Greene and Coppelia Kahn, Editors. London: Methuen.

767. Martin, Wallace. (1986). *Recent Theories of Narrative*. Ithaca, NY: Cornell University Press.

768. Meese, Elizabeth. (1986). *Crossing the Double-Cross: The Practice of Feminist Criticism*. Chapel Hill, NC: University of North Carolina Press.

769. Miller, Bruce E. (1980). *Teaching the Art of Literature*. Urbana, IL: National Council of Teachers of English.

770. Miller, J. Hillis. (1982). *Fiction and Repetition: Seven English Novels*. Cambridge, MA: Harvard University Press.

771. Mills, Gordon. (1976). *Hamlet's Castle: The Study of Literature as a Social Experience*. Austin, TX: University of Texas Press.

772. Moi, Toril. (1985). *Sexual/Textual Politics: Feminist Literary Theory*. London: Methuen.

773. *The New Feminist Criticism: Essays on Women, Literature & Theory*. (1985). Elaine Showalter, Editor. New York: Pantheon Books.

774. Norris, Christopher. (1982). *Deconstruction: Theory and Practice*. New York: Methuen.

775. *Northrop Frye in Modern Criticism*. (1966). Murray Krieger, Editor. New York: Columbia University Press.

776. Novarr, David. (1986). *The Lines of Life: Theories of Biography, 1880-1970*. Lafayette, IN: Purdue University Press.

777. Ogden, C. K., and I. A. Richards. (1923). *The Meaning of Meaning*. New York: Harcourt Brace.

778. Ong, W. J. (1982). *Orality and Literacy*. New York: Methuen.

779. *On Text and Context*. (1980). Eduardo Forastieri-Braschi and others, Editors. Rio Piedras, Puerto Rico: Editorial Universitaria.

780. *Play Language and Stories*. (1985). Lee Galda, and Anthony Pellegrini, Editors. Norwood, NJ: Ablex Publishing.

781. *The Poetics of Gender*. (1986). Nancy K. Miller, Editor. New York: Columbia University Press.

782. Poovey, Mary. (1984). *The Proper Lady and the Woman Writer*. Chicago, IL: University of Chicago Press.

783. Pratt, Annis, and others. (1981). *Archetypal Patterns in Women's Fiction*. Bloomington, IN: Indiana University Press.

784. Pratt, Mary Louise. (1977). *Toward a Speech Act Theory of Literary Discourse*. Bloomington, IN: Indiana University Press.

785. Propp, Vladimir. (1968). *Morphology of the Folktale*. Translated by Louis A. Wagner. Austin, TX: University of Texas Press. (First published in 1928; first English translation in 1958).

786. *Psychoanalysis and the Literary Process*. (1970). Frederick C. Crews, Editor. Berkeley, CA: University of California Press.

787. *Psychoanalysis and the Question of the Text*. (1978). Geoffrey Hartman, Editor. Baltimore, MD: The Johns Hopkins University Press.

788. Purves, Alan C., and Victoria Rippere. (1968). *Elements of Writing about a Literary Work: A Study of Responses to Literature*. Urbana, IL: National Council of Teachers of English.

789. Purves, Alan C., and Richard Beach. (1972). *Literature and the Reader: Research in Response to Literature, Reading Interests, and the Teaching of Literature*. Urbana, IL: National Council of Teachers of English.

790. Purves, Alan C. (1981). *Reading and Literature: American Achievement in International Perspective*. Urbana, IL: National Council of Teachers of English.

791. Rabin, Eric S. (1976). *The Fantastic in Literature*. Princeton, NJ: Princeton University Press.

792. Rabine, Leslie W. (1985). *Reading the Romantic Heroine: Text, History, Ideology*. Ann Arbor, MI: University of Michigan Press.

793. Radway, Janice A. (1984). *Reading the Romance: Women, Patriarchy, and Popular Literature*. Chapel Hill, NC: University of North Carolina Press.

794. Ransom, John Crowe. (1938). *The World's Body*. New York: Scribner's.

795. Raval, Suresh. (1981). *Metacriticism*. Athens, GA: University of Georgia Press.

796. *The Reader and the Text: Essays on Audience and Interpretation*. (1980). Susan Suleiman and Inge Crosman, Editors. Princeton, NJ: Princeton University Press.

797. *Reader-Response Criticism: From Formalism to Post-Structuralism*. (1980). Jane P. Tompkins, Editor. Baltimore, MD: The Johns Hopkins University Press.

798. Reichert, John. (1977). *Making Sense of Literature*. Chicago, IL: University of Chicago Press.

799. *The Representation of Women in Fiction*. (1983). Carolyn G. Heilbrun and Margaret R. Higonnet, Editors. Baltimore, MD: The Johns Hopkins University Press.

800. Richards, I. A. (1935). *Practical Criticism: A Study of Literary Judgment*. New York: Harcourt Brace and Co.

801. _____. (1959). *Principles of Literary Criticism*. New York: Harcourt Brace and Co. (Originally published in 1924).

802. Rosenblatt, Louise M. (1981). *The Journey Itself*. The Leland B. Jacobs Lecture, 1981. New York: School of Library Service, Columbia University.

803. _____. (1976). *Literature as Exploration*. 3rd Edition. New York: Noble & Noble Publishers, Inc. (First published in 1938).

804. _____. (1978). *The Reader, The Text, The Poem*. Carbondale, IL: Southern Illinois University Press.

805. *Russian Formalist Criticism: Four Essays*. (1965). Lee T. Lemon and Marion J. Reis, Editors. Lincoln, NB: University of Nebraska Press.

806. Ruthven, K. K. (1984). *Feminist Literary Studies*. Cambridge, England: Cambridge University Press.

807. Said, Edward W. (1983). *The World, The Text and the Critic*. Cambridge, MA: Harvard University Press.

808. Saussure, Ferdinand de. (1967). *Cours de Linguistique Generale*. 3rd Edition. Paris: Payot.

809. Sartre, Jean-Paul. (1949). *What Is Literature?* Translated by Bernard Frechtman from the 1948 French edition. New York: Philosophical Library.

810. Scholes, Robert, and Robert Kellogg. (1966). *The Nature of Narrative*. Oxford, England: Oxford University Press.

811. Scholes, Robert. (1974). *Structuralism in Literature*. New Haven, CT: Yale University Press.

812. Selden, Raman. (1984). *Criticism and Objectivity*. London: George Allen & Unwin.

813. Silverman, Kaja. (1983). *The Subject of Semiotics*. New York: Oxford University Press.

814. Slatoff, Walter. (1970). *With Respect to Readers: Dimensions of Literary Response*. Ithaca, NY: Cornell University Press.

815. Smith, Frank. (1988). *Joining the Literacy Club*. Portsmouth, NH: Heinemann Educational Books.

816. _____. (1971). *Understanding Reading: A Psycholinguistic Analysis of Reading and Learning to Read*. New York: Holt, Rinehart and Winston.

817. Sollors, Werner. (1986). *Beyond Ethnicity: Consent and Descent in American Culture.* New York: Oxford University Press.

818. Sontag, Susan. (1967). *Against Interpretation.* New York: Farrar, Straus & Giroux.

819. Spacks, Patricia Meyer. (1975). *The Female Imagination.* New York: Alfred A. Knopf.

820. Steiner, George. (1967). *Language and Silence: Essays on Language, Literature and the Inhuman.* New York: Atheneum.

821. *Structuralism and Since.* (1979). John Sturrock, Editor. New York: Oxford University Press.

822. *The Structuralist Controversy: The Languages of Criticism and the Sciences of Man.* (1972). Richard A. Macksey and Eugenio Donato, Editors. Baltimore, MD: The Johns Hopkins University Press.

823. Tate, Allen. (1936). *Reactionary Essays in Poetry and Ideas.* New York: Scribner's.

824. *Teaching the Text.* (1983). Edited by Susanne Kappeler and Norman Bryson. London: Routledge & Kegan Paul.

825. *Theoretical Models and Processes of Reading.* (1976). Harry Singer and Robert B. Ruddell, Editors. Newark, DE: International Reading Association.

826. *Theory and Practice of Feminist Literary Criticism.* (1982). Gabriela Mora and Karen S. Van Hooft, Editors. Ypsilanti, MI: Bilingual Press.

827. Todorov, Tzvetan. (1975). *The Fantastic: A Structural Approach to a Literary Genre.* Ithaca, NY: Cornell University Press.

828. _____. (1977). *The Poetics of Prose.* Ithaca, NY: Cornell University Press. (First published in French in 1971).

829. _____. (1982). *Theories of the Symbol.* Translated by C. Porter. Ithaca, NY: Cornell University Press.

830. Tolstoy, Leo N. (1953). *What Is Art?* Translated by Aylmer Maude. New York: Bobbs-Merrill.

831. *Towards a Poetics of Fiction.* (1977). Mark Spilka, Editor. Bloomington, IN: Indiana University Press.

832. Trilling, Lionel. (1965). *Beyond Culture: Essays on Literature and Learning.* New York: Viking Press.

833. *Understanding Poetry.* (1976). Cleanth Brooks and Robert Penn Warren, Editors. 4th Edition. New York: Holt.

834. *Untying the Text: A Post-Structuralist Reader.* (1981). Robert Young, Editor. Boston, MA: Routledge & Kegan Paul.

835. Van DeWeghe, Richard. (1987). "Making and Remaking Meaning: Developing Literary Responses Through Purposeful, Informal Writing," *English Writing.* 20, 38-51.

836. Weldon, Fay. (1984). *Letters to Alice: On First Reading Jane Austen.* New York: Harcourt Brace Jovanovich.

837. Wellek, Rene, and Austin Warren. (1977). *Theory of Literature.* New Revised Edition. New York: Harcourt Brace Jovanovich.

838. Wellek, Rene. (1982). *The Attack on Literature and Other Essays.* Chapel Hill, NC: University of North Carolina Press.

839. *What Is Literature?* (1978). Paul Hernadi, Editor. Bloomington, IN: Indiana University Press.

840. Wicker, Brian. (1975). *The Story-Shaped World.* Notre Dame, IN: University of Notre Dame Press.

841. Wilson, Anne Deidre. (1976). *Traditional Romance and Tale: How Stories Mean.* Cambridge, England: Rowman & Littlefield.

842. Wimmers, Inge Crosman. (1988). *Poetics of Reading: Approaches to the Novel.* Princeton, NJ: Princeton University Press.

843.   Wimsatt, William K. (1965). *Hateful Contraries: Studies in Literature and Criticism*. Lexington, KY: University of Kentucky Press.

844.   Wimsatt, William K. and Cleanth Brooks. (1957). *Literary Criticism: A Short History*. New York: Knopf.

845.   Wimsatt, William K. and Monroe C. Beardsley. (1954). *The Verbal Icon: Studies in the Meaning of Poetry*. Lexington, KY: University of Kentucky Press.

846.   Winters, Ivor. (1947). *In Defense of Reason*. New York: Swallow.

Selected Bibliography of Teaching

Although this list concentrates on works about teaching in higher education, it also includes monographs from the fields of elementary and secondary education when contents seem highly transferable. Several philosophical and general works are included that have added a dimension to my own thinking about teaching. Also included within this section are works with a feminist approach to human development and teaching as well as representative works on reading and critical thinking.

847. Aik, Kam Chuan, and Stephen Edmonds. (1976). *Critical Thinking: Selected Topics for Discussion and Analysis.* Singapore: Longman Malaysia SDN. Berhad.

848. Altbach, Philip G. (1987). *The Knowledge Context: Comparative Perspectives on the Distribution of Knowledge.* Albany, NY: State University of New York Press.

849. Arnheim, Rudolf. (1964). *Art and Visual Perception.* Berkeley, CA: University of California Press.

850. _____. (1969). *Visual Thinking.* London: Faber and Faber.

851. *The Art and Craft of Teaching.* (1982). Margaret Morganroth Gullette, Editor. Cambridge, MA: Harvard-Danforth Center for Teaching and Learning.

852. Astin, Alexander W. (1985). *Achieving Educational Excellence.* San Francisco, CA: Jossey Bass.

853. Axelrod, Joseph. (1973). *The University Teacher as Artist.* San Francisco, CA: Jossey Bass.

854. Berger, Peter L. and Thomas Luckman. (1966). *The Social Construction of Reality.* Garden City, NY: Doubleday.

855. Bloom, Allan. (1987). *The Closing of the American Mind.* New York: Simon and Schuster.

856. Brackamp, Larry A. (1984). *Evaluating Teaching Effectiveness: A Practical Guide.* Beverly Hills, CA: Sage.

857. Brand, Stewart. (1987). *The Media Lab: Inventing the Future at MIT.* New York: Viking Press.

858. Britton, James. (1970). *Language and Learning.* Harmondsworth, Middlesex, England: Penguin Books.

859. Brookfield, Stephen D. (1987). *Developing Critical Thinkers: Challenging Adults to Explore Alternative Ways of Thinking and Acting.* San Francisco, CA: Jossey Bass.

860. _____. (1986). *Understanding and Facilitating Adult Learning.* San Francisco, CA: Jossey Bass.

861. Bruner, Jerome S. (1960). *The Process of Education.* Cambridge, MA: Harvard University Press.

862. Bruner, Jerome S. and others. (1986). *A Study of Thinking*. New Brunswick, NJ: Transaction Books.

863. Carin, Arthur, and Robert B. Sund. (1971). *Developing Questioning Techniques: A Self-Concept Approach*. Columbus, OH: Charles Merrill.

864. Cassirer, Ernst. (1944). *An Essay on Man: An Introduction to a Philosophy of Human Culture*. New Haven, CT: Yale University Press.

865. _____. (1946). *Language and Myth*. New York: Harper & Row.

866. *Changing Instructional Strategies*. (1977). James O. Hammons, Editor. San Francisco, CA: Jossey Bass.

867. Chazan, Barry I. (1985). *Contemporary Approaches to Moral Education: Analyzing Alternative Theories*. New York: Teachers College Press.

868. Chomsky, Noam. (1972). *Language and Mind*. New York: Harcourt Brace Jovanovich.

869. Clark, E. H., and Herbert Clark. (1977). *Psychology and Language: An Introduction to Psycholinguistics*. New York: Harcourt Brace Jovanovich.

870. Claxton, Charles Sydney, and Yvonne Ralston. (1978). *Learning Styles: Their Impact on Teaching and Administration*. Washington, DC: American Association for Higher Education.

871. Commission on the Humanities. (1980). *The Humanities in American Life*. Berkeley, CA: University of California Press.

872. *The Compleat Academic: A Practical Guide for the Beginning Social Scientist*. (1987). Mark P. Zanna and John M. Darley, Editors. New York: Random House.

873. *Contemporary Thought on Teaching*. (1971). Ronald T. Hyman, Editor. Englewood Cliffs, NJ: Prentice Hall.

874. Cooper, Jan and others. (1985). *Teaching College Students to Read Analytically*. Urbana, IL: National Council of Teachers of English.

875. *A Critical Dictionary of Educational Concepts: An Appraisal of Selected Issues in Educational Theory and Practice*. (1987). Robin Barrow and Geoffrey Milburn, Editors. New York: St. Martin's Press.

876. Daloz, Laurent A. (1986). *Effective Teaching and Mentoring*. San Francisco, CA: Jossey Bass.

877. Davis, James R. (1976). *Teaching Strategies for the College Classroom*. Boulder, CO: Westview Press.

878. *Designing and Implementing Effective Workshops*. (1984). Thomas J. Sork, Editor. San Francisco, CA: Jossey Bass.

879. *Developing Minds: A Resource Book for Teaching Thinking*. (1985). Arthur Costa, Editor. Alexandria, VA: Association for Supervision and Curriculum Development.

880. Dewey, John. (1933). *How We Think*. Boston, MA: D. C. Heath.

881. *Dewey on Education*. (1961). Martin S. Dworkin, Editor. New York: Bureau of Publications, Teachers College, Columbia University.

882. Dressel, Paul Leroy. (1982). *On Teaching and Learning in College*. San Francisco, CA: Jossey Bass.

883. Dunkin, Michael J., and Bruce J. Biddle. (1974). *The Study of Teaching*. New York: Holt, Rinehart and Winston.

884. Eble, Kenneth E. (1988). *The Craft of Teaching*. Revised Edition. San Francisco, CA: Jossey Bass.

885. Elbow, Peter. (1986). *Embracing Contraries: Explorations in Learning and Teaching*. New York: Oxford University Press.

886. Ericksen, Stanford C. (1984). *The Essence of Good Teaching*. San Francisco, CA: Jossey Bass.

887. Fenstermacher, Gary, and Jonas F. Soltis. (1986). *Approaches to Teaching*. New York: Teachers College Press.

888. Fullan, Michael. (1982). *The Meaning of Educational Change*. New York: Teachers College Press.

889. *The Future of State Universities: Issues in Teaching Research and Public Service*. (1985). Leslie W. Koepplin and David A. Wilson, Editors. New Brunswick, NJ: Rutgers University Press.

890. Gage, N. L. (1978). *The Scientific Basis of the Art of Teaching*. New York: Teachers College Press.

891. Gardner, Howard. (1987). *The Mind's New Science: A History of the Cognitive Revolution*. New York: Basic Books.

892. *Gendered Subjects: The Dynamics of Feminist Teaching*. (1985). Margo Culley and Catherine Portuges, Editors. Boston, MA: Routledge & Kegan Paul.

893. Gilligan, Carol. (1982). *In a Different Voice: Psychological Theory and Women's Development*. Cambridge, MA: Harvard University Press.

894. Grant, Carl A. (1984). *Preparing for Reflective Teaching*. Boston, MA: Allyn and Bacon.

895. Greene, Maxine. (1973). *Teacher as Stranger*. Belmont, CA: Wadsworth.

896. Gribble, James. (1983). *Literary Education: A Revaluation*. Cambridge, England: Cambridge University Press.

897. *Guide to Effective Teaching: A National Report on Eighty-One Outstanding College Teachers and How They Teach*. (1978). New Rochelle, NY: Change Magazine Press.

898. Hansen, Jane. (1987). *When Writers Read*. Portsmith, NH: Heinemann.

899. Hare, William. (1985). *In Defense of Open-Mindedness*. Kingston, Canada: McGill-Queen's University Press.

900. Harms, Jeanne McLain. (1982). *Comprehension and Literature*. Dubuque, IA: Kendall Hunt Publishing.

901. Hildebrand, Milton. (1971). *Evaluating University Teaching*. Berkeley, CA: Center for Research and Development in Higher Education, University of California.

902. Hirsch, E. D. (1987). *Cultural Literacy: What Every American Needs to Know*. Boston, MA: Houghton Mifflin.

903. Huizinga, J. (1949). *Homo Ludens*. London: Routledge & Kegan Paul.

904. Hunkins, Francis P. (1972). *Questioning Strategies and Techniques*. Boston, MA: Allyn and Bacon.

905. *Interaction Analysis: Theory, Research and Application*. (1967). E. J. Amidon and J. B. Hough, Editors. Reading, MA: Addison-Wesley.

906. Jackson, Philip W. (1986). *The Practice of Teaching*. New York: Teachers College Press.

907. James, Thomas. (1987). *Exile Within: The Schooling of Japanese Americans, 1942-1945*. Cambridge, MA: Harvard University Press.

908. Johnson, Katie. (1987). *Doing Words: Using the Creative Power of Children's Personal Images to Teach Reading and Writing*. Boston, MA: Houghton Mifflin.

909. Joyce, Bruce, and Marsha Weil. (1980). *Models of Teaching*. 2nd Edition. Englewood Cliffs, NJ: Prentice Hall.

910. Joyce, Bruce, and B. Showers. (1983). *Power in Staff Development through Research on Training*. Alexandria, VA: Association for Supervision and Curriculum Development.

911. Kindsvatter, Richard, and others. (1988). *Dynamics of Effective Teaching*. White Plains, NY: Longman.

912. Knox, Alan B. (1986). *Helping Adults Learn*. San Francisco, CA: Jossey Bass.

913. Kolstoe, Oliver P. (1975). *College Professoring: Or, Through Academia with Gun and Camera*. Carbondale, IL: Southern Illinois University Press.

914. Komarovsky, Mirra. (1985). *Women in College: Shaping New Feminist Identities*. New York: Basic Books.

915. Kozma, Robert B. (1978). *Instructional Techniques in Higher Education*. Englewood Cliffs, NJ: Educational Technology Publication.

916. Kuhn, T. S. (1962). *The Structure of Scientific Revolutions*. Chicago, IL: University of Chicago Press.

917. Langer, Susanne K. (1953). *Feeling and Form*. New York: Charles Scribner's Sons.

918. _____. (1942). *Philosophy in a New Key*. Cambridge, MA: Harvard University Press.

919. *Language and Concepts in Education*. (1961). B. O. Smith and R. H. Ennis, Editors. Chicago, IL: Rand McNally.

920. Lawler, Robert. (1985). *Computer Experience and Cognitive Development: A Child's Learning in a Computer Culture*. Chichester, England: Horwood.

921. Lott, Bernice. (1987). *Women's Lives: Themes and Variations in Gender Learning*. Monterey, CA: Brooks/Cole.

922. Lowman, Joseph. (1984). *Mastering the Techniques of Teaching*. San Francisco, CA: Jossey Bass.

923. Luria, A. R. (1979). *The Making of the Mind*. Cambridge, MA: Harvard University Press.

924. Lynton, Ernest, and Sandra E. Elman. (1987). *New Priorities for the University*. San Francisco, CA: Jossey Bass.

925. McKeachie, Wilbert James. (1986). *Teaching Tips: A Guidebook for the Beginning College Teacher*. 8th Edition. Lexington, MA: D. C. Heath.

926. Mandell, Richard D. (1977). *The Professor Game*. Garden City, NY: Doubleday.

927. Marzano, Robert, and others. (1988). *Dimensions of Thinking: A Framework for Curriculum and Instruction*. Alexandria, VA: Association for Supervision and Curriculum Development.

928. *Measuring Faculty Research Performance*. (1986). John W. Creswell, Editor. San Francisco, CA: Jossey Bass.

929. Meyers, Chet. (1986). *Teaching Students to Think Critically*. San Francisco, CA: Jossey Bass.

930. Miller, Richard I. (1987). *Evaluating Faculty for Promotion and Tenure*. San Francisco, CA: Jossey Bass.

931. Milton, Ohmer. (1972). *Alternatives to the Traditional: How Professors Teach and How Students Learn*. San Francisco, CA: Jossey Bass.

932. Milton, Ohmer, and others. (1978). *On College Teaching: A Guide to Contemporary Practices*. San Francisco, CA: Jossey Bass.

933. Moffett, James. (1968). *Teaching the Universe of Discourse*. Boston, MA: Houghton Mifflin.

934. Morrill, Paul. (1982). *The Academic Profession: Teaching in Higher Education*. New York: Human Sciences Press.

935. *Motivating Professors to Teach Effectively*. (1982). James L. Bess, Editor. San Francisco, CA: Jossey Bass.

936. Pace, Charles Robert. (1973). *Evaluating Learning and Teaching.* San Francisco, CA: Jossey Bass.

937. Paulos, John Allen. (1988). *Innumeracy: Mathematical Illiteracy and Its Consequences.* New York: Hill & Wang.

938. Perkins, D. N. (1986). *Knowledge as Design.* Hillsdale, NJ: Lawrence Erlbaum Associates.

939. _____. (1981). *The Mind's Best Work.* Cambridge, MA: Harvard University Press.

940. *Perspectives on Effective Teaching and the Cooperative Classroom.* (1984). Judy Reinhartz, Editor. Washington, DC: National Education Association.

941. Phenix, Philip H. (1964). *Realms of Meaning.* New York: McGraw-Hill.

942. Piaget, Jean. (1968). *Six Psychological Studies.* Translated by David Elkin. New York: Vintage Books.

943. *Play Language and Stories: The Development of Children's Literate Behavior.* (1985). Lee Galda and Anthony Pellegrini, Editors. Norwood, NJ: Ablex Publishing.

944. Pool, Ithiel de Sola. (1983). *Technologies of Freedom: On Free Speech in an Electronic Age.* Cambridge, MA: Harvard University Press.

945. Presseisen, Barbara Z. (1986). *Thinking Skills: Research and Practice.* Washington, DC: National Education Association.

946. *Promoting Reading Comprehension.* (1984). James Flood, Editor. Newark, DE: International Reading Association.

947. Raths, Louis E. and others. (1986). *Teaching for Thinking.* 2nd Edition. New York: Teachers College Press.

948. Ravitch, Diane, and Chester Finn, Jr. (1987). *What Do Our 17-Year-Olds Know?* New York: Harper & Row.

949. *Readers, Texts, Teachers.* (1987). Bill Corcoran and Emrys Evans, Editors. Upper Montclair, NJ: Boynton/Cook.

950. *Research within Reach Secondary School Reading: A Research Guided Response to Concerns of Reading Educators.* (1987). Donna E. Alvermann and others, Editors. Newark, DE: International Reading Association.

951. Ross, Stephen David. (1981). *Learning and Discovery: The University and the Development of the Mind.* New York: Gordon & Breach.

952. Roueche, John E. (1979). *College Teaching: Putting the Pieces Together.* New York: National League for Nursing.

953. Rumelhart, David E. (1980). "Schemata: The Building Blocks of Cognition," in *Theoretical Issues in Reading Comprehension.* R. J. Spiro and others, Editors. Hillsdale, NJ: Erlbaum, 33-58.

954. Samples, Bob, and others. (1977). *The Wholeschool Book: Teaching and Learning in the 20th Century.* Reading, MA: Addison-Wesley.

955. Schank, Roger C. (1984). *The Cognitive Computer: On Language, Learning, and Artificial Intelligence.* Reading, MA: Addison-Wesley.

956. Scheffler, Israel. (1985). *Of Human Potential: An Essay in the Philosophy of Education.* New York: Routledge & Kegan Paul.

957. Schon, Donald. (1983). *The Reflective Practitioner: How Professionals Think in Action.* New York: Basic Books.

958. _____. (1987). *Educating the Reflective Practitioner: Toward a New Design for Teaching and Learning in the Professions.* San Francisco, CA: Jossey Bass.

959. Showers, B. (1984). *Peer Coaching: A Strategy for Facilitating Transfer of Training.* Eugene, OR: University of Oregon, Center for Educational Policy and Management.

960. Skinner, B. F. (1968). *The Technology of Teaching*. New York: Appleton-Century-Crofts.

961. Smith, Frank. (1986). *Insult to Intelligence: The Bureaucratic Invasion of Our Classrooms*. New York: Arbor House.

962. _____. (1979). *Reading without Nonsense*. New York: Teachers College Press.

963. _____. (1982). *Understanding Reading: A Psycholinguistic Analysis of Reading and Learning to Read*. 3rd Edition. New York: Holt, Rinehart and Winston.

964. Stiggins, Richard J. (1986). *Measuring Thinking Skills in the Classroom*. Washington, DC: National Education Association.

965. Strike, Kenneth A., and Jonas Soltis. (1985). *The Ethics of Teaching*. New York: Teachers College Press.

966. *Teaching Large Classes Well*. (1987). Maryellen Gleason Weiner, Editor. San Francisco, CA: Jossey Bass.

967. *Teaching Literature: What Is Needed Now*. (1988). James Engell and David Perkins, Editors. Cambridge, MA: Harvard University Press.

968. Theodore, Athena. (1986). *The Campus Troublemakers: Academic Women in Protest*. Houston, TX: Cap & Gown Press.

969. *Toward the Recovery of Wholeness: Knowledge, Education, and Human Values*. (1984). Douglas Sloan, Editor. New York: Teachers College Press.

970. *Using Research to Improve Teaching*. (1985). Janet G. Donald and Arthur M. Sullivan, Editors. San Francisco, CA: Jossey Bass.

971. Vygotsky, L. (1963). *Language and Thought*. Cambridge, MA: The MIT Press.

972. _____. (1978). *Mind in Society*. Cambridge, MA: Harvard University Press.

973. Wells, C. Gordon. (1986). *The Meaning Makers: Children Learning Language and Using Language to Learn*. Portsmouth, NH: Heinemann.

974. Westmeyer, Paul. (1988). *Effective Teaching in Adult and Higher Education*. Springfield, IL: Charles C. Thomas.

975. White, Edward M. (1985). *Teaching and Assessing Writing*. San Francisco, CA: Jossey Bass.

976. Whitehead, Alfred North. (1929). *The Aims of Education*. New York: Macmillan.

977. *Women's Place in the Academy: Transforming the Liberal Arts Curriculum*. (1985). Marilyn R. Schuster and Susan R. Van Dyne, Editors. Totowa, NJ: Rowman & Allanheld.

Index